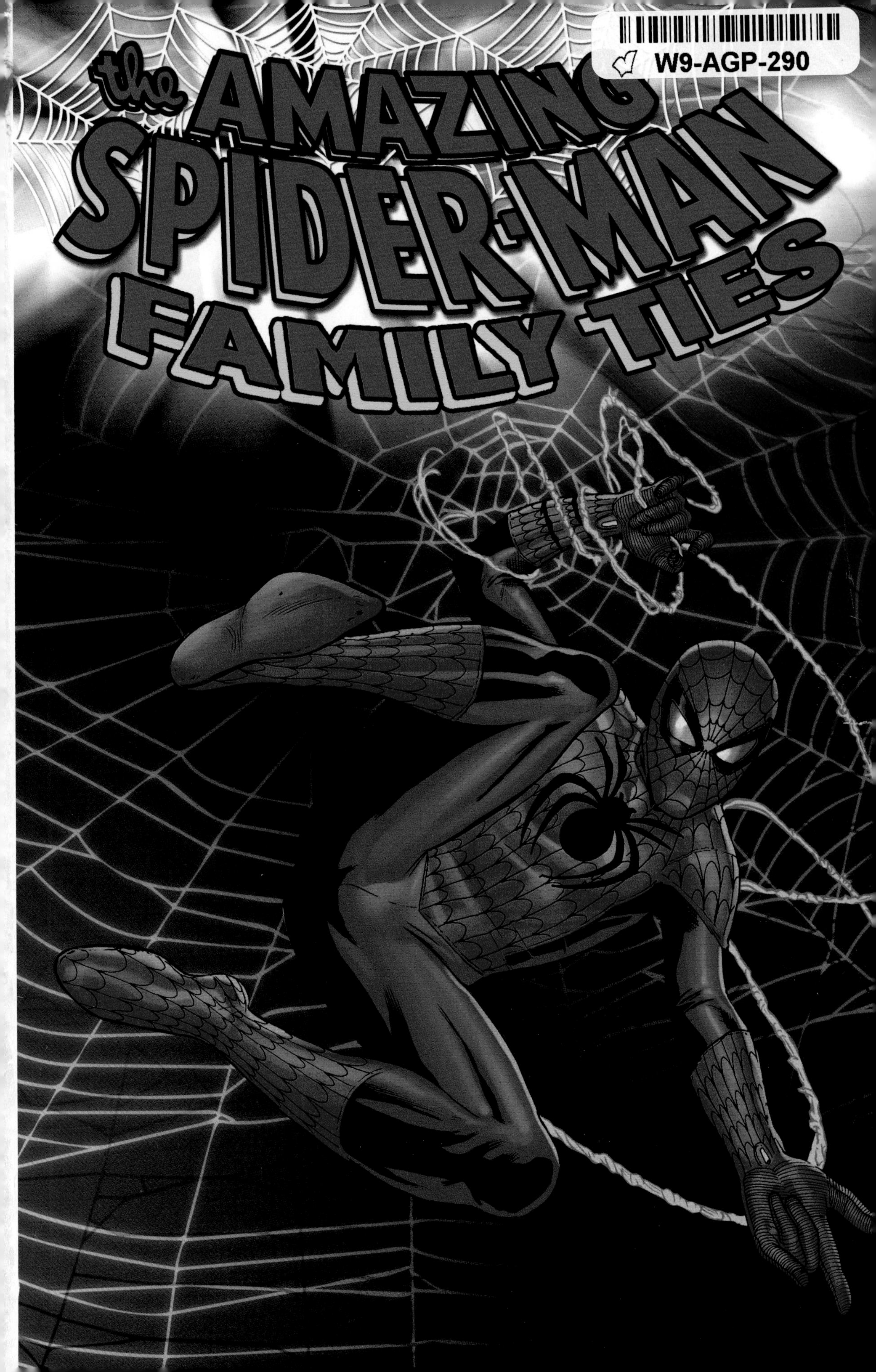
the AMAZING SPIDER-MAN
FAMILY TIES

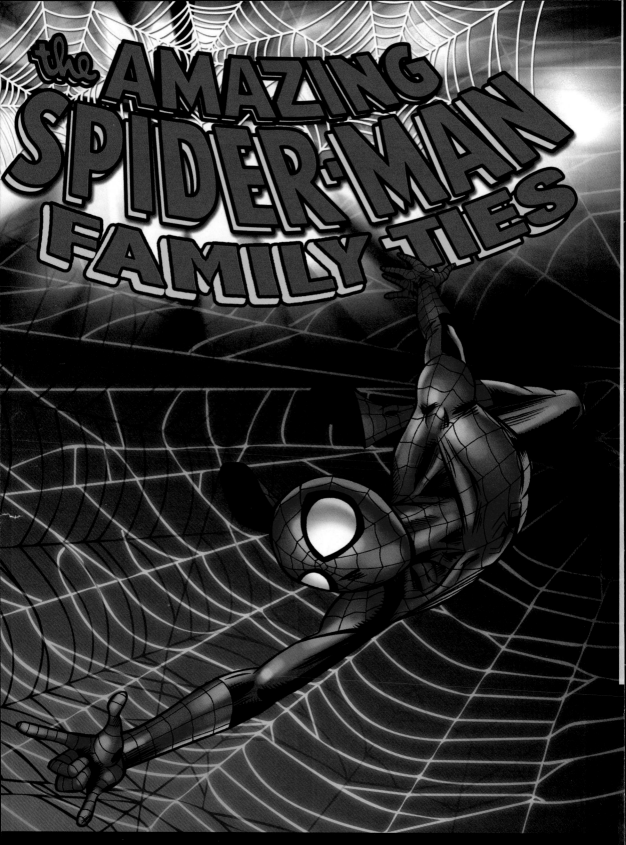

the AMAZING SPIDER-MAN FAMILY TIES

SPIDER-MAN: FAMILY TIES. Contains material originally published in magazine form as AMAZING SPIDER-MAN FAMILY #1-3 and SPIDER-MAN: FEAR ITSELF. First printing 2009. Hardcover ISBN# 978-0-7851-3825-9. Softcover ISBN# 978-0-7851-3517-3. Published by MARVEL PUBLISHING, INC., a subsidiary of MARVEL ENTERTAINMENT, INC. OFFICE OF PUBLICATION: 417 5th Avenue, New York, NY 10016. Copyright © 2008 and 2009 Marvel Characters, Inc. All rights reserved. Hardcover: $19.99 per copy in the U.S. (GST #R127032852). Softcover: $14.99 per copy in the U.S. (GST #R127032852). Canadian Agreement #40668537. All characters featured in this issue and the distinctive names and likenesses thereof, and all related indicia are trademarks of Marvel Characters, Inc. No similarity between any of the names, characters, persons, and/or institutions in this magazine with those of any living or dead person or institution is intended, and any such similarity which may exist is purely coincidental. **Printed in the U.S.A.** ALAN FINE, CEO Marvel Toys & Publishing Divisions and CMO Marvel Characters, Inc.; JIM SOKOLOWSKI, Chief Operating Officer; DAVID GABRIEL, SVP of Publishing Sales & Circulation; DAVID BOGART, SVP of Business Affairs & Talent Management; MICHAEL PASCIULLO, VP Merchandising & Communications; JIM O'KEEFE, VP of Operations & Logistics; DAN CARR, Executive Director of Publishing Technology; JUSTIN F. GABRIE, Director of Publishing & Editorial Operations; SUSAN CRESPI, Editorial Operations Manager; ALEX MORALES, Publishing Operations Manager; STAN LEE, Chairman Emeritus. For information regarding advertising in Marvel Comics or on Marvel.com, please contact Mitch Dane, Advertising Director, at mdane@marvel.com. For Marvel subscription inquiries, please call 800-217-9158.

10 9 8 7 6 5 4 3 2 1

SPIDER-MAN FAMILY

Writers: **J.M. DEMATTEIS, KARL KESEL, KEITH CHAMPAGNE, JOHN ARCUDI, PAUL BENJAMIN, ABBY DENSON & STUART MOORE**

Artists: **ALEX CAL, RAMON BACHS, SHAWN MOLL AND KEITH CHAMPAGNE, VAL SEMEIKS AND VICTOR OLAZABA, ANDY LANNING, KRIS JUSTICE, COLLEEN COOVER & MARK IRWIN**

Colorists: **RAIN BEREDO, JAVIER MENA GUERRERO, ROB RO, ALLEN PASSALAQUA, SOTOCOLOR'S A. STREET, ANDREW CROSSLEY & ANDRES MOSSA**

Letterers: **SIMON BOWLAND, JARED K. FLETCHER, BLAMBOT'S NATE PIEKOS & DAVE SHARPE**

Editors: **TOM BRENNAN & STEPHEN WACKER**

Cover Artists: **ADI GRANOV, MIKE DEODATO JR. & PAT OLLIFFE**

FEAR ITSELF

Writer: **STUART MOORE**

Artist: **JOE SUITOR**

Letterer: **JARED K. FLETCHER**

Assistant Editor: **TOM BRENNAN**

Editor: **STEPHEN WACKER**

Cover Artists: **MICO SUAYAN & FRANK D'ARMATA**

Collection Editor: **CORY LEVINE**
Editorial Assistant: **ALEX STARBUCK**
Assistant Editor: **JOHN DENNING**
Editors, Special Projects: **JENNIFER GRÜNWALD & MARK D. BEAZLEY**
Senior Editor, Special Projects: **JEFF YOUNGQUIST**
Senior Vice President of Sales: **DAVID GABRIEL**
Production: **CARRIE BEADLE & JERRY KALINOWSKI**

Editor in Chief: **JOE QUESADA**
Publisher: **DAN BUCKLEY**
Executive Producer: **ALAN FINE**

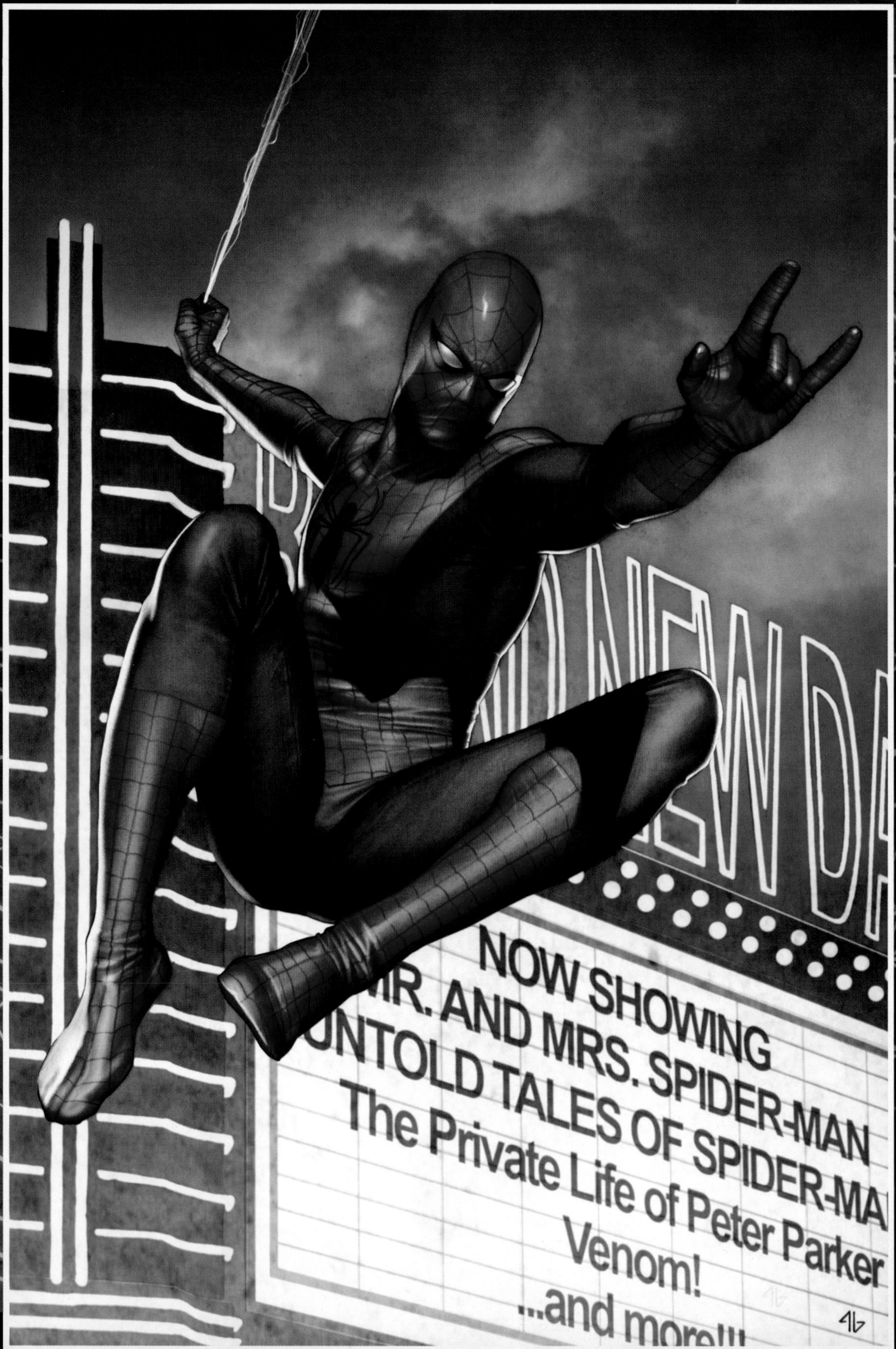
NOW SHOWING
MR. AND MRS. SPIDER-MAN
UNTOLD TALES OF SPIDER-MAN
The Private Life of Peter Parker
Venom!
...and more!!!

AMAZING SPIDER-MAN FAMILY #1

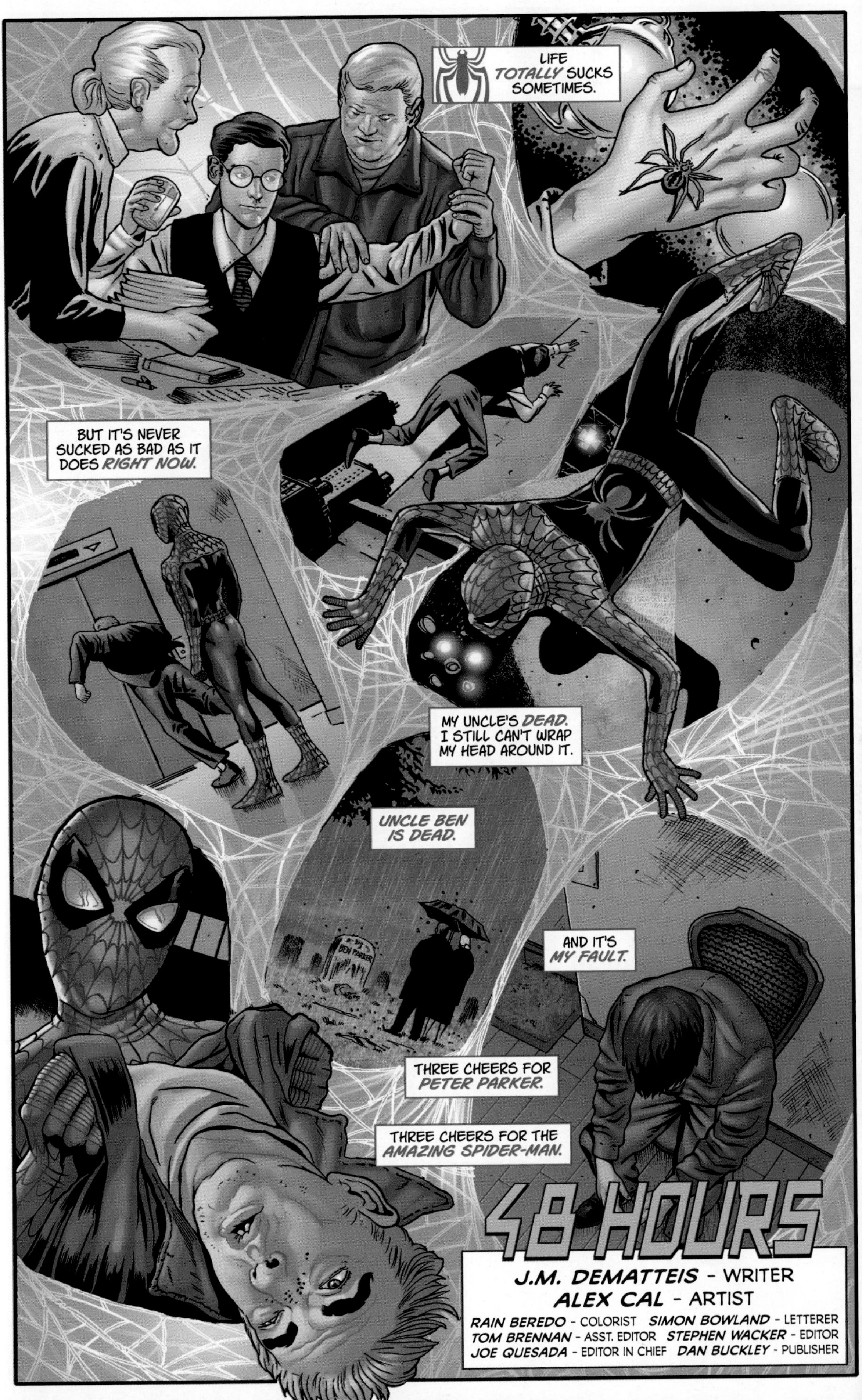
LIFE TOTALLY SUCKS SOMETIMES.
BUT IT'S NEVER SUCKED AS BAD AS IT DOES RIGHT NOW.
MY UNCLE'S DEAD. I STILL CAN'T WRAP MY HEAD AROUND IT.
UNCLE BEN IS DEAD.
BEN PARKER
AND IT'S MY FAULT.
THREE CHEERS FOR PETER PARKER.
THREE CHEERS FOR THE AMAZING SPIDER-MAN.
48 HOURS
J.M. DEMATTEIS - WRITER
ALEX CAL - ARTIST
RAIN BEREDO - COLORIST SIMON BOWLAND - LETTERER
TOM BRENNAN - ASST. EDITOR STEPHEN WACKER - EDITOR
JOE QUESADA - EDITOR IN CHIEF DAN BUCKLEY - PUBLISHER

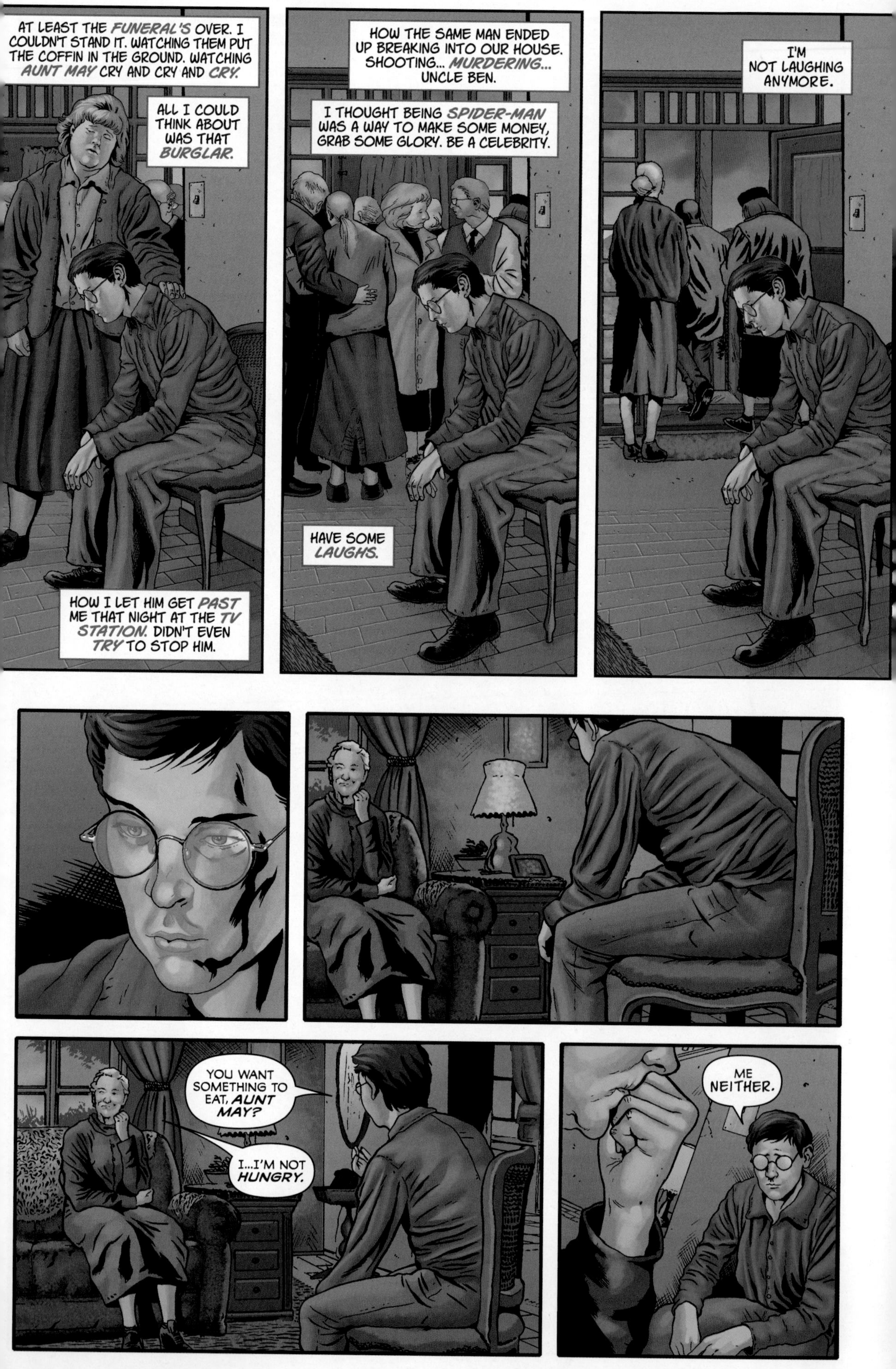

AT LEAST THE FUNERAL'S OVER. I COULDN'T STAND IT. WATCHING THEM PUT THE COFFIN IN THE GROUND. WATCHING AUNT MAY CRY AND CRY AND CRY.
ALL I COULD THINK ABOUT WAS THAT BURGLAR.
HOW I LET HIM GET PAST ME THAT NIGHT AT THE TV STATION. DIDN'T EVEN TRY TO STOP HIM.
HOW THE SAME MAN ENDED UP BREAKING INTO OUR HOUSE. SHOOTING... MURDERING... UNCLE BEN.
I THOUGHT BEING SPIDER-MAN WAS A WAY TO MAKE SOME MONEY, GRAB SOME GLORY. BE A CELEBRITY.
HAVE SOME LAUGHS.
I'M NOT LAUGHING ANYMORE.
YOU WANT SOMETHING TO EAT, AUNT MAY?
I...I'M NOT HUNGRY.
ME NEITHER.

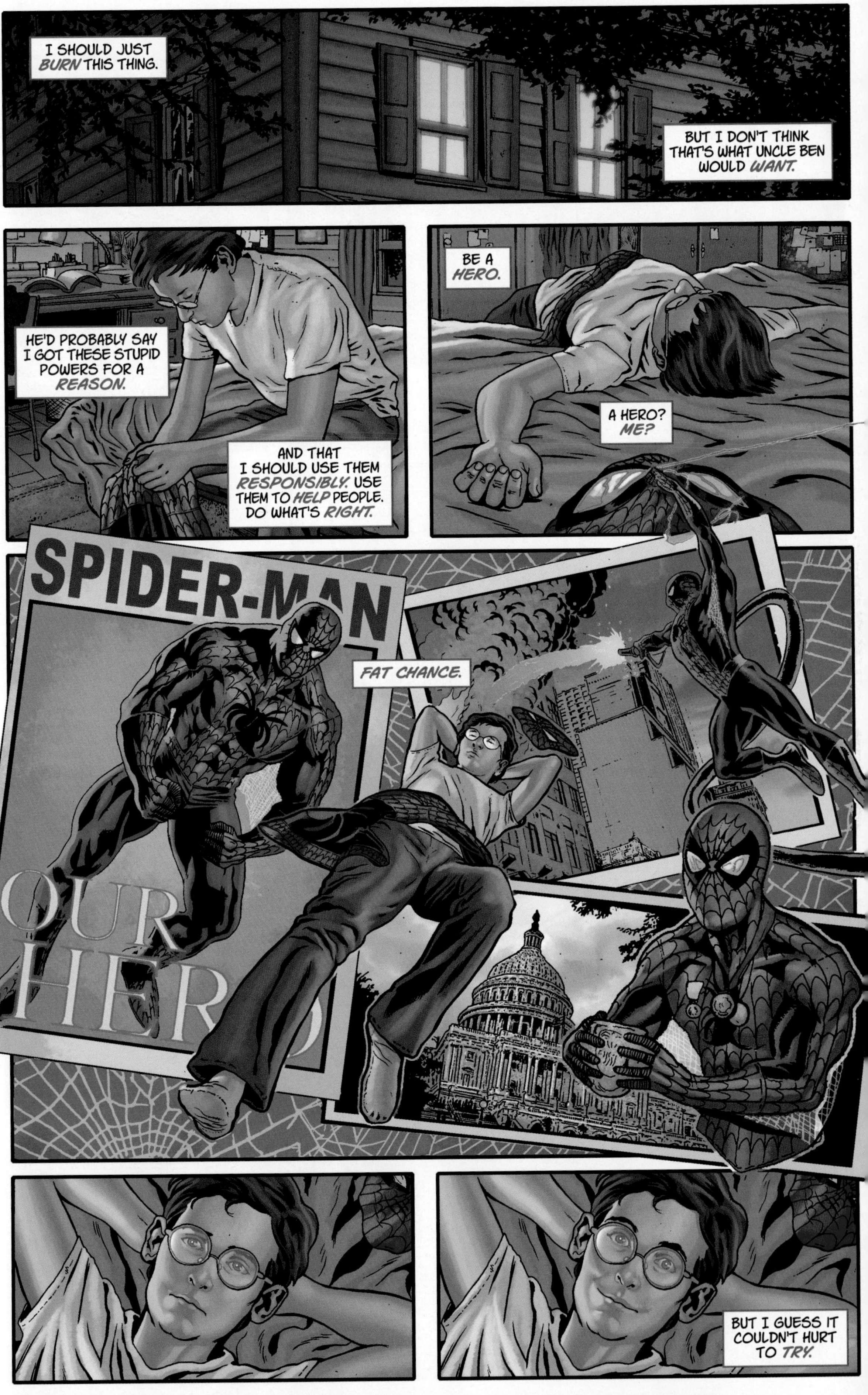
I SHOULD JUST BURN THIS THING.
BUT I DON'T THINK THAT'S WHAT UNCLE BEN WOULD WANT.
HE'D PROBABLY SAY I GOT THESE STUPID POWERS FOR A REASON.
AND THAT I SHOULD USE THEM RESPONSIBLY. USE THEM TO HELP PEOPLE. DO WHAT'S RIGHT.
BE A HERO.
A HERO? ME?
SPIDER-MAN
OUR HERO
FAT CHANCE.
BUT I GUESS IT COULDN'T HURT TO TRY.

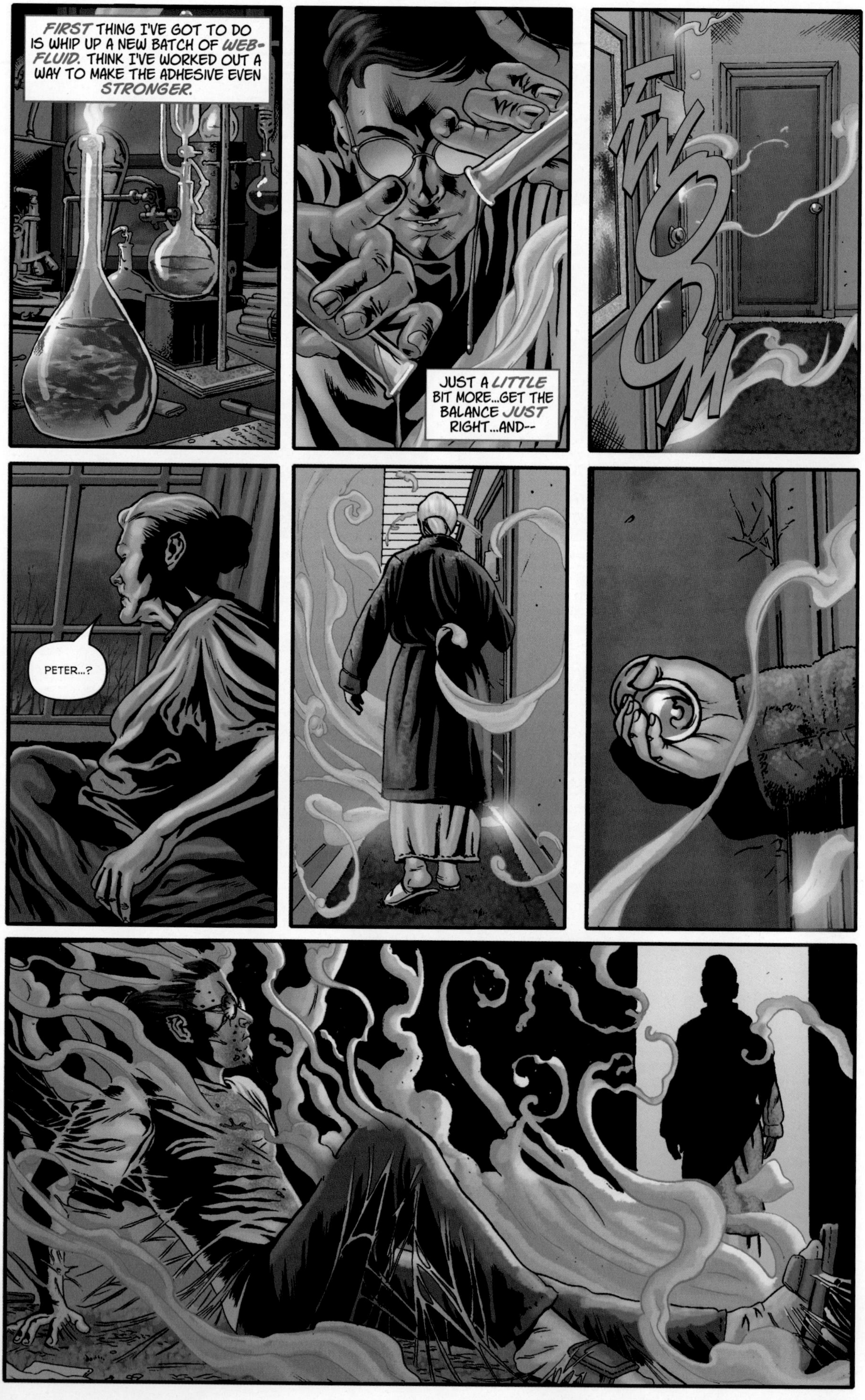
FIRST THING I'VE GOT TO DO IS WHIP UP A NEW BATCH OF WEB-FLUID. THINK I'VE WORKED OUT A WAY TO MAKE THE ADHESIVE EVEN STRONGER.
JUST A LITTLE BIT MORE...GET THE BALANCE JUST RIGHT...AND--
FWOOOM
PETER...?

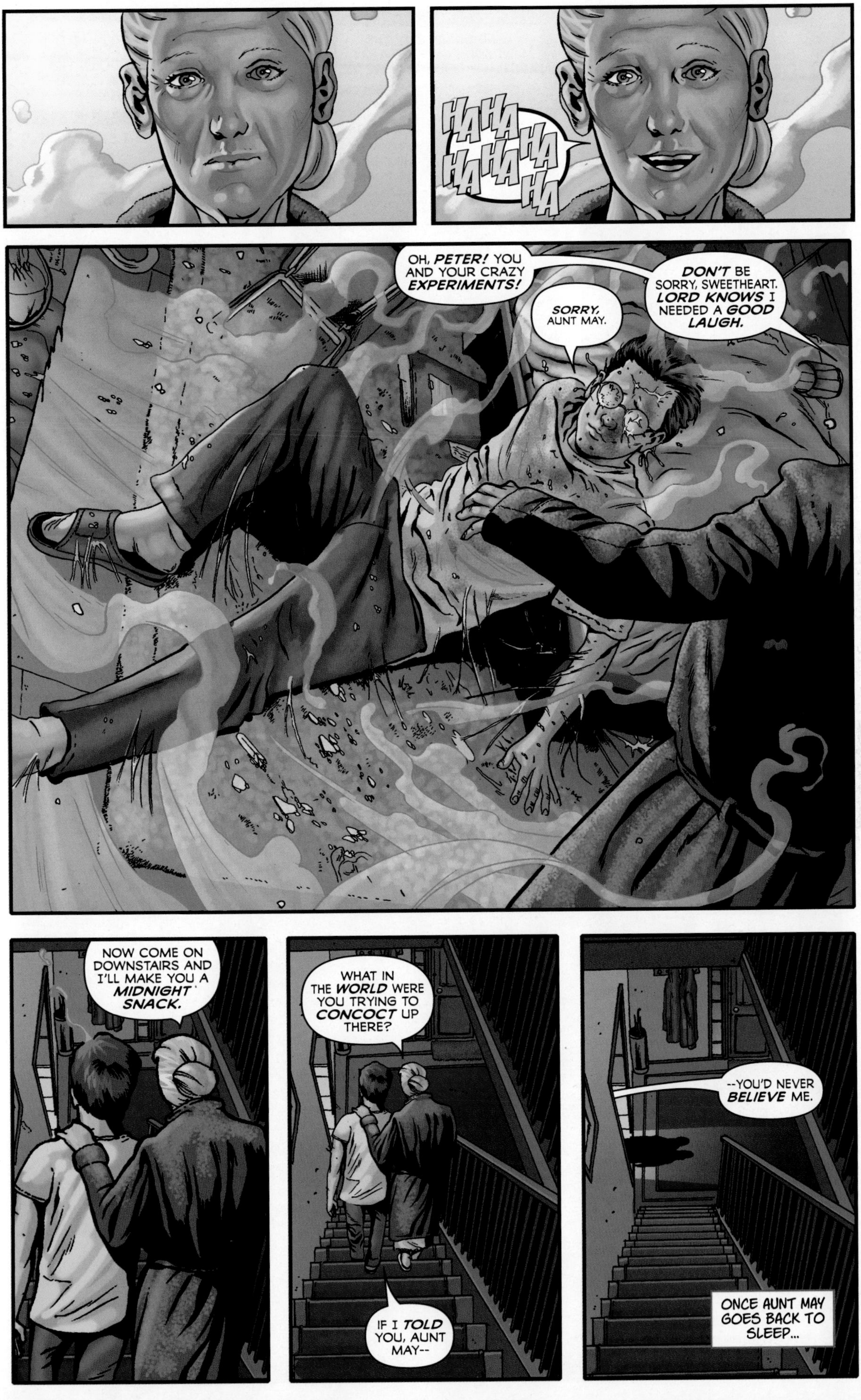
HAHAHAHAHAHAHA
OH, PETER! YOU AND YOUR CRAZY EXPERIMENTS!
SORRY, AUNT MAY.
DON'T BE SORRY, SWEETHEART. LORD KNOWS I NEEDED A GOOD LAUGH.
NOW COME ON DOWNSTAIRS AND I'LL MAKE YOU A MIDNIGHT SNACK.
WHAT IN THE WORLD WERE YOU TRYING TO CONCOCT UP THERE?
IF I TOLD YOU, AUNT MAY--
--YOU'D NEVER BELIEVE ME.
ONCE AUNT MAY GOES BACK TO SLEEP...

...I SLAP ON THE WEB-SHOOTERS (GOOD THING I'VE GOT A LITTLE OF THE *OLD FORMULA* LEFT), SLIP ON THE COSTUME (WHICH COULD USE A *WASH*: IT KINDA *REEKS*)...

...AND SNEAK OUT THE WINDOW--*PRAYING* THAT AUNT MAY DOESN'T HEAR ME.

IT'D BE JUST AS BAD IF ONE OF THE *NEIGHBORS* SAW ME. I CAN JUST IMAGINE *MRS. WATSON* FROM NEXT DOOR CALLING AUNT MAY TOMORROW MORNING...

...TO ASK *WHAT*, EXACTLY, HER *GEEKAZOID NEPHEW* WAS DOING CRAWLING DOWN THE WALL IN A HALLOWEEN COSTUME LAST NIGHT?

MAYBE I SHOULD BUILD A *SECRET TUNNEL* UNDER THE HOUSE.

NOT THAT I HAVE A *CLUE* HOW TO *DO* THAT.

IN FACT, I HAVEN'T GOT A CLUE ABOUT *ANY* OF THIS.

I MEAN, I KNOW HOW TO WORK A *CROWD*...PUT ON A *SHOW*. BUT THIS IS *WAY DIFFERENT*.

THIS ISN'T *ENTERTAINMENT*. THIS IS *REAL LIFE*.

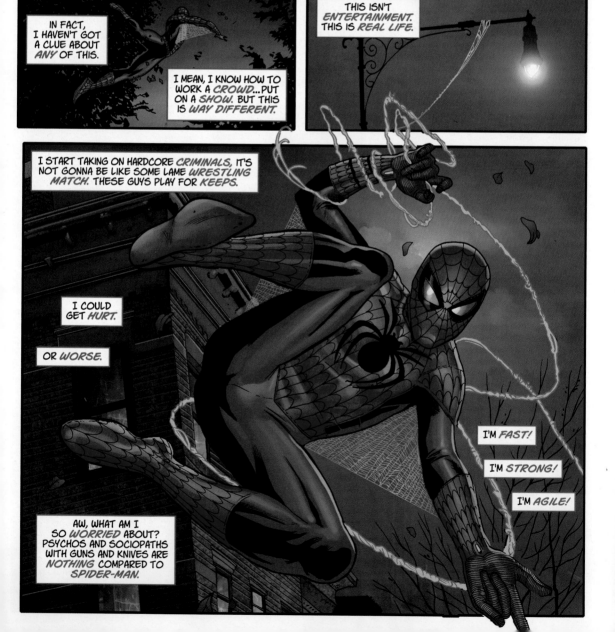

I START TAKING ON HARDCORE *CRIMINALS*, IT'S NOT GONNA BE LIKE SOME LAME *WRESTLING MATCH*. THESE GUYS PLAY FOR *KEEPS*.

I COULD GET *HURT*.

OR *WORSE*.

I'M *FAST*!

I'M *STRONG*!

I'M *AGILE*!

AW, WHAT AM I SO *WORRIED* ABOUT? PSYCHOS AND SOCIOPATHS WITH GUNS AND KNIVES ARE *NOTHING* COMPARED TO *SPIDER-MAN*.

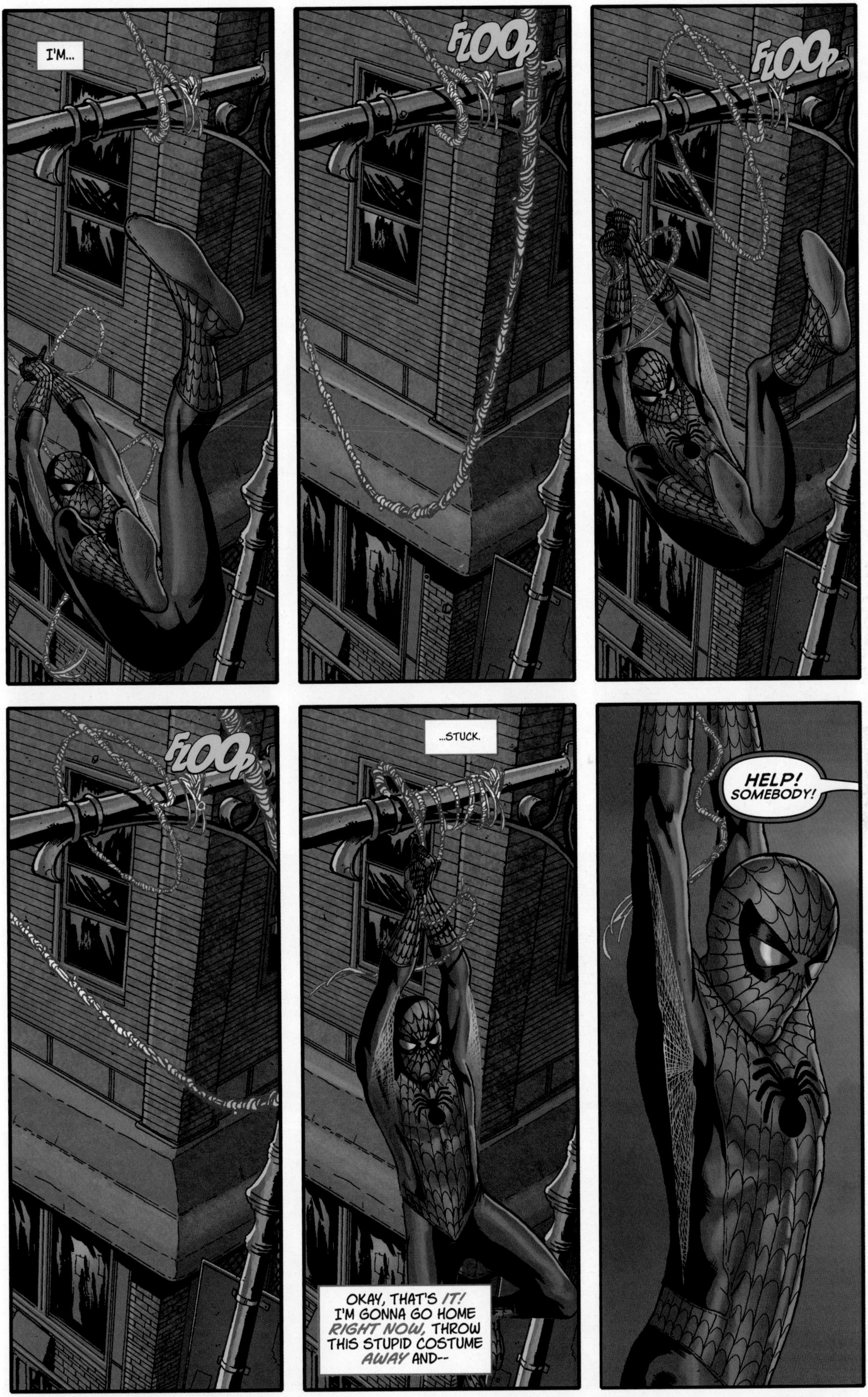
I'M...
FZOOp
FZOOp
FZOOp
...STUCK.
OKAY, THAT'S IT! I'M GONNA GO HOME RIGHT NOW, THROW THIS STUPID COSTUME AWAY AND--
HELP! SOMEBODY!

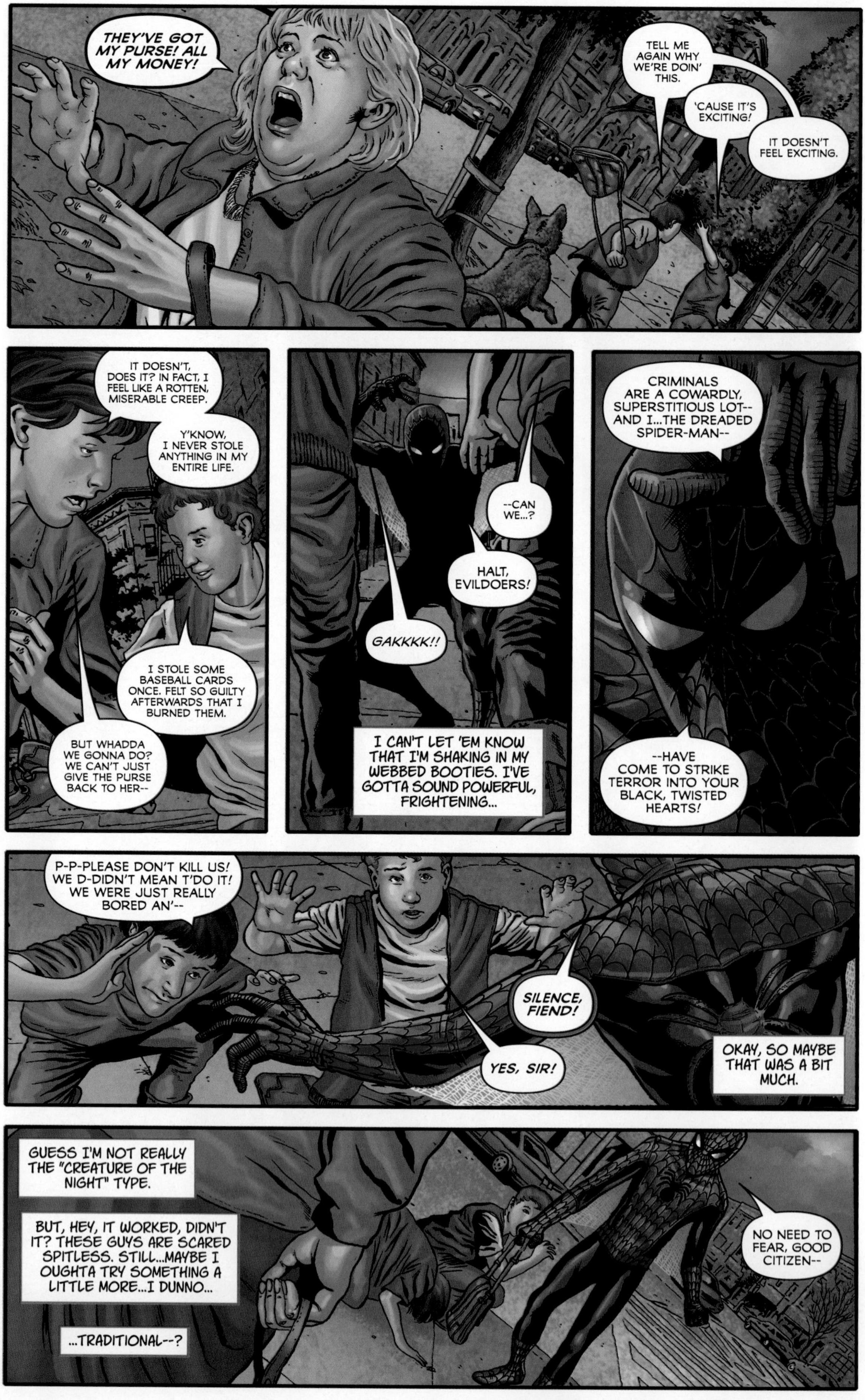
THEY'VE GOT MY PURSE! ALL MY MONEY!
TELL ME AGAIN WHY WE'RE DOIN' THIS.
'CAUSE IT'S EXCITING!
IT DOESN'T FEEL EXCITING.
IT DOESN'T, DOES IT? IN FACT, I FEEL LIKE A ROTTEN, MISERABLE CREEP.
Y'KNOW, I NEVER STOLE ANYTHING IN MY ENTIRE LIFE.
I STOLE SOME BASEBALL CARDS ONCE. FELT SO GUILTY AFTERWARDS THAT I BURNED THEM.
BUT WHADDA WE GONNA DO? WE CAN'T JUST GIVE THE PURSE BACK TO HER--
--CAN WE...?
HALT, EVILDOERS!
GAKKKK!!
I CAN'T LET 'EM KNOW THAT I'M SHAKING IN MY WEBBED BOOTIES. I'VE GOTTA SOUND POWERFUL, FRIGHTENING...
CRIMINALS ARE A COWARDLY, SUPERSTITIOUS LOT-- AND I...THE DREADED SPIDER-MAN--
--HAVE COME TO STRIKE TERROR INTO YOUR BLACK, TWISTED HEARTS!
P-P-PLEASE DON'T KILL US! WE D-DIDN'T MEAN T'DO IT! WE WERE JUST REALLY BORED AN'--
SILENCE, FIEND!
YES, SIR!
OKAY, SO MAYBE THAT WAS A BIT MUCH.
GUESS I'M NOT REALLY THE "CREATURE OF THE NIGHT" TYPE.
BUT, HEY, IT WORKED, DIDN'T IT? THESE GUYS ARE SCARED SPITLESS. STILL...MAYBE I OUGHTA TRY SOMETHING A LITTLE MORE...I DUNNO...
...TRADITIONAL--?
NO NEED TO FEAR, GOOD CITIZEN--

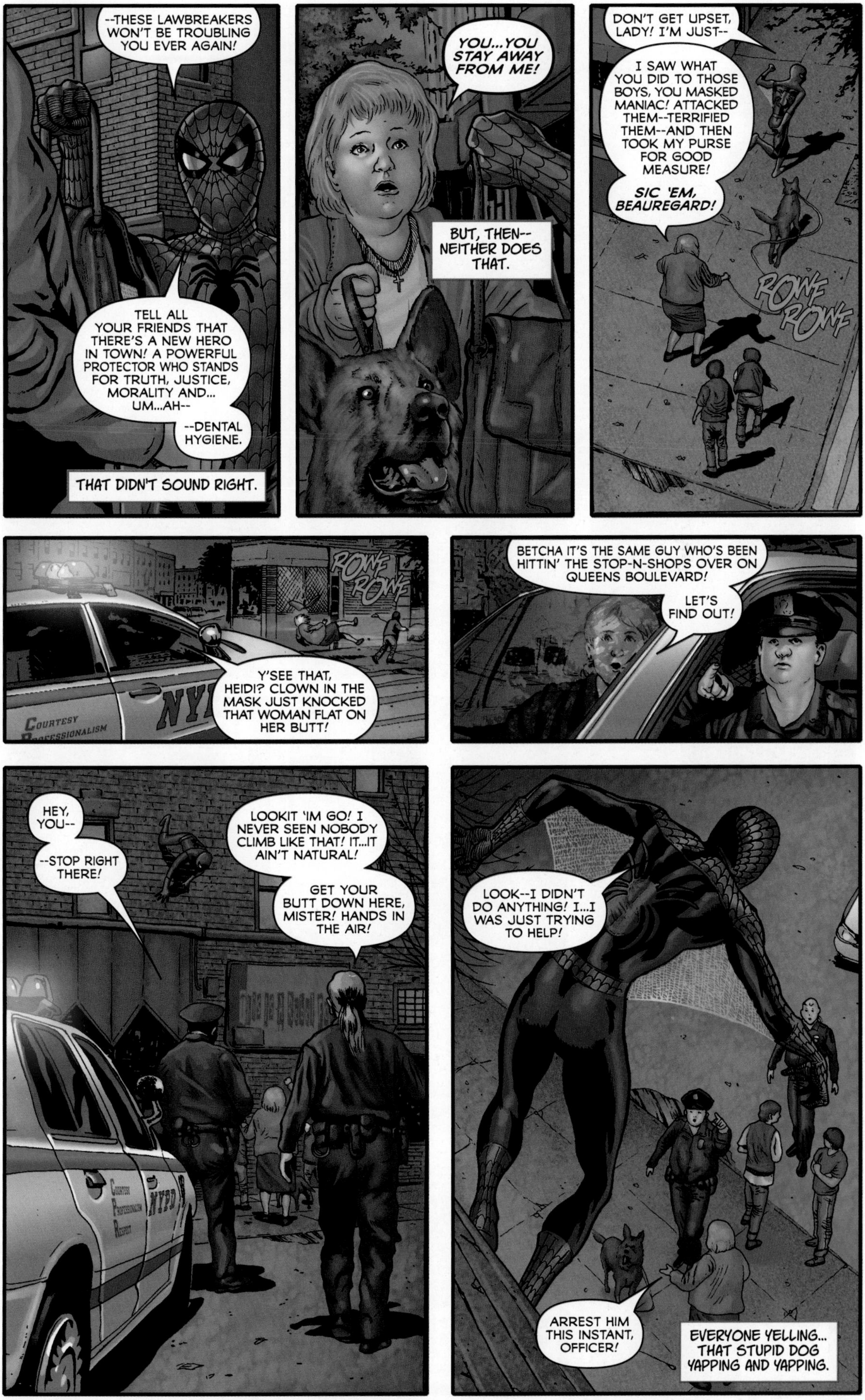
--THESE LAWBREAKERS WON'T BE TROUBLING YOU EVER AGAIN!
TELL ALL YOUR FRIENDS THAT THERE'S A NEW HERO IN TOWN! A POWERFUL PROTECTOR WHO STANDS FOR TRUTH, JUSTICE, MORALITY AND... UM...AH--
--DENTAL HYGIENE.
THAT DIDN'T SOUND RIGHT.
YOU...YOU STAY AWAY FROM ME!
BUT, THEN-- NEITHER DOES THAT.
DON'T GET UPSET, LADY! I'M JUST--
I SAW WHAT YOU DID TO THOSE BOYS, YOU MASKED MANIAC! ATTACKED THEM--TERRIFIED THEM--AND THEN TOOK MY PURSE FOR GOOD MEASURE!
SIC 'EM, BEAUREGARD!
ROWF ROWF
ROWF ROWF
Y'SEE THAT, HEIDI? CLOWN IN THE MASK JUST KNOCKED THAT WOMAN FLAT ON HER BUTT!
NYPD
BETCHA IT'S THE SAME GUY WHO'S BEEN HITTIN' THE STOP-N-SHOPS OVER ON QUEENS BOULEVARD!
LET'S FIND OUT!
HEY, YOU--
--STOP RIGHT THERE!
LOOKIT 'IM GO! I NEVER SEEN NOBODY CLIMB LIKE THAT! IT...IT AIN'T NATURAL!
GET YOUR BUTT DOWN HERE, MISTER! HANDS IN THE AIR!
NYPD
LOOK--I DIDN'T DO ANYTHING! I...I WAS JUST TRYING TO HELP!
ARREST HIM THIS INSTANT, OFFICER!
EVERYONE YELLING... THAT STUPID DOG YAPPING AND YAPPING.

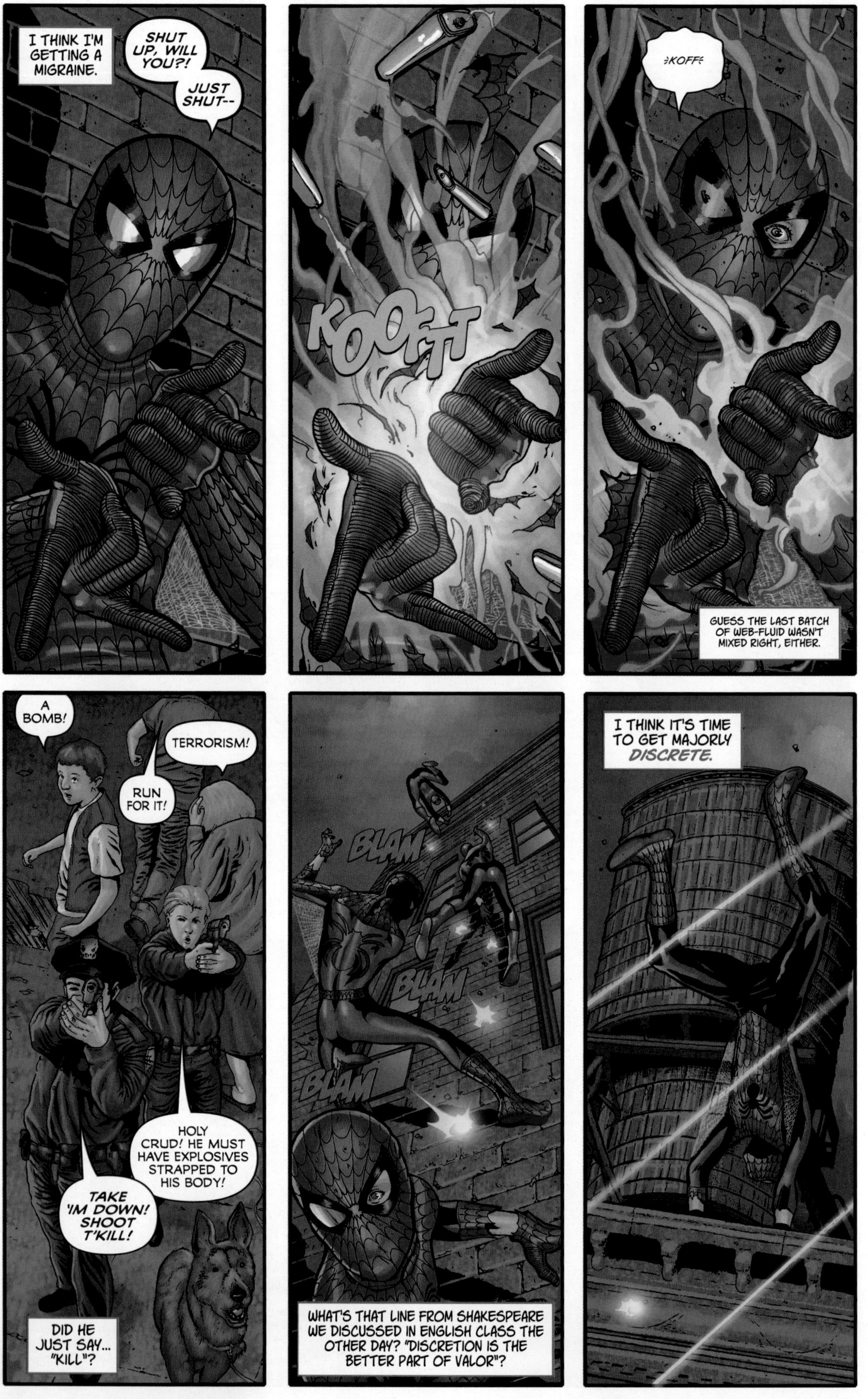
I THINK I'M GETTING A MIGRAINE.
SHUT UP, WILL YOU?!
JUST SHUT--
KOOFTT
KOFF
GUESS THE LAST BATCH OF WEB-FLUID WASN'T MIXED RIGHT, EITHER.
A BOMB!
TERRORISM!
RUN FOR IT!
HOLY CRUD! HE MUST HAVE EXPLOSIVES STRAPPED TO HIS BODY!
TAKE 'IM DOWN! SHOOT T'KILL!
DID HE JUST SAY... "KILL"?
BLAM
BLAM
BLAM
WHAT'S THAT LINE FROM SHAKESPEARE WE DISCUSSED IN ENGLISH CLASS THE OTHER DAY? "DISCRETION IS THE BETTER PART OF VALOR"?
I THINK IT'S TIME TO GET MAJORLY DISCRETE.

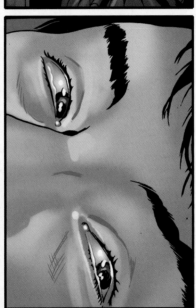

I THOUGHT COMING TO SCHOOL TODAY WOULD HELP GET MY MIND OFF UNCLE BEN.

NOT TO MENTION MY HUMILIATING PERFORMANCE LAST NIGHT.

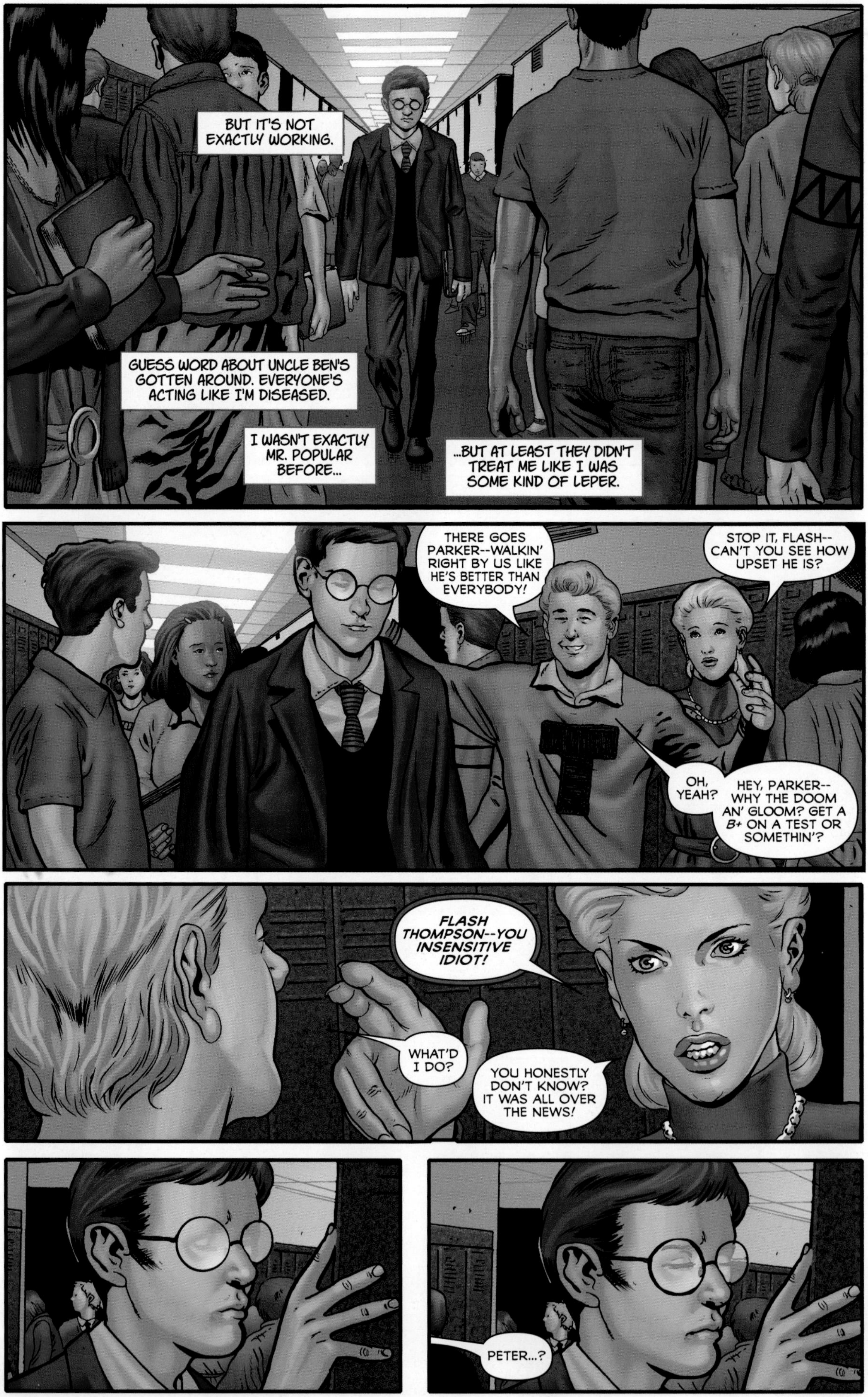
BUT IT'S NOT EXACTLY WORKING.
GUESS WORD ABOUT UNCLE BEN'S GOTTEN AROUND. EVERYONE'S ACTING LIKE I'M DISEASED.
I WASN'T EXACTLY MR. POPULAR BEFORE...
...BUT AT LEAST THEY DIDN'T TREAT ME LIKE I WAS SOME KIND OF LEPER.
THERE GOES PARKER--WALKIN' RIGHT BY US LIKE HE'S BETTER THAN EVERYBODY!
STOP IT, FLASH-- CAN'T YOU SEE HOW UPSET HE IS?
OH, YEAH?
HEY, PARKER-- WHY THE DOOM AN' GLOOM? GET A B+ ON A TEST OR SOMETHIN'?
FLASH THOMPSON--YOU INSENSITIVE IDIOT!
WHAT'D I DO?
YOU HONESTLY DON'T KNOW? IT WAS ALL OVER THE NEWS!
PETER...?

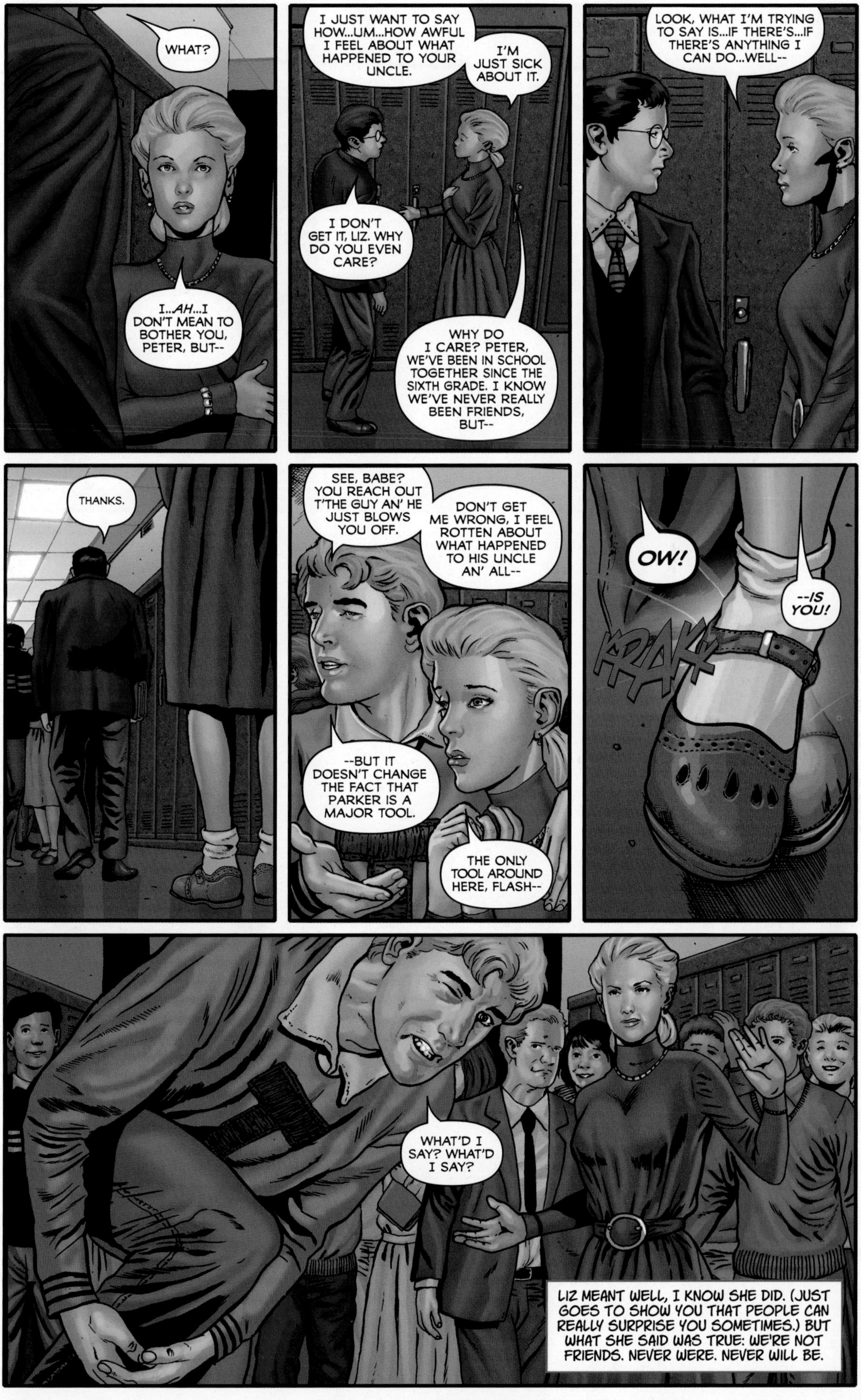
WHAT?
I...AH...I DON'T MEAN TO BOTHER YOU, PETER, BUT--
I JUST WANT TO SAY HOW...UM...HOW AWFUL I FEEL ABOUT WHAT HAPPENED TO YOUR UNCLE.
I'M JUST SICK ABOUT IT.
I DON'T GET IT, LIZ. WHY DO YOU EVEN CARE?
WHY DO I CARE? PETER, WE'VE BEEN IN SCHOOL TOGETHER SINCE THE SIXTH GRADE. I KNOW WE'VE NEVER REALLY BEEN FRIENDS, BUT--
LOOK, WHAT I'M TRYING TO SAY IS...IF THERE'S...IF THERE'S ANYTHING I CAN DO...WELL--
THANKS.
SEE, BABE? YOU REACH OUT T'THE GUY AN' HE JUST BLOWS YOU OFF.
DON'T GET ME WRONG, I FEEL ROTTEN ABOUT WHAT HAPPENED TO HIS UNCLE AN' ALL--
--BUT IT DOESN'T CHANGE THE FACT THAT PARKER IS A MAJOR TOOL.
THE ONLY TOOL AROUND HERE, FLASH--
OW!
--IS YOU!
KRAK!
WHAT'D I SAY? WHAT'D I SAY?
LIZ MEANT WELL, I KNOW SHE DID. (JUST GOES TO SHOW YOU THAT PEOPLE CAN REALLY SURPRISE YOU SOMETIMES.) BUT WHAT SHE SAID WAS TRUE: WE'RE NOT FRIENDS. NEVER WERE. NEVER WILL BE.

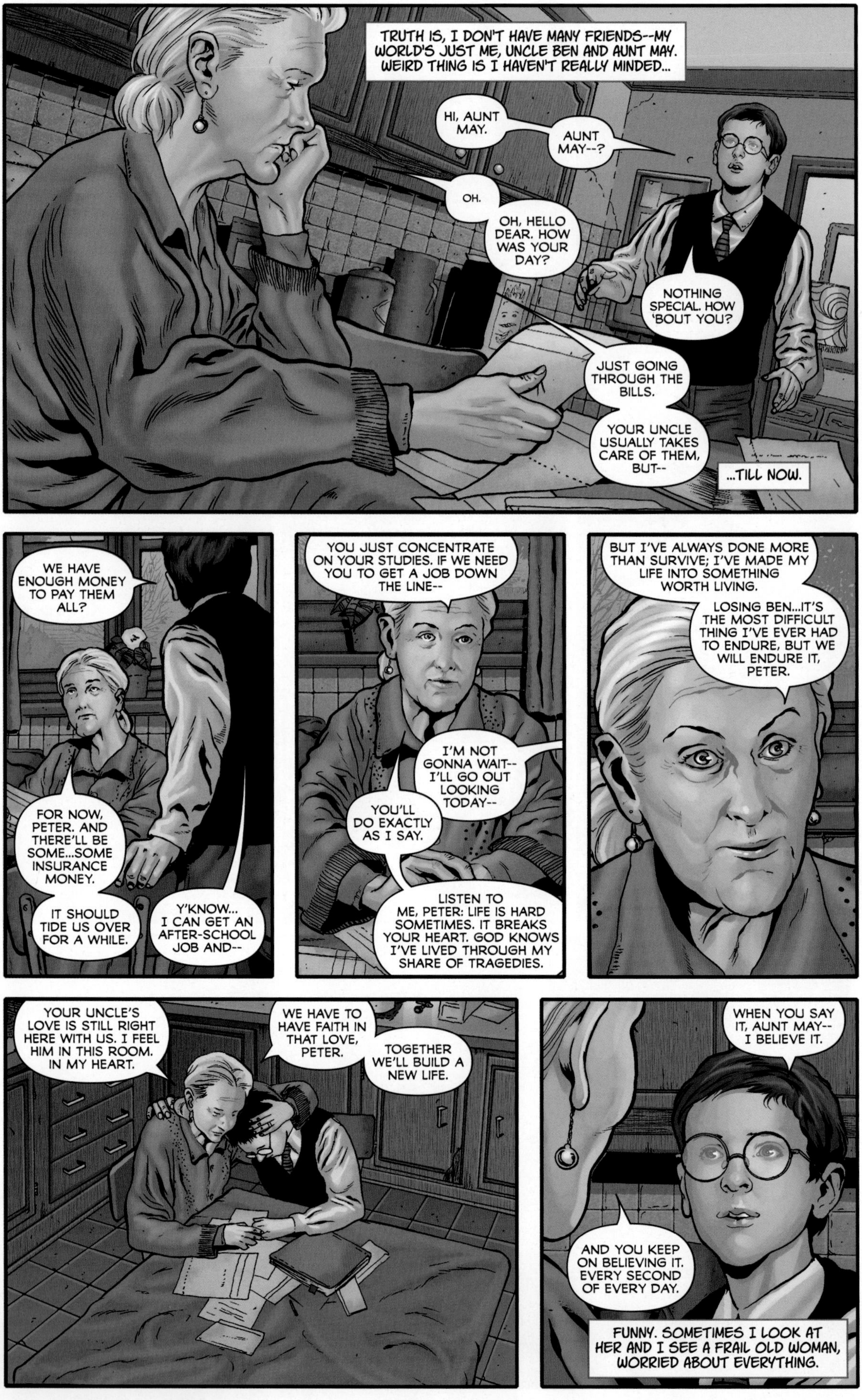
TRUTH IS, I DON'T HAVE MANY FRIENDS--MY WORLD'S JUST ME, UNCLE BEN AND AUNT MAY. WEIRD THING IS I HAVEN'T REALLY MINDED...
HI, AUNT MAY.
AUNT MAY--?
OH.
OH, HELLO DEAR. HOW WAS YOUR DAY?
NOTHING SPECIAL. HOW 'BOUT YOU?
JUST GOING THROUGH THE BILLS.
YOUR UNCLE USUALLY TAKES CARE OF THEM, BUT--
...TILL NOW.
WE HAVE ENOUGH MONEY TO PAY THEM ALL?
FOR NOW, PETER. AND THERE'LL BE SOME...SOME INSURANCE MONEY.
IT SHOULD TIDE US OVER FOR A WHILE.
Y'KNOW... I CAN GET AN AFTER-SCHOOL JOB AND--
YOU JUST CONCENTRATE ON YOUR STUDIES. IF WE NEED YOU TO GET A JOB DOWN THE LINE--
I'M NOT GONNA WAIT-- I'LL GO OUT LOOKING TODAY--
YOU'LL DO EXACTLY AS I SAY.
LISTEN TO ME, PETER: LIFE IS HARD SOMETIMES. IT BREAKS YOUR HEART. GOD KNOWS I'VE LIVED THROUGH MY SHARE OF TRAGEDIES.
BUT I'VE ALWAYS DONE MORE THAN SURVIVE; I'VE MADE MY LIFE INTO SOMETHING WORTH LIVING.
LOSING BEN...IT'S THE MOST DIFFICULT THING I'VE EVER HAD TO ENDURE, BUT WE WILL ENDURE IT, PETER.
YOUR UNCLE'S LOVE IS STILL RIGHT HERE WITH US. I FEEL HIM IN THIS ROOM. IN MY HEART.
WE HAVE TO HAVE FAITH IN THAT LOVE, PETER.
TOGETHER WE'LL BUILD A NEW LIFE.
WHEN YOU SAY IT, AUNT MAY-- I BELIEVE IT.
AND YOU KEEP ON BELIEVING IT. EVERY SECOND OF EVERY DAY.
FUNNY. SOMETIMES I LOOK AT HER AND I SEE A FRAIL OLD WOMAN, WORRIED ABOUT EVERYTHING.

AND, YEAH, I GUESS THAT'S A PART OF WHO SHE IS.

NOW ON YOUR WAY. GO DO YOUR HOMEWORK WHILE I FINISH WITH THESE BILLS.

OK, AUNT MAY.

BUT THERE'S MORE TO HER...

SO MUCH MORE.

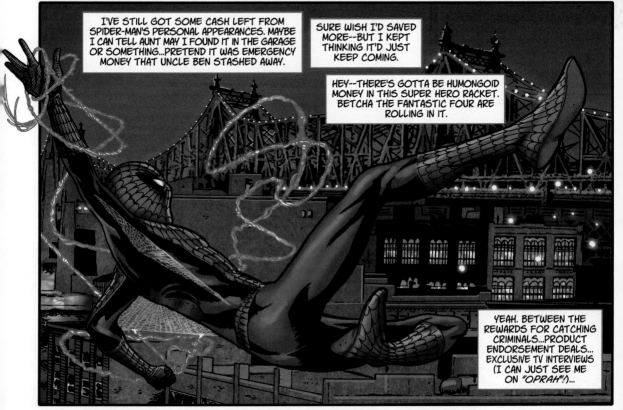

I'VE STILL GOT SOME CASH LEFT FROM SPIDER-MAN'S PERSONAL APPEARANCES. MAYBE I CAN TELL AUNT MAY I FOUND IT IN THE GARAGE OR SOMETHING...PRETEND IT WAS EMERGENCY MONEY THAT UNCLE BEN STASHED AWAY.

SURE WISH I'D SAVED MORE--BUT I KEPT THINKING IT'D JUST KEEP COMING.

HEY--THERE'S GOTTA BE HUMONGOID MONEY IN THIS SUPER HERO RACKET. BETCHA THE FANTASTIC FOUR ARE ROLLING IN IT.

YEAH. BETWEEN THE REWARDS FOR CATCHING CRIMINALS...PRODUCT ENDORSEMENT DEALS... EXCLUSIVE TV INTERVIEWS (I CAN JUST SEE ME ON "OPRAH"!)...

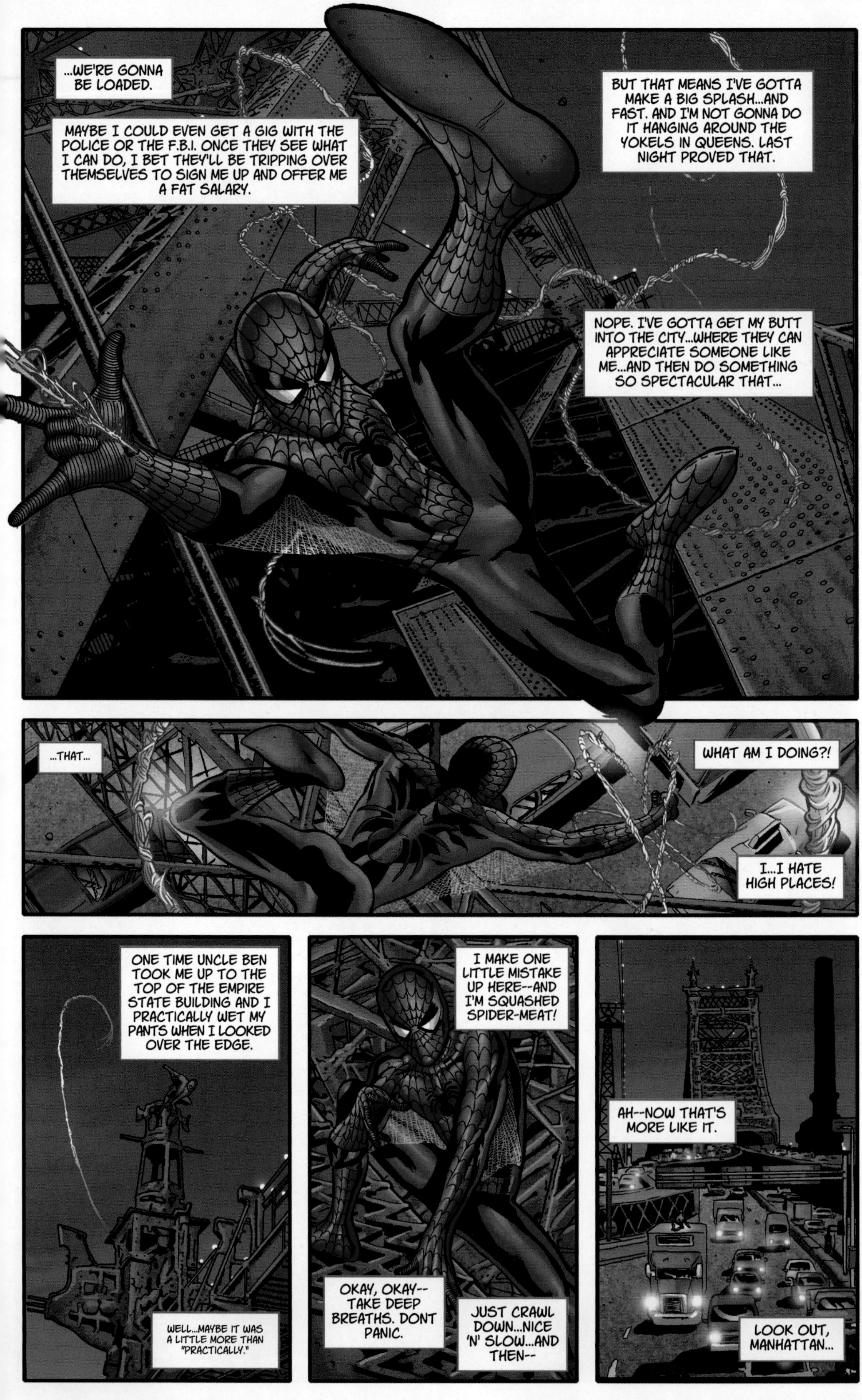
...WE'RE GONNA BE LOADED.
MAYBE I COULD EVEN GET A GIG WITH THE POLICE OR THE F.B.I. ONCE THEY SEE WHAT I CAN DO, I BET THEY'LL BE TRIPPING OVER THEMSELVES TO SIGN ME UP AND OFFER ME A FAT SALARY.
BUT THAT MEANS I'VE GOTTA MAKE A BIG SPLASH...AND FAST. AND I'M NOT GONNA DO IT HANGING AROUND THE YOKELS IN QUEENS. LAST NIGHT PROVED THAT.
NOPE. I'VE GOTTA GET MY BUTT INTO THE CITY...WHERE THEY CAN APPRECIATE SOMEONE LIKE ME...AND THEN DO SOMETHING SO SPECTACULAR THAT...
...THAT...
WHAT AM I DOING?!
I...I HATE HIGH PLACES!
ONE TIME UNCLE BEN TOOK ME UP TO THE TOP OF THE EMPIRE STATE BUILDING AND I PRACTICALLY WET MY PANTS WHEN I LOOKED OVER THE EDGE.
WELL...MAYBE IT WAS A LITTLE MORE THAN "PRACTICALLY."
I MAKE ONE LITTLE MISTAKE UP HERE--AND I'M SQUASHED SPIDER-MEAT!
OKAY, OKAY-- TAKE DEEP BREATHS. DONT PANIC.
JUST CRAWL DOWN...NICE 'N' SLOW...AND THEN--
AH--NOW THAT'S MORE LIKE IT.
LOOK OUT, MANHATTAN...

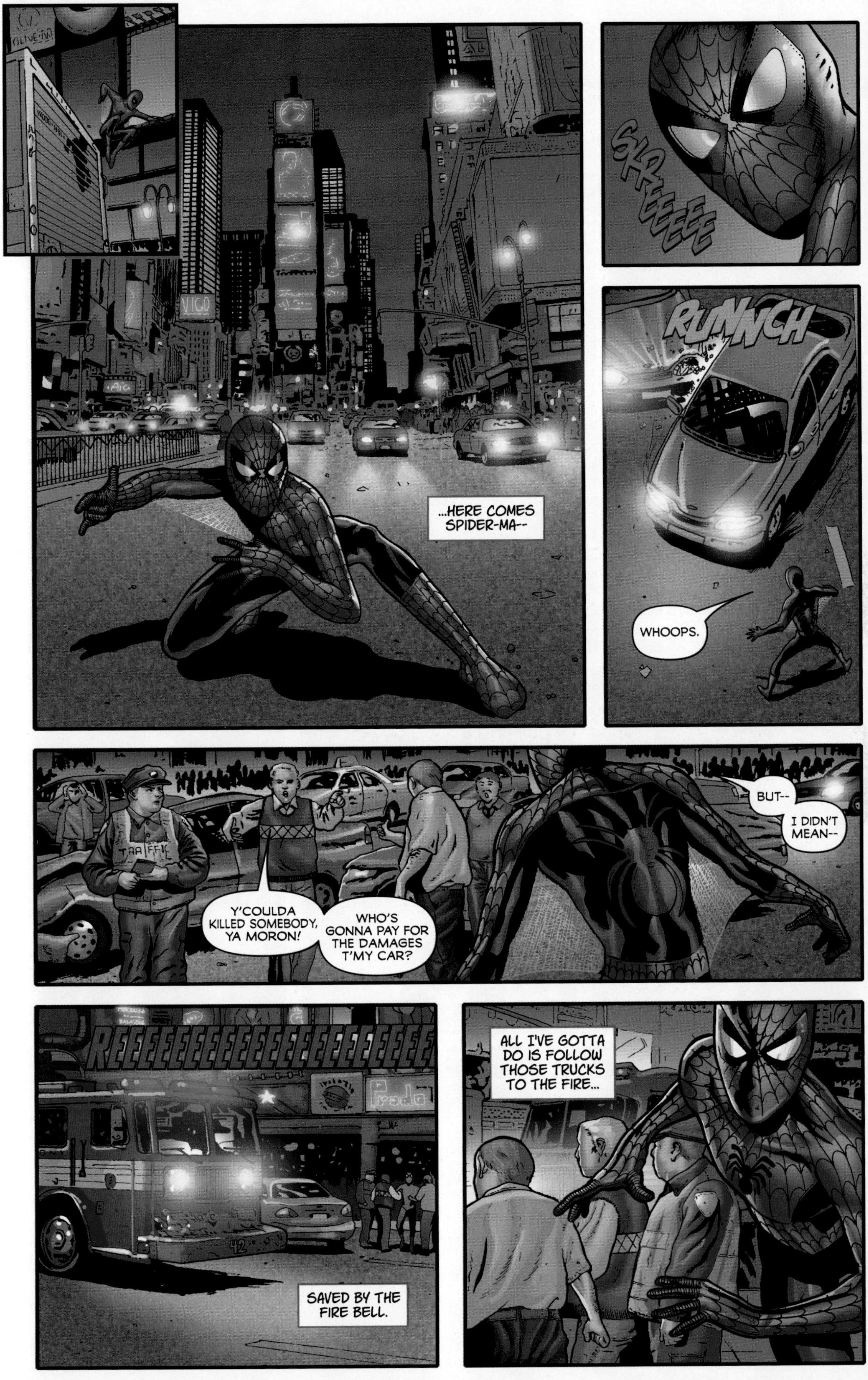

...HERE COMES SPIDER-MA--
SKREEEEEE
RUNNCH
WHOOPS.
BUT--
I DIDN'T MEAN--
Y'COULDA KILLED SOMEBODY, YA MORON!
WHO'S GONNA PAY FOR THE DAMAGES T'MY CAR?
REEEEEEEEEEEEEEEEEEEEE
SAVED BY THE FIRE BELL.
ALL I'VE GOTTA DO IS FOLLOW THOSE TRUCKS TO THE FIRE...

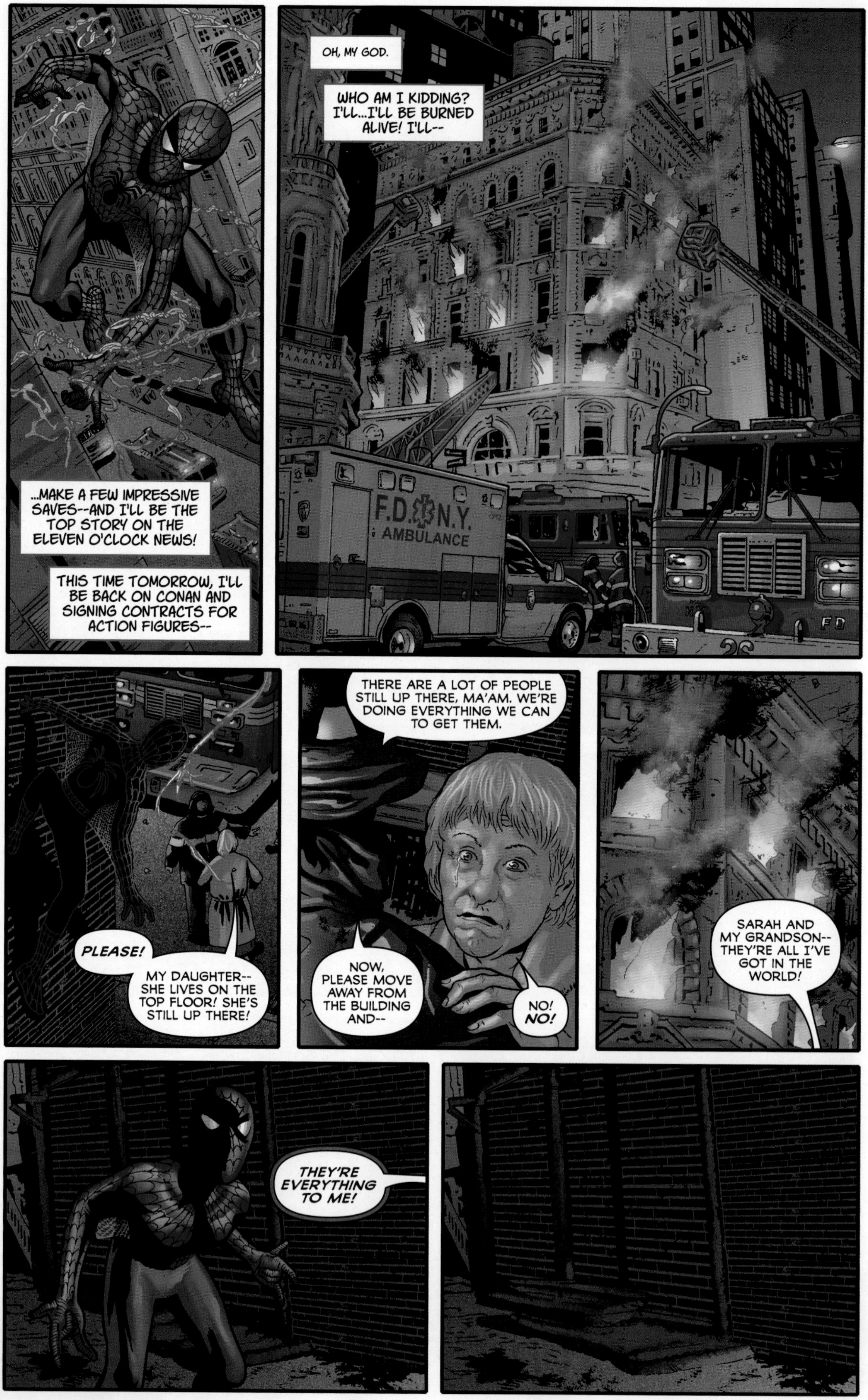
...MAKE A FEW IMPRESSIVE SAVES--AND I'LL BE THE TOP STORY ON THE ELEVEN O'CLOCK NEWS!
THIS TIME TOMORROW, I'LL BE BACK ON CONAN AND SIGNING CONTRACTS FOR ACTION FIGURES--
OH, MY GOD.
WHO AM I KIDDING? I'LL...I'LL BE BURNED ALIVE! I'LL--
F.D.N.Y.
AMBULANCE
FD
PLEASE!
MY DAUGHTER-- SHE LIVES ON THE TOP FLOOR! SHE'S STILL UP THERE!
THERE ARE A LOT OF PEOPLE STILL UP THERE, MA'AM. WE'RE DOING EVERYTHING WE CAN TO GET THEM.
NOW, PLEASE MOVE AWAY FROM THE BUILDING AND--
NO! NO!
SARAH AND MY GRANDSON-- THEY'RE ALL I'VE GOT IN THE WORLD!
THEY'RE EVERYTHING TO ME!

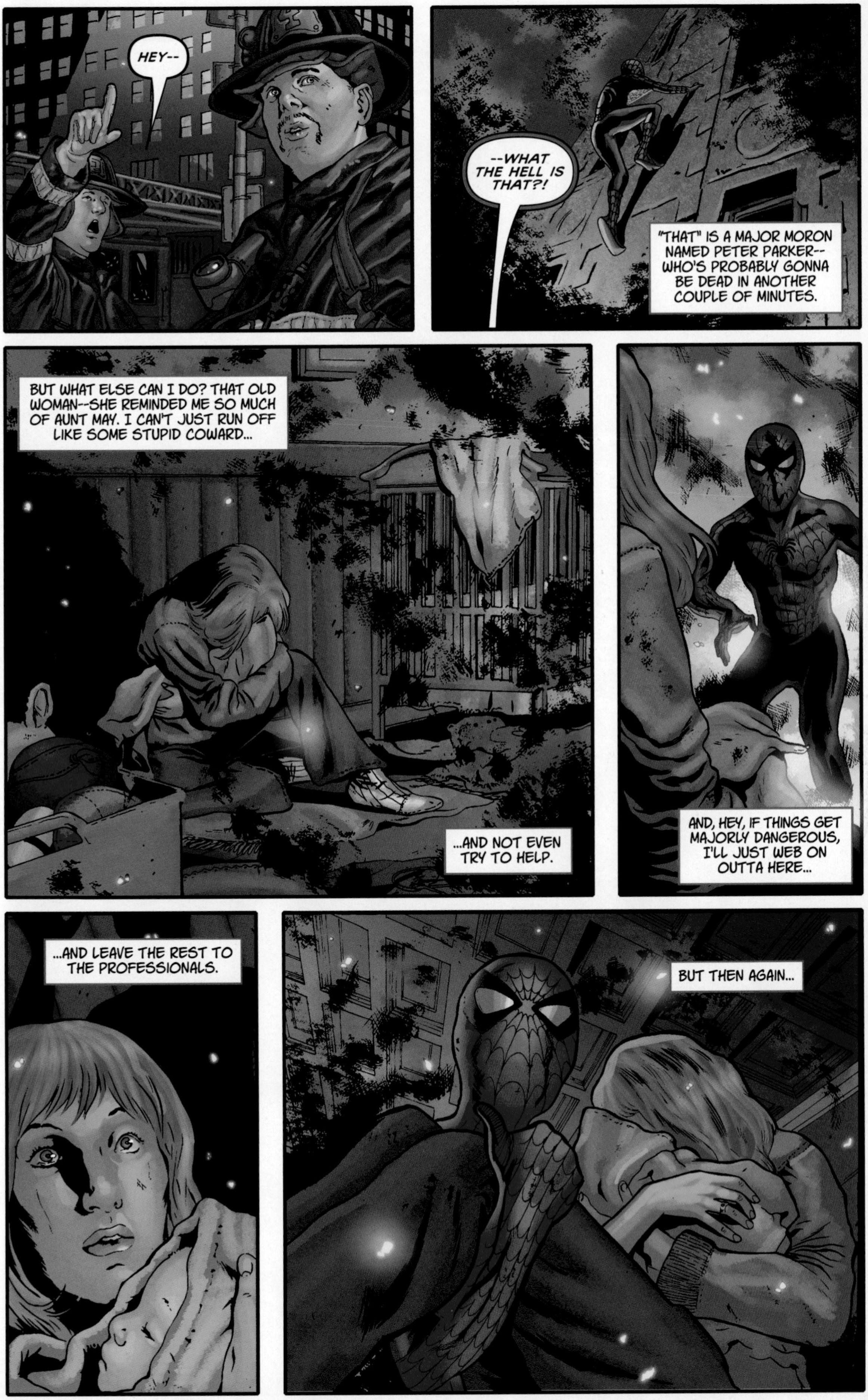
HEY--
--WHAT THE HELL IS THAT?!
"THAT" IS A MAJOR MORON NAMED PETER PARKER--WHO'S PROBABLY GONNA BE DEAD IN ANOTHER COUPLE OF MINUTES.
BUT WHAT ELSE CAN I DO? THAT OLD WOMAN--SHE REMINDED ME SO MUCH OF AUNT MAY. I CAN'T JUST RUN OFF LIKE SOME STUPID COWARD...
...AND NOT EVEN TRY TO HELP.
AND, HEY, IF THINGS GET MAJORLY DANGEROUS, I'LL JUST WEB ON OUTTA HERE...
...AND LEAVE THE REST TO THE PROFESSIONALS.
BUT THEN AGAIN...

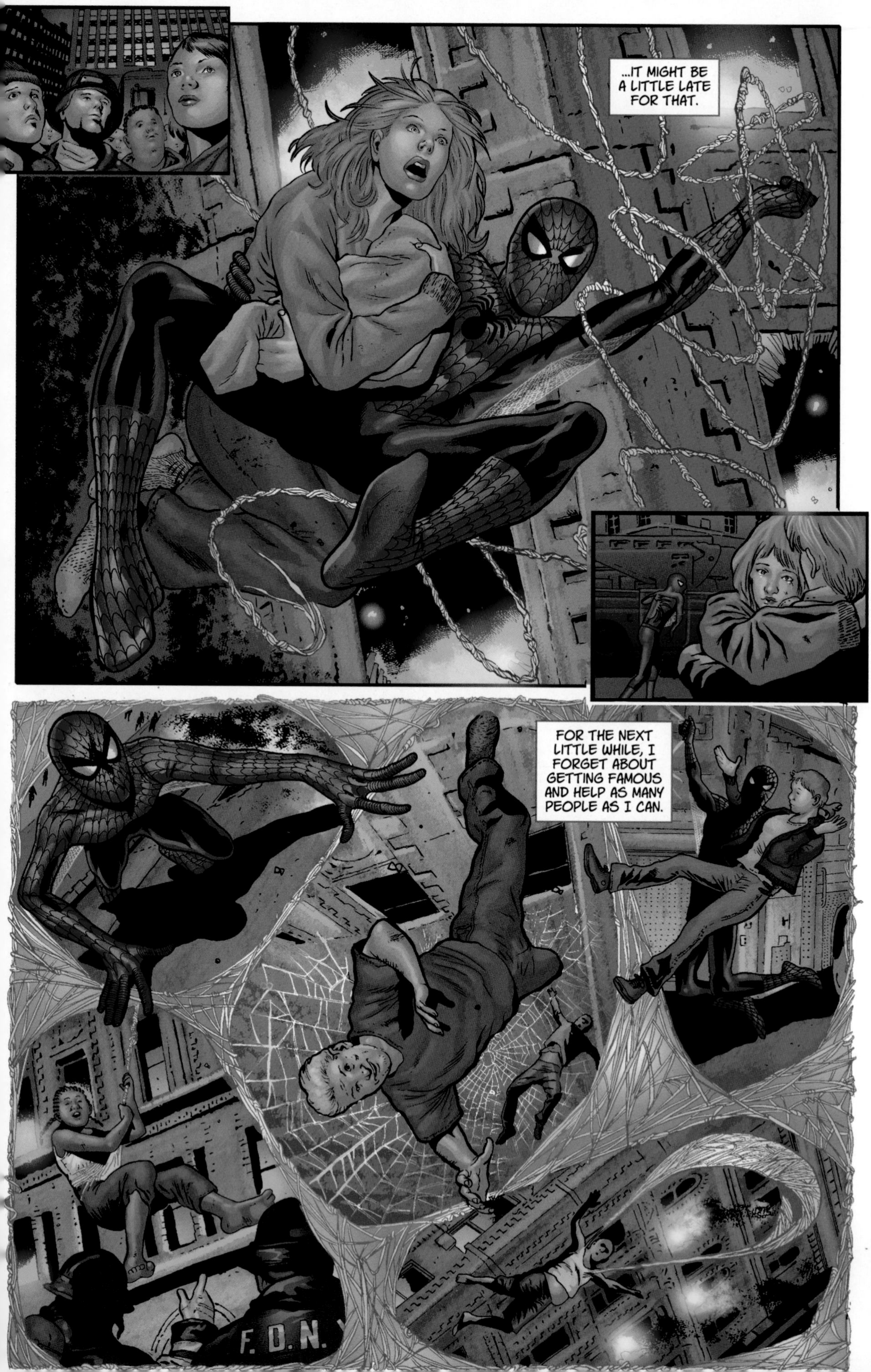
...IT MIGHT BE A LITTLE LATE FOR THAT.
FOR THE NEXT LITTLE WHILE, I FORGET ABOUT GETTING FAMOUS AND HELP AS MANY PEOPLE AS I CAN.
F.D.N.

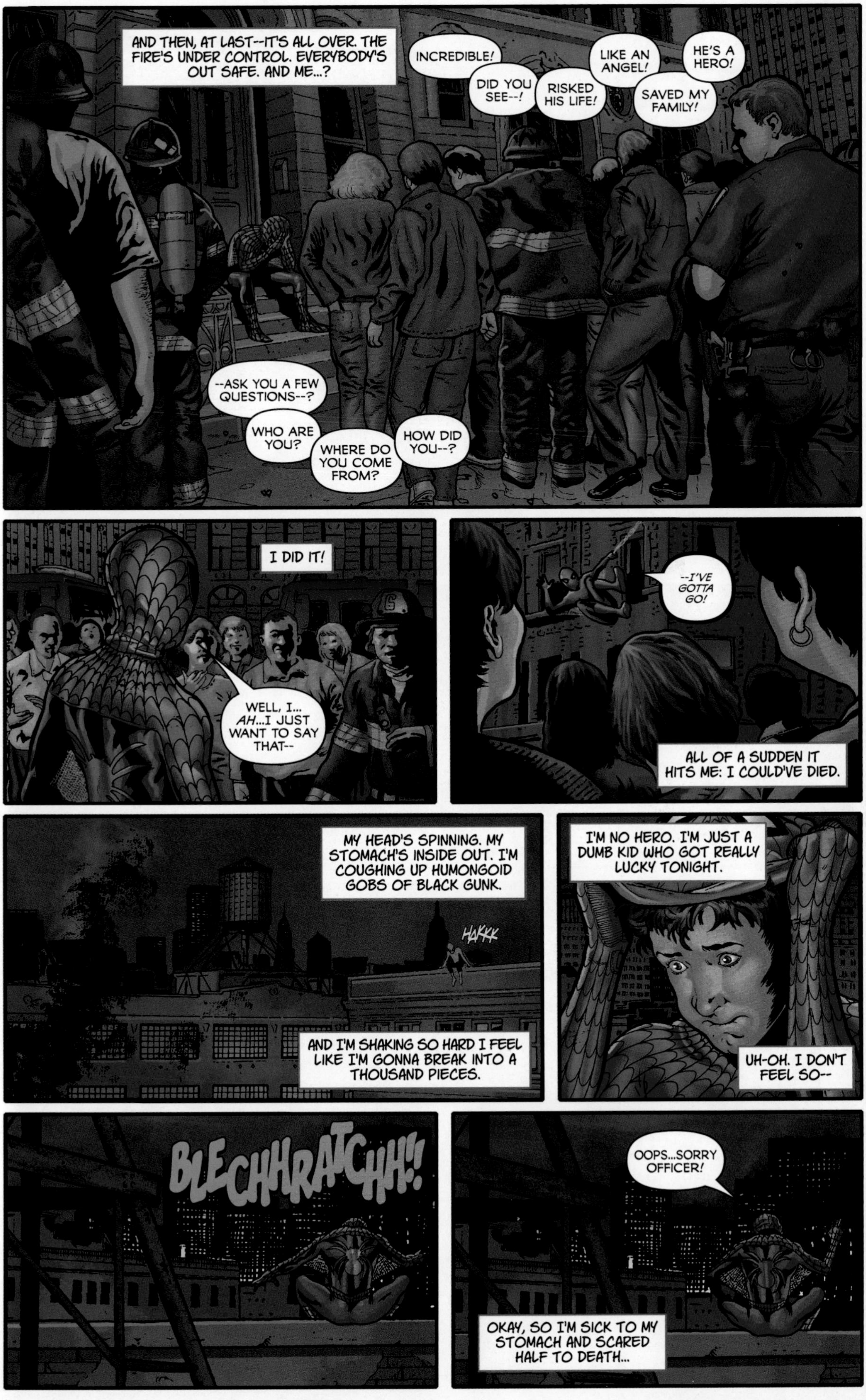
AND THEN, AT LAST--IT'S ALL OVER. THE FIRE'S UNDER CONTROL. EVERYBODY'S OUT SAFE. AND ME...?
INCREDIBLE!
DID YOU SEE--!
RISKED HIS LIFE!
LIKE AN ANGEL!
HE'S A HERO!
SAVED MY FAMILY!
--ASK YOU A FEW QUESTIONS--?
WHO ARE YOU?
WHERE DO YOU COME FROM?
HOW DID YOU--?
I DID IT!
WELL, I... AH...I JUST WANT TO SAY THAT--
--I'VE GOTTA GO!
ALL OF A SUDDEN IT HITS ME: I COULD'VE DIED.
MY HEAD'S SPINNING. MY STOMACH'S INSIDE OUT. I'M COUGHING UP HUMONGOID GOBS OF BLACK GUNK.
HAKKK
AND I'M SHAKING SO HARD I FEEL LIKE I'M GONNA BREAK INTO A THOUSAND PIECES.
I'M NO HERO. I'M JUST A DUMB KID WHO GOT REALLY LUCKY TONIGHT.
UH-OH. I DON'T FEEL SO--
BLECHHRATCHH!!
OOPS...SORRY OFFICER!
OKAY, SO I'M SICK TO MY STOMACH AND SCARED HALF TO DEATH...

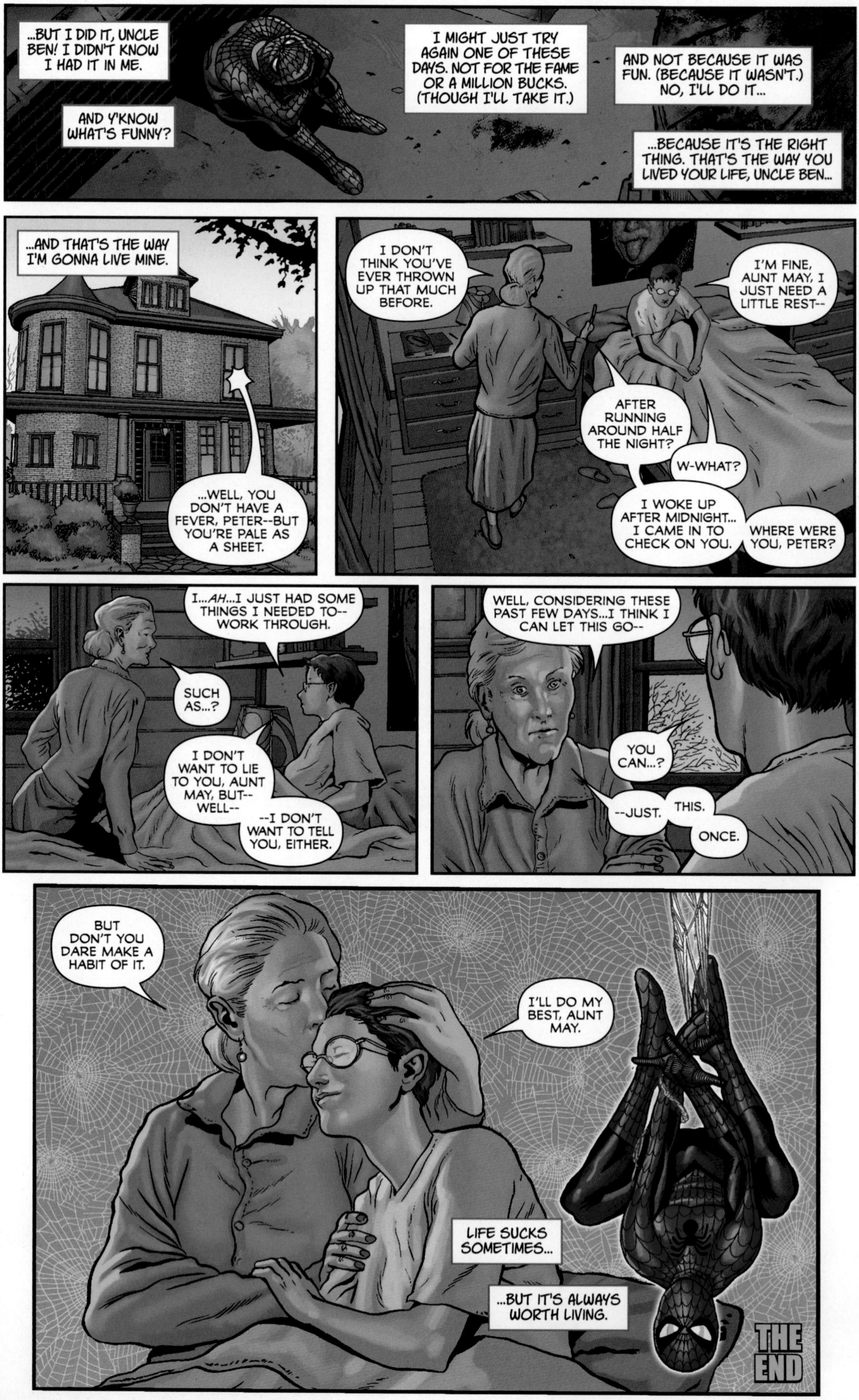
...BUT I DID IT, UNCLE BEN! I DIDN'T KNOW I HAD IT IN ME.
AND Y'KNOW WHAT'S FUNNY?
I MIGHT JUST TRY AGAIN ONE OF THESE DAYS. NOT FOR THE FAME OR A MILLION BUCKS. (THOUGH I'LL TAKE IT.)
AND NOT BECAUSE IT WAS FUN. (BECAUSE IT WASN'T.) NO, I'LL DO IT...
...BECAUSE IT'S THE RIGHT THING. THAT'S THE WAY YOU LIVED YOUR LIFE, UNCLE BEN...
...AND THAT'S THE WAY I'M GONNA LIVE MINE.
...WELL, YOU DON'T HAVE A FEVER, PETER--BUT YOU'RE PALE AS A SHEET.
I DON'T THINK YOU'VE EVER THROWN UP THAT MUCH BEFORE.
I'M FINE, AUNT MAY, I JUST NEED A LITTLE REST--
AFTER RUNNING AROUND HALF THE NIGHT?
W-WHAT?
I WOKE UP AFTER MIDNIGHT... I CAME IN TO CHECK ON YOU.
WHERE WERE YOU, PETER?
I...AH...I JUST HAD SOME THINGS I NEEDED TO--WORK THROUGH.
SUCH AS...?
I DON'T WANT TO LIE TO YOU, AUNT MAY, BUT--WELL--
--I DON'T WANT TO TELL YOU, EITHER.
WELL, CONSIDERING THESE PAST FEW DAYS...I THINK I CAN LET THIS GO--
YOU CAN...?
--JUST.
THIS.
ONCE.
BUT DON'T YOU DARE MAKE A HABIT OF IT.
I'LL DO MY BEST, AUNT MAY.
LIFE SUCKS SOMETIMES...
...BUT IT'S ALWAYS WORTH LIVING.
THE END

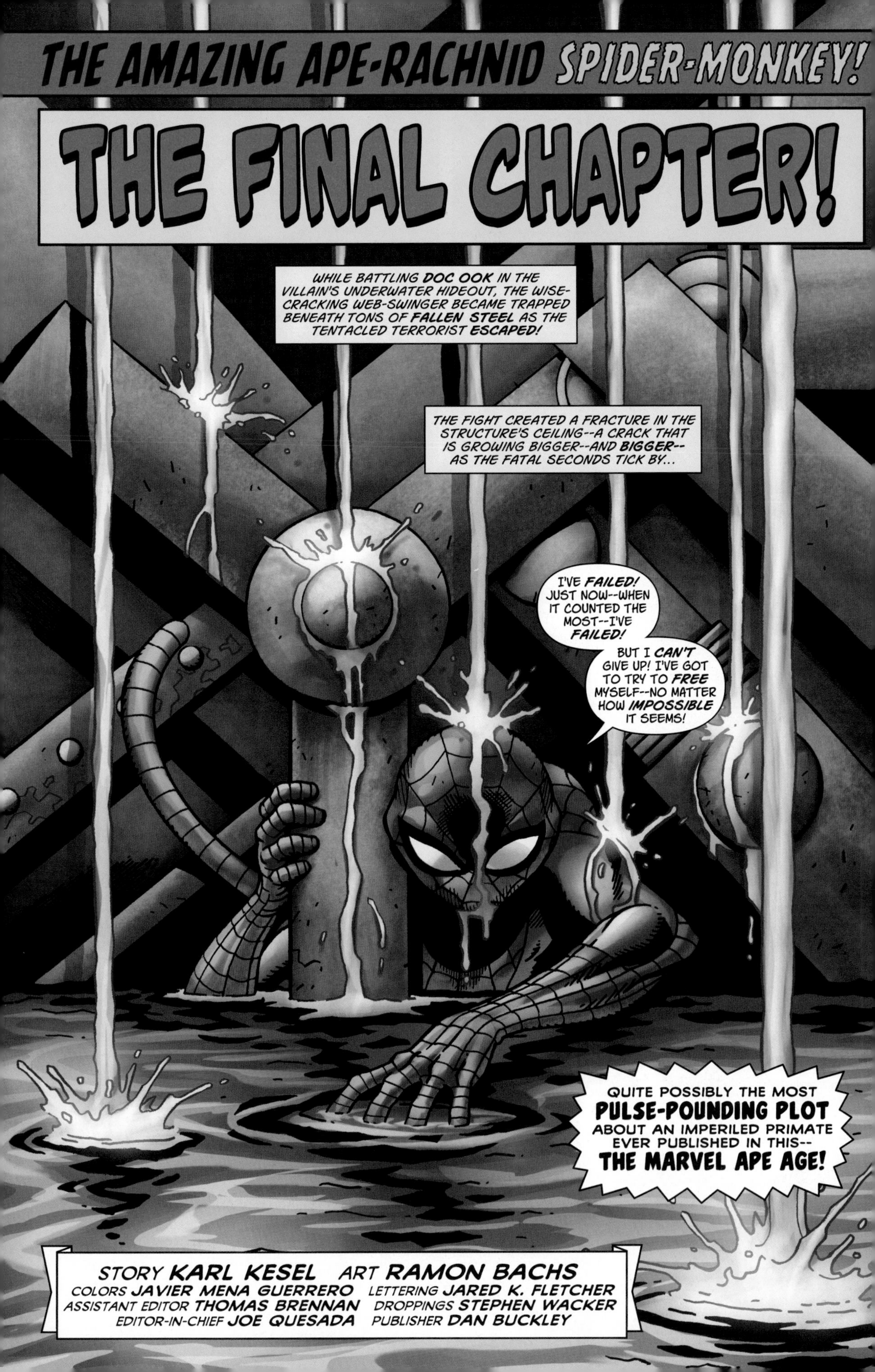

THE AMAZING APE-RACHNID SPIDER-MONKEY!
THE FINAL CHAPTER!
WHILE BATTLING DOC OOK IN THE VILLAIN'S UNDERWATER HIDEOUT, THE WISE-CRACKING WEB-SWINGER BECAME TRAPPED BENEATH TONS OF FALLEN STEEL AS THE TENTACLED TERRORIST ESCAPED!
THE FIGHT CREATED A FRACTURE IN THE STRUCTURE'S CEILING--A CRACK THAT IS GROWING BIGGER--AND BIGGER--AS THE FATAL SECONDS TICK BY...
I'VE FAILED! JUST NOW--WHEN IT COUNTED THE MOST--I'VE FAILED!
BUT I CAN'T GIVE UP! I'VE GOT TO TRY TO FREE MYSELF--NO MATTER HOW IMPOSSIBLE IT SEEMS!
QUITE POSSIBLY THE MOST PULSE-POUNDING PLOT ABOUT AN IMPERILED PRIMATE EVER PUBLISHED IN THIS-- THE MARVEL APE AGE!
STORY KARL KESEL ART RAMON BACHS
COLORS JAVIER MENA GUERRERO LETTERING JARED K. FLETCHER
ASSISTANT EDITOR THOMAS BRENNAN DROPPINGS STEPHEN WACKER
EDITOR-IN-CHIEF JOE QUESADA PUBLISHER DAN BUCKLEY

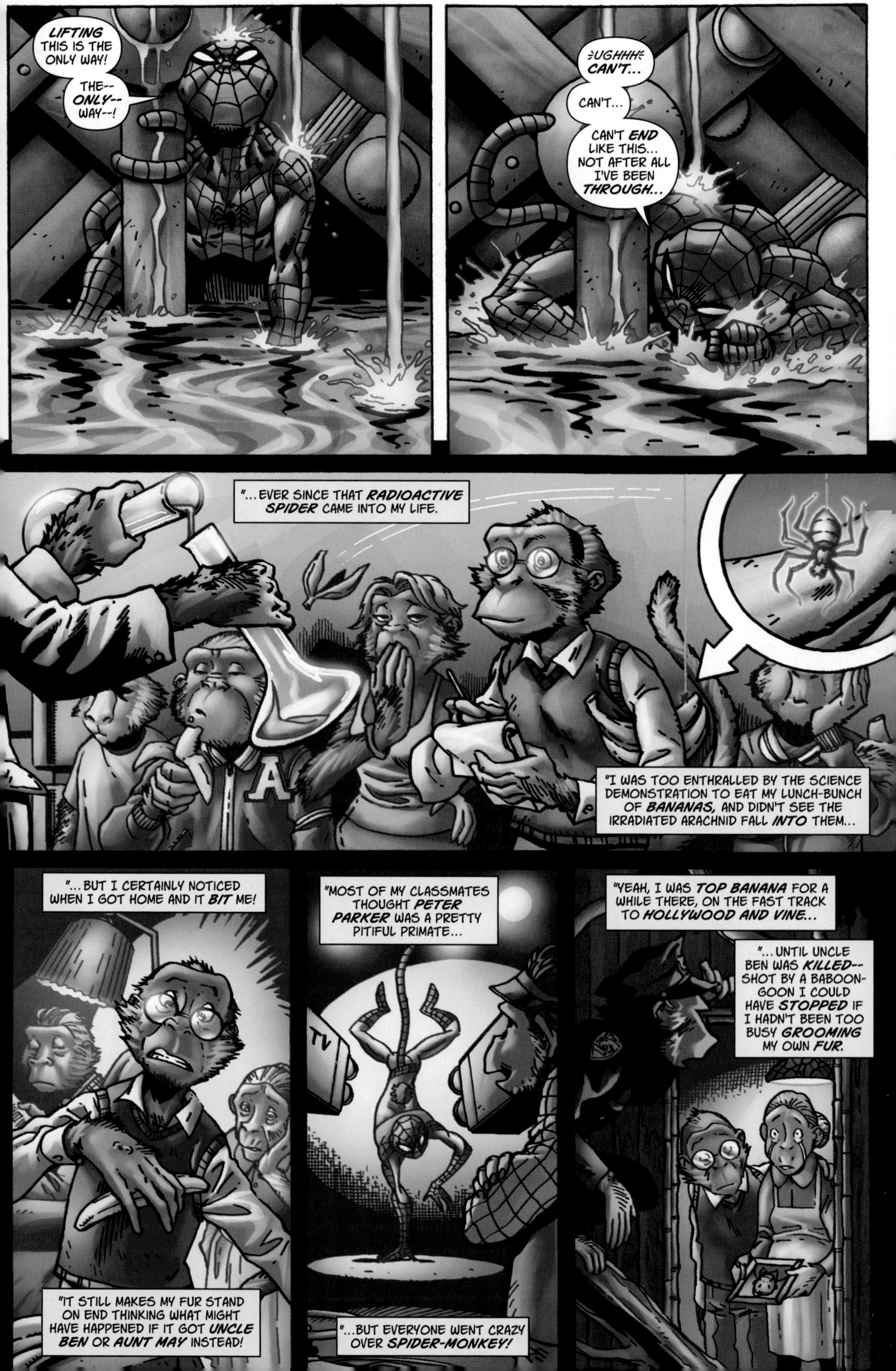
LIFTING THIS IS THE ONLY WAY!
THE-- ONLY-- WAY--!
UGHHH CAN'T...
CAN'T...
CAN'T END LIKE THIS... NOT AFTER ALL I'VE BEEN THROUGH...
"...EVER SINCE THAT RADIOACTIVE SPIDER CAME INTO MY LIFE.
"I WAS TOO ENTHRALLED BY THE SCIENCE DEMONSTRATION TO EAT MY LUNCH-BUNCH OF BANANAS, AND DIDN'T SEE THE IRRADIATED ARACHNID FALL INTO THEM...
"...BUT I CERTAINLY NOTICED WHEN I GOT HOME AND IT BIT ME!
"IT STILL MAKES MY FUR STAND ON END THINKING WHAT MIGHT HAVE HAPPENED IF IT GOT UNCLE BEN OR AUNT MAY INSTEAD!
"MOST OF MY CLASSMATES THOUGHT PETER PARKER WAS A PRETTY PITIFUL PRIMATE...
TV
"...BUT EVERYONE WENT CRAZY OVER SPIDER-MONKEY!
"YEAH, I WAS TOP BANANA FOR A WHILE THERE, ON THE FAST TRACK TO HOLLYWOOD AND VINE...
"...UNTIL UNCLE BEN WAS KILLED-- SHOT BY A BABOON-GOON I COULD HAVE STOPPED IF I HADN'T BEEN TOO BUSY GROOMING MY OWN FUR.

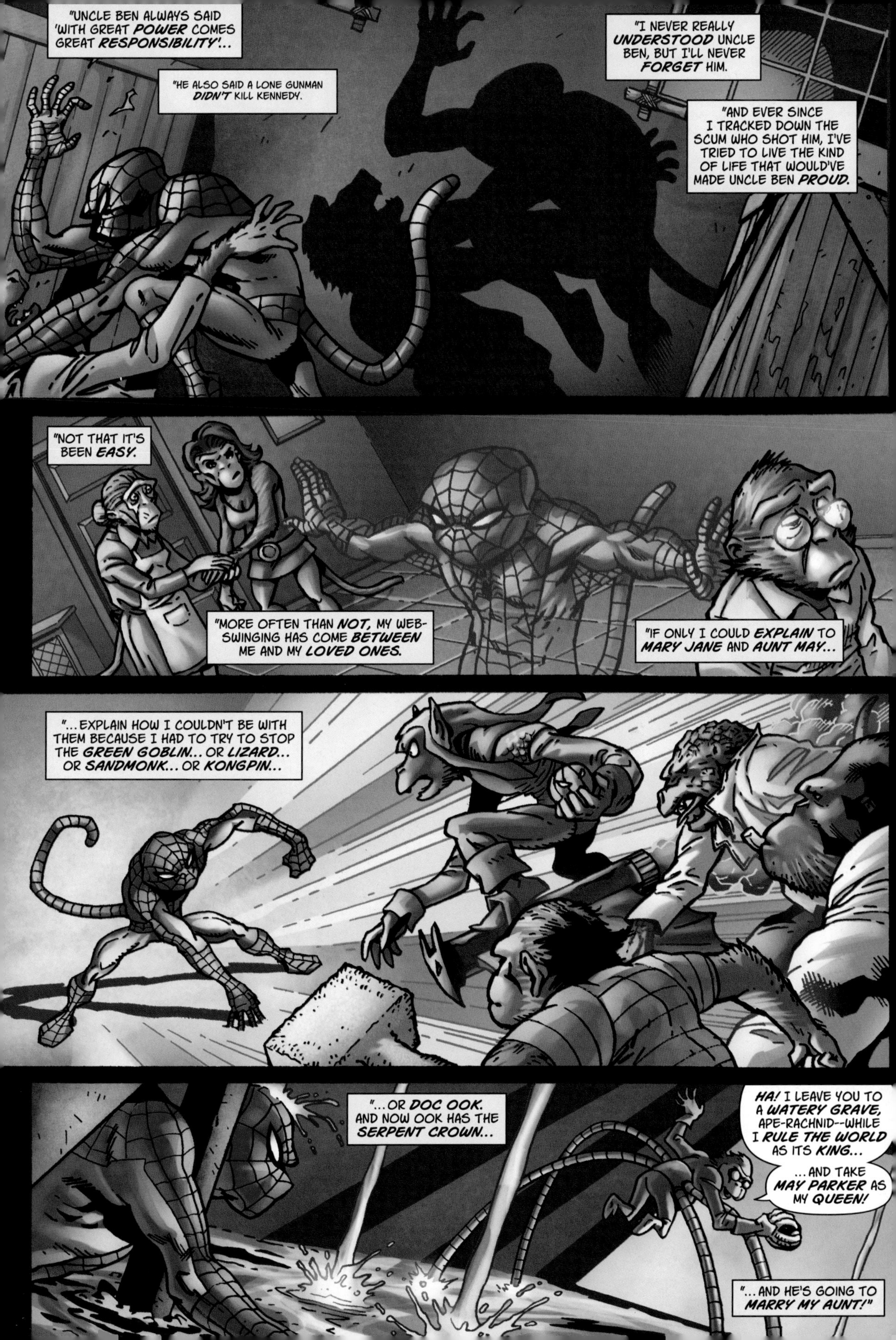

"UNCLE BEN ALWAYS SAID 'WITH GREAT POWER COMES GREAT RESPONSIBILITY'...
"HE ALSO SAID A LONE GUNMAN DIDN'T KILL KENNEDY.
"I NEVER REALLY UNDERSTOOD UNCLE BEN, BUT I'LL NEVER FORGET HIM.
"AND EVER SINCE I TRACKED DOWN THE SCUM WHO SHOT HIM, I'VE TRIED TO LIVE THE KIND OF LIFE THAT WOULD'VE MADE UNCLE BEN PROUD.
"NOT THAT IT'S BEEN EASY.
"MORE OFTEN THAN NOT, MY WEB-SWINGING HAS COME BETWEEN ME AND MY LOVED ONES.
"IF ONLY I COULD EXPLAIN TO MARY JANE AND AUNT MAY...
"...EXPLAIN HOW I COULDN'T BE WITH THEM BECAUSE I HAD TO TRY TO STOP THE GREEN GOBLIN... OR LIZARD... OR SANDMONK... OR KONGPIN...
"...OR DOC OOK. AND NOW OOK HAS THE SERPENT CROWN...
HA! I LEAVE YOU TO A WATERY GRAVE, APE-RACHNID--WHILE I RULE THE WORLD AS ITS KING...
...AND TAKE MAY PARKER AS MY QUEEN!
"...AND HE'S GOING TO MARRY MY AUNT!"

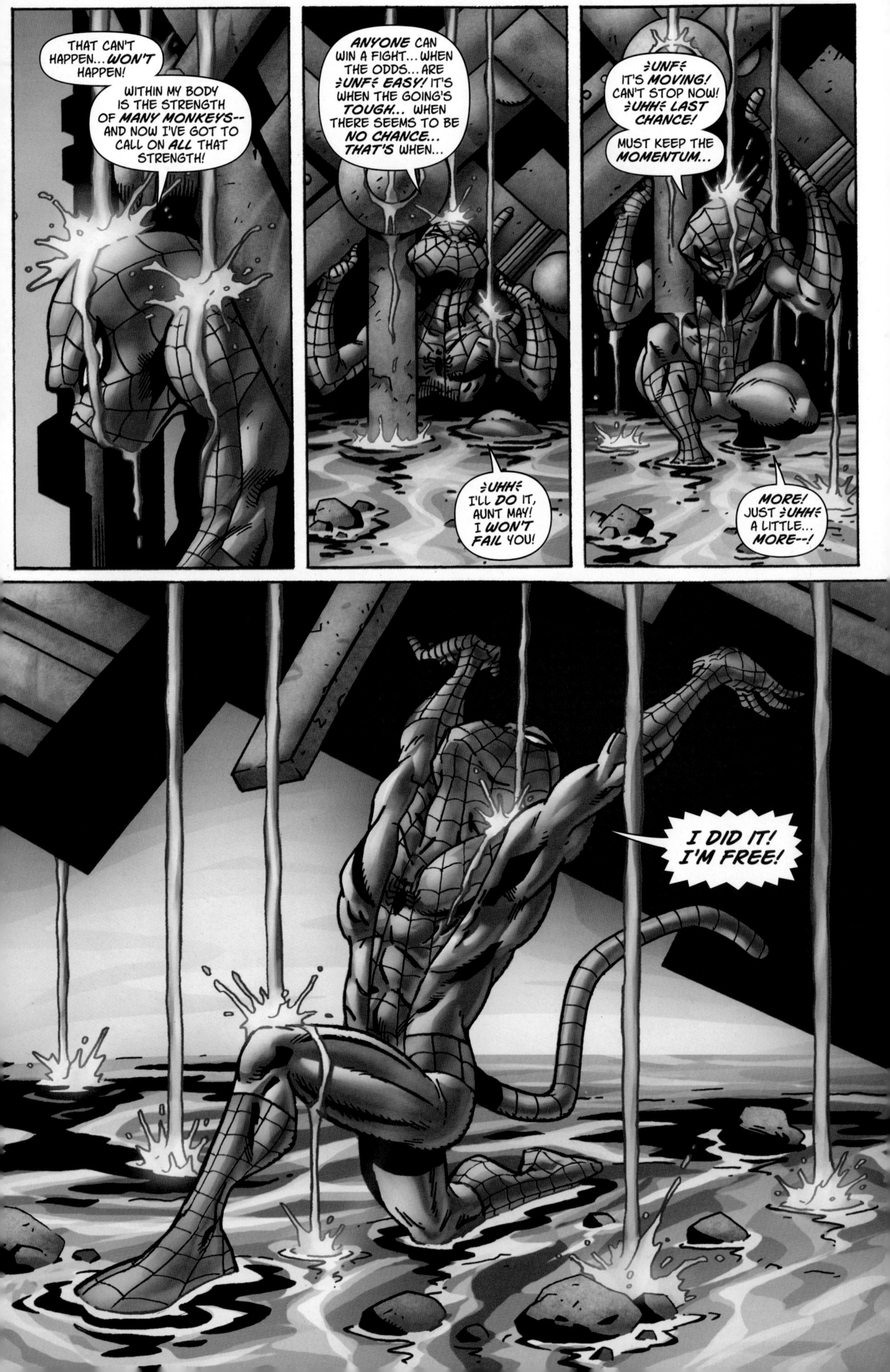
THAT CAN'T HAPPEN... WON'T HAPPEN!
WITHIN MY BODY IS THE STRENGTH OF MANY MONKEYS-- AND NOW I'VE GOT TO CALL ON ALL THAT STRENGTH!
ANYONE CAN WIN A FIGHT... WHEN THE ODDS... ARE UNF EASY! IT'S WHEN THE GOING'S TOUGH... WHEN THERE SEEMS TO BE NO CHANCE... THAT'S WHEN...
UHH I'LL DO IT, AUNT MAY! I WON'T FAIL YOU!
UNF IT'S MOVING! CAN'T STOP NOW! UHH LAST CHANCE!
MUST KEEP THE MOMENTUM...
MORE! JUST UHH A LITTLE... MORE--!
I DID IT! I'M FREE!

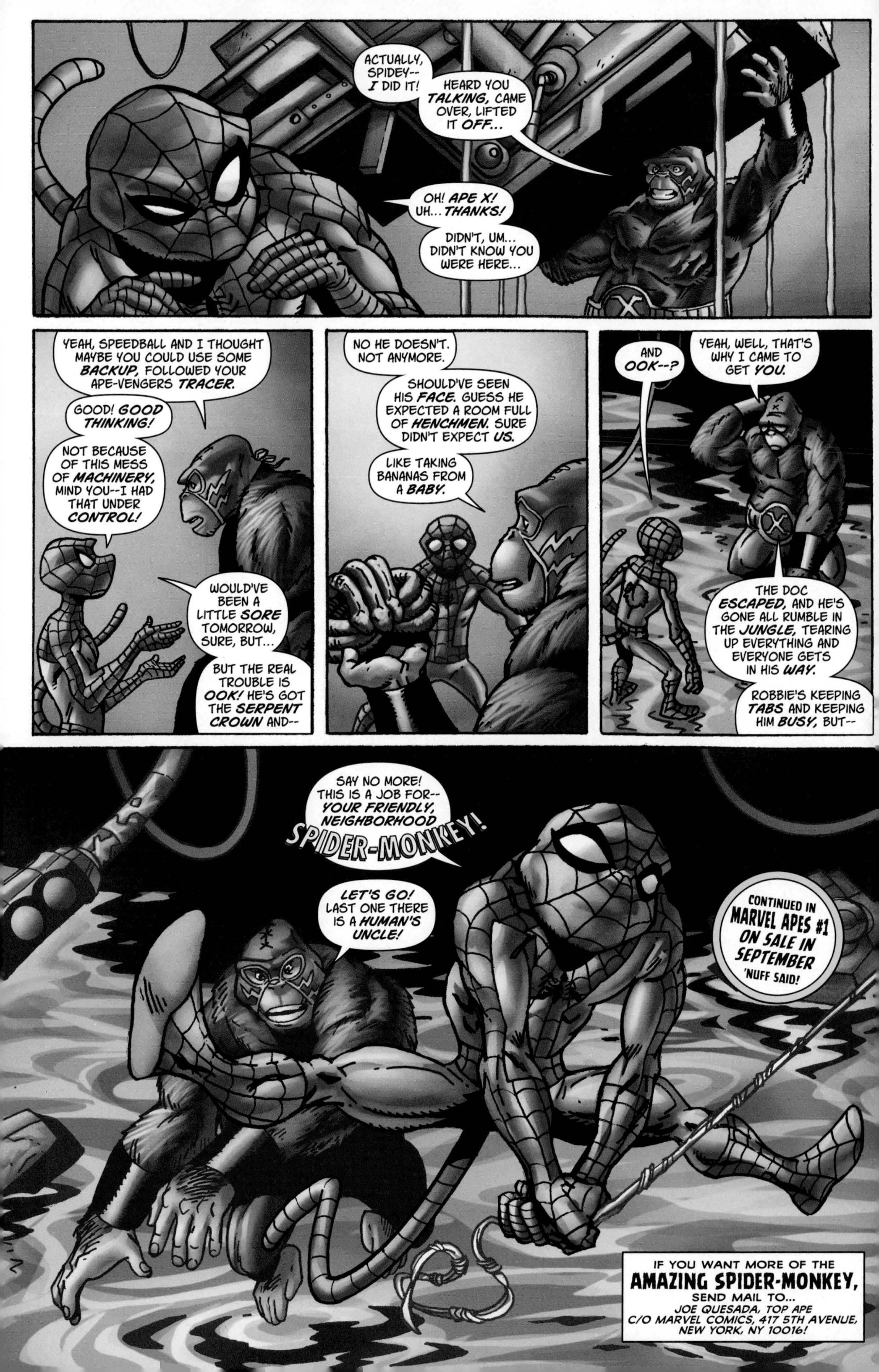
ACTUALLY, SPIDEY-- I DID IT!
HEARD YOU TALKING, CAME OVER, LIFTED IT OFF...
OH! APE X! UH... THANKS!
DIDN'T, UM... DIDN'T KNOW YOU WERE HERE...
YEAH, SPEEDBALL AND I THOUGHT MAYBE YOU COULD USE SOME BACKUP, FOLLOWED YOUR APE-VENGERS TRACER.
GOOD! GOOD THINKING!
NOT BECAUSE OF THIS MESS OF MACHINERY, MIND YOU--I HAD THAT UNDER CONTROL!
WOULD'VE BEEN A LITTLE SORE TOMORROW, SURE, BUT...
BUT THE REAL TROUBLE IS OOK! HE'S GOT THE SERPENT CROWN AND--
NO HE DOESN'T. NOT ANYMORE.
SHOULD'VE SEEN HIS FACE. GUESS HE EXPECTED A ROOM FULL OF HENCHMEN. SURE DIDN'T EXPECT US.
LIKE TAKING BANANAS FROM A BABY.
AND OOK--?
YEAH, WELL, THAT'S WHY I CAME TO GET YOU.
THE DOC ESCAPED, AND HE'S GONE ALL RUMBLE IN THE JUNGLE, TEARING UP EVERYTHING AND EVERYONE GETS IN HIS WAY.
ROBBIE'S KEEPING TABS AND KEEPING HIM BUSY, BUT--
SAY NO MORE! THIS IS A JOB FOR-- YOUR FRIENDLY, NEIGHBORHOOD SPIDER-MONKEY!
LET'S GO! LAST ONE THERE IS A HUMAN'S UNCLE!
CONTINUED IN MARVEL APES #1 ON SALE IN SEPTEMBER 'NUFF SAID!
IF YOU WANT MORE OF THE AMAZING SPIDER-MONKEY, SEND MAIL TO... JOE QUESADA, TOP APE C/O MARVEL COMICS, 417 5TH AVENUE, NEW YORK, NY 10016!

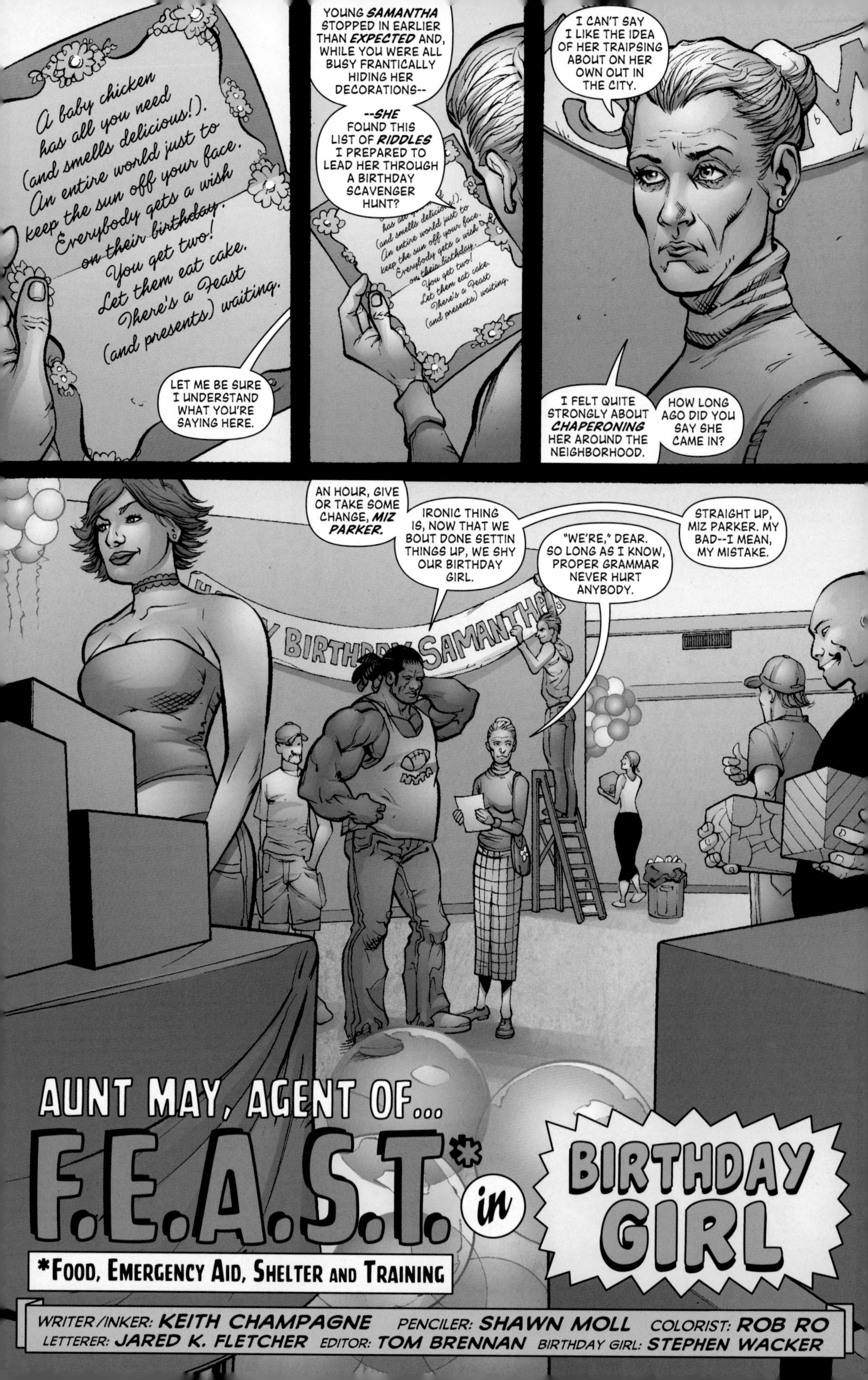
A baby chicken has all you need (and smells delicious!). An entire world just to keep the sun off your face. Everybody gets a wish on their birthday. You get two! Let them eat cake. There's a Feast (and presents) waiting.
LET ME BE SURE I UNDERSTAND WHAT YOU'RE SAYING HERE.
YOUNG SAMANTHA STOPPED IN EARLIER THAN EXPECTED AND, WHILE YOU WERE ALL BUSY FRANTICALLY HIDING HER DECORATIONS--
--SHE FOUND THIS LIST OF RIDDLES I PREPARED TO LEAD HER THROUGH A BIRTHDAY SCAVENGER HUNT?
I CAN'T SAY I LIKE THE IDEA OF HER TRAIPSING ABOUT ON HER OWN OUT IN THE CITY.
I FELT QUITE STRONGLY ABOUT CHAPERONING HER AROUND THE NEIGHBORHOOD.
HOW LONG AGO DID YOU SAY SHE CAME IN?
AN HOUR, GIVE OR TAKE SOME CHANGE, MIZ PARKER.
IRONIC THING IS, NOW THAT WE BOUT DONE SETTIN THINGS UP, WE SHY OUR BIRTHDAY GIRL.
"WE'RE," DEAR. SO LONG AS I KNOW, PROPER GRAMMAR NEVER HURT ANYBODY.
STRAIGHT UP, MIZ PARKER. MY BAD--I MEAN, MY MISTAKE.
BIRTHDAY SAMANTHA
AUNT MAY, AGENT OF...
F.E.A.S.T.* in
BIRTHDAY GIRL
*FOOD, EMERGENCY AID, SHELTER AND TRAINING
WRITER/INKER: KEITH CHAMPAGNE PENCILER: SHAWN MOLL COLORIST: ROB RO
LETTERER: JARED K. FLETCHER EDITOR: TOM BRENNAN BIRTHDAY GIRL: STEPHEN WACKER

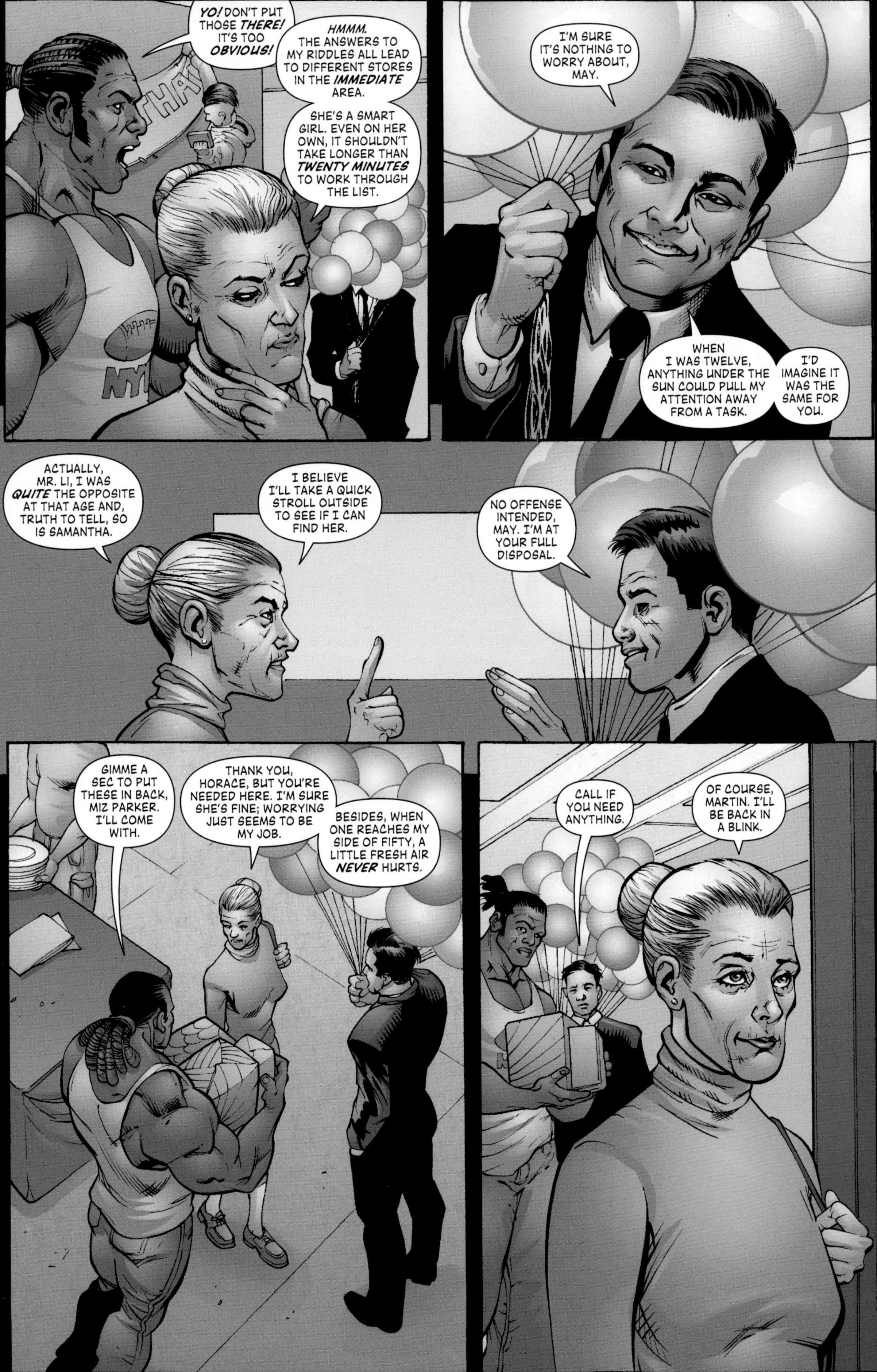
YO! DON'T PUT THOSE THERE! IT'S TOO OBVIOUS!
HMMM. THE ANSWERS TO MY RIDDLES ALL LEAD TO DIFFERENT STORES IN THE IMMEDIATE AREA.
SHE'S A SMART GIRL. EVEN ON HER OWN, IT SHOULDN'T TAKE LONGER THAN TWENTY MINUTES TO WORK THROUGH THE LIST.
I'M SURE IT'S NOTHING TO WORRY ABOUT, MAY.
WHEN I WAS TWELVE, ANYTHING UNDER THE SUN COULD PULL MY ATTENTION AWAY FROM A TASK.
I'D IMAGINE IT WAS THE SAME FOR YOU.
ACTUALLY, MR. LI, I WAS QUITE THE OPPOSITE AT THAT AGE AND, TRUTH TO TELL, SO IS SAMANTHA.
I BELIEVE I'LL TAKE A QUICK STROLL OUTSIDE TO SEE IF I CAN FIND HER.
NO OFFENSE INTENDED, MAY. I'M AT YOUR FULL DISPOSAL.
GIMME A SEC TO PUT THESE IN BACK, MIZ PARKER. I'LL COME WITH.
THANK YOU, HORACE, BUT YOU'RE NEEDED HERE. I'M SURE SHE'S FINE; WORRYING JUST SEEMS TO BE MY JOB.
BESIDES, WHEN ONE REACHES MY SIDE OF FIFTY, A LITTLE FRESH AIR NEVER HURTS.
CALL IF YOU NEED ANYTHING.
OF COURSE, MARTIN. I'LL BE BACK IN A BLINK.

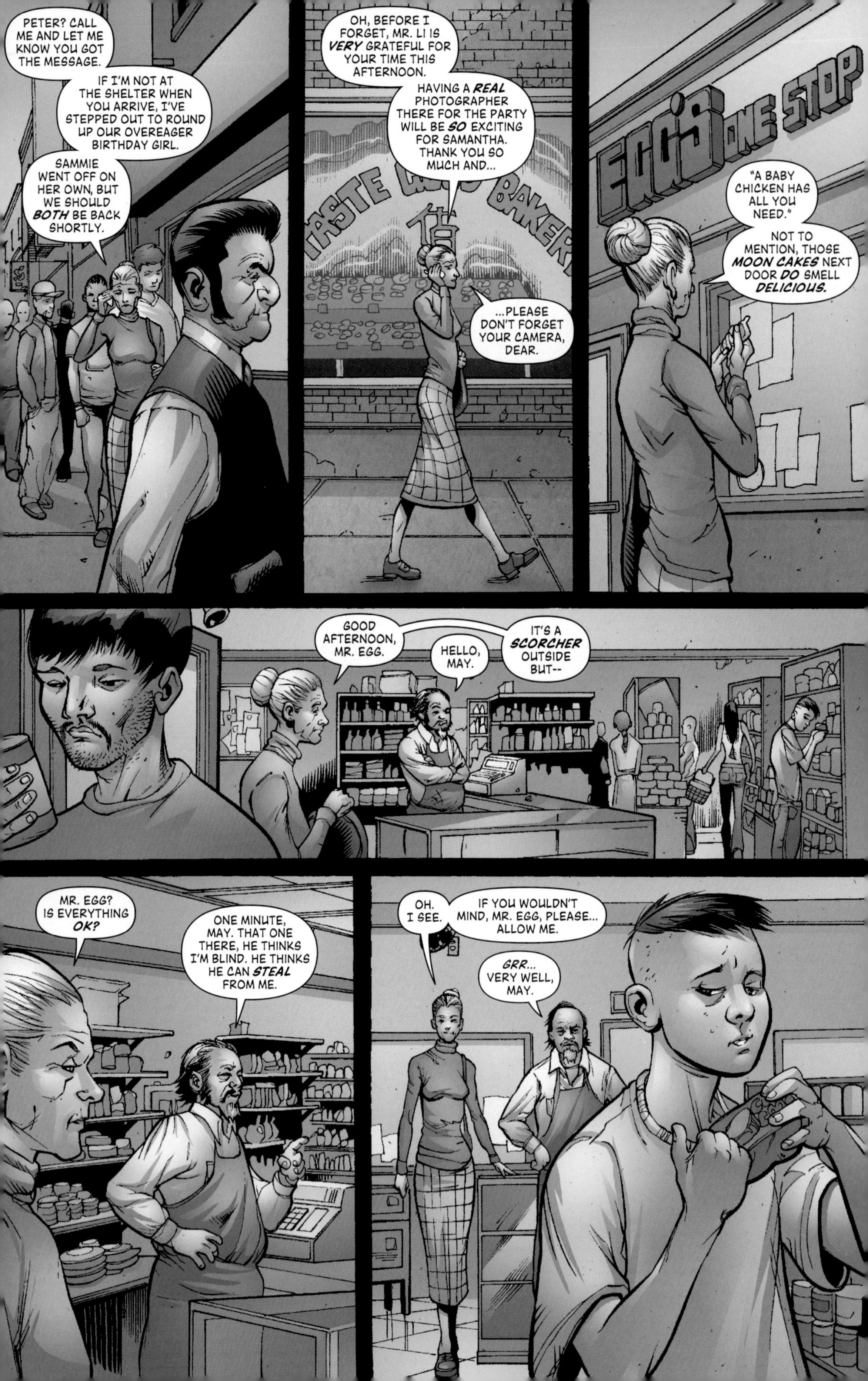
PETER? CALL ME AND LET ME KNOW YOU GOT THE MESSAGE.
IF I'M NOT AT THE SHELTER WHEN YOU ARRIVE, I'VE STEPPED OUT TO ROUND UP OUR OVEREAGER BIRTHDAY GIRL.
SAMMIE WENT OFF ON HER OWN, BUT WE SHOULD BOTH BE BACK SHORTLY.
OH, BEFORE I FORGET, MR. LI IS VERY GRATEFUL FOR YOUR TIME THIS AFTERNOON.
HAVING A REAL PHOTOGRAPHER THERE FOR THE PARTY WILL BE SO EXCITING FOR SAMANTHA. THANK YOU SO MUCH AND...
...PLEASE DON'T FORGET YOUR CAMERA, DEAR.
EGG'S ONE STOP
"A BABY CHICKEN HAS ALL YOU NEED."
NOT TO MENTION, THOSE MOON CAKES NEXT DOOR DO SMELL DELICIOUS.
GOOD AFTERNOON, MR. EGG.
HELLO, MAY.
IT'S A SCORCHER OUTSIDE BUT--
MR. EGG? IS EVERYTHING OK?
ONE MINUTE, MAY. THAT ONE THERE, HE THINKS I'M BLIND. HE THINKS HE CAN STEAL FROM ME.
OH. I SEE.
IF YOU WOULDN'T MIND, MR. EGG, PLEASE... ALLOW ME.
GRR... VERY WELL, MAY.

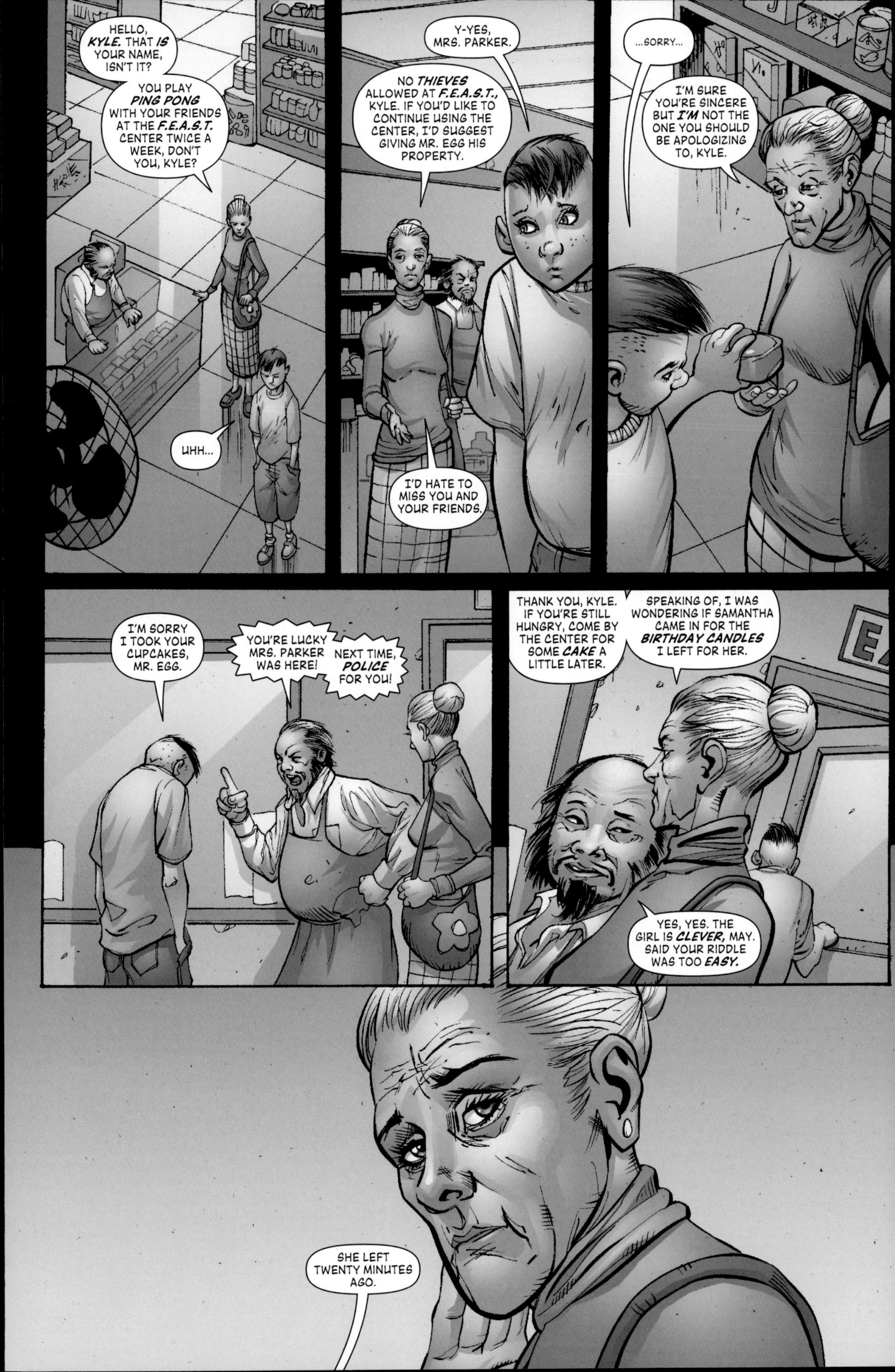
HELLO, KYLE. THAT IS YOUR NAME, ISN'T IT?
YOU PLAY PING PONG WITH YOUR FRIENDS AT THE F.E.A.S.T. CENTER TWICE A WEEK, DON'T YOU, KYLE?
UHH...
Y-YES, MRS. PARKER.
NO THIEVES ALLOWED AT F.E.A.S.T., KYLE. IF YOU'D LIKE TO CONTINUE USING THE CENTER, I'D SUGGEST GIVING MR. EGG HIS PROPERTY.
I'D HATE TO MISS YOU AND YOUR FRIENDS.
...SORRY...
I'M SURE YOU'RE SINCERE BUT I'M NOT THE ONE YOU SHOULD BE APOLOGIZING TO, KYLE.
I'M SORRY I TOOK YOUR CUPCAKES, MR. EGG.
YOU'RE LUCKY MRS. PARKER WAS HERE!
NEXT TIME, POLICE FOR YOU!
THANK YOU, KYLE. IF YOU'RE STILL HUNGRY, COME BY THE CENTER FOR SOME CAKE A LITTLE LATER.
SPEAKING OF, I WAS WONDERING IF SAMANTHA CAME IN FOR THE BIRTHDAY CANDLES I LEFT FOR HER.
YES, YES. THE GIRL IS CLEVER, MAY. SAID YOUR RIDDLE WAS TOO EASY.
SHE LEFT TWENTY MINUTES AGO.

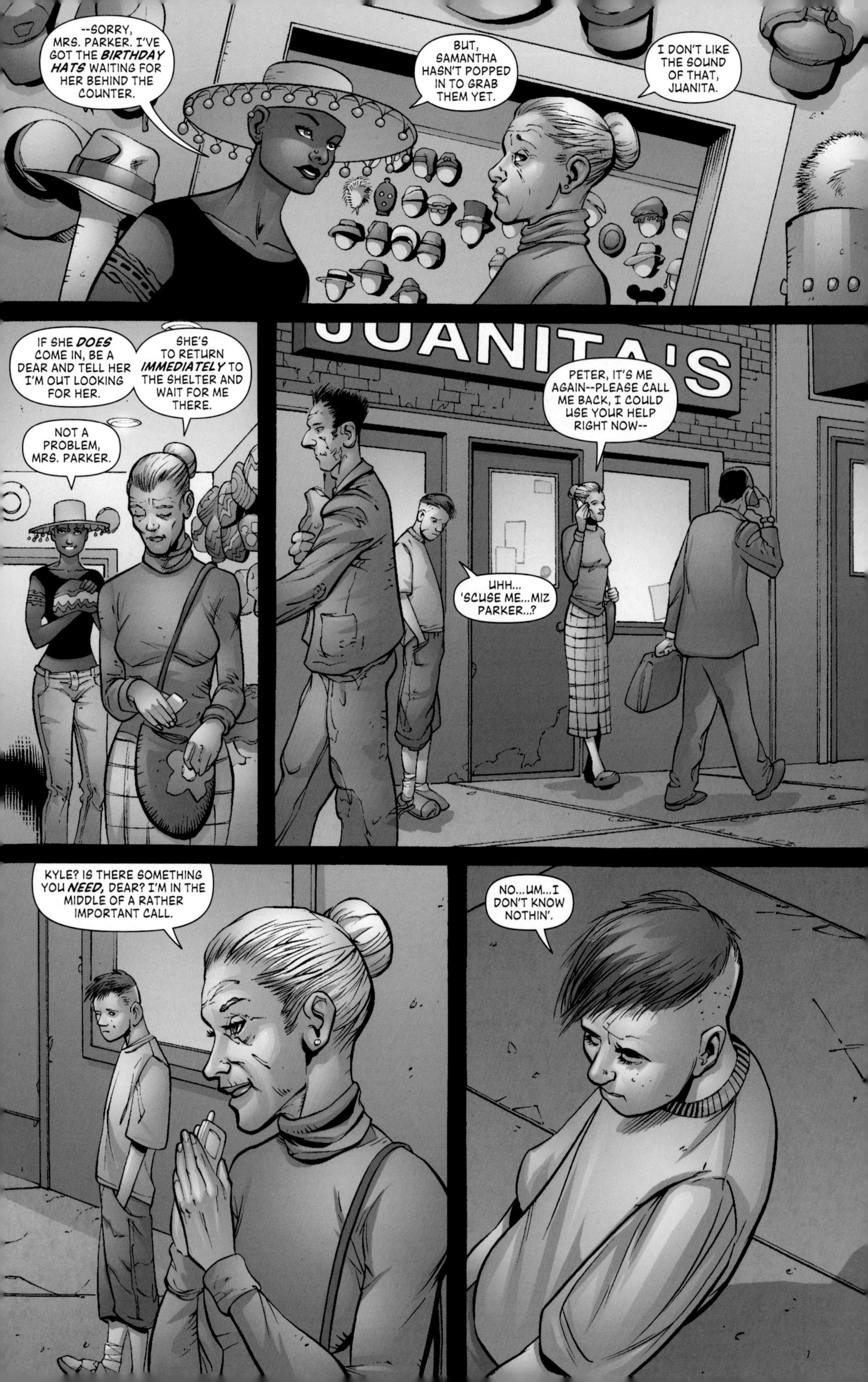
--SORRY, MRS. PARKER. I'VE GOT THE BIRTHDAY HATS WAITING FOR HER BEHIND THE COUNTER.
BUT, SAMANTHA HASN'T POPPED IN TO GRAB THEM YET.
I DON'T LIKE THE SOUND OF THAT, JUANITA.
IF SHE DOES COME IN, BE A DEAR AND TELL HER I'M OUT LOOKING FOR HER.
SHE'S TO RETURN IMMEDIATELY TO THE SHELTER AND WAIT FOR ME THERE.
NOT A PROBLEM, MRS. PARKER.
JUANITA'S
PETER, IT'S ME AGAIN--PLEASE CALL ME BACK, I COULD USE YOUR HELP RIGHT NOW--
UHH... 'SCUSE ME...MIZ PARKER...?
KYLE? IS THERE SOMETHING YOU NEED, DEAR? I'M IN THE MIDDLE OF A RATHER IMPORTANT CALL.
NO...UM...I DON'T KNOW NOTHIN'.

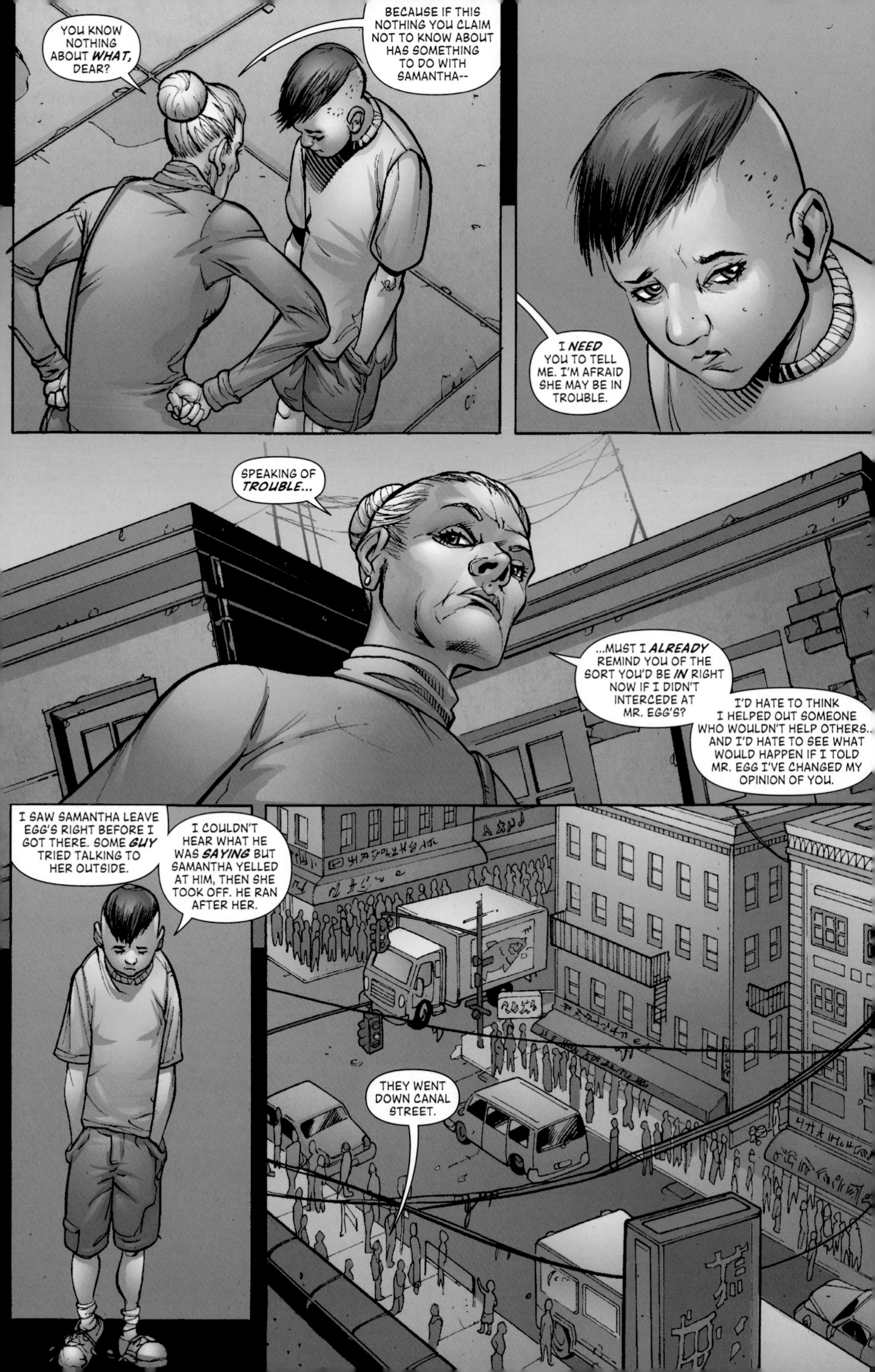
YOU KNOW NOTHING ABOUT WHAT, DEAR?
BECAUSE IF THIS NOTHING YOU CLAIM NOT TO KNOW ABOUT HAS SOMETHING TO DO WITH SAMANTHA--
I NEED YOU TO TELL ME. I'M AFRAID SHE MAY BE IN TROUBLE.
SPEAKING OF TROUBLE...
...MUST I ALREADY REMIND YOU OF THE SORT YOU'D BE IN RIGHT NOW IF I DIDN'T INTERCEDE AT MR. EGG'S?
I'D HATE TO THINK I HELPED OUT SOMEONE WHO WOULDN'T HELP OTHERS. AND I'D HATE TO SEE WHAT WOULD HAPPEN IF I TOLD MR. EGG I'VE CHANGED MY OPINION OF YOU.
I SAW SAMANTHA LEAVE EGG'S RIGHT BEFORE I GOT THERE. SOME GUY TRIED TALKING TO HER OUTSIDE.
I COULDN'T HEAR WHAT HE WAS SAYING BUT SAMANTHA YELLED AT HIM, THEN SHE TOOK OFF. HE RAN AFTER HER.
THEY WENT DOWN CANAL STREET.

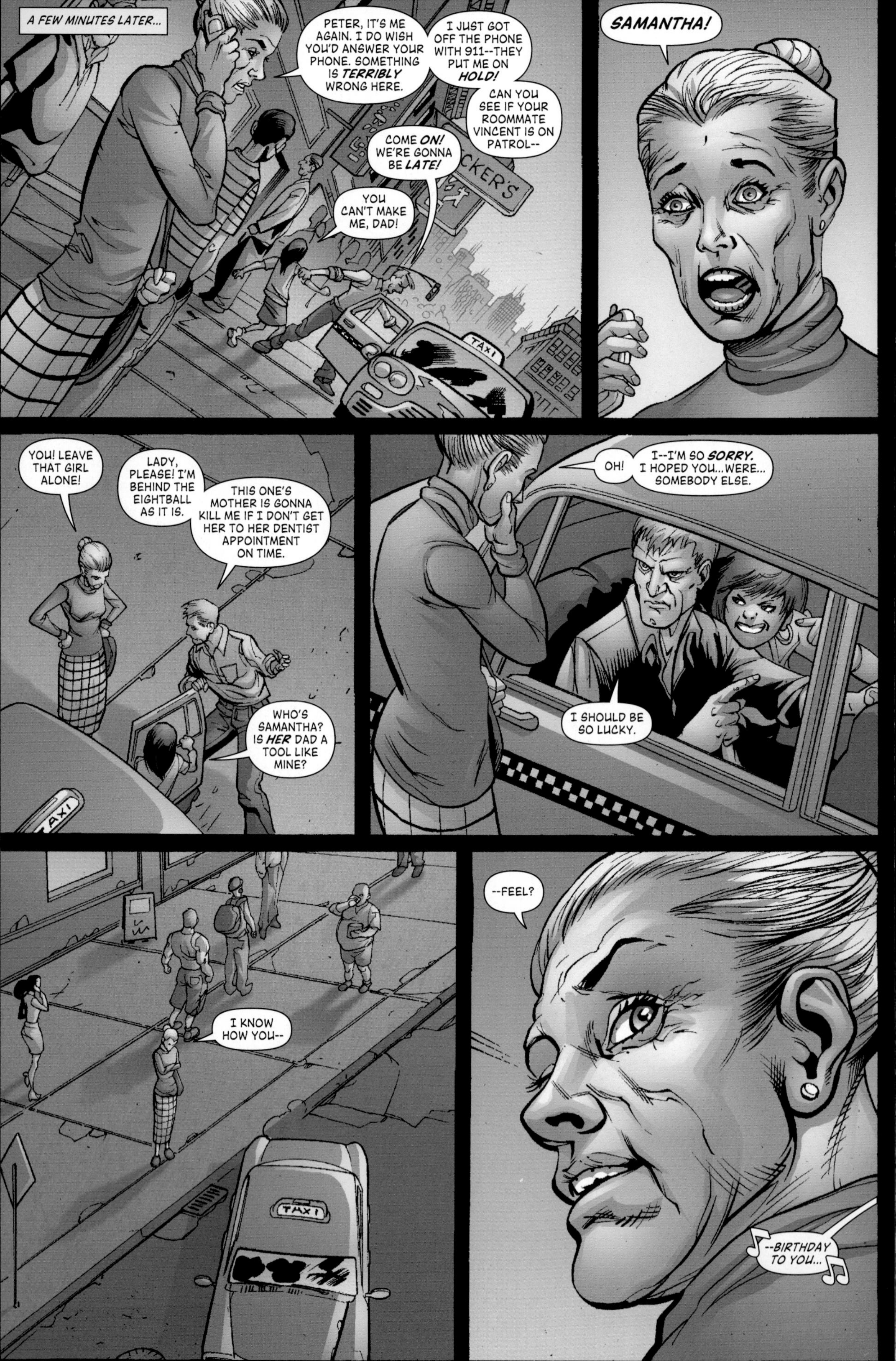
A FEW MINUTES LATER...
PETER, IT'S ME AGAIN. I DO WISH YOU'D ANSWER YOUR PHONE. SOMETHING IS TERRIBLY WRONG HERE.
I JUST GOT OFF THE PHONE WITH 911--THEY PUT ME ON HOLD!
CAN YOU SEE IF YOUR ROOMMATE VINCENT IS ON PATROL--
COME ON! WE'RE GONNA BE LATE!
YOU CAN'T MAKE ME, DAD!
SAMANTHA!
YOU! LEAVE THAT GIRL ALONE!
LADY, PLEASE! I'M BEHIND THE EIGHTBALL AS IT IS.
THIS ONE'S MOTHER IS GONNA KILL ME IF I DON'T GET HER TO HER DENTIST APPOINTMENT ON TIME.
WHO'S SAMANTHA? IS HER DAD A TOOL LIKE MINE?
OH!
I--I'M SO SORRY. I HOPED YOU...WERE... SOMEBODY ELSE.
I SHOULD BE SO LUCKY.
I KNOW HOW YOU--
--FEEL?
--BIRTHDAY TO YOU...

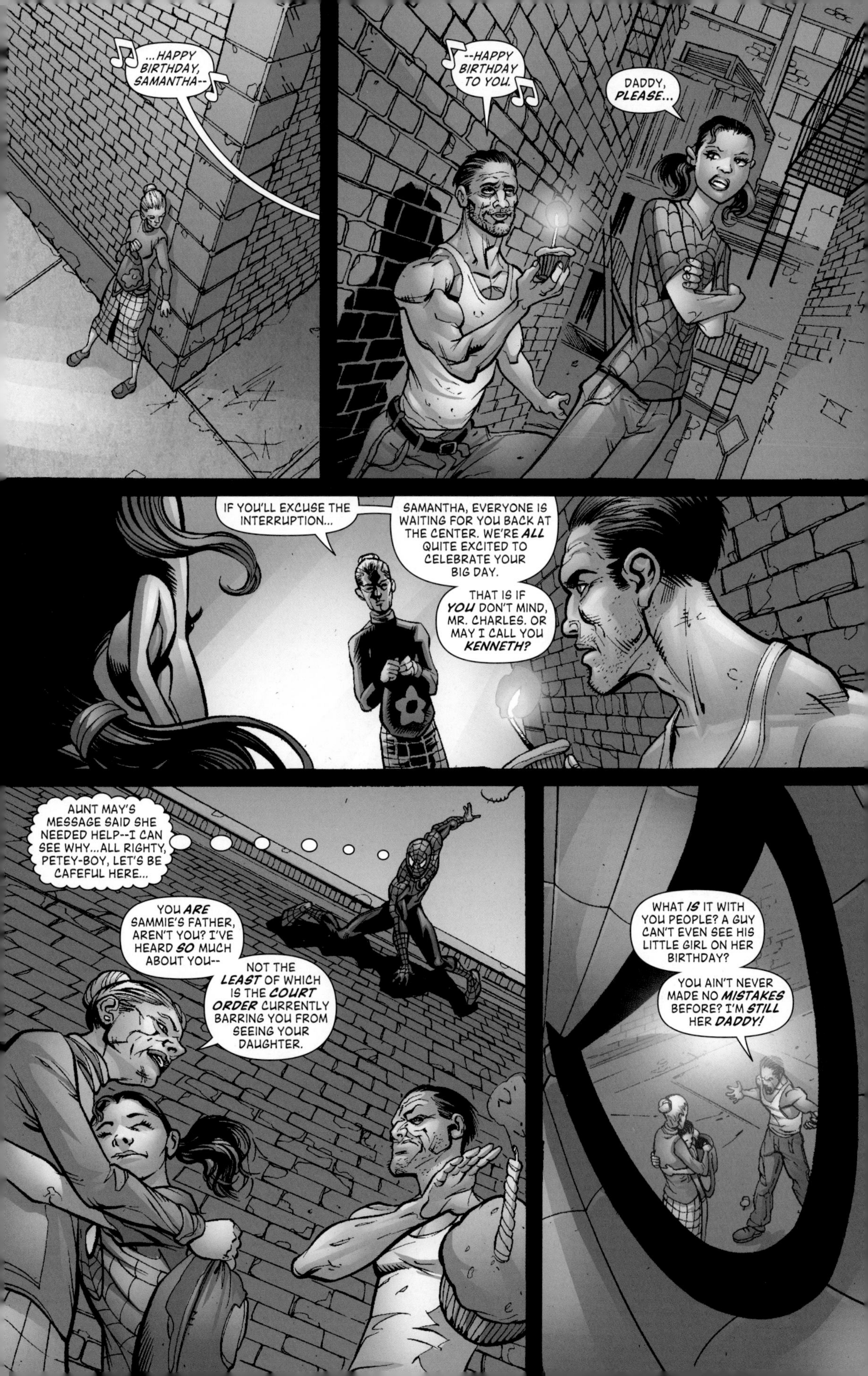
...HAPPY BIRTHDAY, SAMANTHA--
--HAPPY BIRTHDAY TO YOU.
DADDY, PLEASE...
IF YOU'LL EXCUSE THE INTERRUPTION...
SAMANTHA, EVERYONE IS WAITING FOR YOU BACK AT THE CENTER. WE'RE ALL QUITE EXCITED TO CELEBRATE YOUR BIG DAY.
THAT IS IF YOU DON'T MIND, MR. CHARLES. OR MAY I CALL YOU KENNETH?
AUNT MAY'S MESSAGE SAID SHE NEEDED HELP--I CAN SEE WHY...ALL RIGHTY, PETEY-BOY, LET'S BE CAREFUL HERE...
YOU ARE SAMMIE'S FATHER, AREN'T YOU? I'VE HEARD SO MUCH ABOUT YOU--
NOT THE LEAST OF WHICH IS THE COURT ORDER CURRENTLY BARRING YOU FROM SEEING YOUR DAUGHTER.
WHAT IS IT WITH YOU PEOPLE? A GUY CAN'T EVEN SEE HIS LITTLE GIRL ON HER BIRTHDAY?
YOU AIN'T NEVER MADE NO MISTAKES BEFORE? I'M STILL HER DADDY!

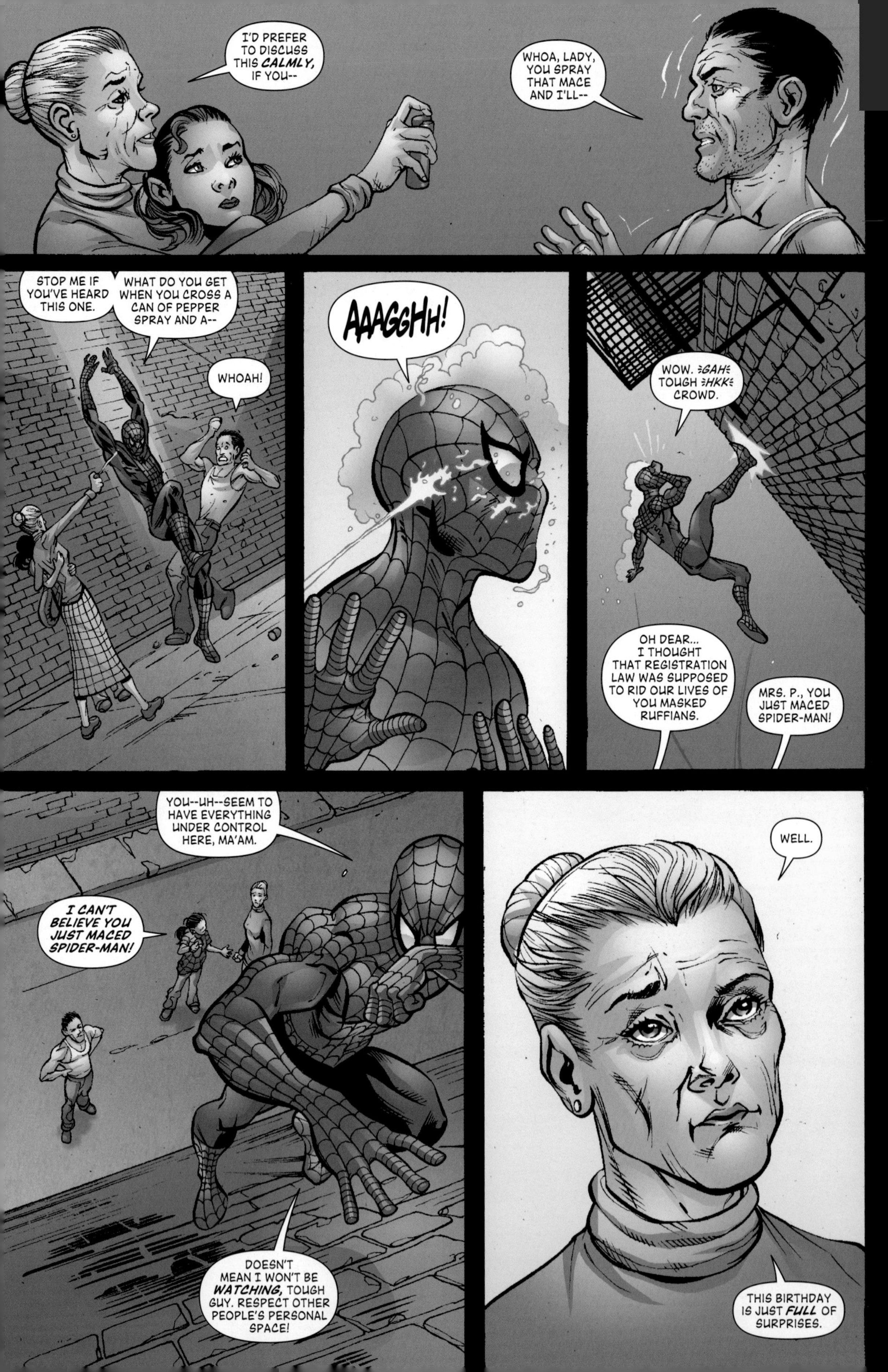
I'D PREFER TO DISCUSS THIS CALMLY, IF YOU--
WHOA, LADY, YOU SPRAY THAT MACE AND I'LL--
STOP ME IF YOU'VE HEARD THIS ONE.
WHAT DO YOU GET WHEN YOU CROSS A CAN OF PEPPER SPRAY AND A--
WHOAH!
AAAGGHH!
WOW. GAH TOUGH HKK CROWD.
OH DEAR... I THOUGHT THAT REGISTRATION LAW WAS SUPPOSED TO RID OUR LIVES OF YOU MASKED RUFFIANS.
MRS. P., YOU JUST MACED SPIDER-MAN!
YOU--UH--SEEM TO HAVE EVERYTHING UNDER CONTROL HERE, MA'AM.
I CAN'T BELIEVE YOU JUST MACED SPIDER-MAN!
DOESN'T MEAN I WON'T BE WATCHING, TOUGH GUY. RESPECT OTHER PEOPLE'S PERSONAL SPACE!
WELL.
THIS BIRTHDAY IS JUST FULL OF SURPRISES.

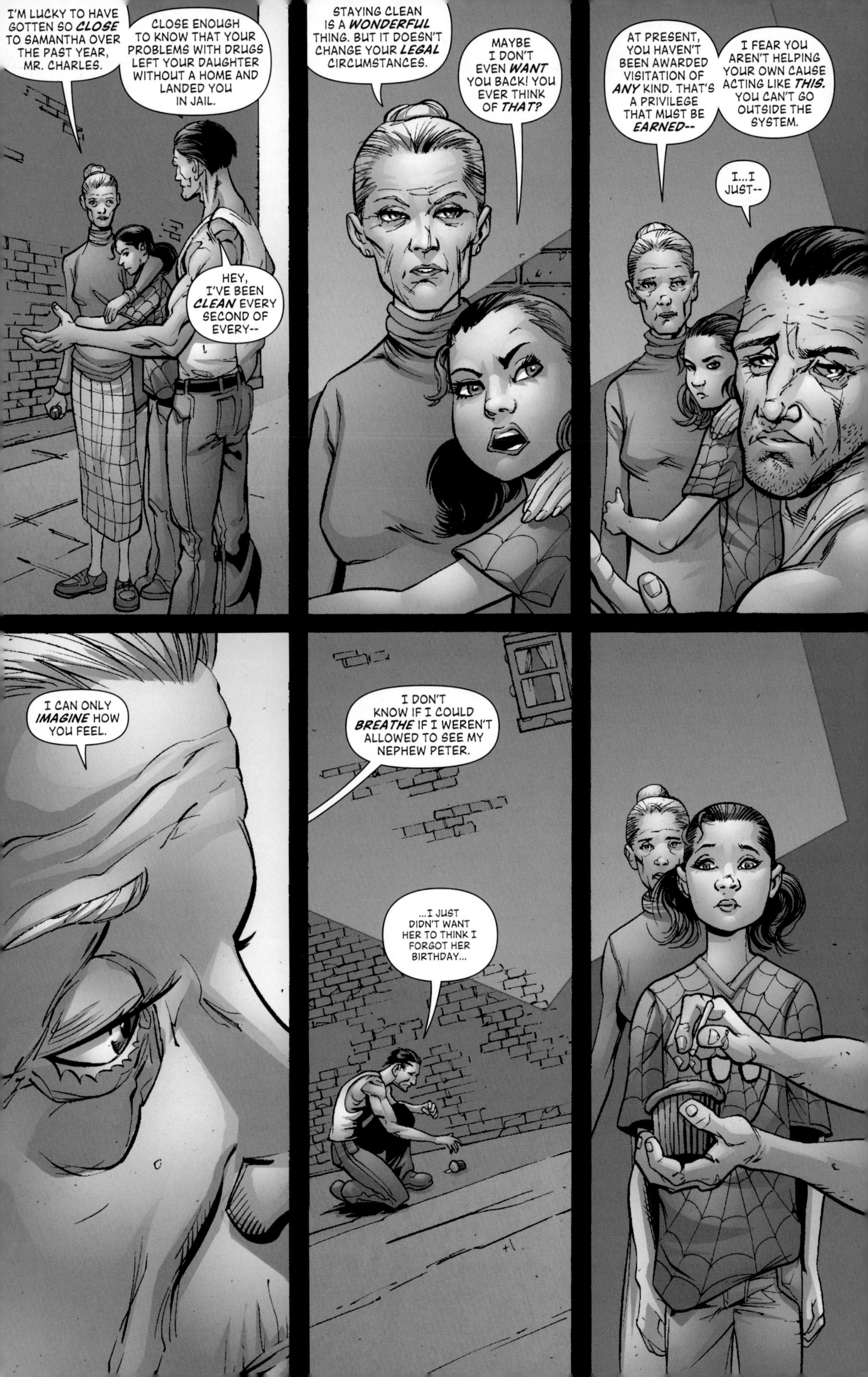
I'M LUCKY TO HAVE GOTTEN SO CLOSE TO SAMANTHA OVER THE PAST YEAR, MR. CHARLES.
CLOSE ENOUGH TO KNOW THAT YOUR PROBLEMS WITH DRUGS LEFT YOUR DAUGHTER WITHOUT A HOME AND LANDED YOU IN JAIL.
HEY, I'VE BEEN CLEAN EVERY SECOND OF EVERY--
STAYING CLEAN IS A WONDERFUL THING. BUT IT DOESN'T CHANGE YOUR LEGAL CIRCUMSTANCES.
MAYBE I DON'T EVEN WANT YOU BACK! YOU EVER THINK OF THAT?
AT PRESENT, YOU HAVEN'T BEEN AWARDED VISITATION OF ANY KIND. THAT'S A PRIVILEGE THAT MUST BE EARNED--
I FEAR YOU AREN'T HELPING YOUR OWN CAUSE ACTING LIKE THIS. YOU CAN'T GO OUTSIDE THE SYSTEM.
I...I JUST--
I CAN ONLY IMAGINE HOW YOU FEEL.
I DON'T KNOW IF I COULD BREATHE IF I WEREN'T ALLOWED TO SEE MY NEPHEW PETER.
...I JUST DIDN'T WANT HER TO THINK I FORGOT HER BIRTHDAY...

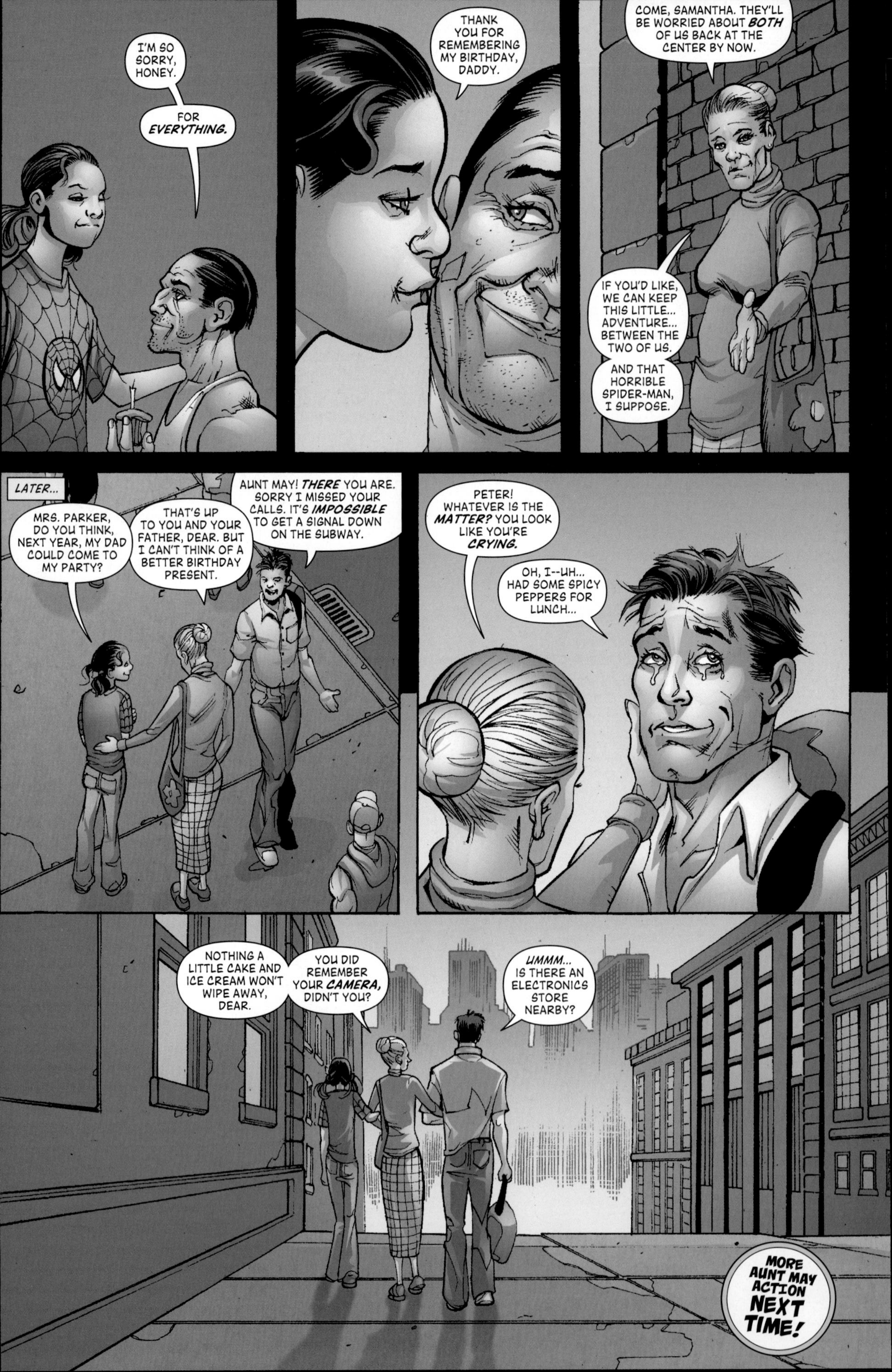
I'M SO SORRY, HONEY.
FOR *EVERYTHING.*
THANK YOU FOR REMEMBERING MY BIRTHDAY, DADDY.
COME, SAMANTHA. THEY'LL BE WORRIED ABOUT *BOTH* OF US BACK AT THE CENTER BY NOW.
IF YOU'D LIKE, WE CAN KEEP THIS LITTLE... ADVENTURE... BETWEEN THE TWO OF US.
AND THAT HORRIBLE SPIDER-MAN, I SUPPOSE.
LATER...
MRS. PARKER, DO YOU THINK, NEXT YEAR, MY DAD COULD COME TO MY PARTY?
THAT'S UP TO YOU AND YOUR FATHER, DEAR. BUT I CAN'T THINK OF A BETTER BIRTHDAY PRESENT.
AUNT MAY! *THERE* YOU ARE. SORRY I MISSED YOUR CALLS. IT'S *IMPOSSIBLE* TO GET A SIGNAL DOWN ON THE SUBWAY.
PETER! WHATEVER IS THE *MATTER?* YOU LOOK LIKE YOU'RE *CRYING.*
OH, I--UH... HAD SOME SPICY PEPPERS FOR LUNCH...
NOTHING A LITTLE CAKE AND ICE CREAM WON'T WIPE AWAY, DEAR.
YOU DID REMEMBER YOUR *CAMERA,* DIDN'T YOU?
UMMM... IS THERE AN ELECTRONICS STORE NEARBY?
MORE AUNT MAY ACTION NEXT TIME!

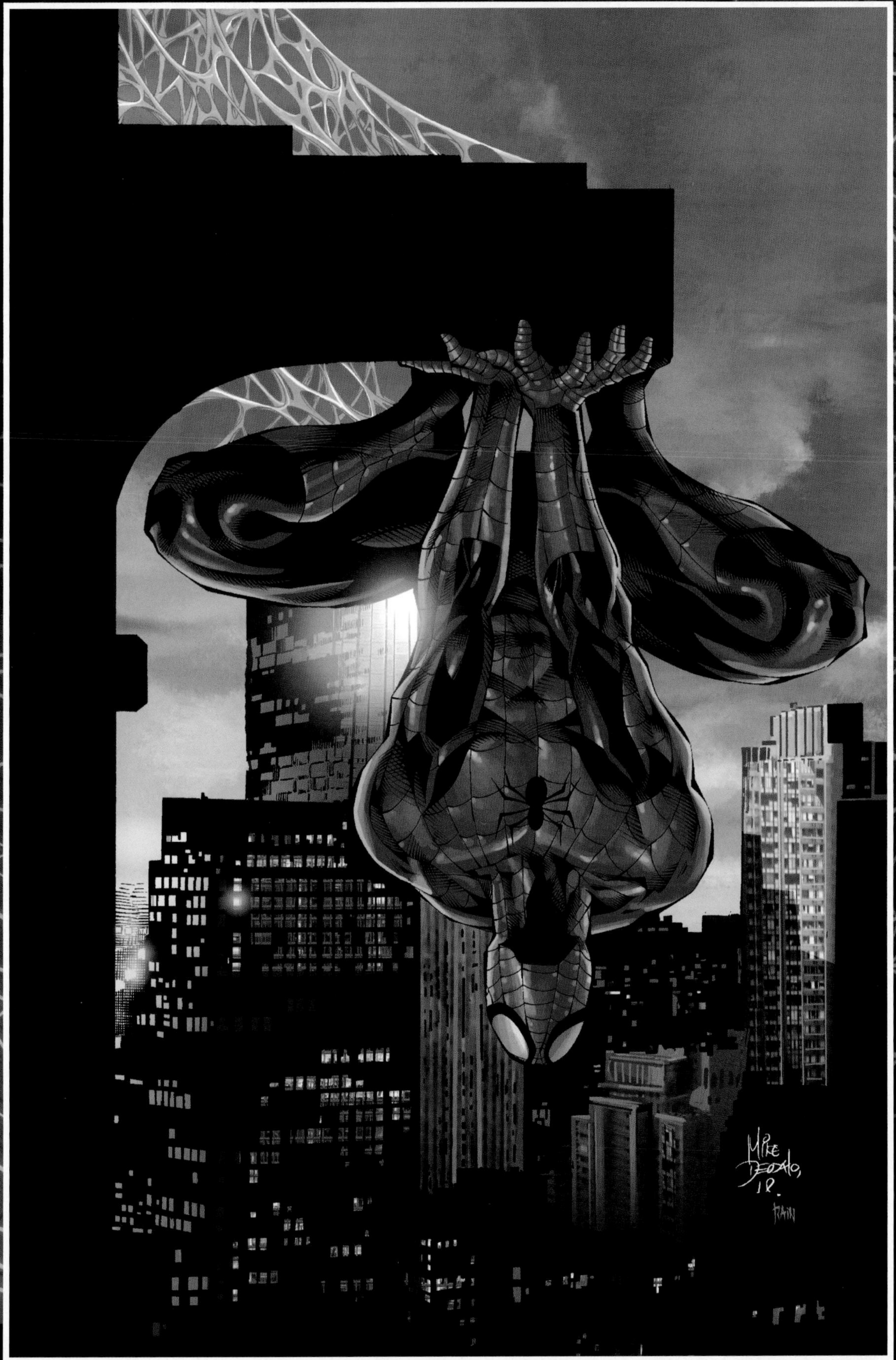

AMAZING SPIDER-MAN FAMILY #2

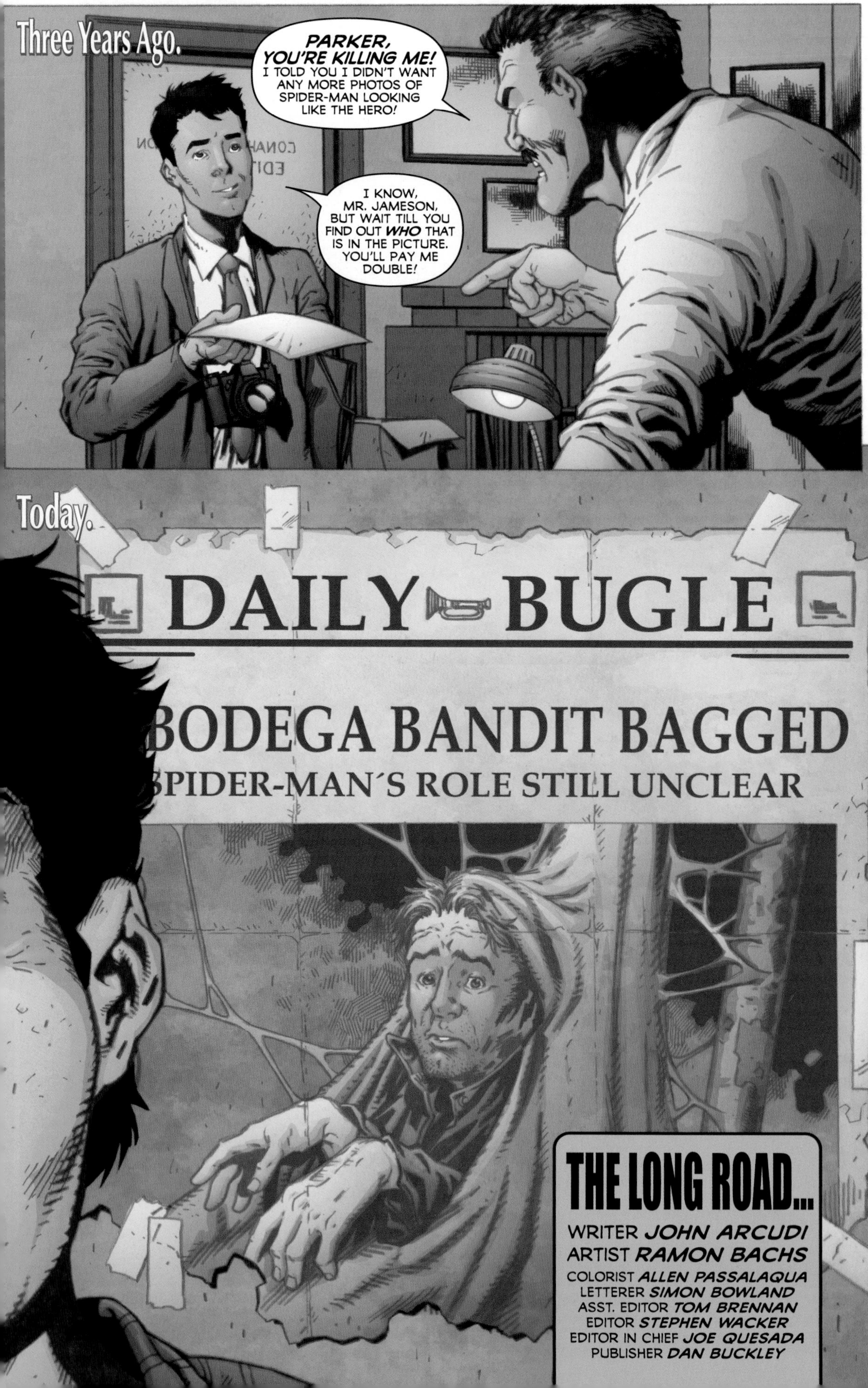
Three Years Ago.
PARKER, YOU'RE KILLING ME! I TOLD YOU I DIDN'T WANT ANY MORE PHOTOS OF SPIDER-MAN LOOKING LIKE THE HERO!
I KNOW, MR. JAMESON, BUT WAIT TILL YOU FIND OUT WHO THAT IS IN THE PICTURE. YOU'LL PAY ME DOUBLE!
Today.
DAILY BUGLE
BODEGA BANDIT BAGGED
SPIDER-MAN´S ROLE STILL UNCLEAR
THE LONG ROAD...
WRITER JOHN ARCUDI
ARTIST RAMON BACHS
COLORIST ALLEN PASSALAQUA
LETTERER SIMON BOWLAND
ASST. EDITOR TOM BRENNAN
EDITOR STEPHEN WACKER
EDITOR IN CHIEF JOE QUESADA
PUBLISHER DAN BUCKLEY

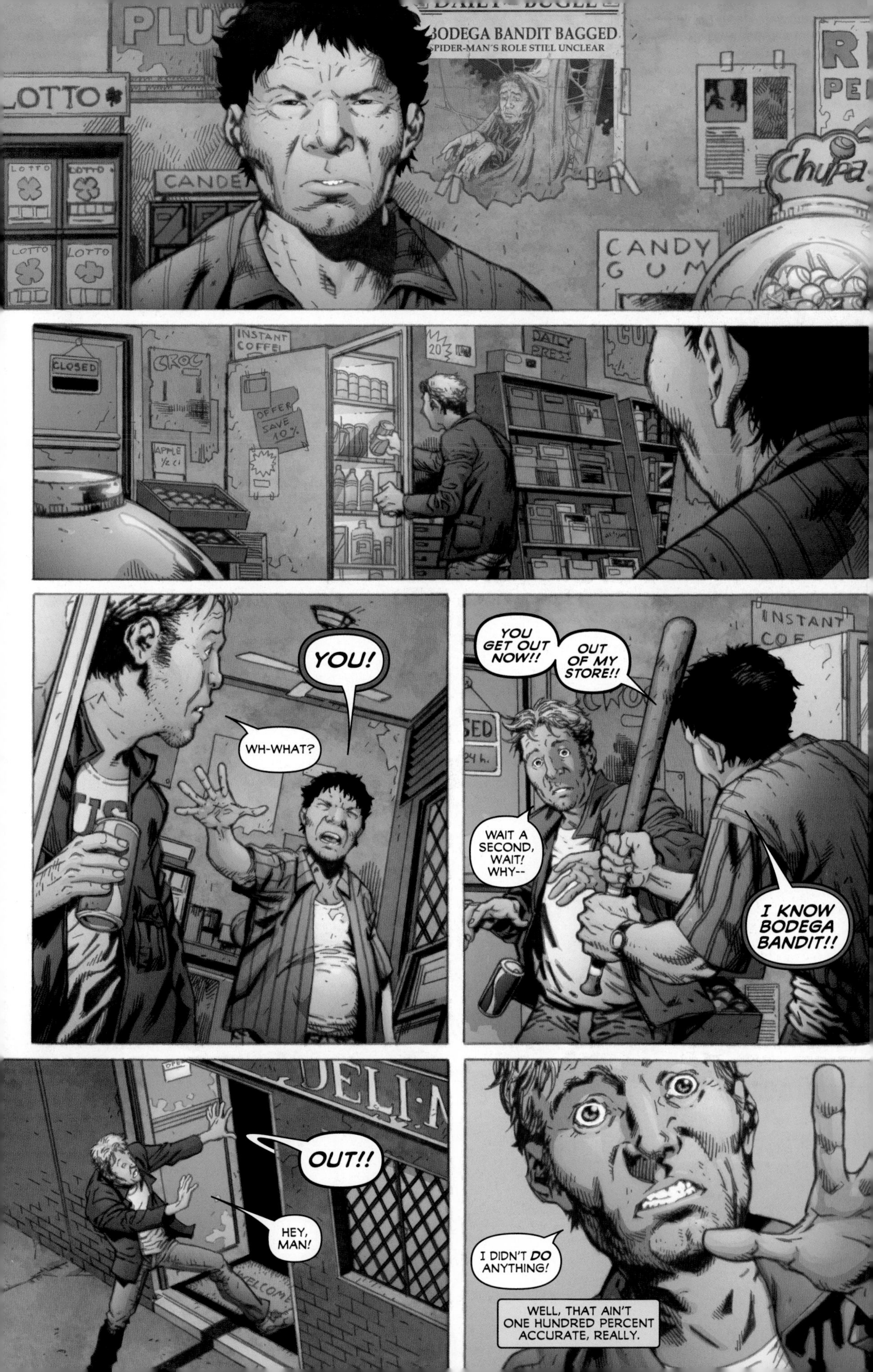

DAILY BUGLE
BODEGA BANDIT BAGGED
SPIDER-MAN'S ROLE STILL UNCLEAR
LOTTO
CANDY GUM
CLOSED
INSTANT COFFEE
OFFER SAVE 10%
YOU!
WH-WHAT?
YOU GET OUT NOW!!
OUT OF MY STORE!!
WAIT A SECOND, WAIT! WHY--
I KNOW BODEGA BANDIT!!
DELI
OUT!!
HEY, MAN!
I DIDN'T *DO* ANYTHING!
WELL, THAT AIN'T ONE HUNDRED PERCENT ACCURATE, REALLY.

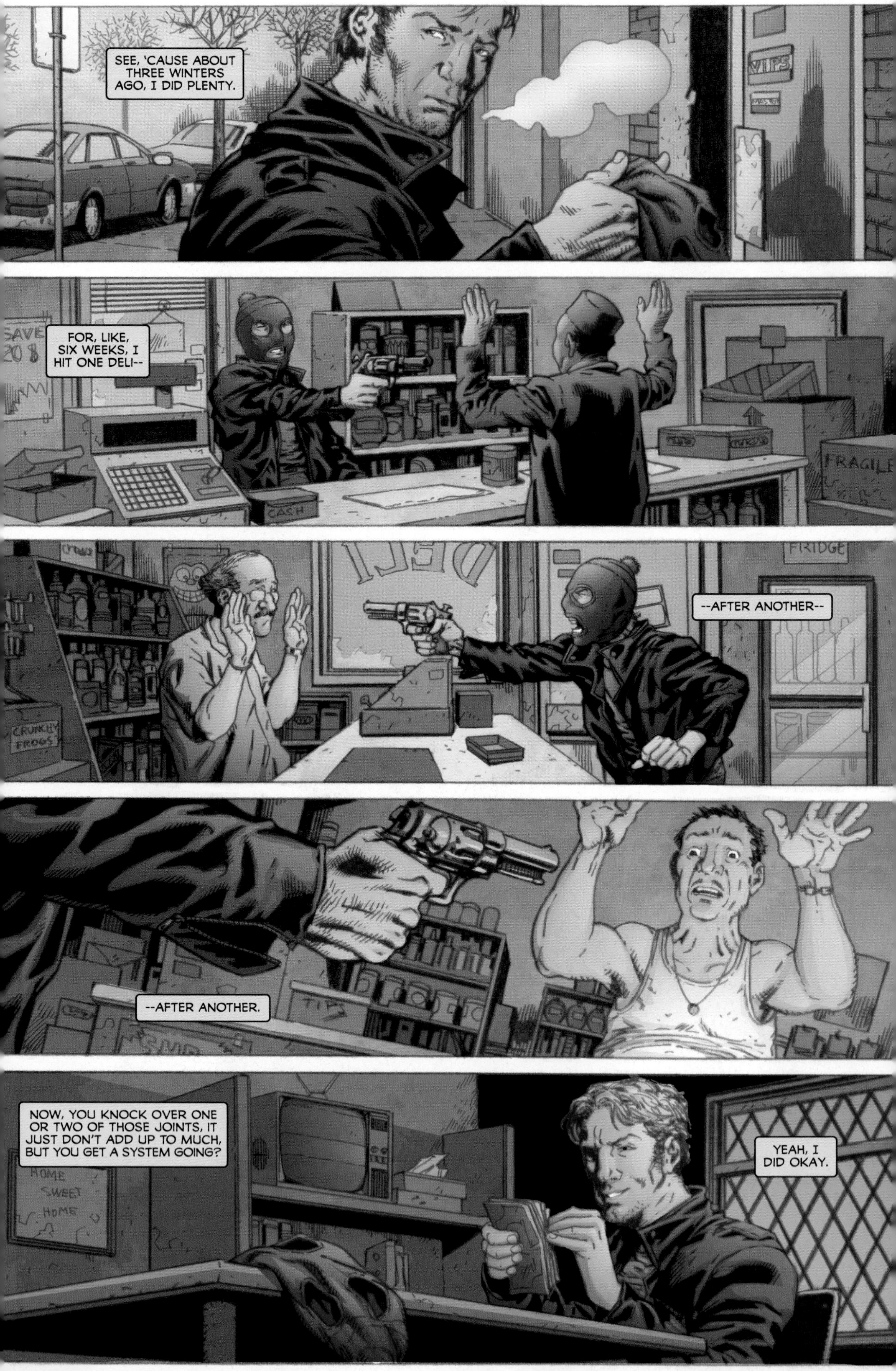
SEE, 'CAUSE ABOUT THREE WINTERS AGO, I DID PLENTY.
VIPS
FOR, LIKE, SIX WEEKS, I HIT ONE DELI--
SAVE 20 $
CASH
FRAGILE
DELI
FRIDGE
CRUNCHY FROGS
--AFTER ANOTHER--
--AFTER ANOTHER.
NOW, YOU KNOCK OVER ONE OR TWO OF THOSE JOINTS, IT JUST DON'T ADD UP TO MUCH, BUT YOU GET A SYSTEM GOING?
HOME SWEET HOME
YEAH, I DID OKAY.

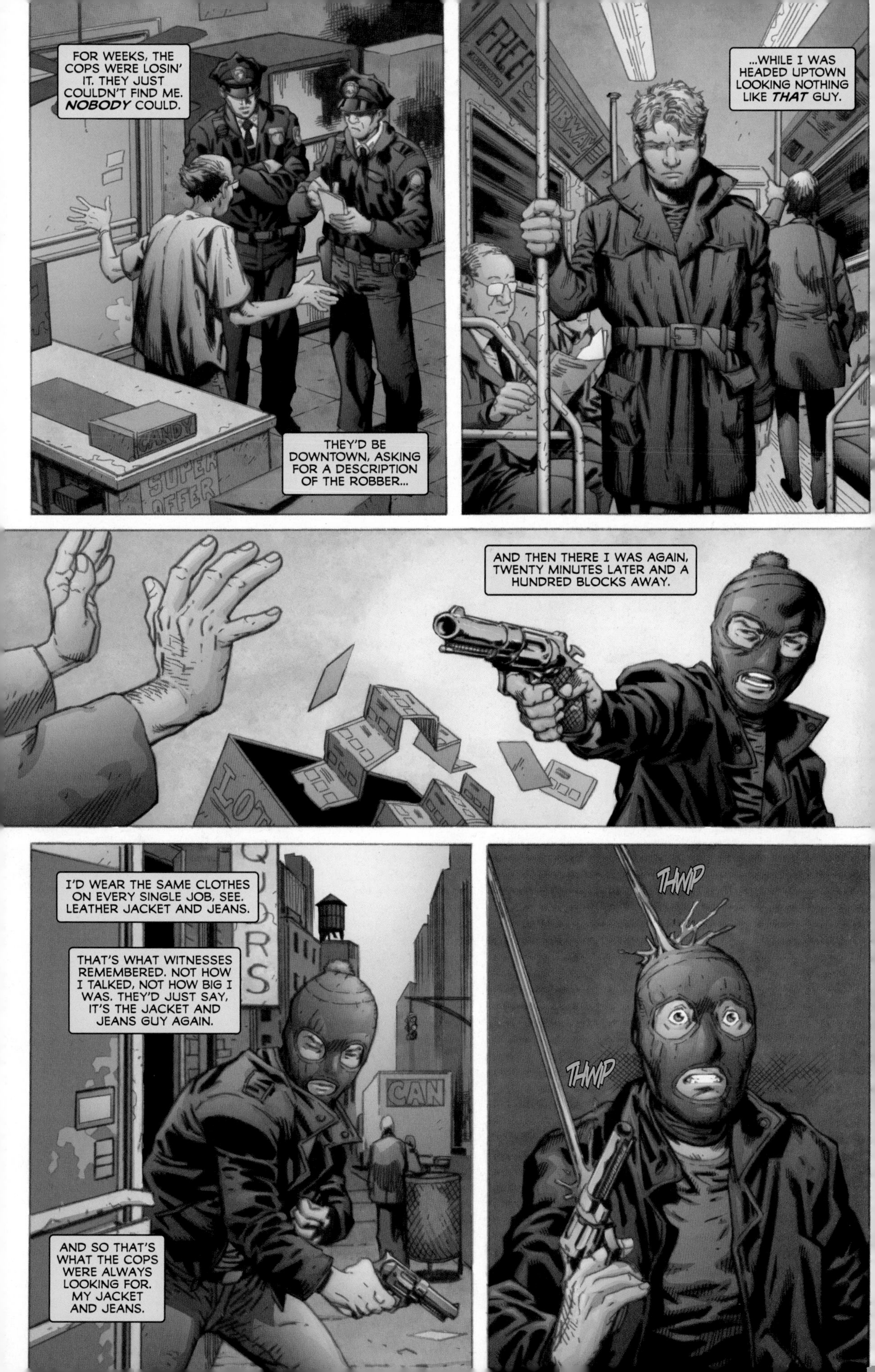
FOR WEEKS, THE COPS WERE LOSIN' IT. THEY JUST COULDN'T FIND ME. NOBODY COULD.
CANDY
SUPER OFFER
THEY'D BE DOWNTOWN, ASKING FOR A DESCRIPTION OF THE ROBBER...
FREE
SUBWAY
...WHILE I WAS HEADED UPTOWN LOOKING NOTHING LIKE THAT GUY.
AND THEN THERE I WAS AGAIN, TWENTY MINUTES LATER AND A HUNDRED BLOCKS AWAY.
LOT
I'D WEAR THE SAME CLOTHES ON EVERY SINGLE JOB, SEE. LEATHER JACKET AND JEANS.
THAT'S WHAT WITNESSES REMEMBERED. NOT HOW I TALKED, NOT HOW BIG I WAS. THEY'D JUST SAY, IT'S THE JACKET AND JEANS GUY AGAIN.
CAN
AND SO THAT'S WHAT THE COPS WERE ALWAYS LOOKING FOR. MY JACKET AND JEANS.
THWIP
THWIP

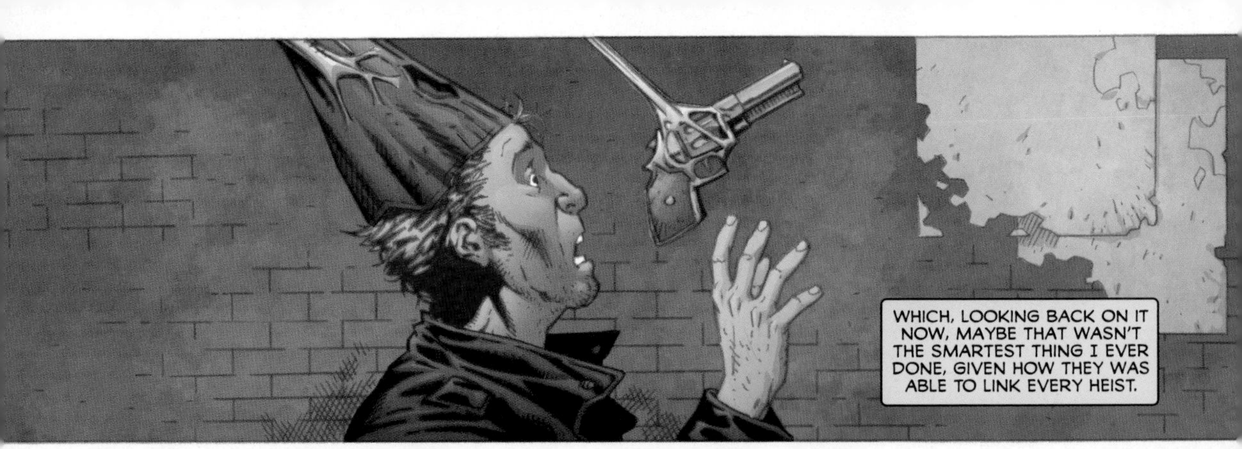
WHICH, LOOKING BACK ON IT NOW, MAYBE THAT WASN'T THE SMARTEST THING I EVER DONE, GIVEN HOW THEY WAS ABLE TO LINK EVERY HEIST.

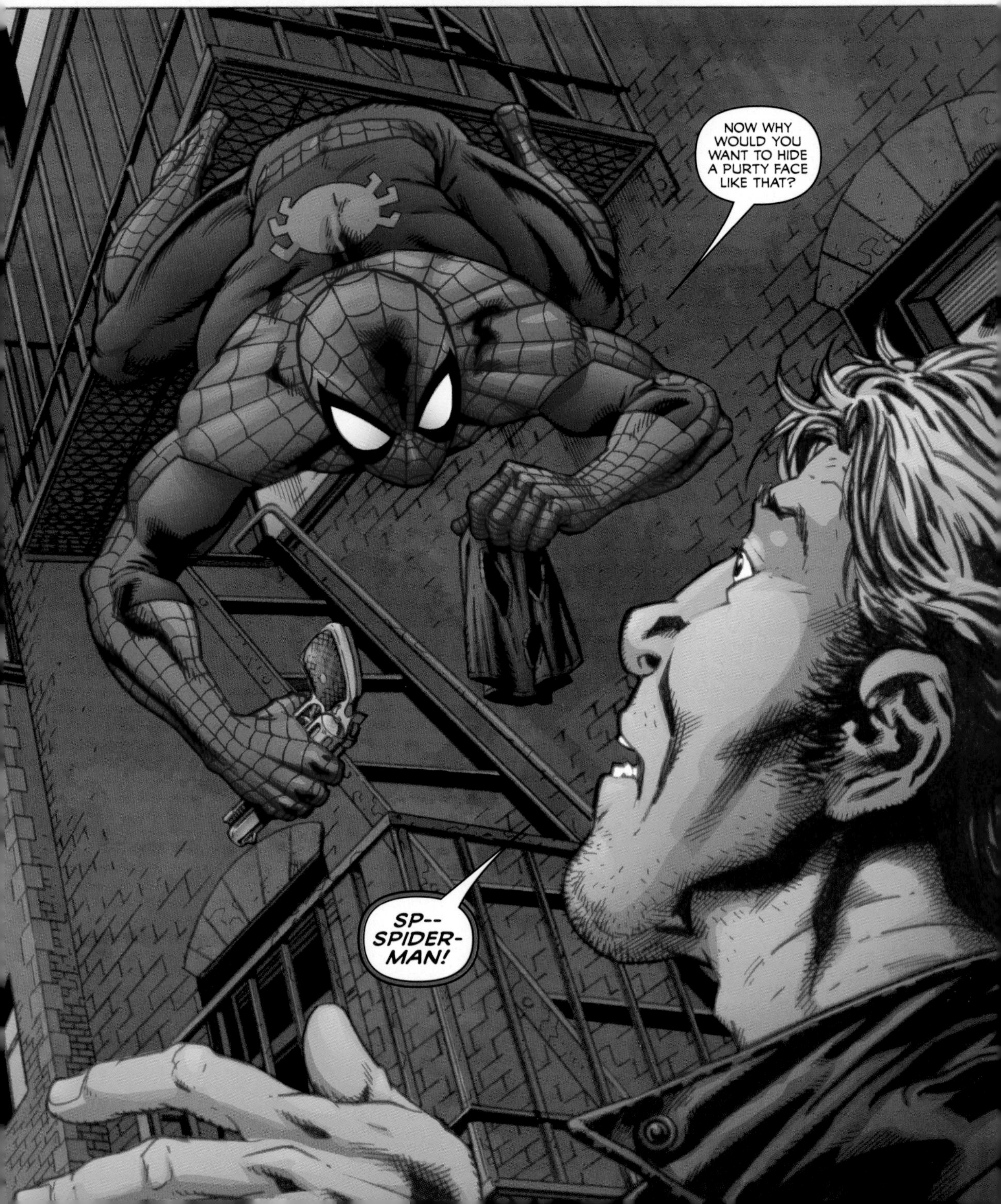
NOW WHY WOULD YOU WANT TO HIDE A PURTY FACE LIKE THAT?
SP-- SPIDER-MAN!

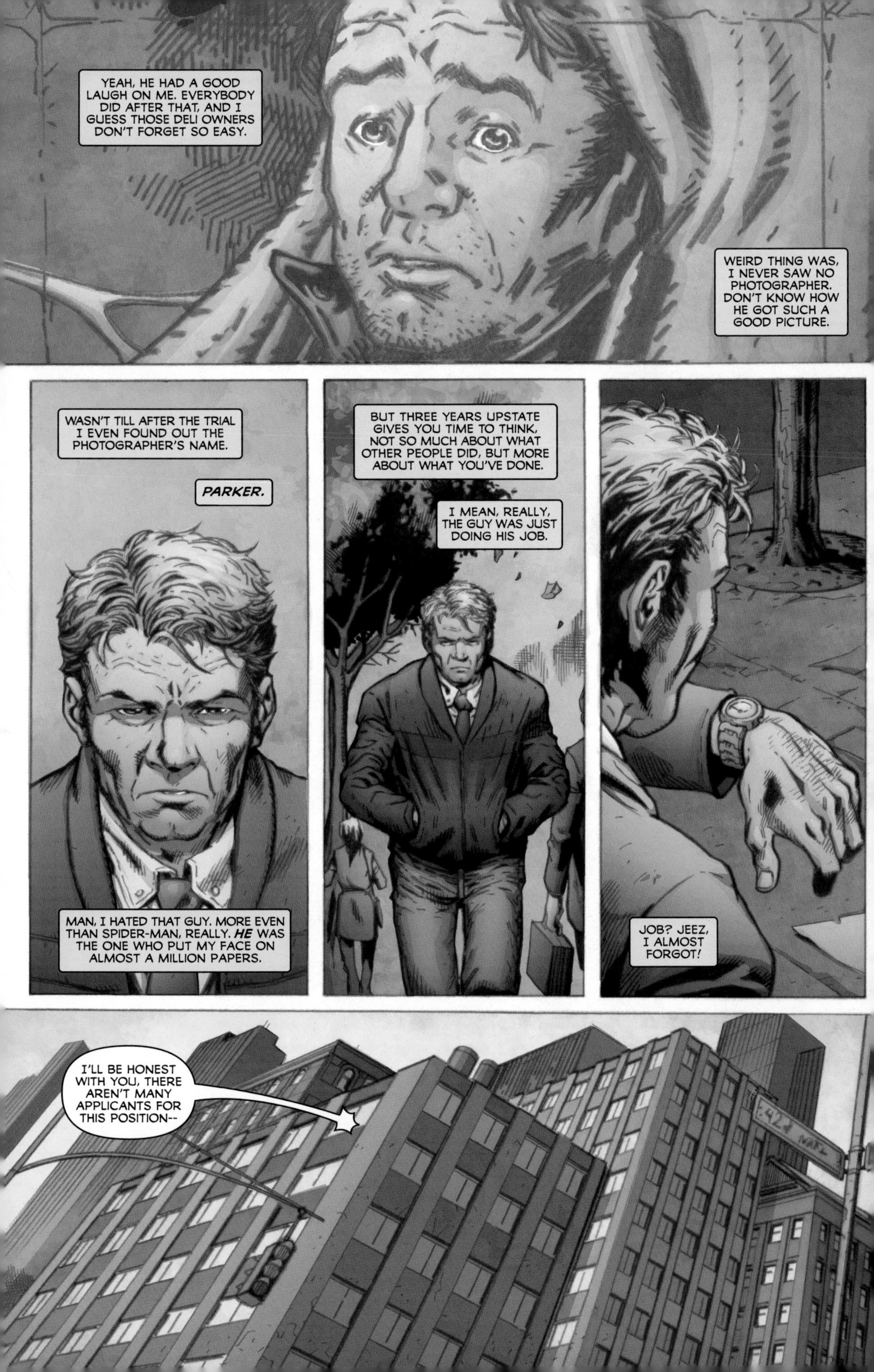
YEAH, HE HAD A GOOD LAUGH ON ME. EVERYBODY DID AFTER THAT, AND I GUESS THOSE DELI OWNERS DON'T FORGET SO EASY.
WEIRD THING WAS, I NEVER SAW NO PHOTOGRAPHER. DON'T KNOW HOW HE GOT SUCH A GOOD PICTURE.
WASN'T TILL AFTER THE TRIAL I EVEN FOUND OUT THE PHOTOGRAPHER'S NAME.
PARKER.
MAN, I HATED THAT GUY. MORE EVEN THAN SPIDER-MAN, REALLY. ***HE*** WAS THE ONE WHO PUT MY FACE ON ALMOST A MILLION PAPERS.
BUT THREE YEARS UPSTATE GIVES YOU TIME TO THINK, NOT SO MUCH ABOUT WHAT OTHER PEOPLE DID, BUT MORE ABOUT WHAT YOU'VE DONE.
I MEAN, REALLY, THE GUY WAS JUST DOING HIS JOB.
JOB? JEEZ, I ALMOST *FORGOT!*
I'LL BE HONEST WITH YOU, THERE AREN'T MANY APPLICANTS FOR THIS POSITION--

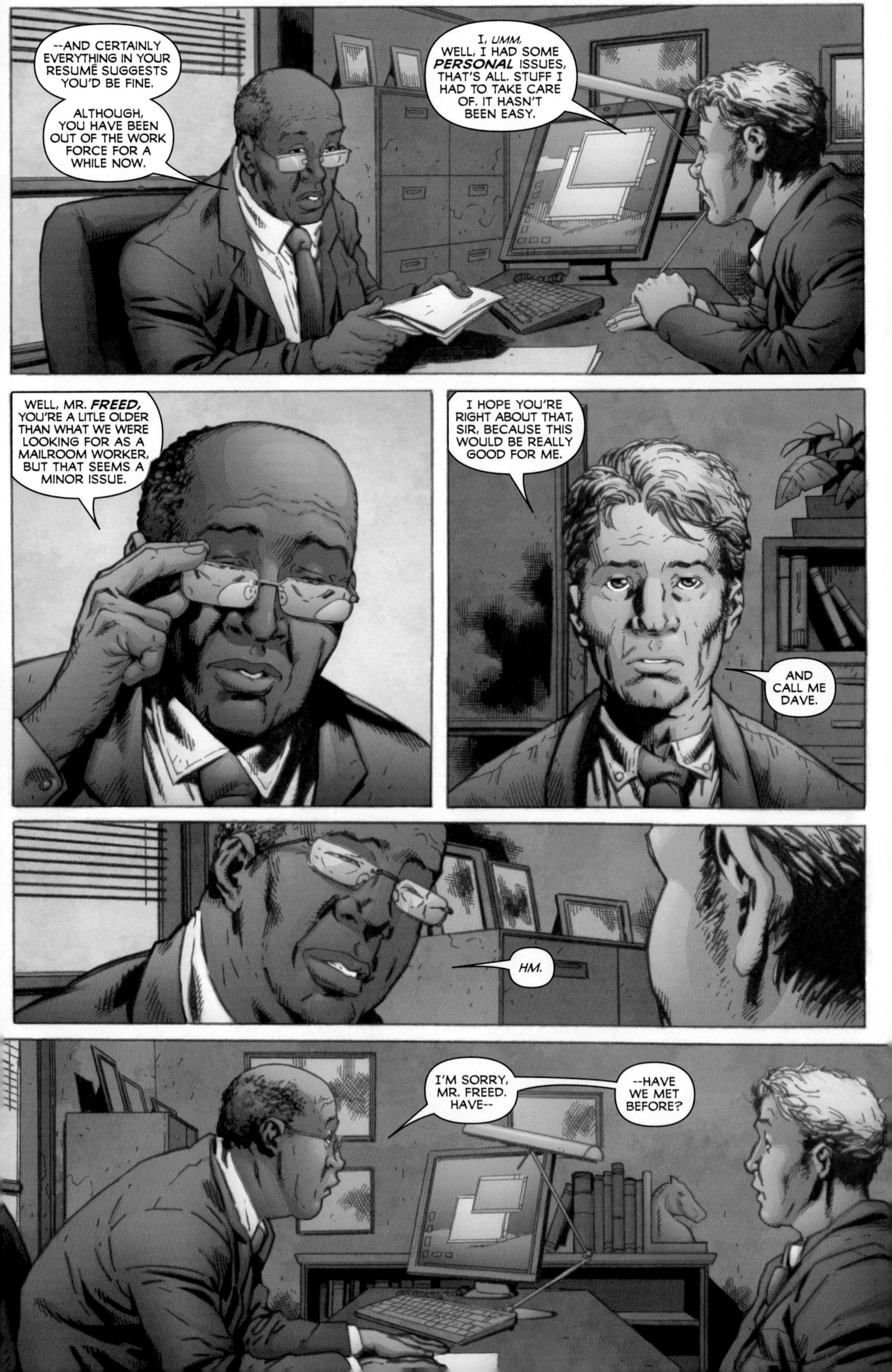
--AND CERTAINLY EVERYTHING IN YOUR RESUMÉ SUGGESTS YOU'D BE FINE.
ALTHOUGH, YOU HAVE BEEN OUT OF THE WORK FORCE FOR A WHILE NOW.
I, UMM, WELL, I HAD SOME PERSONAL ISSUES, THAT'S ALL. STUFF I HAD TO TAKE CARE OF. IT HASN'T BEEN EASY.
WELL, MR. FREED, YOU'RE A LITLE OLDER THAN WHAT WE WERE LOOKING FOR AS A MAILROOM WORKER, BUT THAT SEEMS A MINOR ISSUE.
I HOPE YOU'RE RIGHT ABOUT THAT, SIR, BECAUSE THIS WOULD BE REALLY GOOD FOR ME.
AND CALL ME DAVE.
HM.
I'M SORRY, MR. FREED. HAVE--
--HAVE WE MET BEFORE?

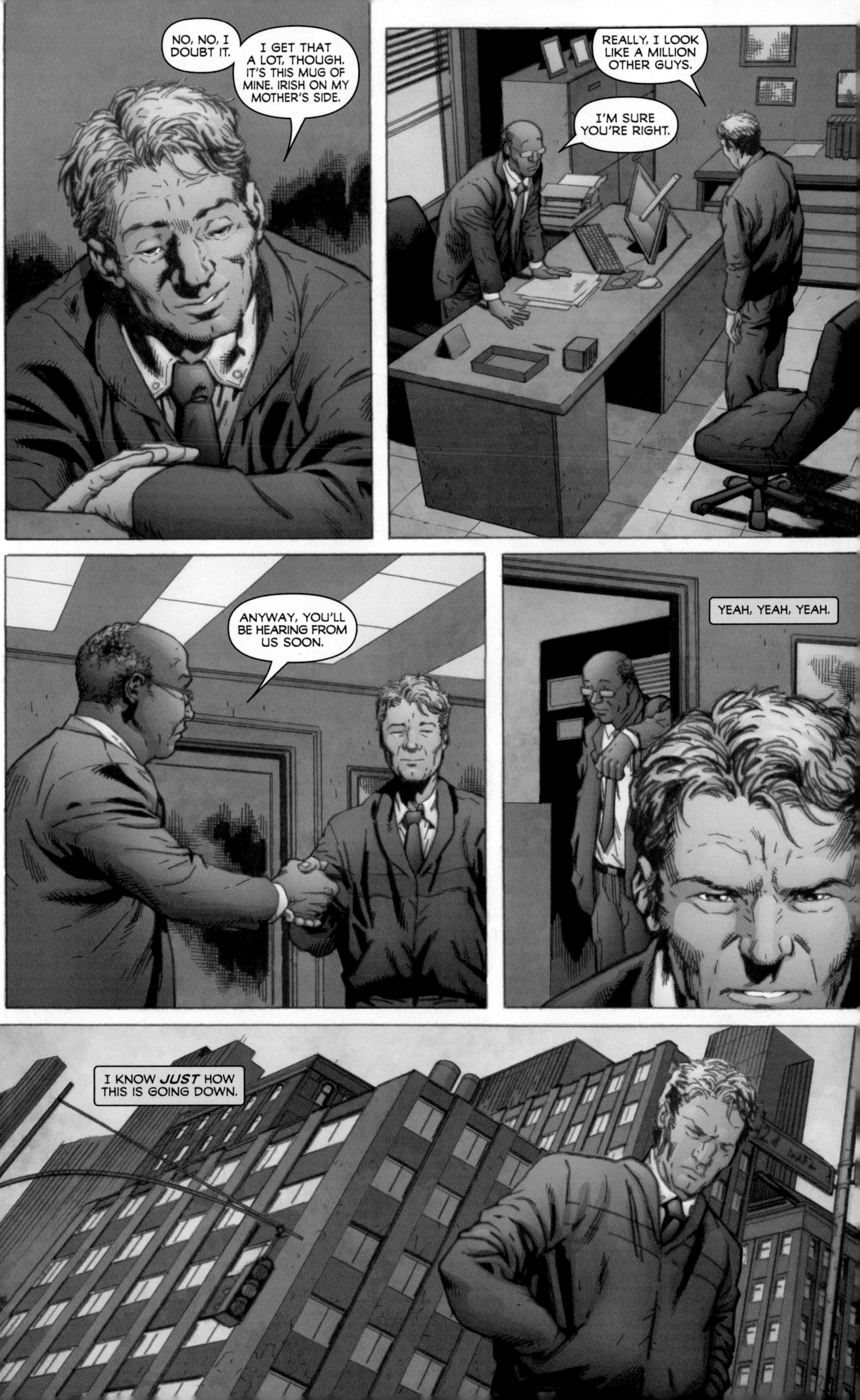
NO, NO, I DOUBT IT.
I GET THAT A LOT, THOUGH. IT'S THIS MUG OF MINE. IRISH ON MY MOTHER'S SIDE.
REALLY, I LOOK LIKE A MILLION OTHER GUYS.
I'M SURE YOU'RE RIGHT.
ANYWAY, YOU'LL BE HEARING FROM US SOON.
YEAH, YEAH, YEAH.
I KNOW JUST HOW THIS IS GOING DOWN.

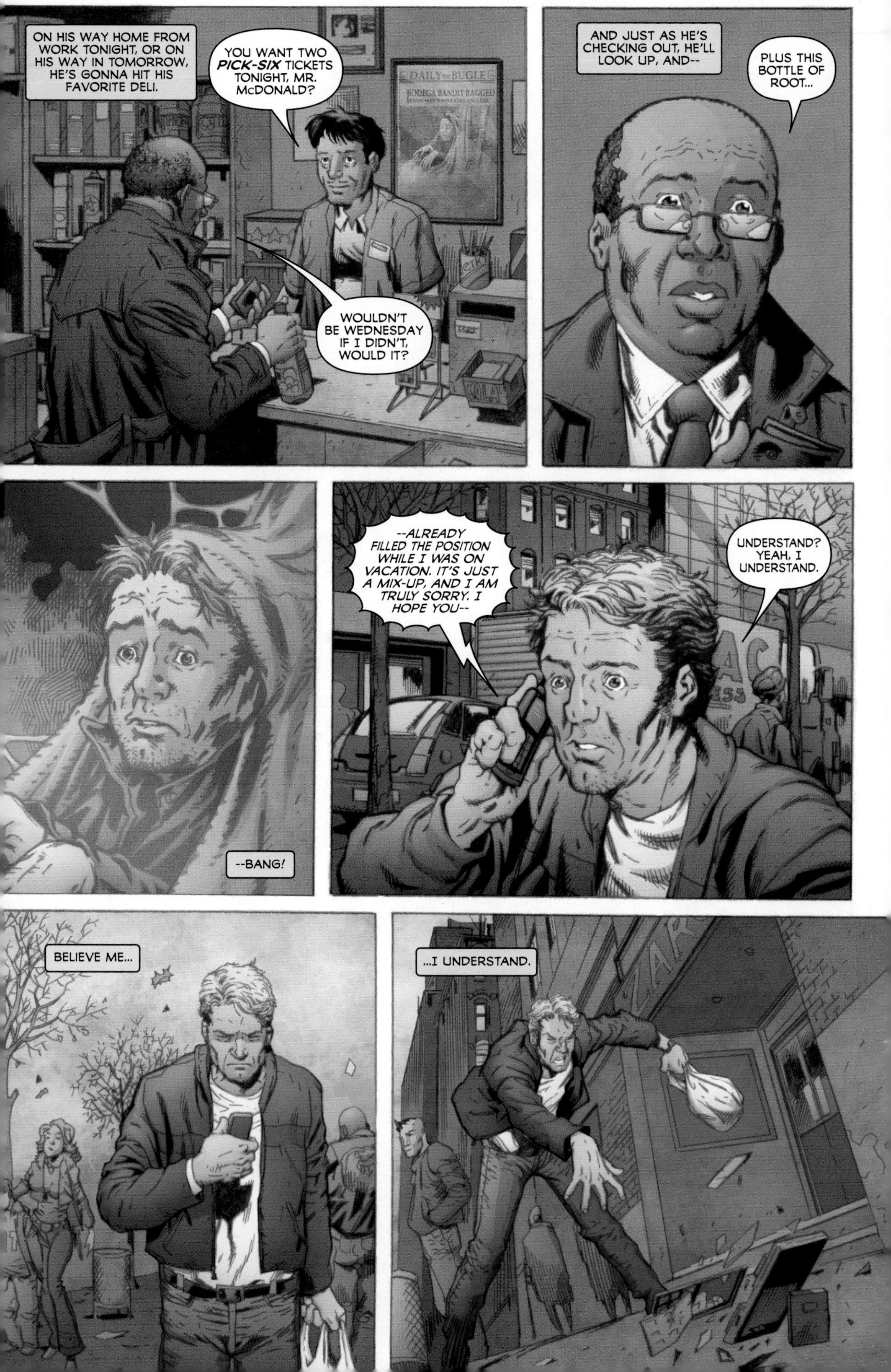
ON HIS WAY HOME FROM WORK TONIGHT, OR ON HIS WAY IN TOMORROW, HE'S GONNA HIT HIS FAVORITE DELI.
YOU WANT TWO PICK-SIX TICKETS TONIGHT, MR. McDONALD?
DAILY BUGLE
BODEGA BANDIT BAGGED
WOULDN'T BE WEDNESDAY IF I DIDN'T, WOULD IT?
AND JUST AS HE'S CHECKING OUT, HE'LL LOOK UP, AND--
PLUS THIS BOTTLE OF ROOT...
--BANG!
--ALREADY FILLED THE POSITION WHILE I WAS ON VACATION. IT'S JUST A MIX-UP, AND I AM TRULY SORRY. I HOPE YOU--
UNDERSTAND? YEAH, I UNDERSTAND.
BELIEVE ME...
...I UNDERSTAND.

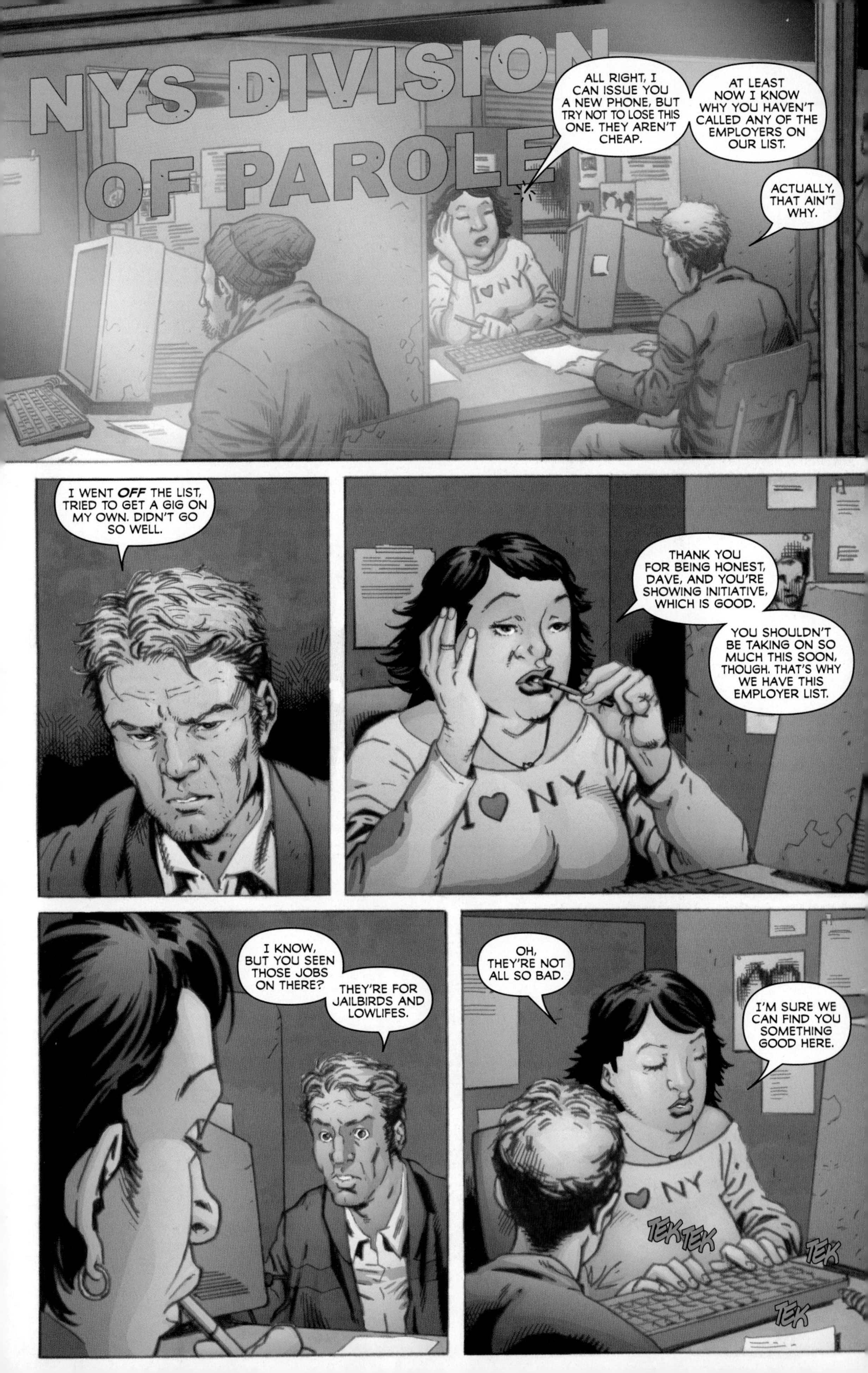
NYS DIVISION OF PAROLE
ALL RIGHT, I CAN ISSUE YOU A NEW PHONE, BUT TRY NOT TO LOSE THIS ONE. THEY AREN'T CHEAP.
AT LEAST NOW I KNOW WHY YOU HAVEN'T CALLED ANY OF THE EMPLOYERS ON OUR LIST.
ACTUALLY, THAT AIN'T WHY.
I WENT OFF THE LIST, TRIED TO GET A GIG ON MY OWN. DIDN'T GO SO WELL.
THANK YOU FOR BEING HONEST, DAVE, AND YOU'RE SHOWING INITIATIVE, WHICH IS GOOD.
YOU SHOULDN'T BE TAKING ON SO MUCH THIS SOON, THOUGH. THAT'S WHY WE HAVE THIS EMPLOYER LIST.
I KNOW, BUT YOU SEEN THOSE JOBS ON THERE?
THEY'RE FOR JAILBIRDS AND LOWLIFES.
OH, THEY'RE NOT ALL SO BAD.
I'M SURE WE CAN FIND YOU SOMETHING GOOD HERE.
TEK TEK
TEK
TEK

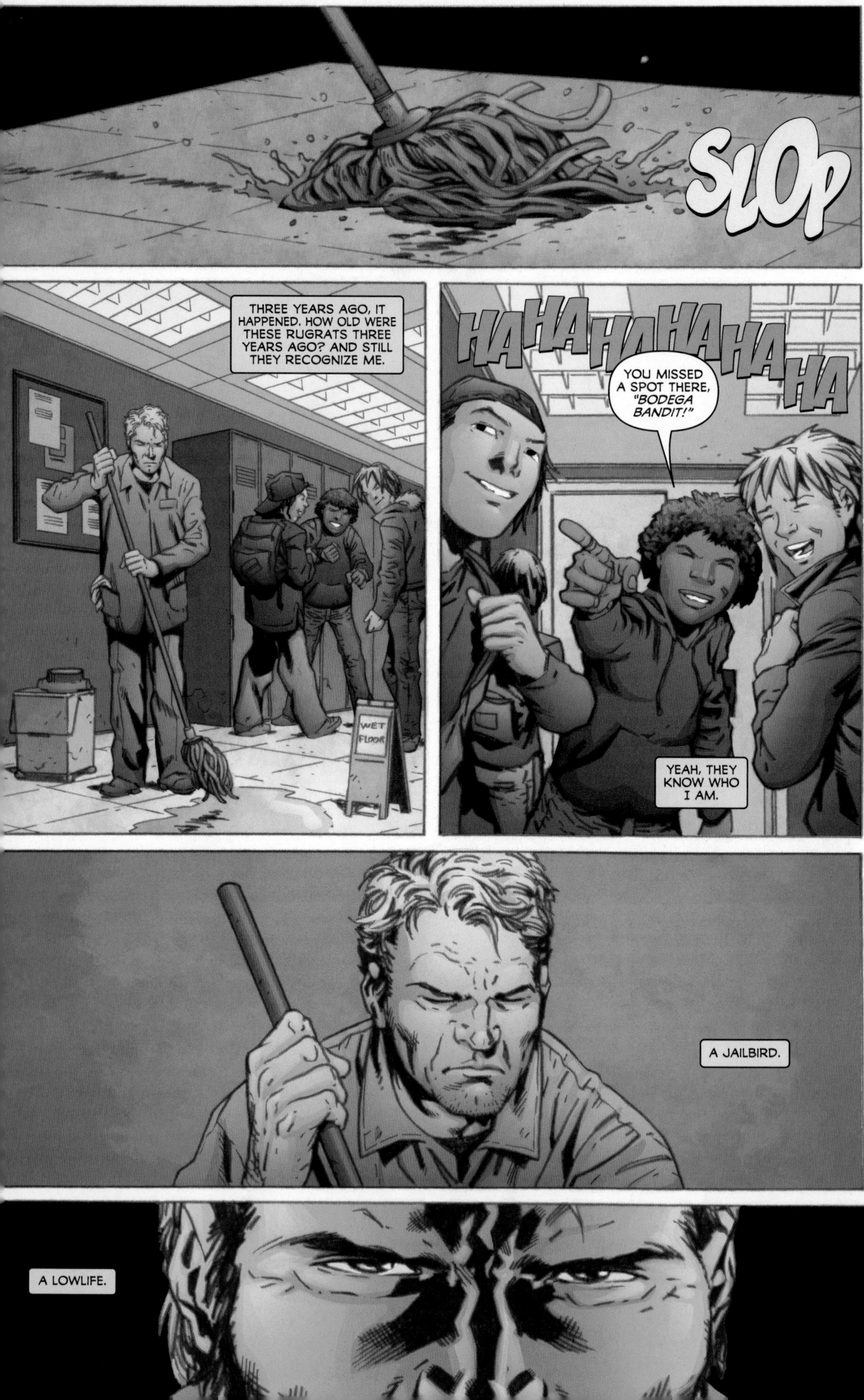
SLOP
THREE YEARS AGO, IT HAPPENED. HOW OLD WERE THESE RUGRATS THREE YEARS AGO? AND STILL THEY RECOGNIZE ME.
WET FLOOR
HAHAHAHAHAHAHAHAHA
YOU MISSED A SPOT THERE, "BODEGA BANDIT!"
YEAH, THEY KNOW WHO I AM.
A JAILBIRD.
A LOWLIFE.

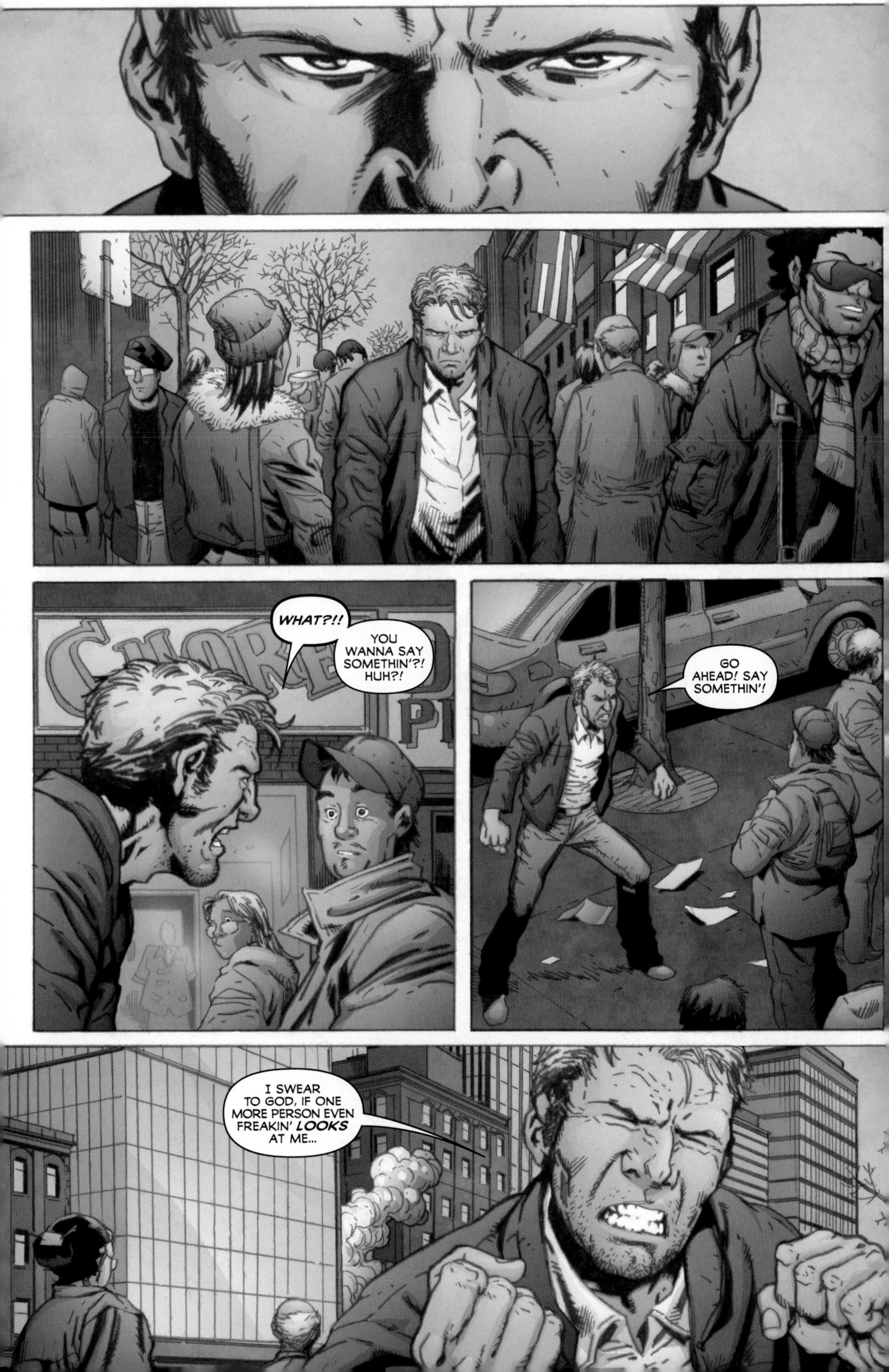
WHAT?!!
YOU WANNA SAY SOMETHIN'?! HUH?!
GO AHEAD! SAY SOMETHIN'!
I SWEAR TO GOD, IF ONE MORE PERSON EVEN FREAKIN' LOOKS AT ME...

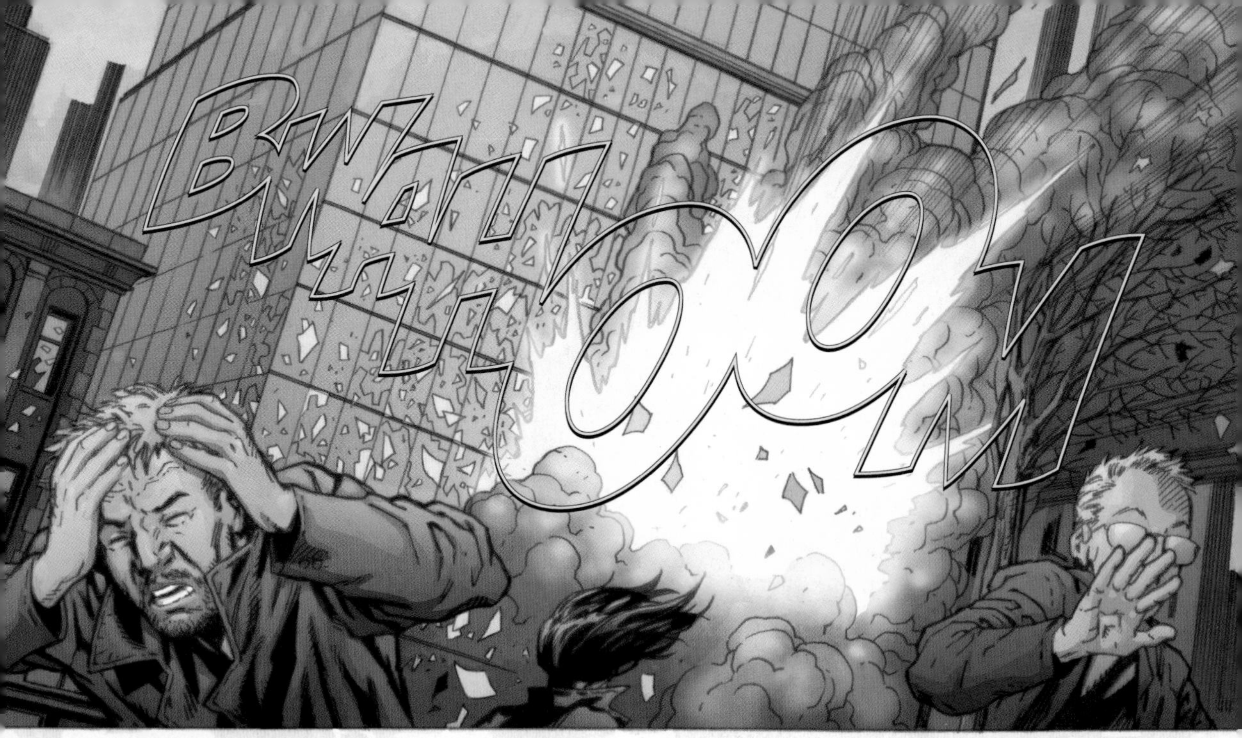
BWHUUOOM

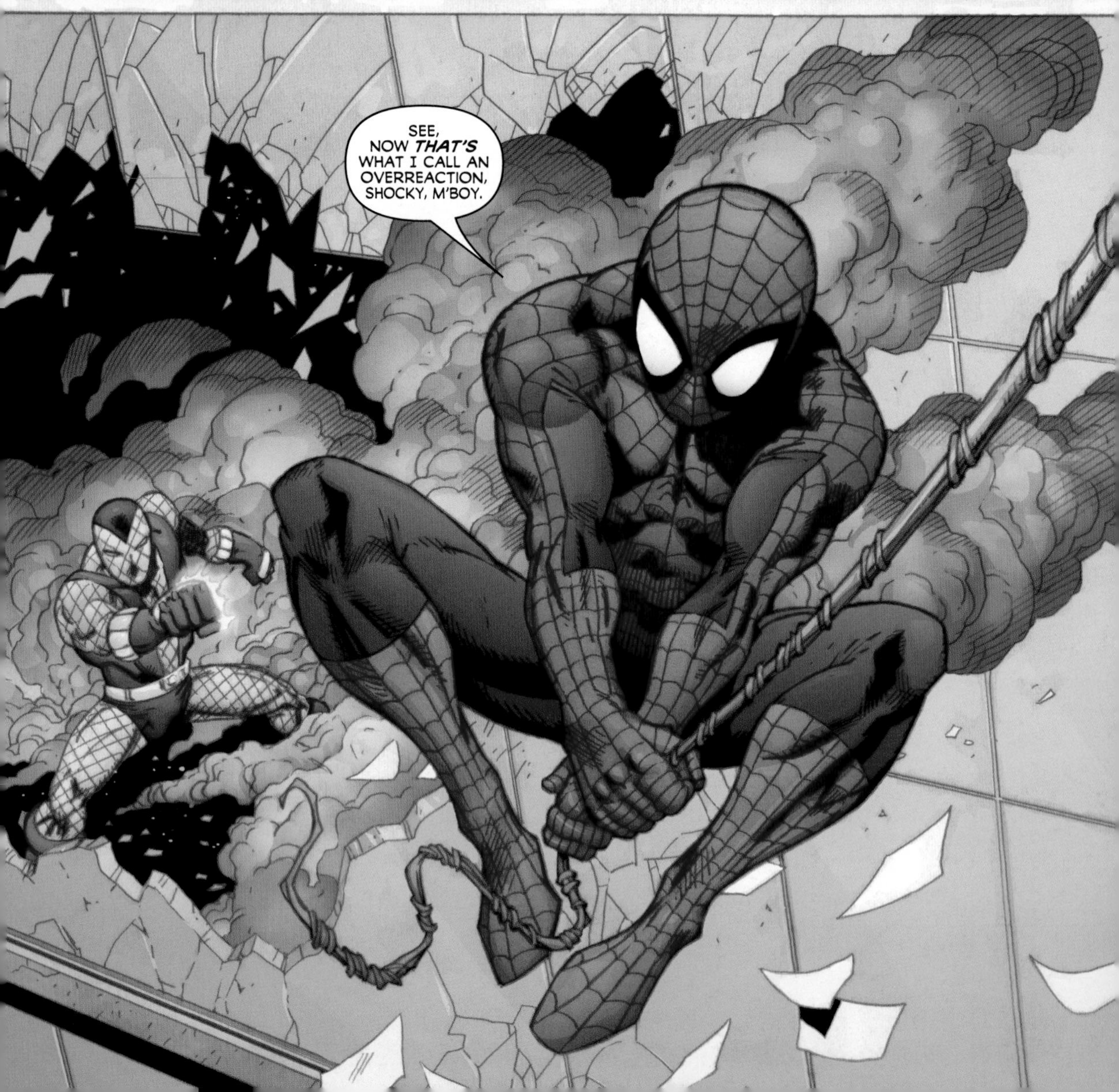
SEE, NOW *THAT'S* WHAT I CALL AN OVERREACTION, SHOCKY, M'BOY.

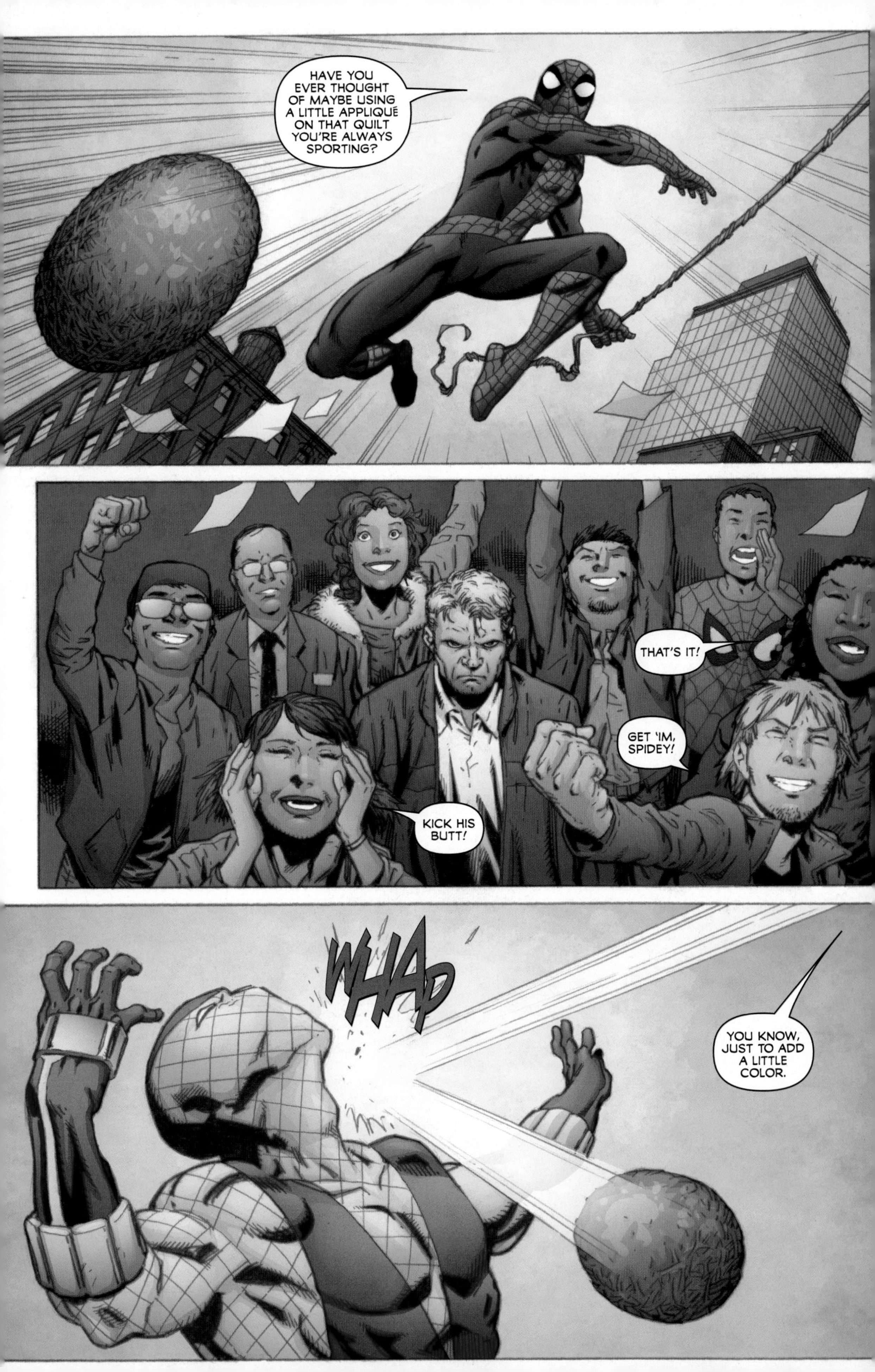
HAVE YOU EVER THOUGHT OF MAYBE USING A LITTLE APPLIQUÉ ON THAT QUILT YOU'RE ALWAYS SPORTING?
THAT'S IT!
GET 'IM, SPIDEY!
KICK HIS BUTT!
WHAP
YOU KNOW, JUST TO ADD A LITTLE COLOR.

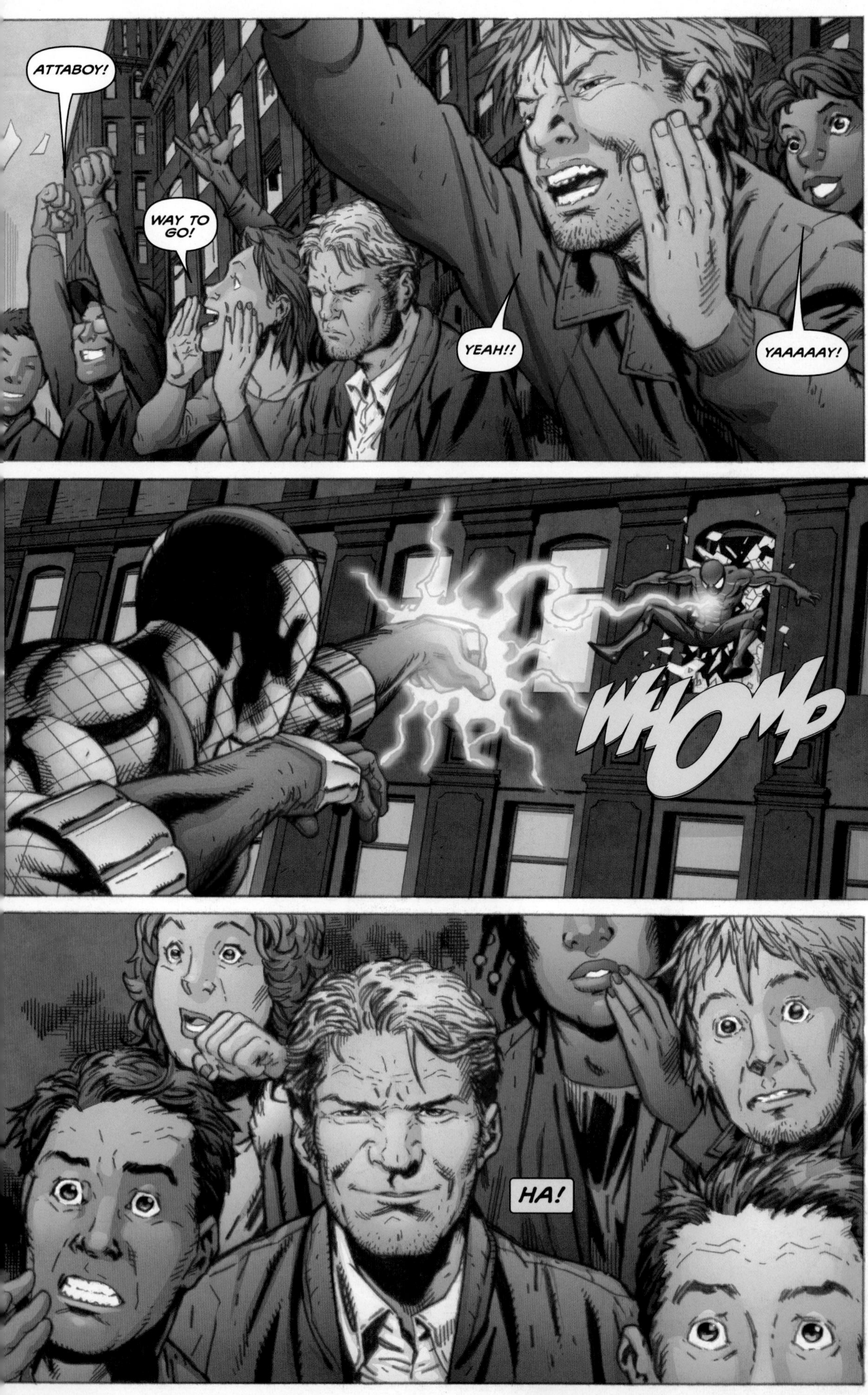
ATTABOY!
WAY TO GO!
YEAH!!
YAAAAAY!
WHOMP
HA!

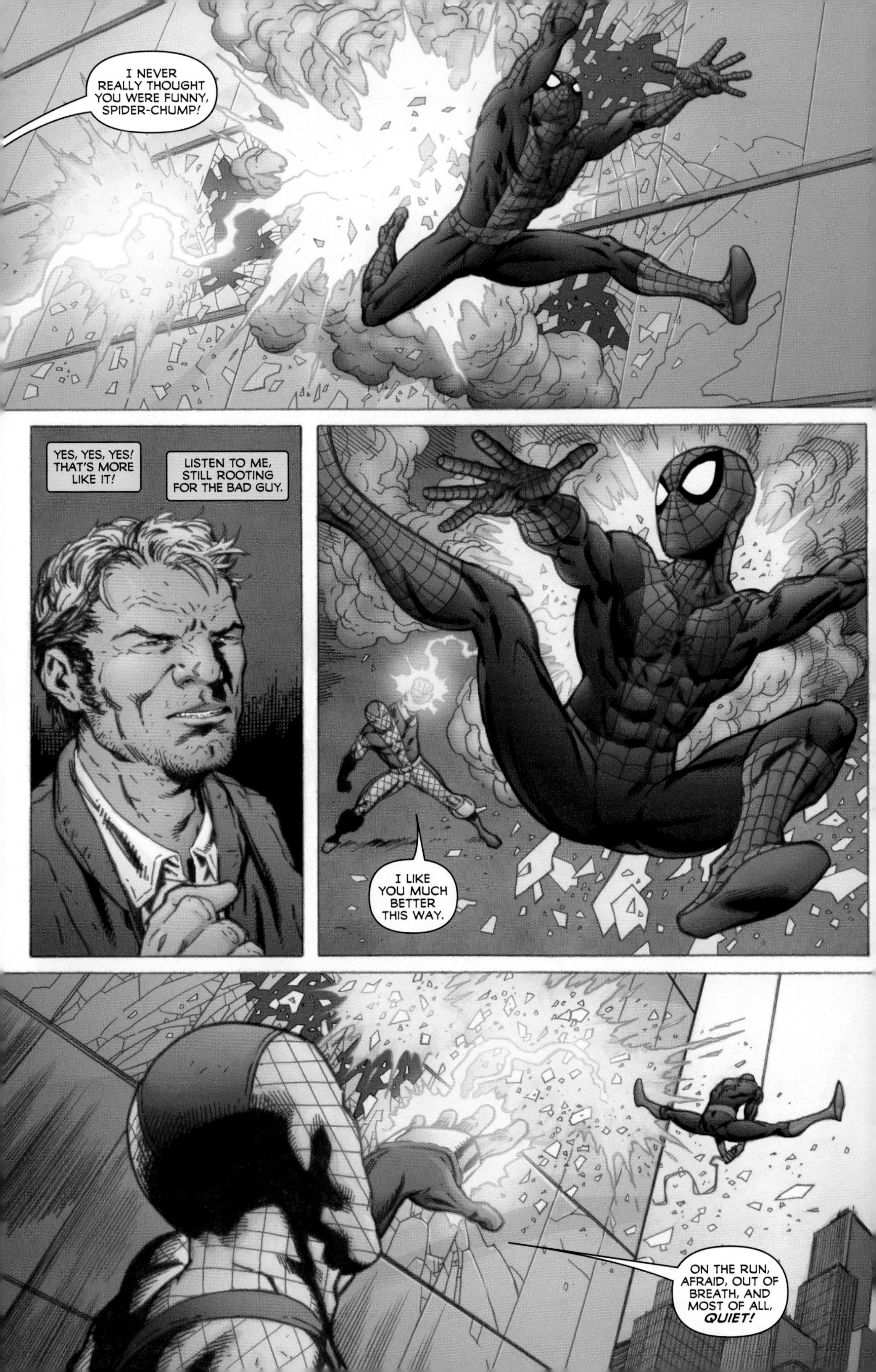
I NEVER REALLY THOUGHT YOU WERE FUNNY, SPIDER-CHUMP!
YES, YES, YES! THAT'S MORE LIKE IT!
LISTEN TO ME, STILL ROOTING FOR THE BAD GUY.
I LIKE YOU MUCH BETTER THIS WAY.
ON THE RUN, AFRAID, OUT OF BREATH, AND MOST OF ALL, *QUIET!*

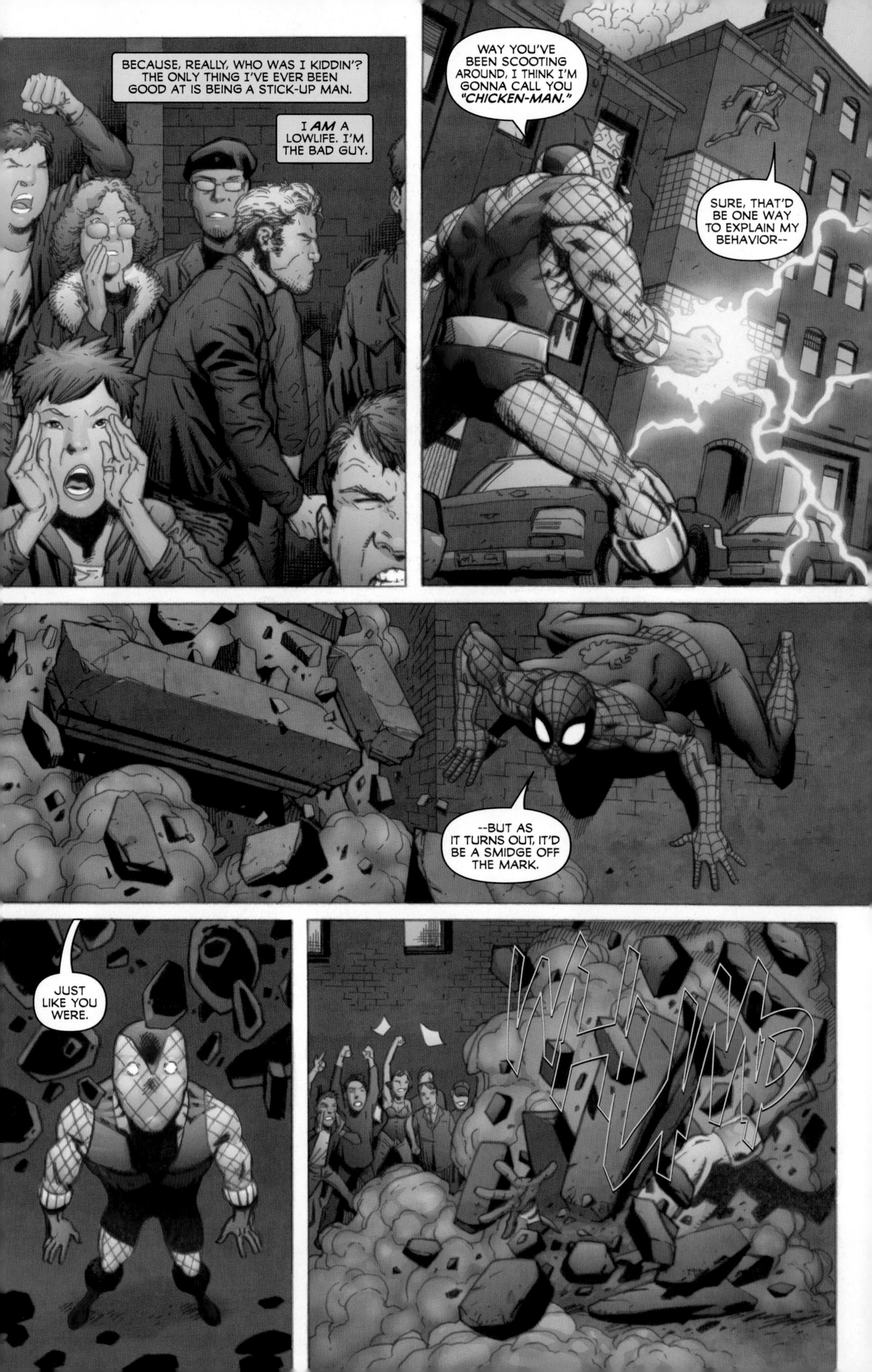
BECAUSE, REALLY, WHO WAS I KIDDIN'? THE ONLY THING I'VE EVER BEEN GOOD AT IS BEING A STICK-UP MAN.
I *AM* A LOWLIFE. I'M THE BAD GUY.
WAY YOU'VE BEEN SCOOTING AROUND, I THINK I'M GONNA CALL YOU *"CHICKEN-MAN."*
SURE, THAT'D BE ONE WAY TO EXPLAIN MY BEHAVIOR--
--BUT AS IT TURNS OUT, IT'D BE A SMIDGE OFF THE MARK.
JUST LIKE YOU WERE.

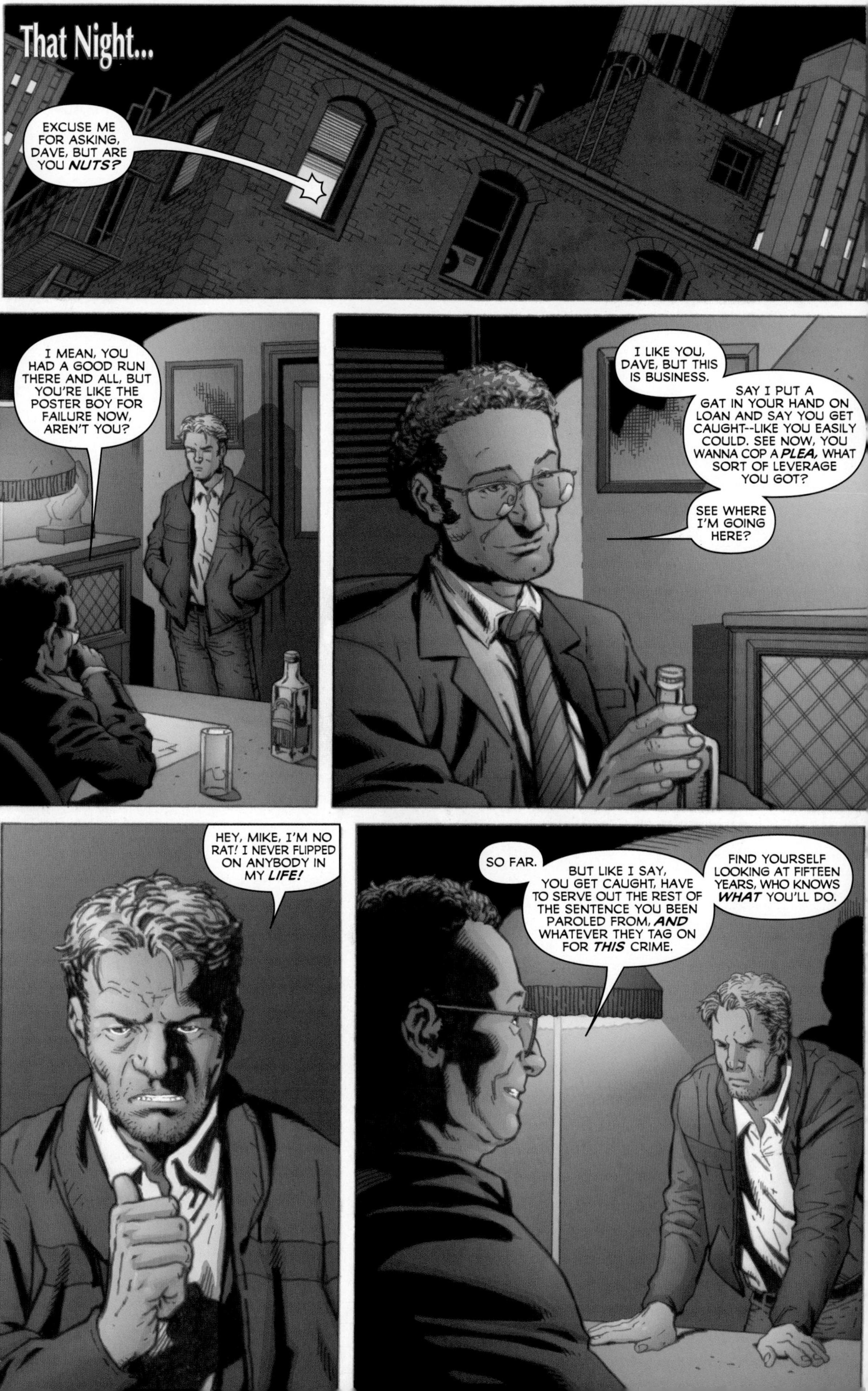
That Night...
EXCUSE ME FOR ASKING, DAVE, BUT ARE YOU NUTS?
I MEAN, YOU HAD A GOOD RUN THERE AND ALL, BUT YOU'RE LIKE THE POSTER BOY FOR FAILURE NOW, AREN'T YOU?
I LIKE YOU, DAVE, BUT THIS IS BUSINESS.
SAY I PUT A GAT IN YOUR HAND ON LOAN AND SAY YOU GET CAUGHT--LIKE YOU EASILY COULD. SEE NOW, YOU WANNA COP A PLEA, WHAT SORT OF LEVERAGE YOU GOT?
SEE WHERE I'M GOING HERE?
HEY, MIKE, I'M NO RAT! I NEVER FLIPPED ON ANYBODY IN MY LIFE!
SO FAR.
BUT LIKE I SAY, YOU GET CAUGHT, HAVE TO SERVE OUT THE REST OF THE SENTENCE YOU BEEN PAROLED FROM, AND WHATEVER THEY TAG ON FOR THIS CRIME.
FIND YOURSELF LOOKING AT FIFTEEN YEARS, WHO KNOWS WHAT YOU'LL DO.

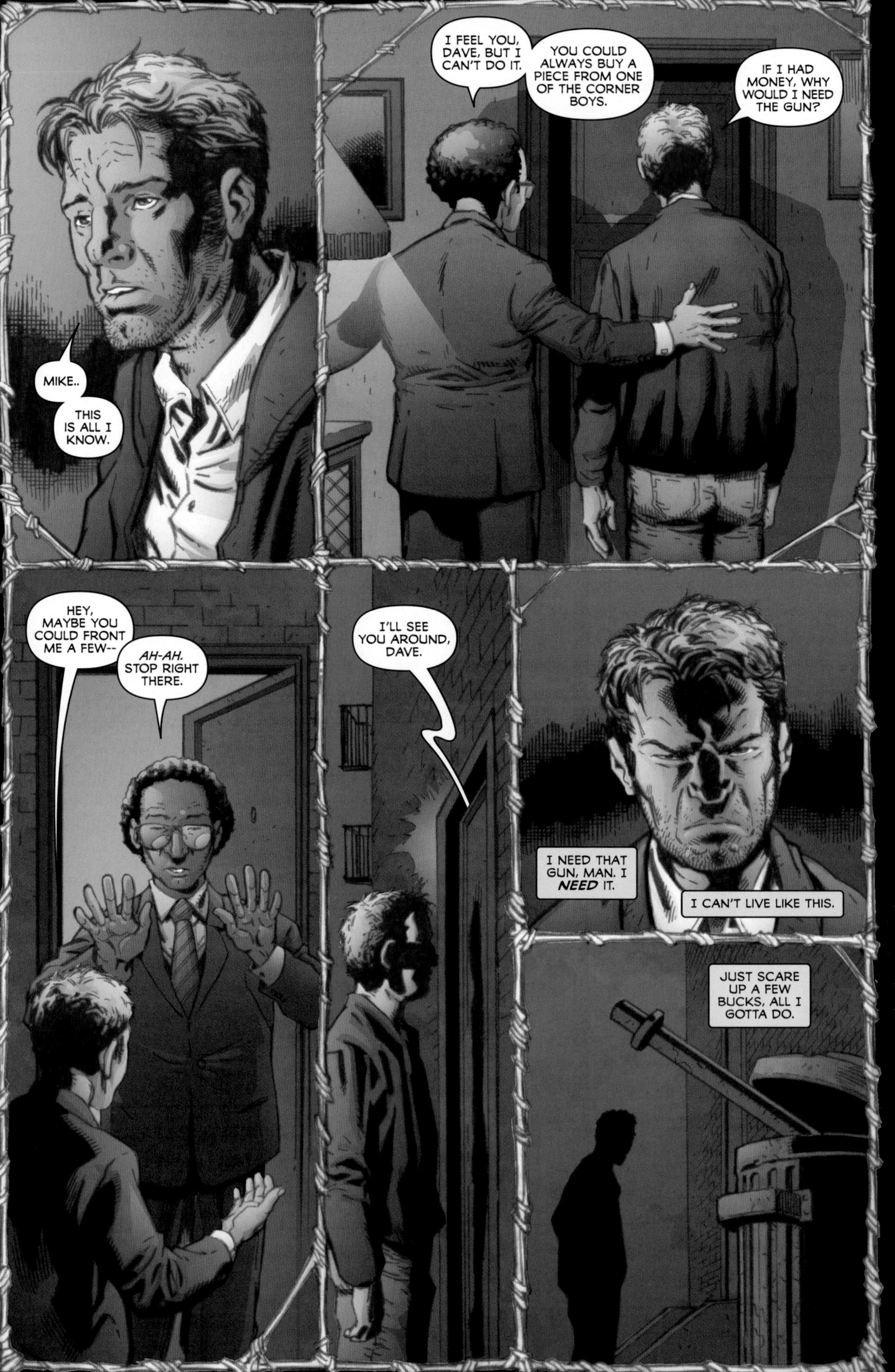
MIKE..
THIS IS ALL I KNOW.
I FEEL YOU, DAVE, BUT I CAN'T DO IT.
YOU COULD ALWAYS BUY A PIECE FROM ONE OF THE CORNER BOYS.
IF I HAD MONEY, WHY WOULD I NEED THE GUN?
HEY, MAYBE YOU COULD FRONT ME A FEW--
AH-AH. STOP RIGHT THERE.
I'LL SEE YOU AROUND, DAVE.
I NEED THAT GUN, MAN. I ***NEED*** IT.
I CAN'T LIVE LIKE THIS.
JUST SCARE UP A FEW BUCKS, ALL I GOTTA DO.

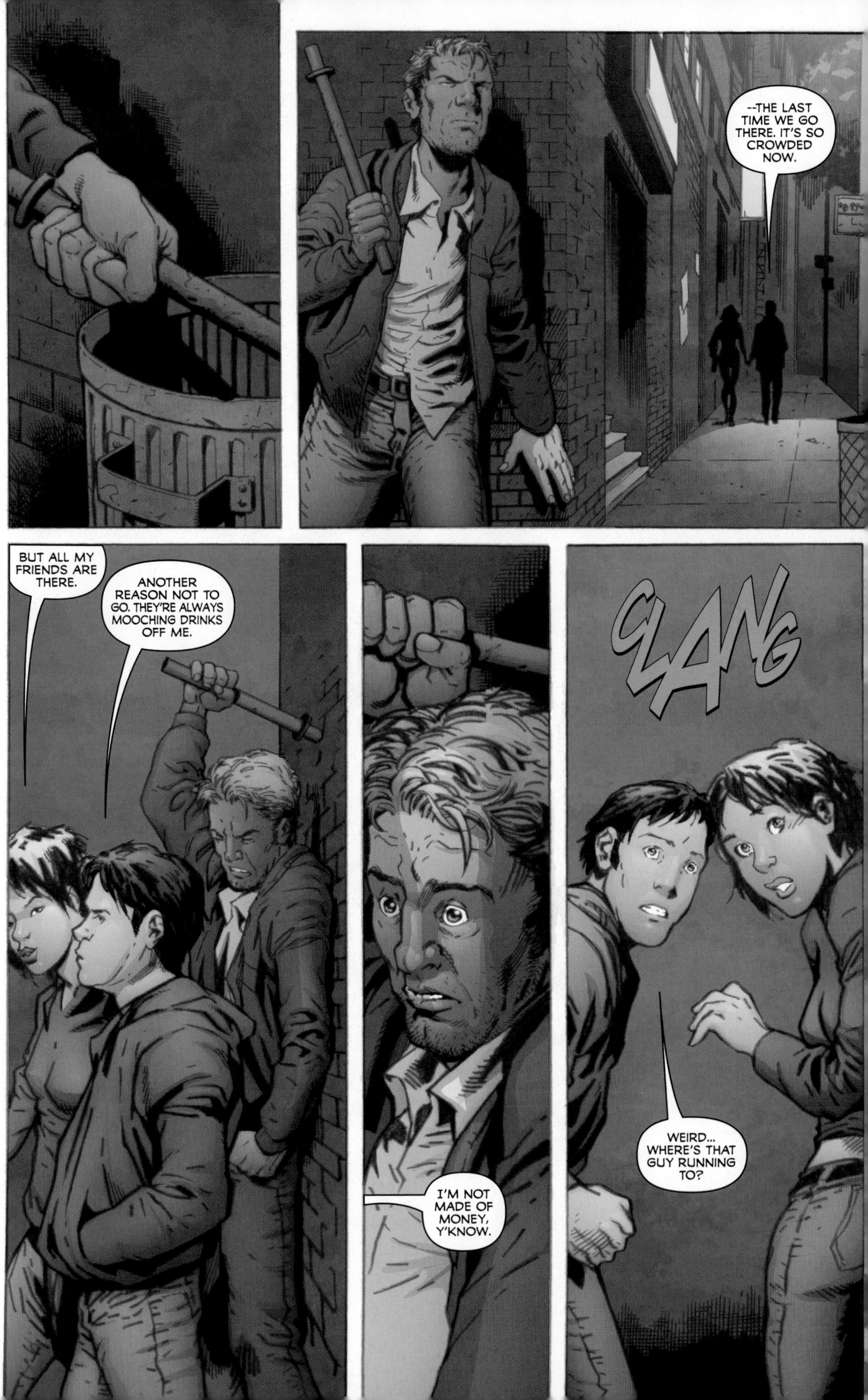
--THE LAST TIME WE GO THERE. IT'S SO CROWDED NOW.
BUT ALL MY FRIENDS ARE THERE.
ANOTHER REASON NOT TO GO. THEY'RE ALWAYS MOOCHING DRINKS OFF ME.
I'M NOT MADE OF MONEY, Y'KNOW.
CLANG
WEIRD... WHERE'S THAT GUY RUNNING TO?

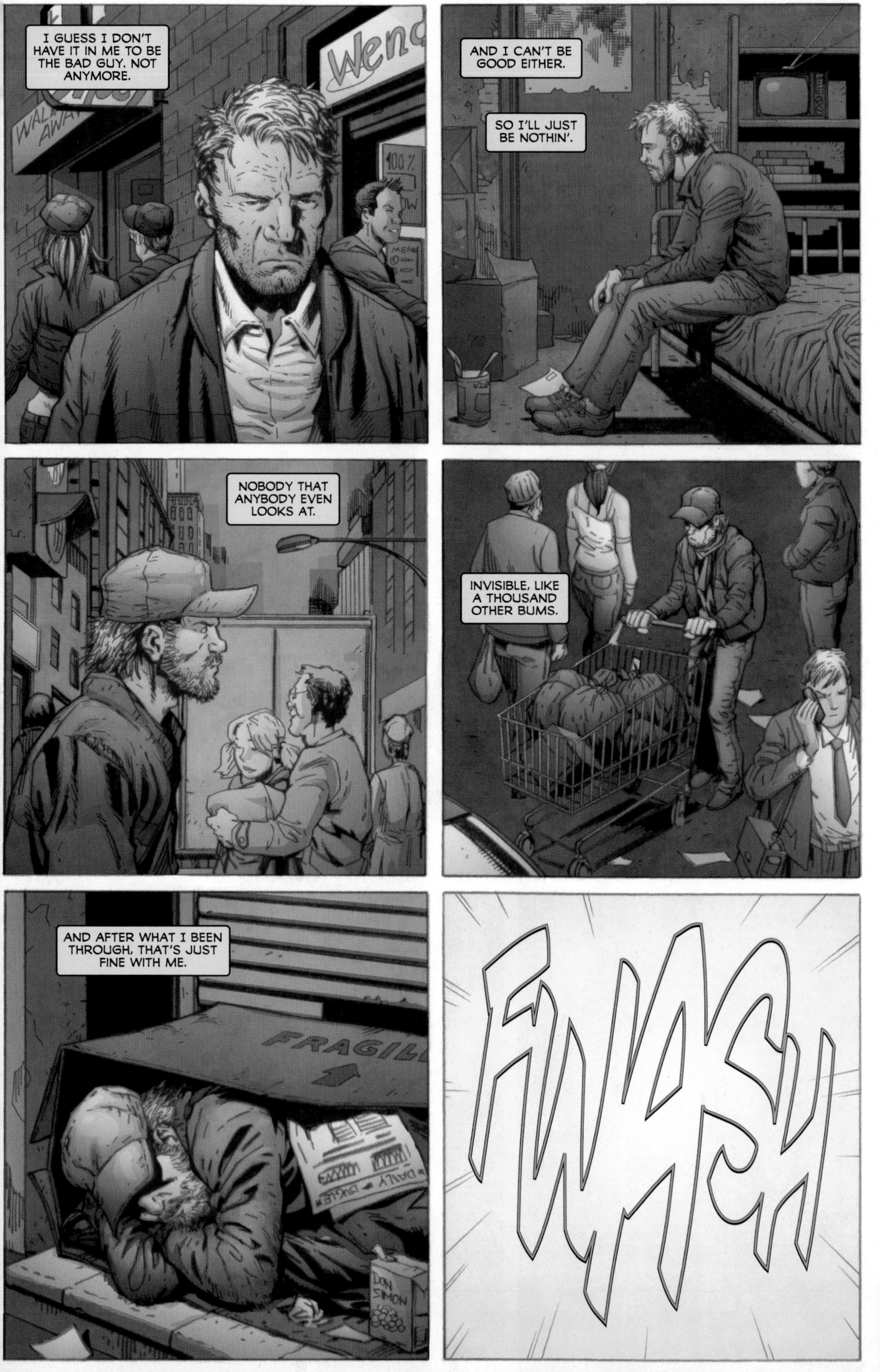
I GUESS I DON'T HAVE IT IN ME TO BE THE BAD GUY. NOT ANYMORE.
AND I CAN'T BE GOOD EITHER.
SO I'LL JUST BE NOTHIN'.
NOBODY THAT ANYBODY EVEN LOOKS AT.
INVISIBLE, LIKE A THOUSAND OTHER BUMS.
AND AFTER WHAT I BEEN THROUGH, THAT'S JUST FINE WITH ME.
DON SIMON

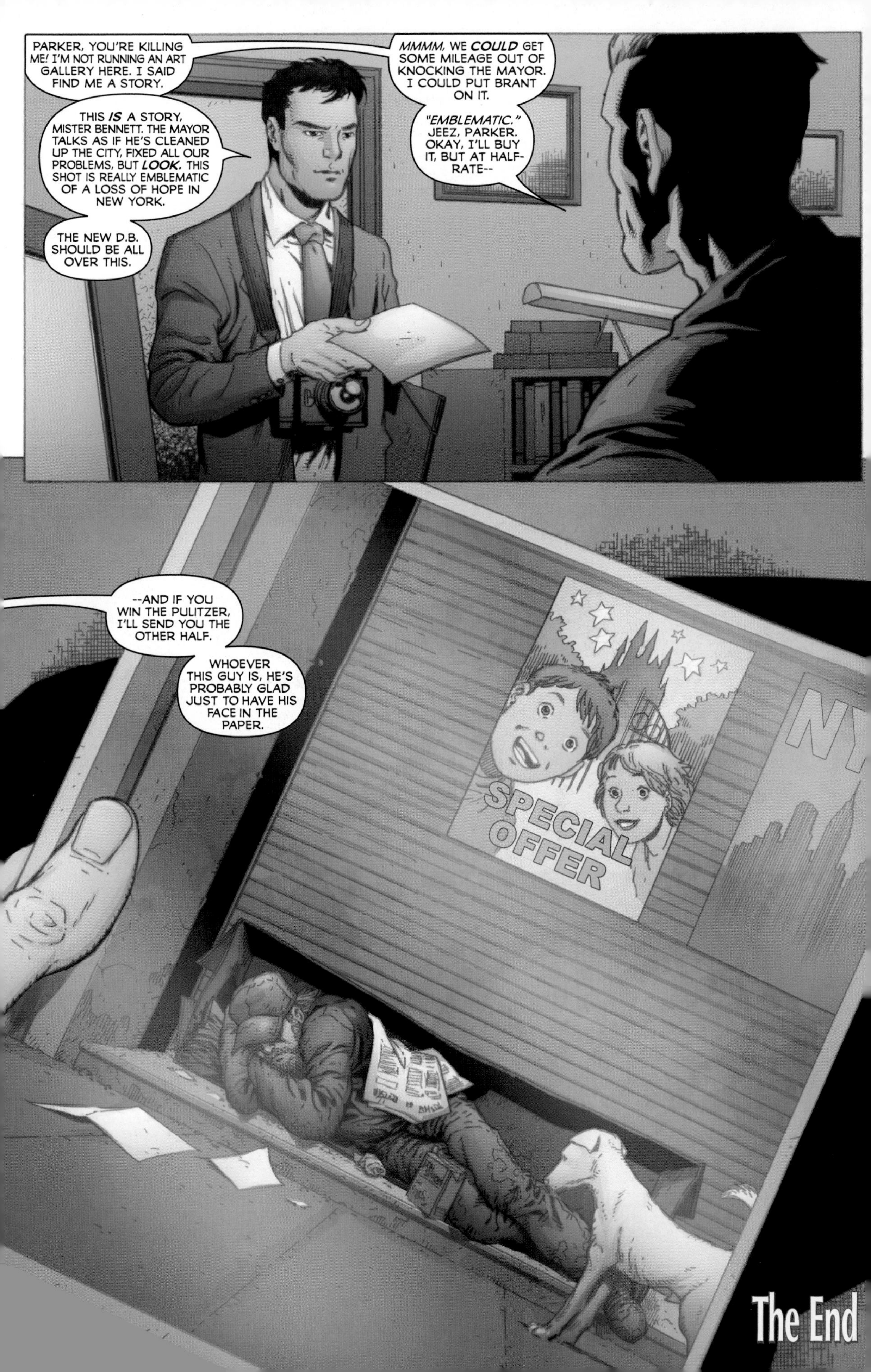
PARKER, YOU'RE KILLING ME! I'M NOT RUNNING AN ART GALLERY HERE. I SAID FIND ME A STORY.
THIS IS A STORY, MISTER BENNETT. THE MAYOR TALKS AS IF HE'S CLEANED UP THE CITY, FIXED ALL OUR PROBLEMS, BUT LOOK. THIS SHOT IS REALLY EMBLEMATIC OF A LOSS OF HOPE IN NEW YORK.
THE NEW D.B. SHOULD BE ALL OVER THIS.
MMMM, WE COULD GET SOME MILEAGE OUT OF KNOCKING THE MAYOR. I COULD PUT BRANT ON IT.
"EMBLEMATIC." JEEZ, PARKER. OKAY, I'LL BUY IT, BUT AT HALF-RATE--
--AND IF YOU WIN THE PULITZER, I'LL SEND YOU THE OTHER HALF.
WHOEVER THIS GUY IS, HE'S PROBABLY GLAD JUST TO HAVE HIS FACE IN THE PAPER.
SPECIAL OFFER
NY
The End

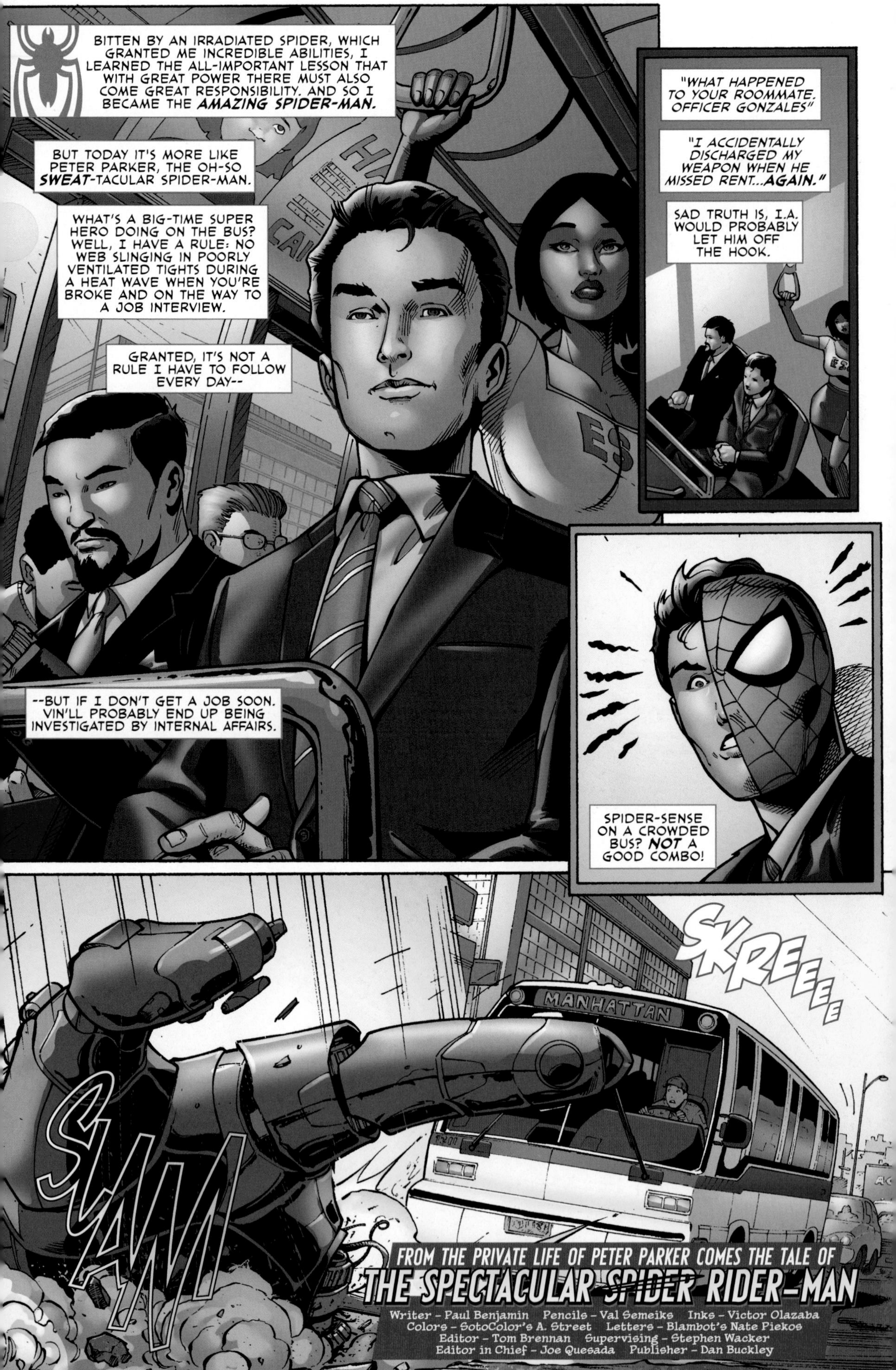
BITTEN BY AN IRRADIATED SPIDER, WHICH GRANTED ME INCREDIBLE ABILITIES, I LEARNED THE ALL-IMPORTANT LESSON THAT WITH GREAT POWER THERE MUST ALSO COME GREAT RESPONSIBILITY. AND SO I BECAME THE AMAZING SPIDER-MAN.
BUT TODAY IT'S MORE LIKE PETER PARKER, THE OH-SO SWEAT-TACULAR SPIDER-MAN.
WHAT'S A BIG-TIME SUPER HERO DOING ON THE BUS? WELL, I HAVE A RULE: NO WEB SLINGING IN POORLY VENTILATED TIGHTS DURING A HEAT WAVE WHEN YOU'RE BROKE AND ON THE WAY TO A JOB INTERVIEW.
GRANTED, IT'S NOT A RULE I HAVE TO FOLLOW EVERY DAY--
--BUT IF I DON'T GET A JOB SOON. VIN'LL PROBABLY END UP BEING INVESTIGATED BY INTERNAL AFFAIRS.
"WHAT HAPPENED TO YOUR ROOMMATE. OFFICER GONZALES"
"I ACCIDENTALLY DISCHARGED MY WEAPON WHEN HE MISSED RENT...AGAIN."
SAD TRUTH IS, I.A. WOULD PROBABLY LET HIM OFF THE HOOK.
SPIDER-SENSE ON A CROWDED BUS? NOT A GOOD COMBO!
SKREEEE
MANHATTAN
SLAM
FROM THE PRIVATE LIFE OF PETER PARKER COMES THE TALE OF
THE SPECTACULAR SPIDER RIDER-MAN
Writer - Paul Benjamin Pencils - Val Semeiks Inks - Victor Olazaba
Colors - SotoColor's A. Street Letters - Blambot's Nate Piekos
Editor - Tom Brennan Supervising - Stephen Wacker
Editor in Chief - Joe Quesada Publisher - Dan Buckley

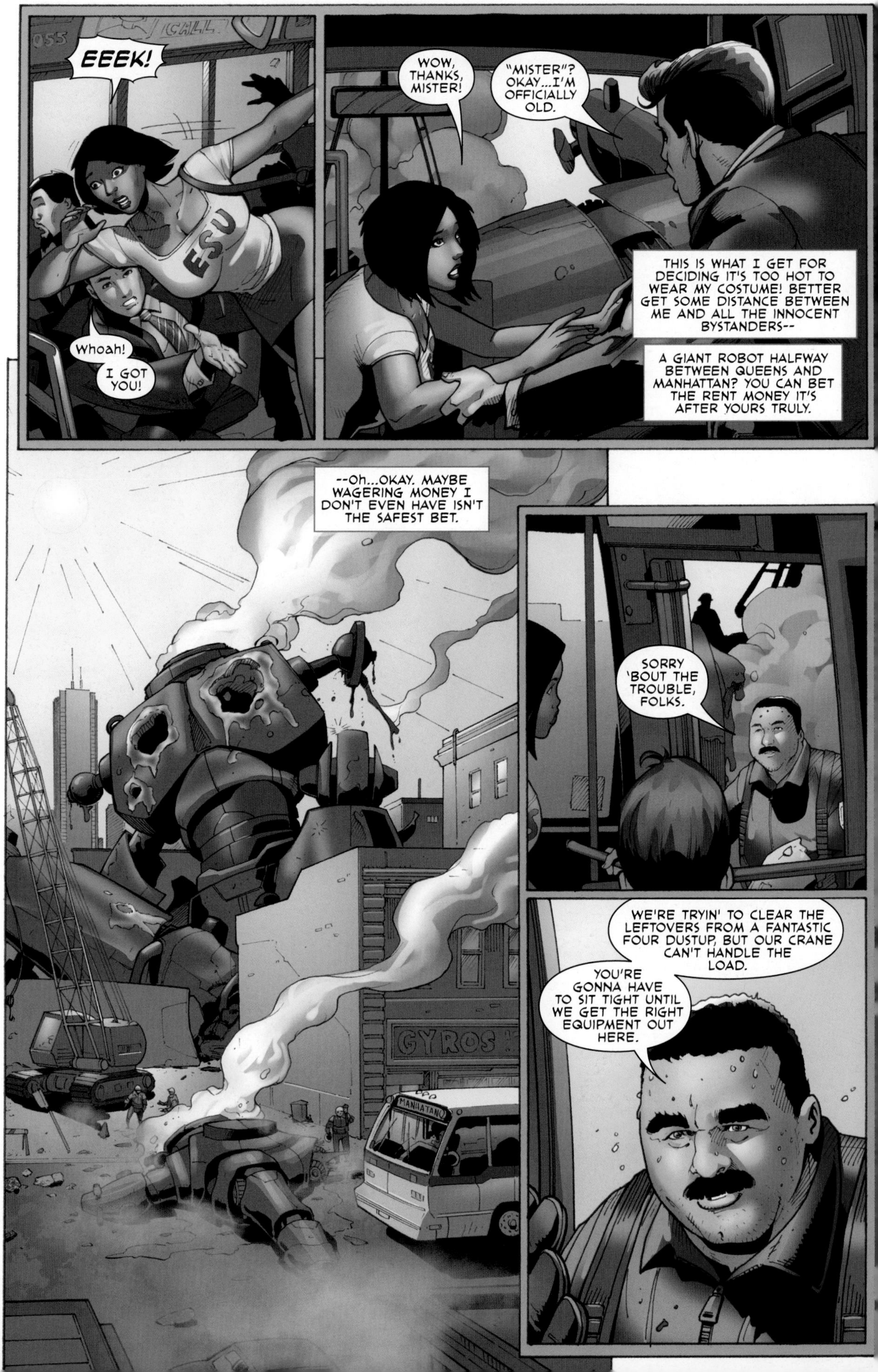

EEEK!
Whoah!
I GOT YOU!
WOW, THANKS, MISTER!
"MISTER"? OKAY...I'M OFFICIALLY OLD.
THIS IS WHAT I GET FOR DECIDING IT'S TOO HOT TO WEAR MY COSTUME! BETTER GET SOME DISTANCE BETWEEN ME AND ALL THE INNOCENT BYSTANDERS--
A GIANT ROBOT HALFWAY BETWEEN QUEENS AND MANHATTAN? YOU CAN BET THE RENT MONEY IT'S AFTER YOURS TRULY.
--Oh...OKAY. MAYBE WAGERING MONEY I DON'T EVEN HAVE ISN'T THE SAFEST BET.
GYROS
MANHATTAN
SORRY 'BOUT THE TROUBLE, FOLKS.
WE'RE TRYIN' TO CLEAR THE LEFTOVERS FROM A FANTASTIC FOUR DUSTUP, BUT OUR CRANE CAN'T HANDLE THE LOAD.
YOU'RE GONNA HAVE TO SIT TIGHT UNTIL WE GET THE RIGHT EQUIPMENT OUT HERE.

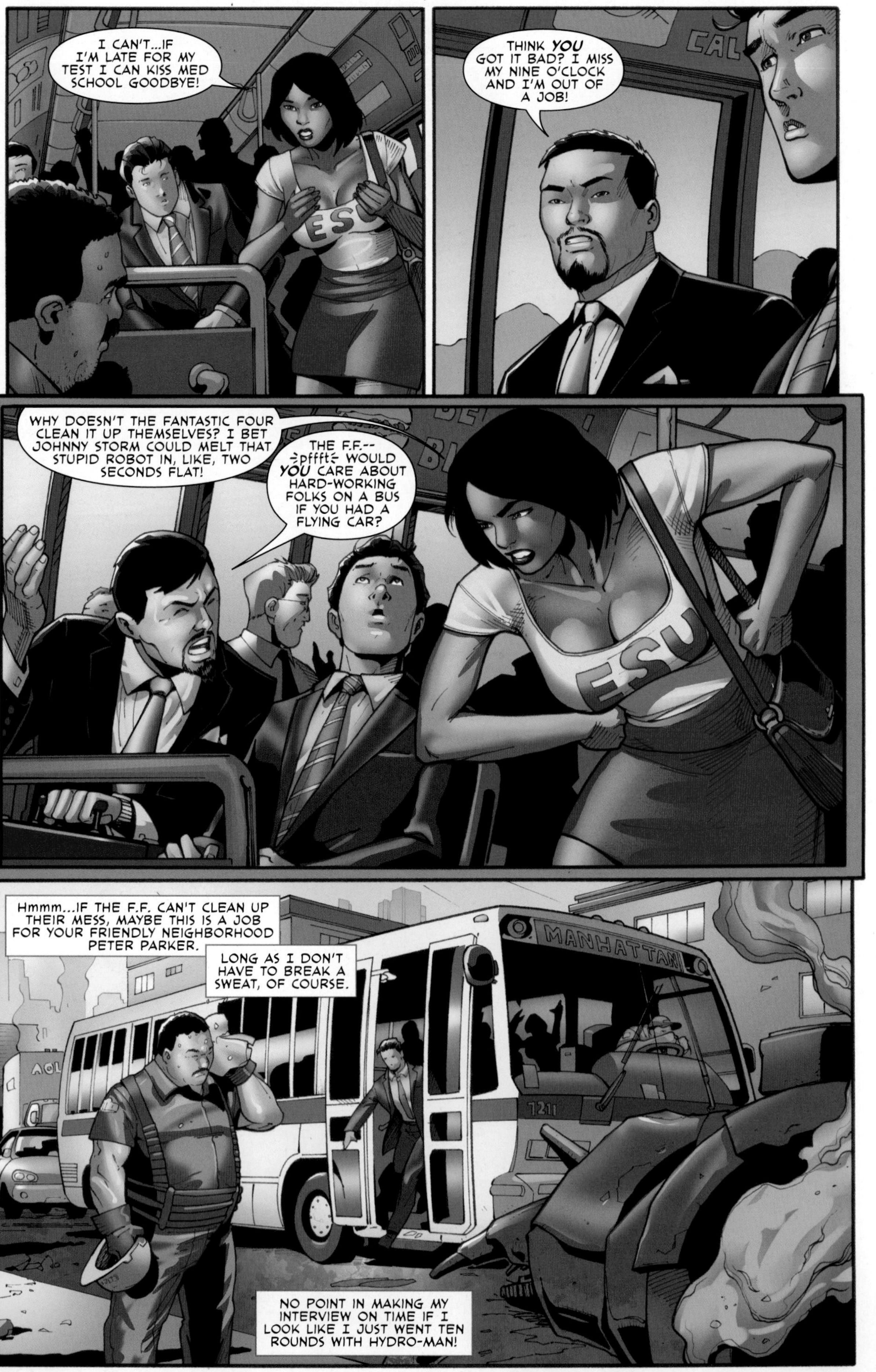
I CAN'T...IF I'M LATE FOR MY TEST I CAN KISS MED SCHOOL GOODBYE!
THINK YOU GOT IT BAD? I MISS MY NINE O'CLOCK AND I'M OUT OF A JOB!
WHY DOESN'T THE FANTASTIC FOUR CLEAN IT UP THEMSELVES? I BET JOHNNY STORM COULD MELT THAT STUPID ROBOT IN, LIKE, TWO SECONDS FLAT!
THE F.F.-- =pffft= WOULD YOU CARE ABOUT HARD-WORKING FOLKS ON A BUS IF YOU HAD A FLYING CAR?
Hmmm...IF THE F.F. CAN'T CLEAN UP THEIR MESS, MAYBE THIS IS A JOB FOR YOUR FRIENDLY NEIGHBORHOOD PETER PARKER.
LONG AS I DON'T HAVE TO BREAK A SWEAT, OF COURSE.
MANHATTAN
NO POINT IN MAKING MY INTERVIEW ON TIME IF I LOOK LIKE I JUST WENT TEN ROUNDS WITH HYDRO-MAN!

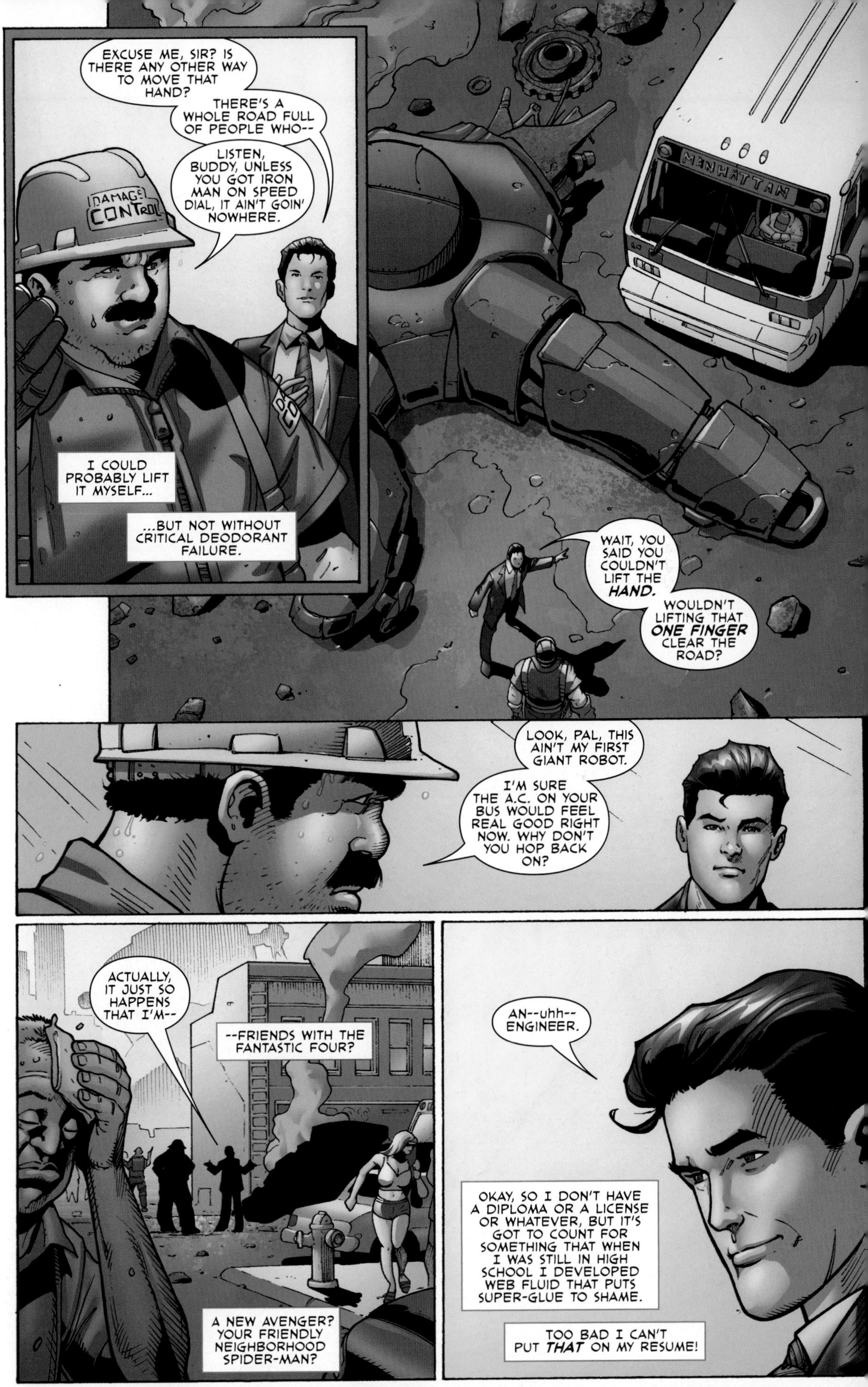
EXCUSE ME, SIR? IS THERE ANY OTHER WAY TO MOVE THAT HAND?
THERE'S A WHOLE ROAD FULL OF PEOPLE WHO--
LISTEN, BUDDY, UNLESS YOU GOT IRON MAN ON SPEED DIAL, IT AIN'T GOIN' NOWHERE.
DAMAGE CONTROL
I COULD PROBABLY LIFT IT MYSELF...
...BUT NOT WITHOUT CRITICAL DEODORANT FAILURE.
MANHATTAN
WAIT, YOU SAID YOU COULDN'T LIFT THE HAND.
WOULDN'T LIFTING THAT ONE FINGER CLEAR THE ROAD?
LOOK, PAL, THIS AIN'T MY FIRST GIANT ROBOT.
I'M SURE THE A.C. ON YOUR BUS WOULD FEEL REAL GOOD RIGHT NOW. WHY DON'T YOU HOP BACK ON?
ACTUALLY, IT JUST SO HAPPENS THAT I'M--
--FRIENDS WITH THE FANTASTIC FOUR?
A NEW AVENGER? YOUR FRIENDLY NEIGHBORHOOD SPIDER-MAN?
AN--uhh-- ENGINEER.
OKAY, SO I DON'T HAVE A DIPLOMA OR A LICENSE OR WHATEVER, BUT IT'S GOT TO COUNT FOR SOMETHING THAT WHEN I WAS STILL IN HIGH SCHOOL I DEVELOPED WEB FLUID THAT PUTS SUPER-GLUE TO SHAME.
TOO BAD I CAN'T PUT THAT ON MY RESUME!

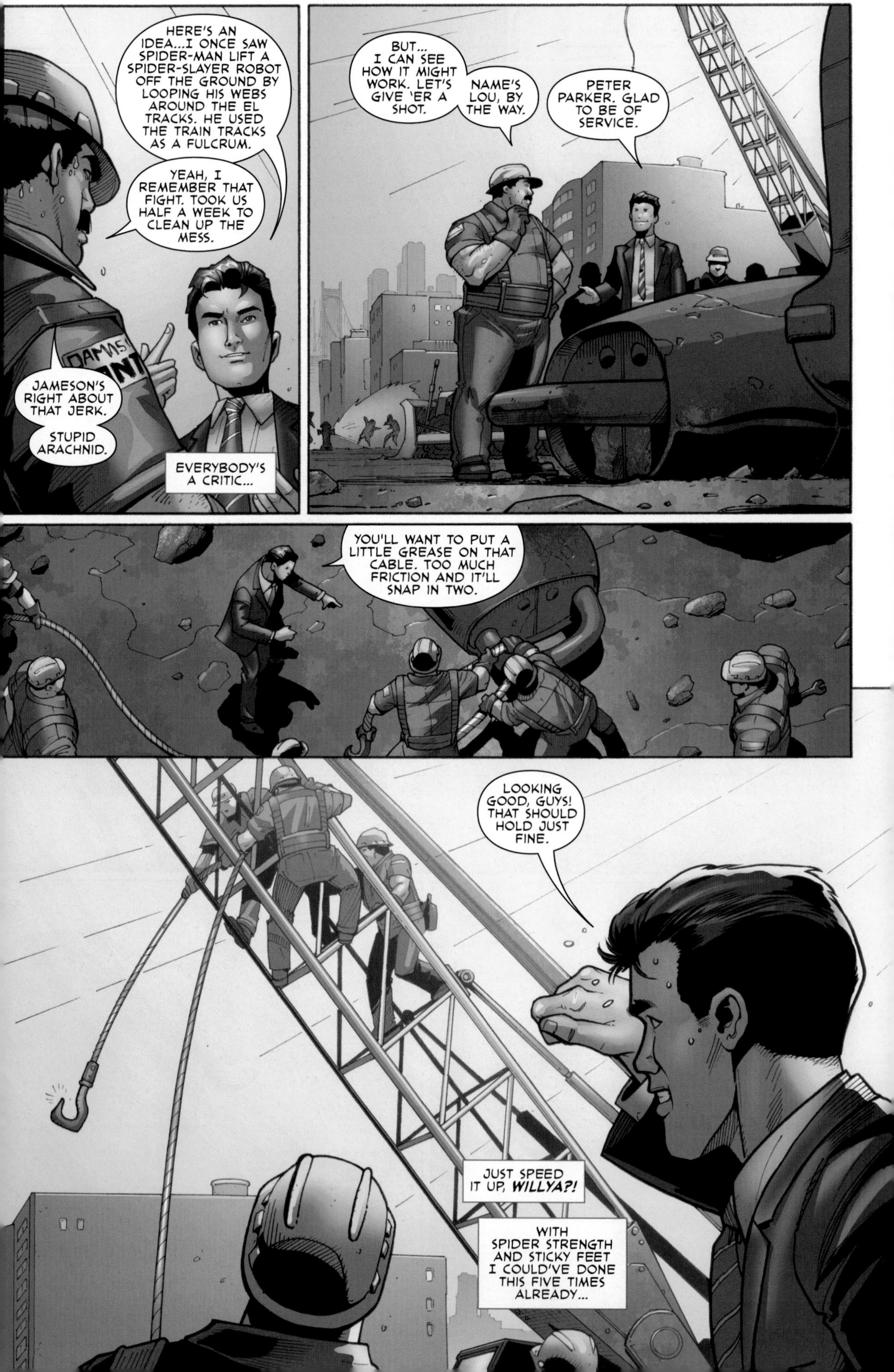
HERE'S AN IDEA...I ONCE SAW SPIDER-MAN LIFT A SPIDER-SLAYER ROBOT OFF THE GROUND BY LOOPING HIS WEBS AROUND THE EL TRACKS. HE USED THE TRAIN TRACKS AS A FULCRUM.
YEAH, I REMEMBER THAT FIGHT. TOOK US HALF A WEEK TO CLEAN UP THE MESS.
JAMESON'S RIGHT ABOUT THAT JERK.
STUPID ARACHNID.
EVERYBODY'S A CRITIC...
BUT... I CAN SEE HOW IT MIGHT WORK. LET'S GIVE 'ER A SHOT.
NAME'S LOU, BY THE WAY.
PETER PARKER. GLAD TO BE OF SERVICE.
YOU'LL WANT TO PUT A LITTLE GREASE ON THAT CABLE. TOO MUCH FRICTION AND IT'LL SNAP IN TWO.
LOOKING GOOD, GUYS! THAT SHOULD HOLD JUST FINE.
JUST SPEED IT UP, WILLYA?!
WITH SPIDER STRENGTH AND STICKY FEET I COULD'VE DONE THIS FIVE TIMES ALREADY...

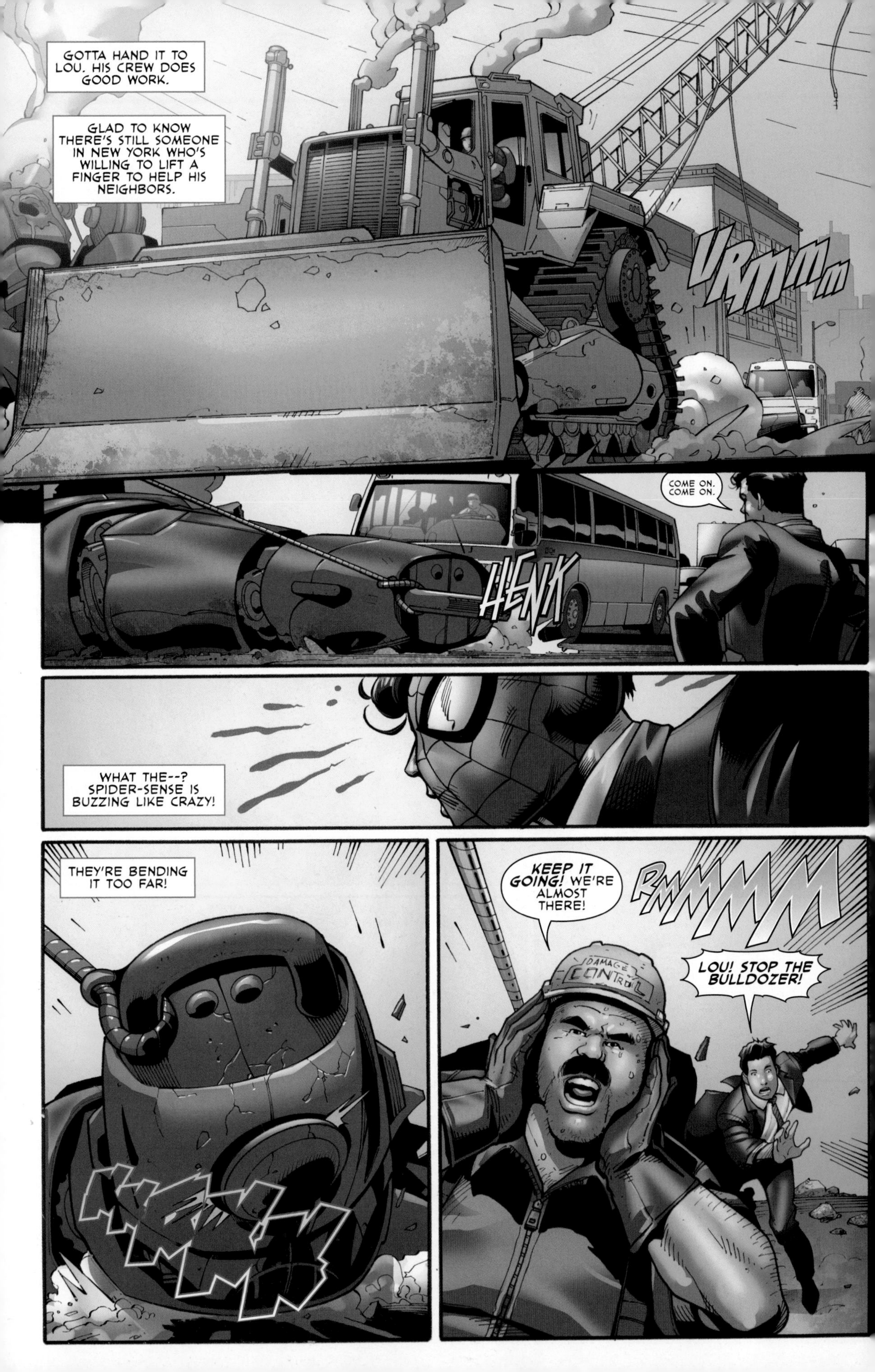
GOTTA HAND IT TO LOU. HIS CREW DOES GOOD WORK.
GLAD TO KNOW THERE'S STILL SOMEONE IN NEW YORK WHO'S WILLING TO LIFT A FINGER TO HELP HIS NEIGHBORS.
COME ON. COME ON.
WHAT THE--? SPIDER-SENSE IS BUZZING LIKE CRAZY!
THEY'RE BENDING IT TOO FAR!
KEEP IT GOING! WE'RE ALMOST THERE!
RMMMMM
DAMAGE CONTROL
LOU! STOP THE BULLDOZER!

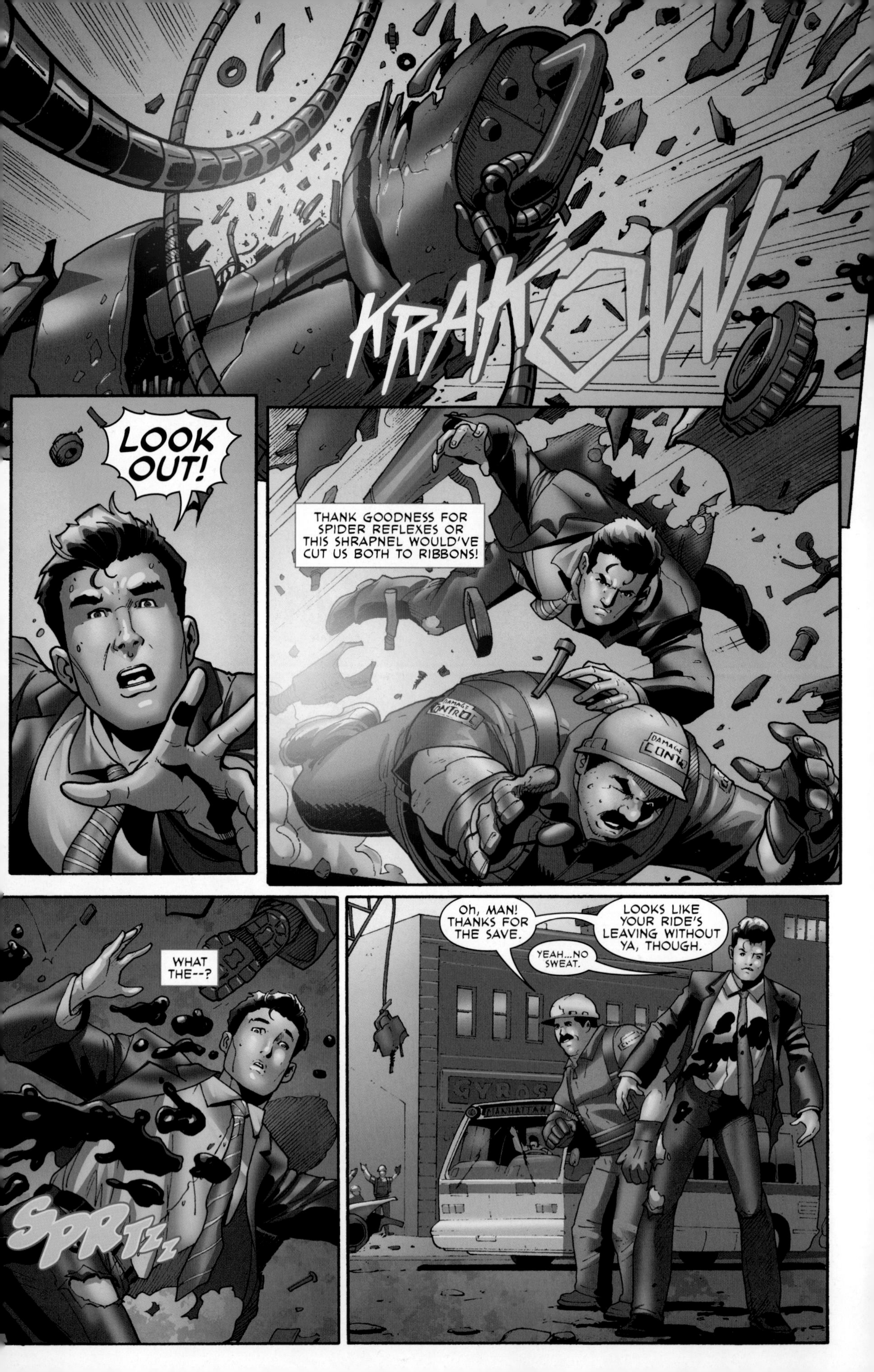
KRAKOW
LOOK OUT!
THANK GOODNESS FOR SPIDER REFLEXES OR THIS SHRAPNEL WOULD'VE CUT US BOTH TO RIBBONS!
DAMAGE CONTROL
WHAT THE--?
SPRTZZ
Oh, MAN! THANKS FOR THE SAVE.
YEAH...NO SWEAT.
LOOKS LIKE YOUR RIDE'S LEAVING WITHOUT YA, THOUGH.
GYROS
MANHATTAN

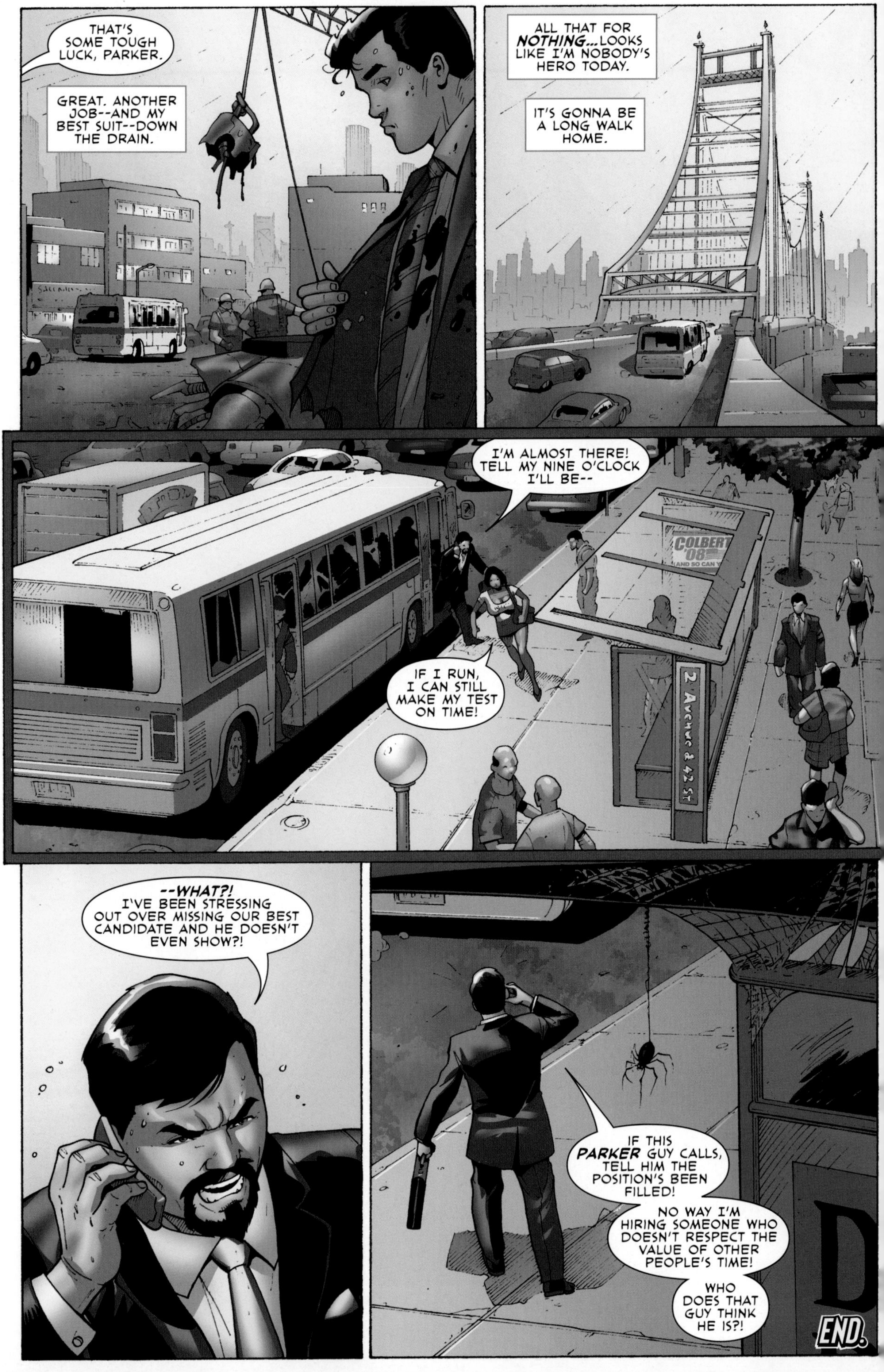
THAT'S SOME TOUGH LUCK, PARKER.
GREAT. ANOTHER JOB--AND MY BEST SUIT--DOWN THE DRAIN.
ALL THAT FOR *NOTHING*... LOOKS LIKE I'M NOBODY'S HERO TODAY.
IT'S GONNA BE A LONG WALK HOME.
I'M ALMOST THERE! TELL MY NINE O'CLOCK I'LL BE--
COLBERT '08
IF I RUN, I CAN STILL MAKE MY TEST ON TIME!
2 Avenue & 42 ST
--WHAT?! I'VE BEEN STRESSING OUT OVER MISSING OUR BEST CANDIDATE AND HE DOESN'T EVEN SHOW?!
IF THIS *PARKER* GUY CALLS, TELL HIM THE POSITION'S BEEN FILLED!
NO WAY I'M HIRING SOMEONE WHO DOESN'T RESPECT THE VALUE OF OTHER PEOPLE'S TIME!
WHO DOES THAT GUY THINK HE IS?!
END.

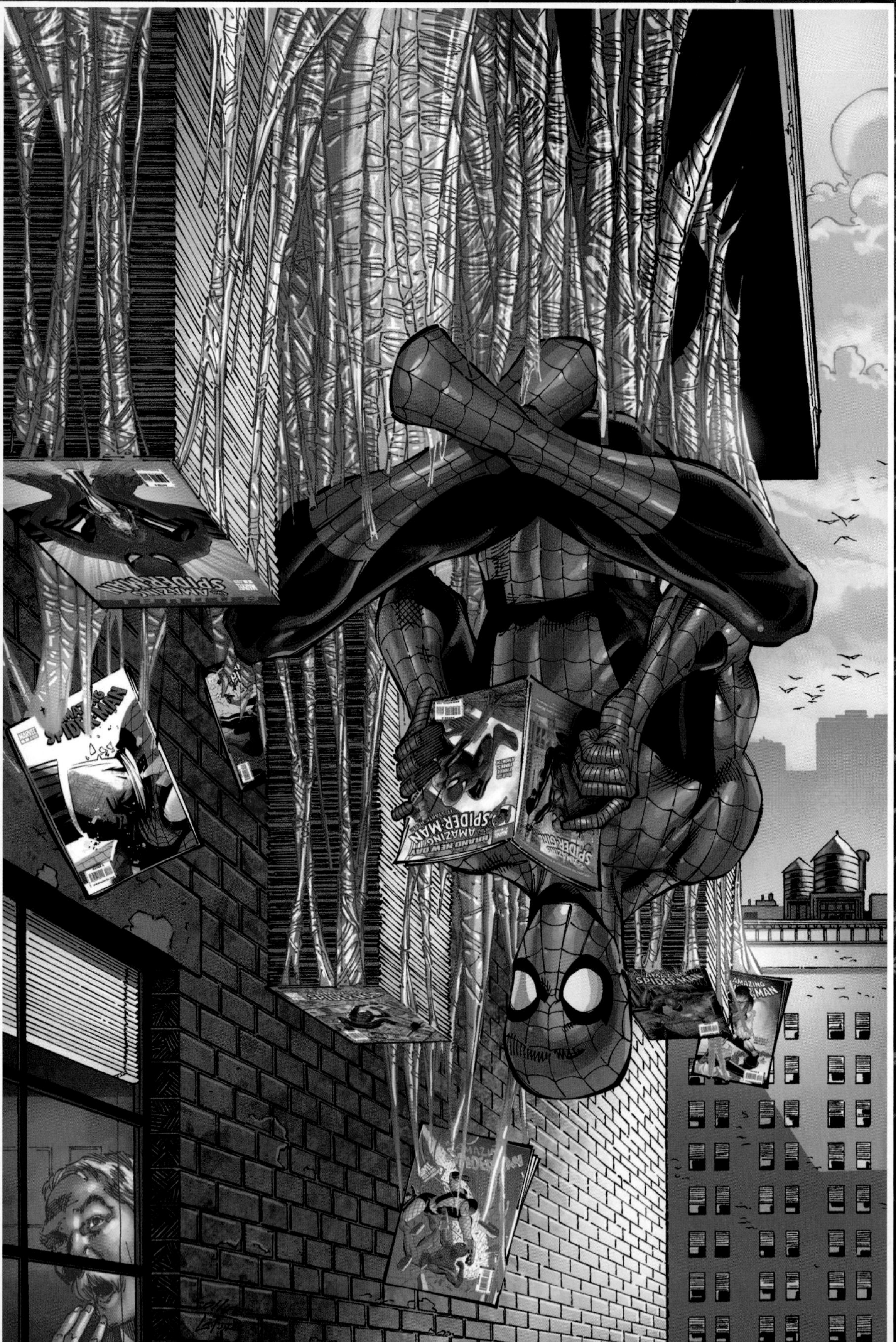
AMAZING SPIDER-MAN

AMAZING SPIDER-MAN FAMILY #3

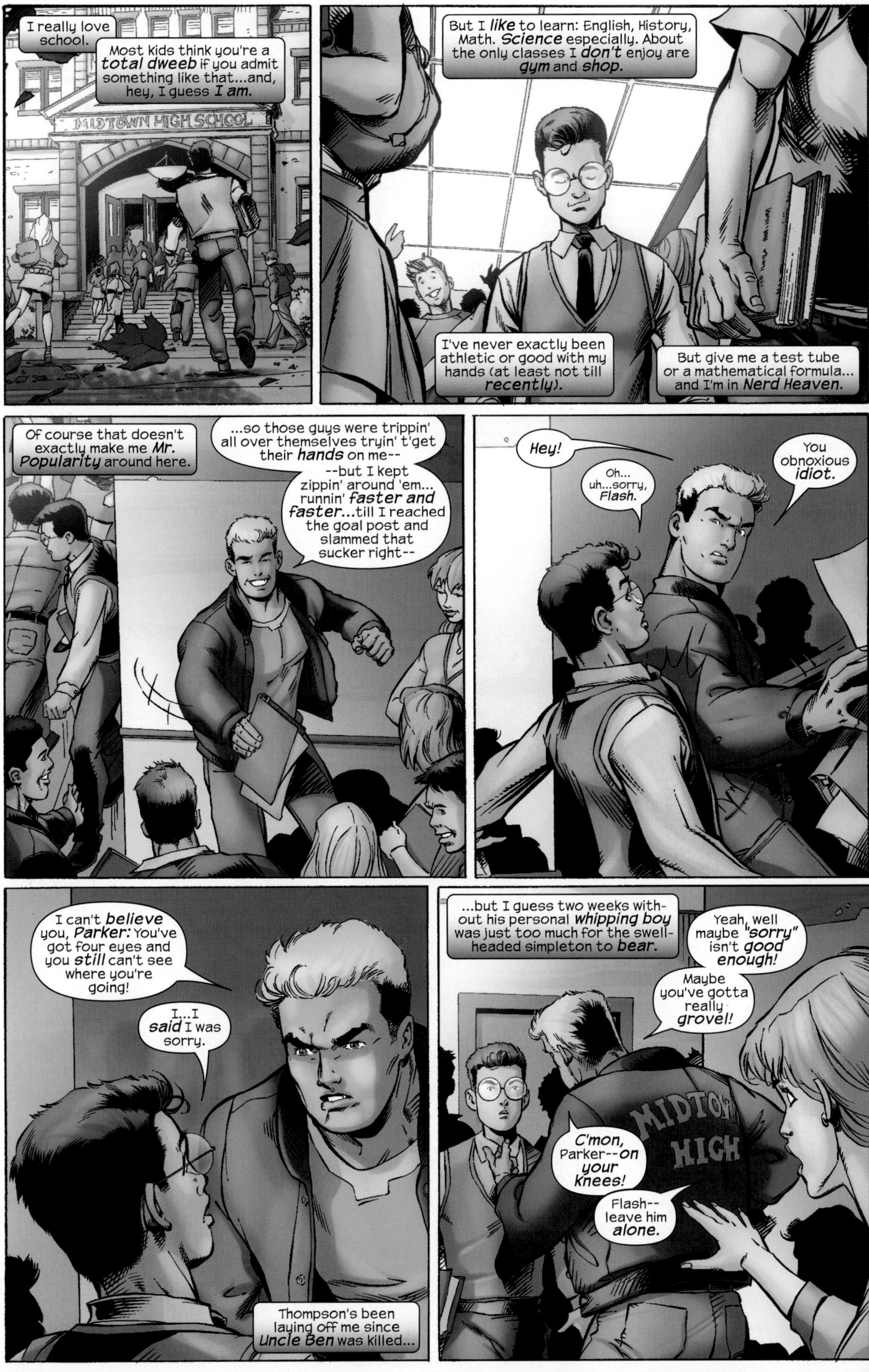

I really love school.
Most kids think you're a total dweeb if you admit something like that...and, hey, I guess I am.
MIDTOWN HIGH SCHOOL
But I like to learn: English, History, Math. Science especially. About the only classes I don't enjoy are gym and shop.
I've never exactly been athletic or good with my hands (at least not till recently).
But give me a test tube or a mathematical formula... and I'm in Nerd Heaven.
Of course that doesn't exactly make me Mr. Popularity around here.
...so those guys were trippin' all over themselves tryin' t'get their hands on me-- --but I kept zippin' around 'em... runnin' faster and faster...till I reached the goal post and slammed that sucker right--
Hey!
Oh... uh...sorry, Flash.
You obnoxious idiot.
I can't believe you, Parker: You've got four eyes and you still can't see where you're going!
I...I said I was sorry.
Thompson's been laying off me since Uncle Ben was killed...
...but I guess two weeks without his personal whipping boy was just too much for the swell-headed simpleton to bear.
Yeah, well maybe "sorry" isn't good enough!
Maybe you've gotta really grovel!
MIDTOWN HIGH
C'mon, Parker--on your knees!
Flash-- leave him alone.

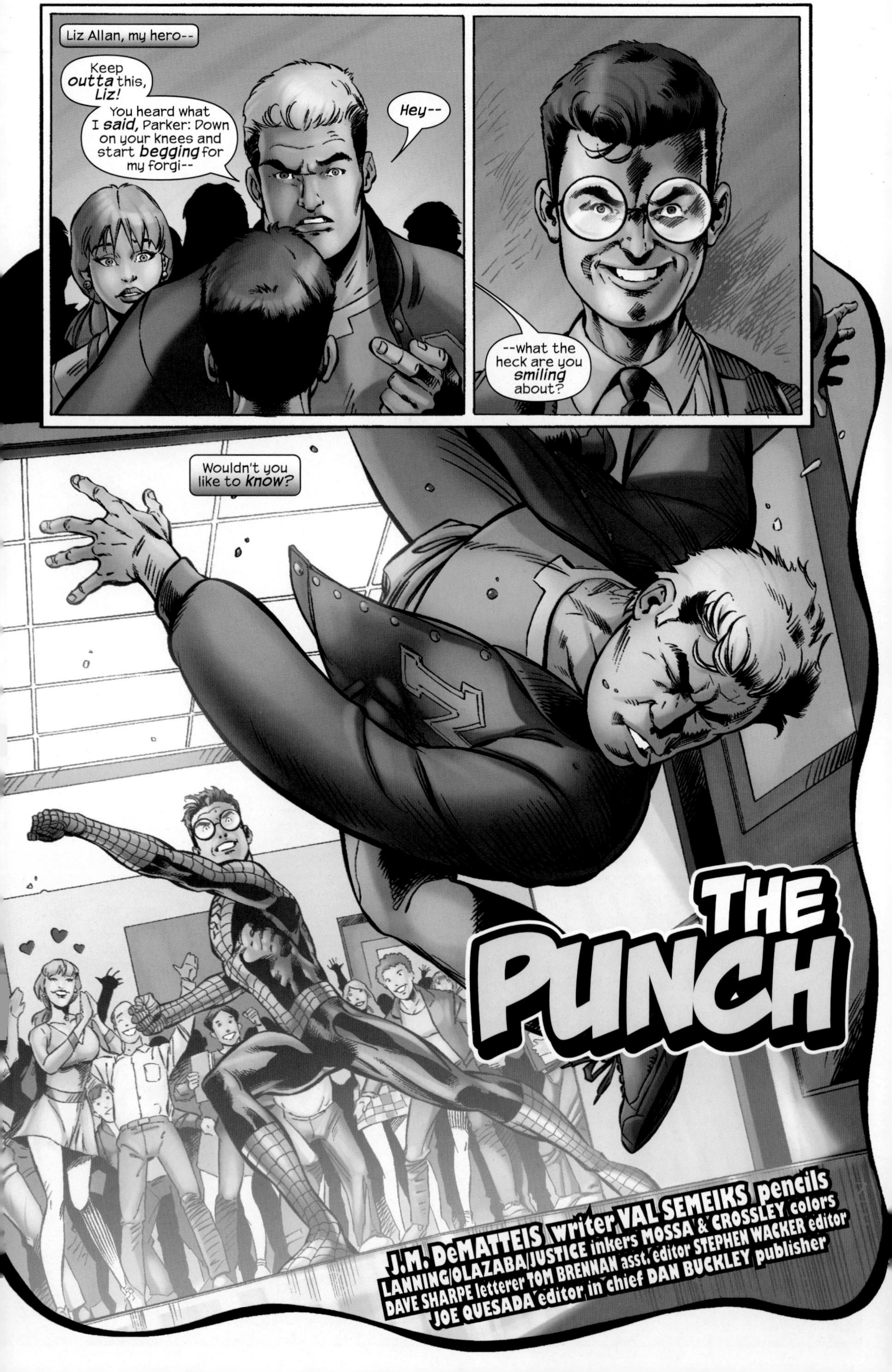

Liz Allan, my hero--
Keep outta this, Liz!
You heard what I said, Parker: Down on your knees and start begging for my forgi--
Hey--
--what the heck are you smiling about?
Wouldn't you like to know?
THE PUNCH
J.M. DeMATTEIS writer VAL SEMEIKS pencils
LANNING/OLAZABA/JUSTICE inkers MOSSA & CROSSLEY colors
DAVE SHARPE letterer TOM BRENNAN asst. editor STEPHEN WACKER editor
JOE QUESADA editor in chief DAN BUCKLEY publisher

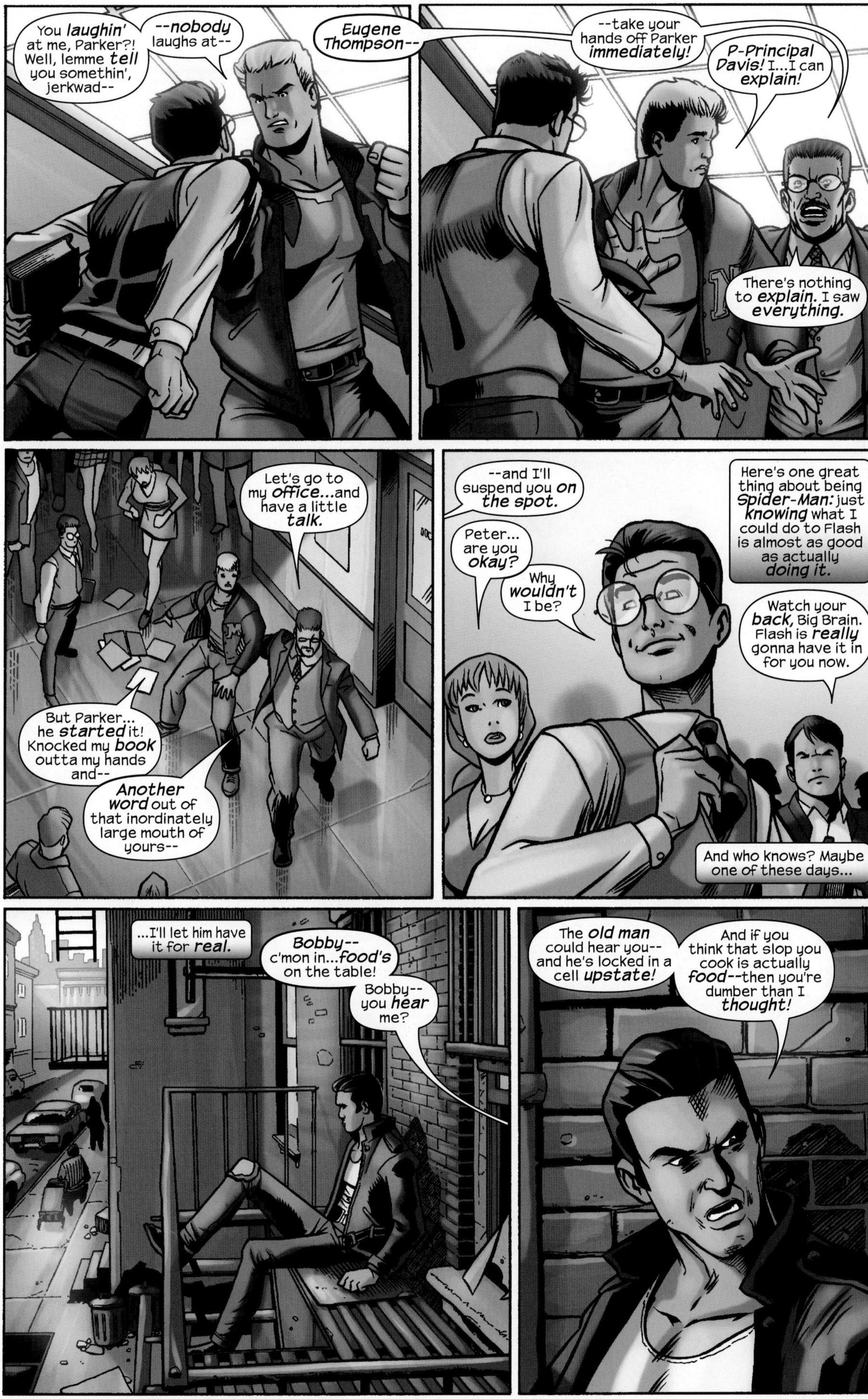
You laughin' at me, Parker?! Well, lemme tell you somethin', jerkwad--
--nobody laughs at--
Eugene Thompson--
--take your hands off Parker immediately!
P-Principal Davis! I...I can explain!
There's nothing to explain. I saw everything.
Let's go to my office...and have a little talk.
But Parker... he started it! Knocked my book outta my hands and--
Another word out of that inordinately large mouth of yours--
--and I'll suspend you on the spot.
Peter... are you okay?
Why wouldn't I be?
Here's one great thing about being Spider-Man: just knowing what I could do to Flash is almost as good as actually doing it.
Watch your back, Big Brain. Flash is really gonna have it in for you now.
And who knows? Maybe one of these days...
...I'll let him have it for real.
Bobby-- c'mon in...food's on the table!
Bobby-- you hear me?
The old man could hear you-- and he's locked in a cell upstate!
And if you think that slop you cook is actually food--then you're dumber than I thought!

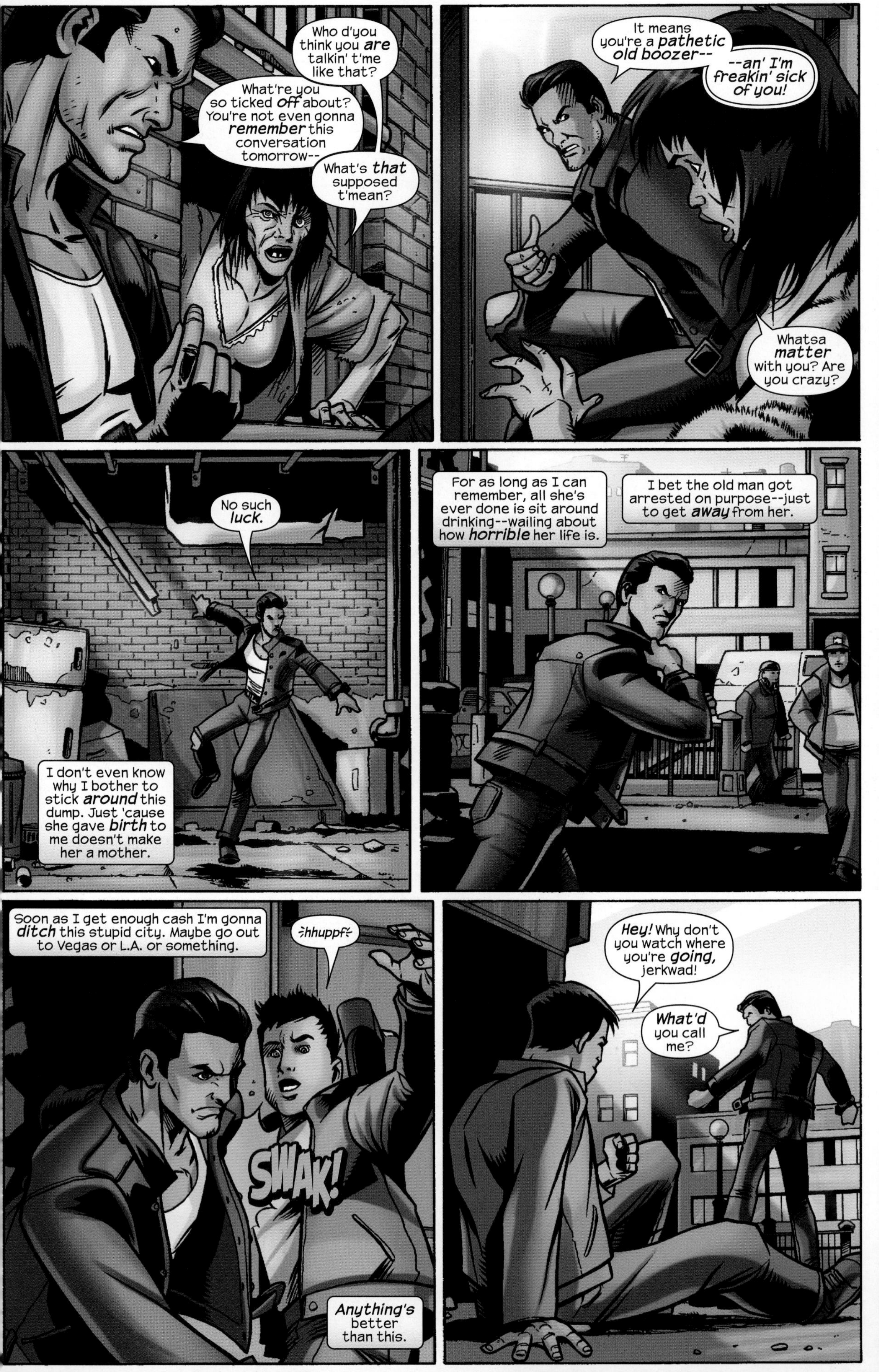
What're you so ticked *off* about? You're not even gonna *remember* this conversation tomorrow--
Who d'you think you *are* talkin' t'me like that?
What's *that* supposed t'mean?
It means you're a *pathetic old boozer*--
--an' I'm freakin' sick of you!
Whatsa *matter* with you? Are you crazy?
No such *luck.*
I don't even know why I bother to stick *around* this dump. Just 'cause she gave *birth* to me doesn't make her a mother.
For as long as I can remember, all she's ever done is sit around drinking--wailing about how *horrible* her life is.
I bet the old man got arrested on purpose--just to get *away* from her.
Soon as I get enough cash I'm gonna *ditch* this stupid city. Maybe go out to Vegas or L.A. or something.
hhuppf
SWAK!
Anything's better than this.
Hey! Why don't you watch where you're *going,* jerkwad!
What'd you call me?

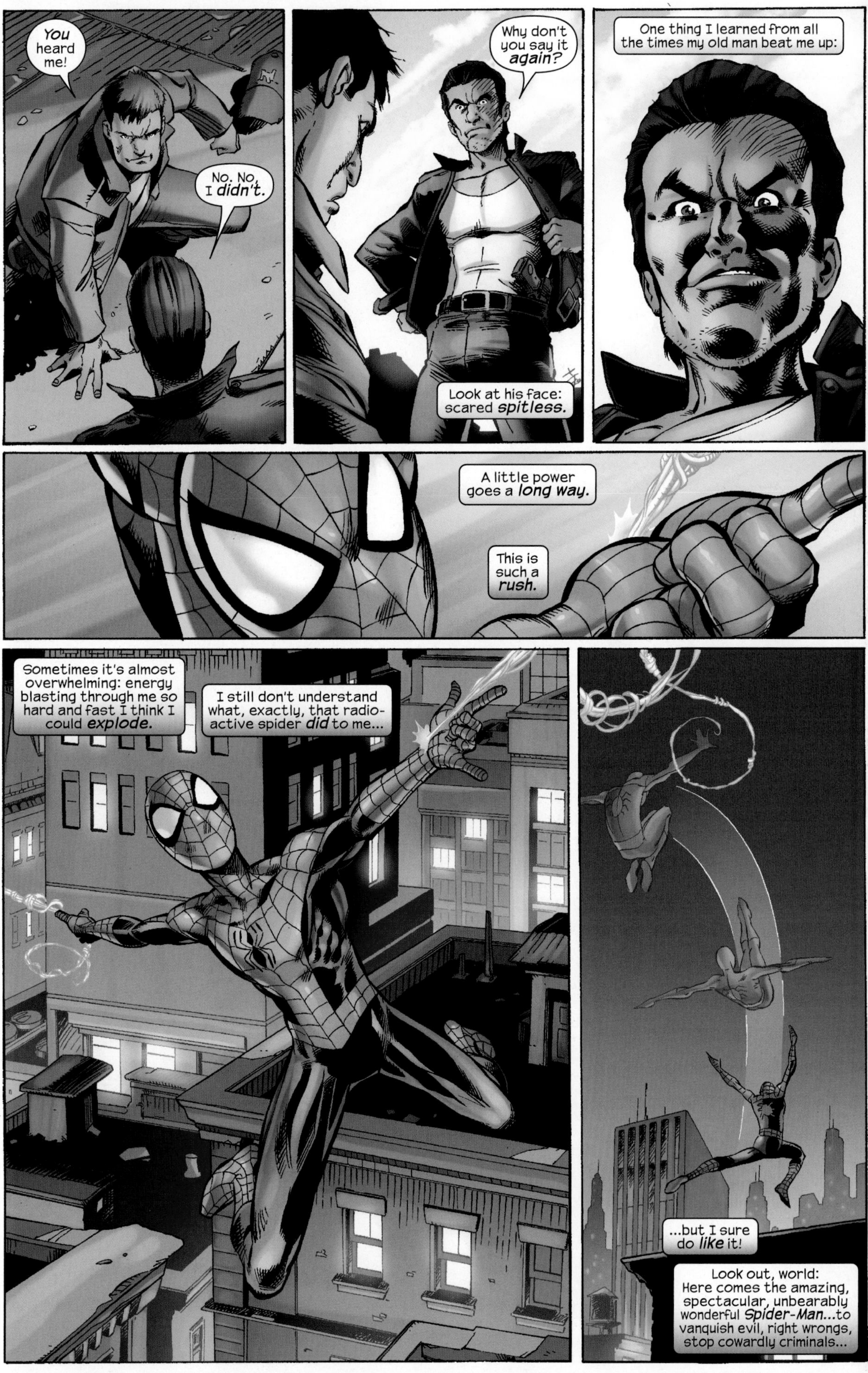
You heard me!
No. No, I didn't.
Why don't you say it again?
Look at his face: scared spitless.
One thing I learned from all the times my old man beat me up:
A little power goes a long way.
This is such a rush.
Sometimes it's almost overwhelming: energy blasting through me so hard and fast I think I could explode.
I still don't understand what, exactly, that radio-active spider did to me...
...but I sure do like it!
Look out, world: Here comes the amazing, spectacular, unbearably wonderful Spider-Man...to vanquish evil, right wrongs, stop cowardly criminals...

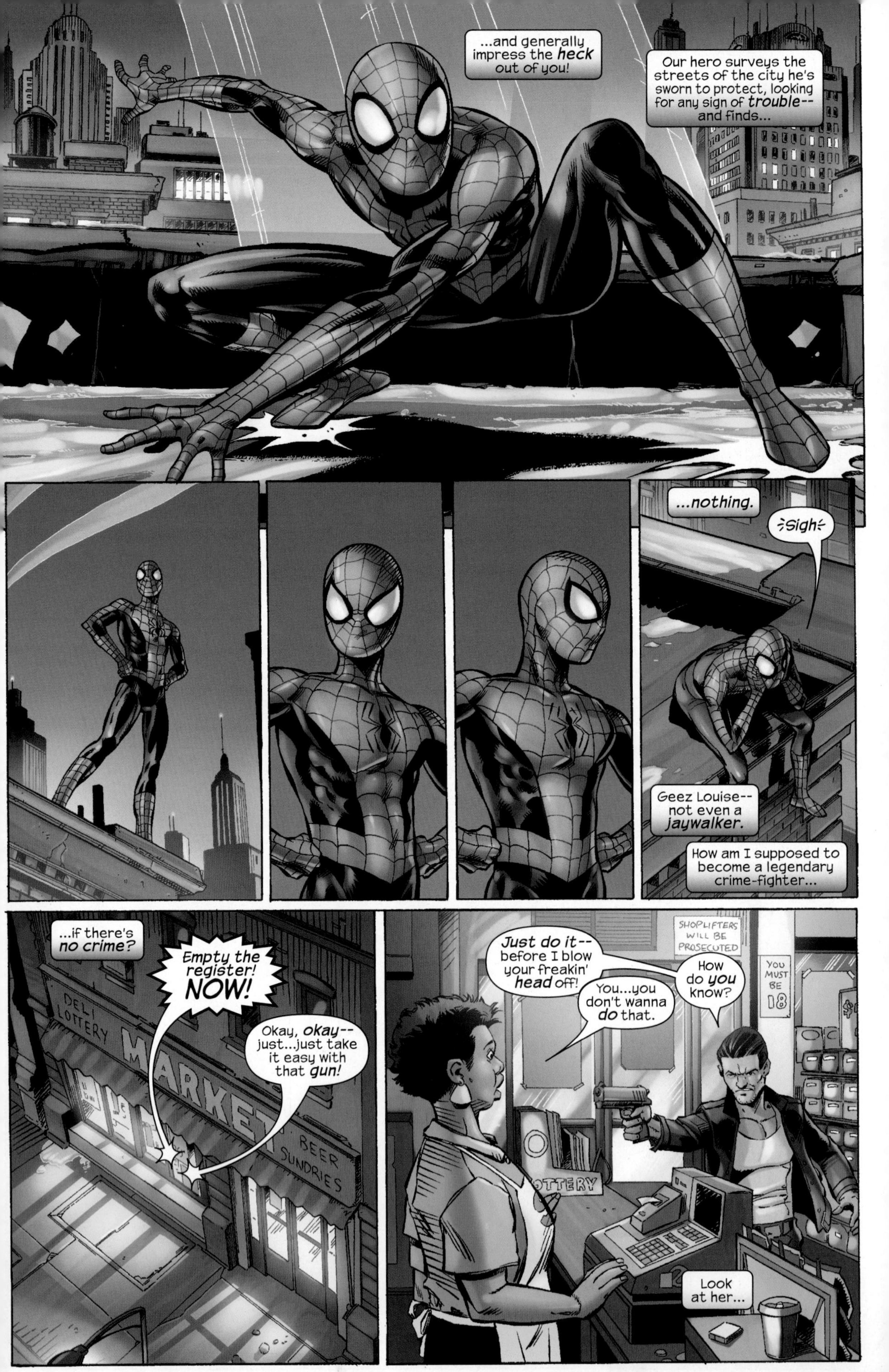
...and generally impress the heck out of you!
Our hero surveys the streets of the city he's sworn to protect, looking for any sign of trouble-- and finds...
...nothing.
Sigh
Geez Louise-- not even a jaywalker.
How am I supposed to become a legendary crime-fighter...
...if there's no crime?
Empty the register! NOW!
Okay, okay-- just...just take it easy with that gun!
DELI LOTTERY MARKET BEER SUNDRIES
SHOPLIFTERS WILL BE PROSECUTED
YOU MUST BE 18
Just do it-- before I blow your freakin' head off!
You...you don't wanna do that.
How do you know?
LOTTERY
Look at her...

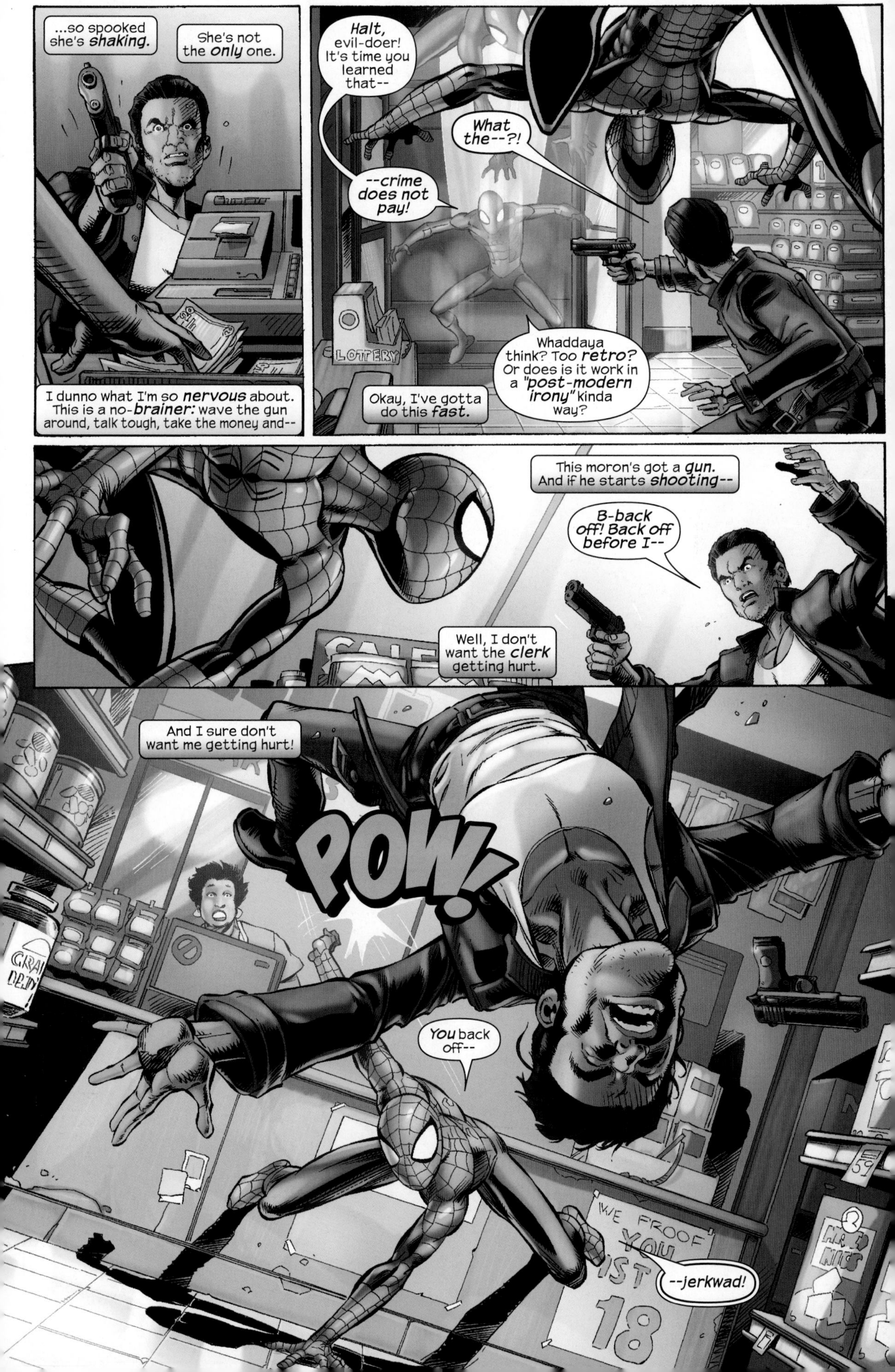
...so spooked she's shaking.
She's not the only one.
I dunno what I'm so nervous about. This is a no-brainer: wave the gun around, talk tough, take the money and--
Halt, evil-doer! It's time you learned that--
What the--?!
--crime does not pay!
Whaddaya think? Too retro? Or does is it work in a "post-modern irony" kinda way?
Okay, I've gotta do this fast.
LOTTERY
This moron's got a gun. And if he starts shooting--
B-back off! Back off before I--
Well, I don't want the clerk getting hurt.
And I sure don't want me getting hurt!
POW!
You back off--
--jerkwad!
18

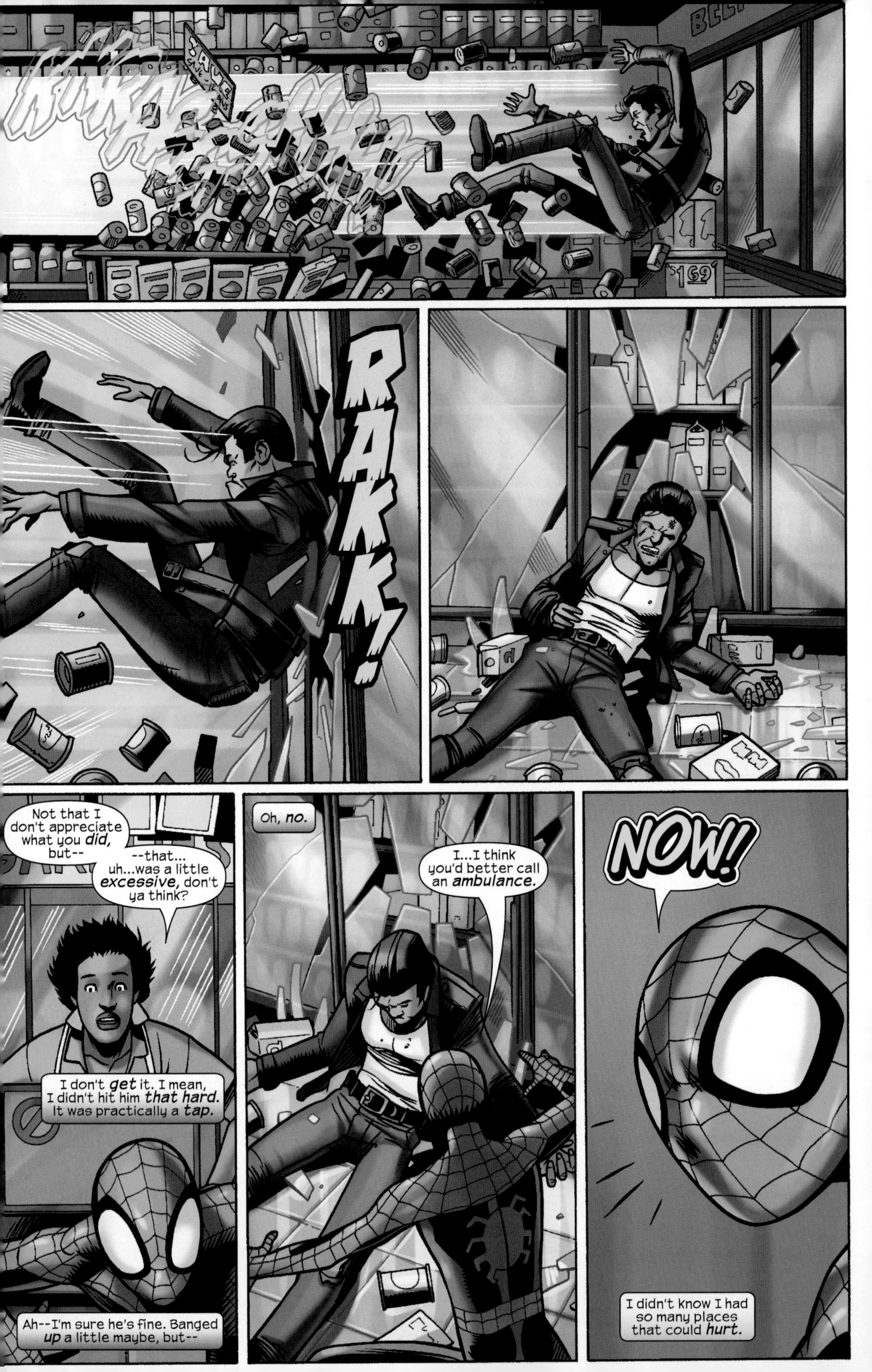

RAKK!
Not that I don't appreciate what you did, but--
--that... uh...was a little excessive, don't ya think?
I don't get it. I mean, I didn't hit him that hard. It was practically a tap.
Ah--I'm sure he's fine. Banged up a little maybe, but--
Oh, no.
I...I think you'd better call an ambulance.
NOW!!
I didn't know I had so many places that could hurt.

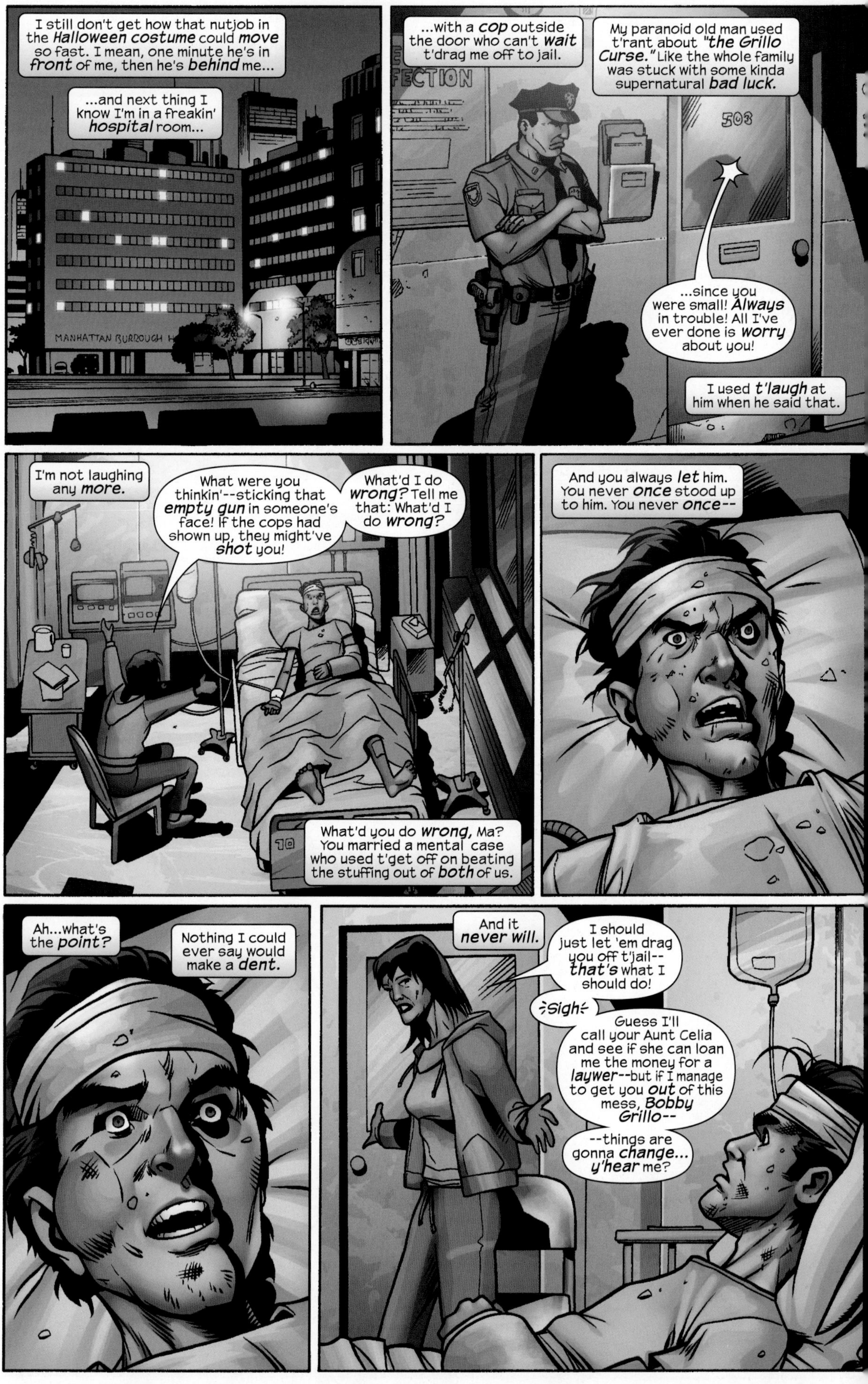

I still don't get how that nutjob in the Halloween costume could move so fast. I mean, one minute he's in front of me, then he's behind me...
...and next thing I know I'm in a freakin' hospital room...
MANHATTAN BURROUGH H
...with a cop outside the door who can't wait t'drag me off to jail.
My paranoid old man used t'rant about "the Grillo Curse." Like the whole family was stuck with some kinda supernatural bad luck.
503
...since you were small! Always in trouble! All I've ever done is worry about you!
I used t'laugh at him when he said that.
I'm not laughing any more.
What were you thinkin'--sticking that empty gun in someone's face! If the cops had shown up, they might've shot you!
What'd I do wrong? Tell me that: What'd I do wrong?
What'd you do wrong, Ma? You married a mental case who used t'get off on beating the stuffing out of both of us.
And you always let him. You never once stood up to him. You never once--
Ah...what's the point?
Nothing I could ever say would make a dent.
And it never will.
I should just let 'em drag you off t'jail--that's what I should do!
Sigh
Guess I'll call your Aunt Celia and see if she can loan me the money for a lawyer--but if I manage to get you out of this mess, Bobby Grillo--
--things are gonna change... y'hear me?

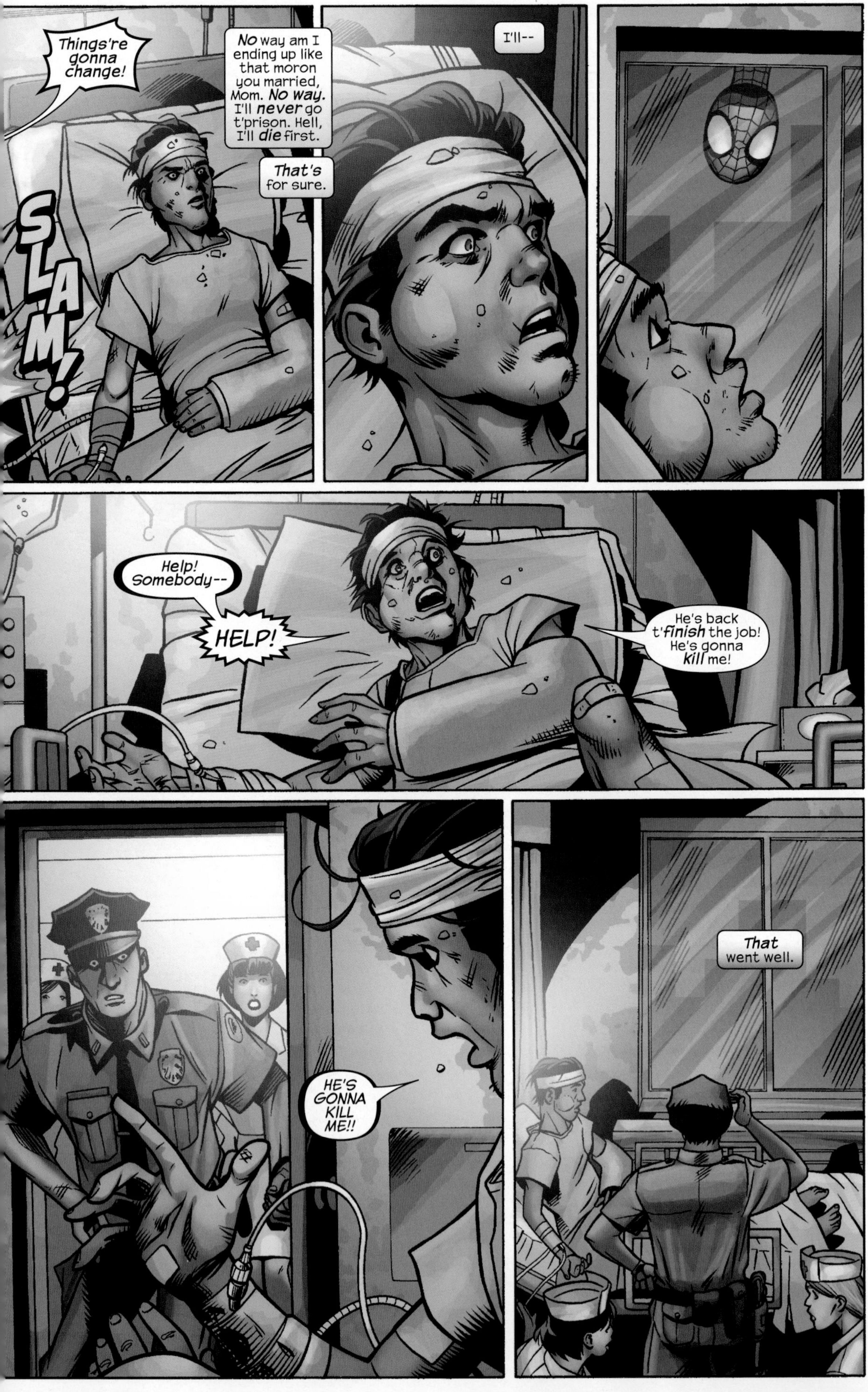
Things're gonna change!
No way am I ending up like that moron you married, Mom. No way. I'll never go t'prison. Hell, I'll die first.
That's for sure.
SLAM!
I'll--
Help! Somebody--
HELP!
He's back t'finish the job! He's gonna kill me!
HE'S GONNA KILL ME!!
That went well.

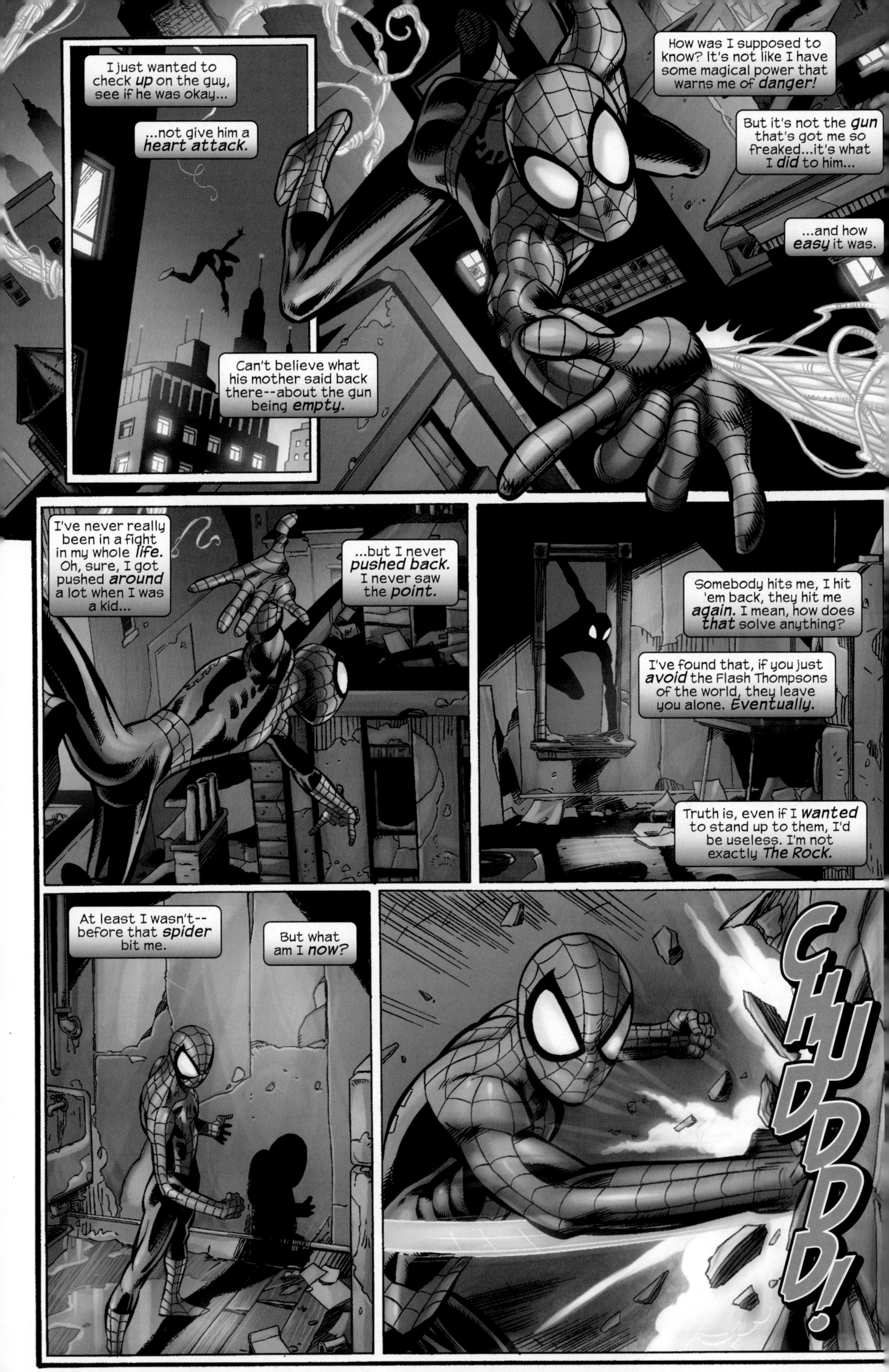
I just wanted to check *up* on the guy, see if he was okay...
...not give him a *heart attack.*
Can't believe what his mother said back there--about the gun being *empty.*
How was I supposed to know? It's not like I have some magical power that warns me of *danger!*
But it's not the *gun* that's got me so freaked...it's what I *did* to him...
...and how *easy* it was.
I've never really been in a fight in my whole *life.* Oh, sure, I got pushed *around* a lot when I was a kid...
...but I never *pushed back.* I never saw the *point.*
Somebody hits me, I hit 'em back, they hit me *again.* I mean, how does *that* solve anything?
I've found that, if you just *avoid* the Flash Thompsons of the world, they leave you alone. *Eventually.*
Truth is, even if I *wanted* to stand up to them, I'd be useless. I'm not exactly *The Rock.*
At least I wasn't--before that *spider* bit me.
But what am I *now?*
CHUDDD!

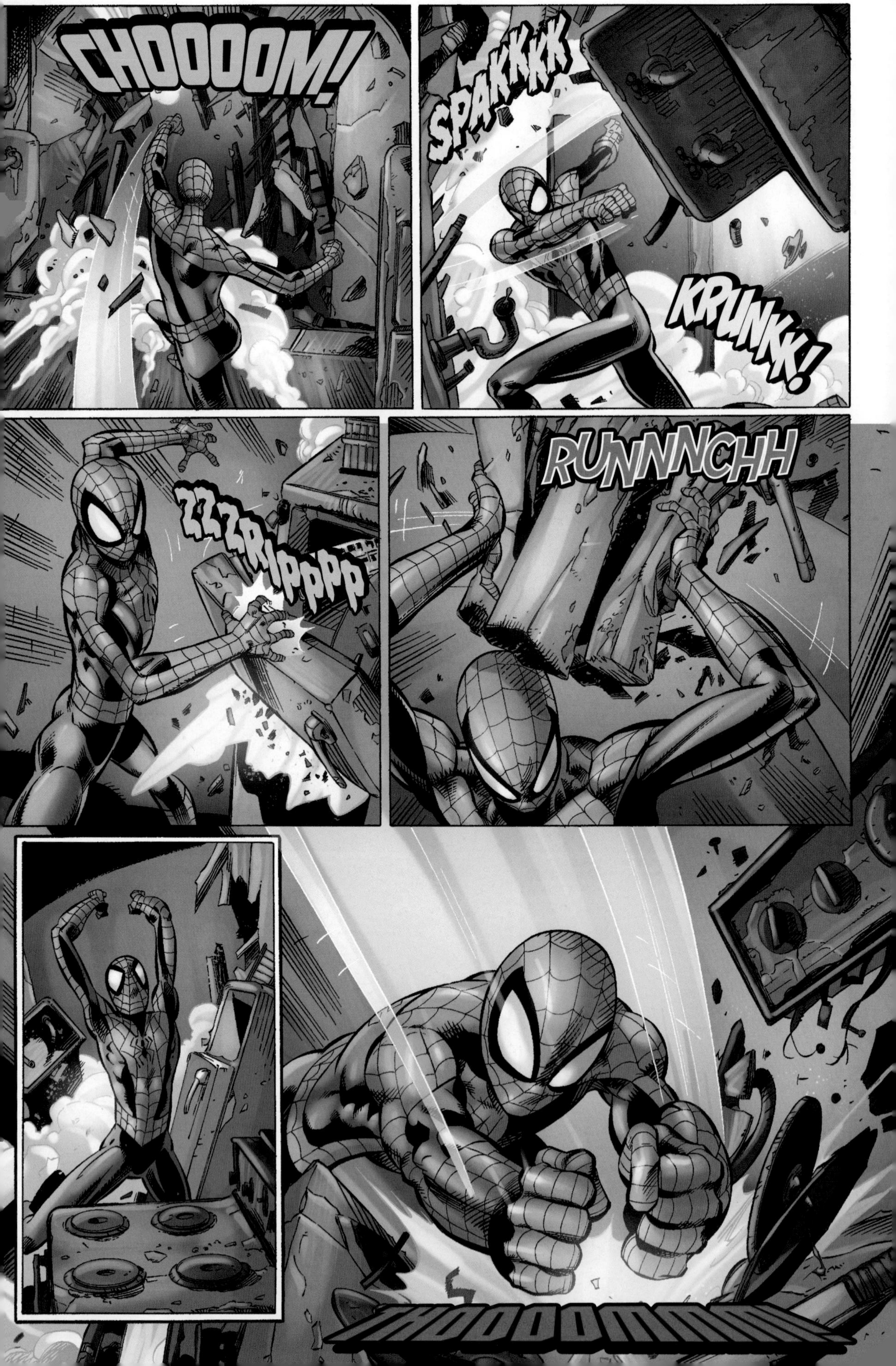
CHOOOOM!
SPAKKKK
KRUNKK!
ZZZZRIPPPP
RUNNNCHH
THOOOOMMM

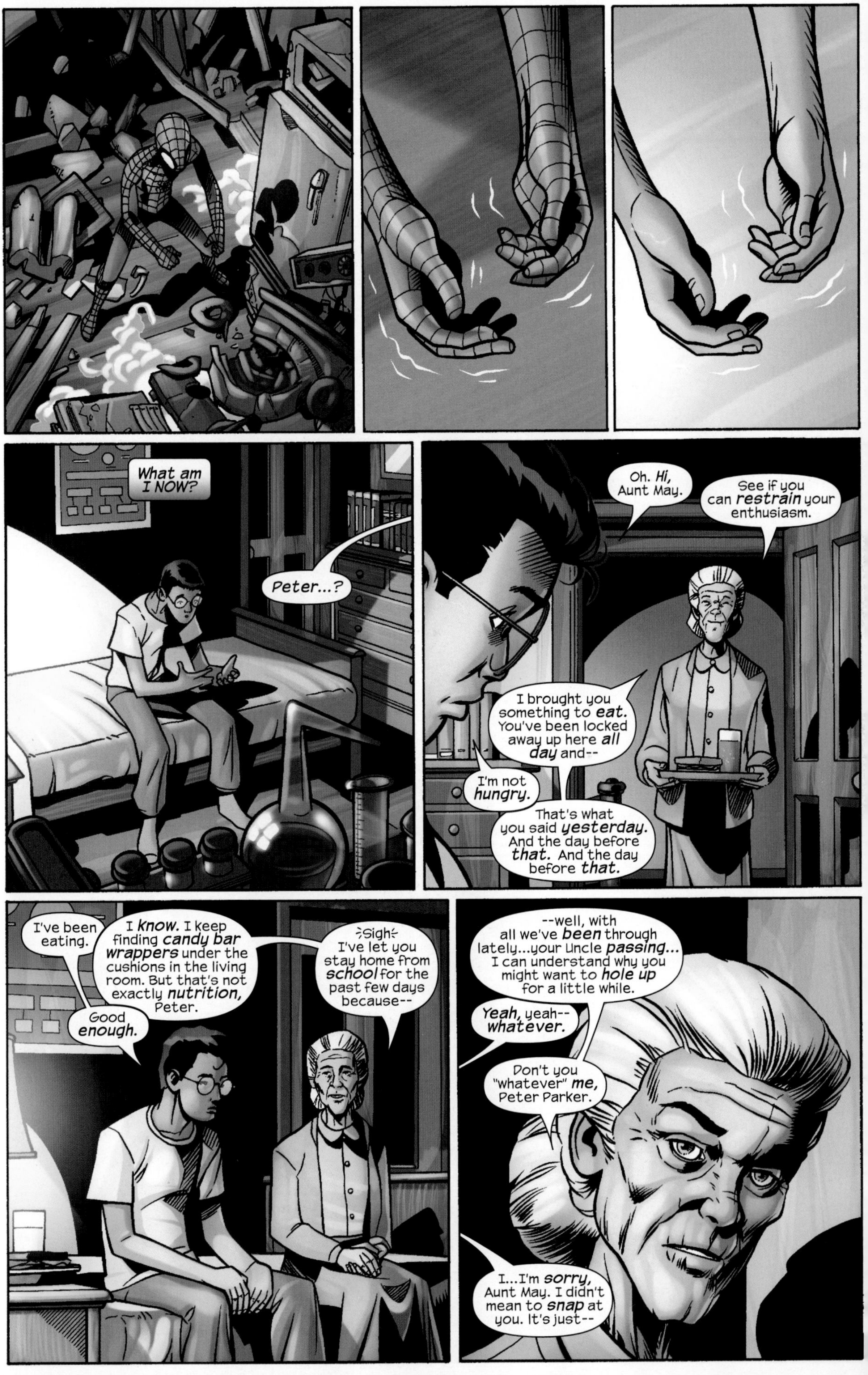
What am I NOW?
Peter...?
Oh. Hi, Aunt May.
See if you can restrain your enthusiasm.
I brought you something to eat. You've been locked away up here all day and--
I'm not hungry.
That's what you said yesterday. And the day before that. And the day before that.
I've been eating.
I know. I keep finding candy bar wrappers under the cushions in the living room. But that's not exactly nutrition, Peter.
Good enough.
Sigh
I've let you stay home from school for the past few days because--
--well, with all we've been through lately...your Uncle passing... I can understand why you might want to hole up for a little while.
Yeah, yeah-- whatever.
Don't you "whatever" me, Peter Parker.
I...I'm sorry, Aunt May. I didn't mean to snap at you. It's just--

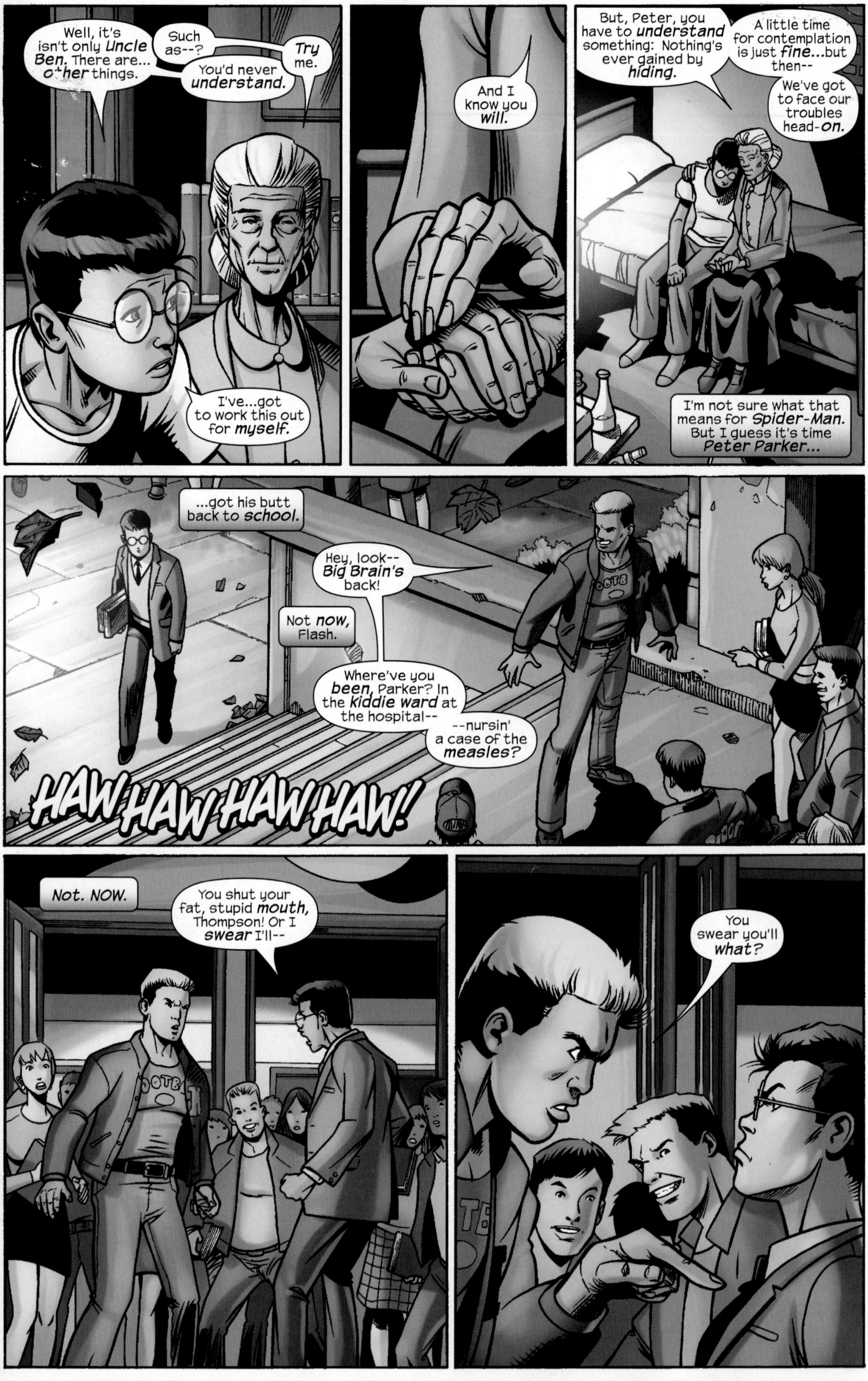

Well, it's isn't only Uncle Ben. There are... other things.
Such as--?
You'd never understand.
Try me.
I've...got to work this out for myself.
And I know you will.
But, Peter, you have to understand something: Nothing's ever gained by hiding.
A little time for contemplation is just fine...but then--
We've got to face our troubles head-on.
I'm not sure what that means for Spider-Man. But I guess it's time Peter Parker...
...got his butt back to school.
Hey, look-- Big Brain's back!
Not now, Flash.
Where've you been, Parker? In the kiddie ward at the hospital--
--nursin' a case of the measles?
HAW HAW HAW HAW!
Not. NOW.
You shut your fat, stupid mouth, Thompson! Or I swear I'll--
You swear you'll what?

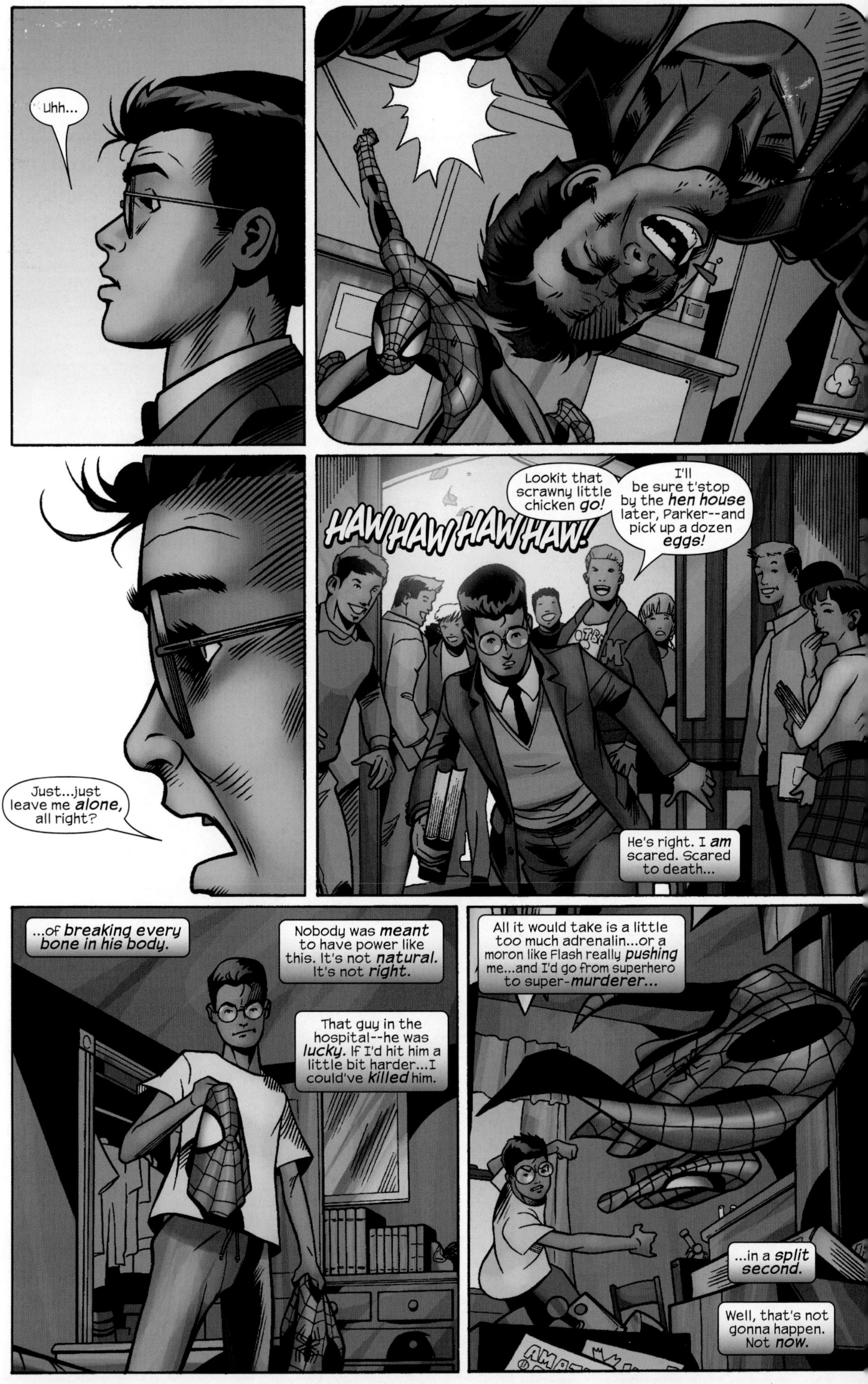

Uhh...
HAW HAW HAW HAW!
Lookit that scrawny little chicken go!
I'll be sure t'stop by the hen house later, Parker--and pick up a dozen eggs!
Just...just leave me alone, all right?
He's right. I am scared. Scared to death...
...of breaking every bone in his body.
Nobody was meant to have power like this. It's not natural. It's not right.
That guy in the hospital--he was lucky. If I'd hit him a little bit harder...I could've killed him.
All it would take is a little too much adrenalin...or a moron like Flash really pushing me...and I'd go from superhero to super-murderer...
...in a split second.
Well, that's not gonna happen. Not now.

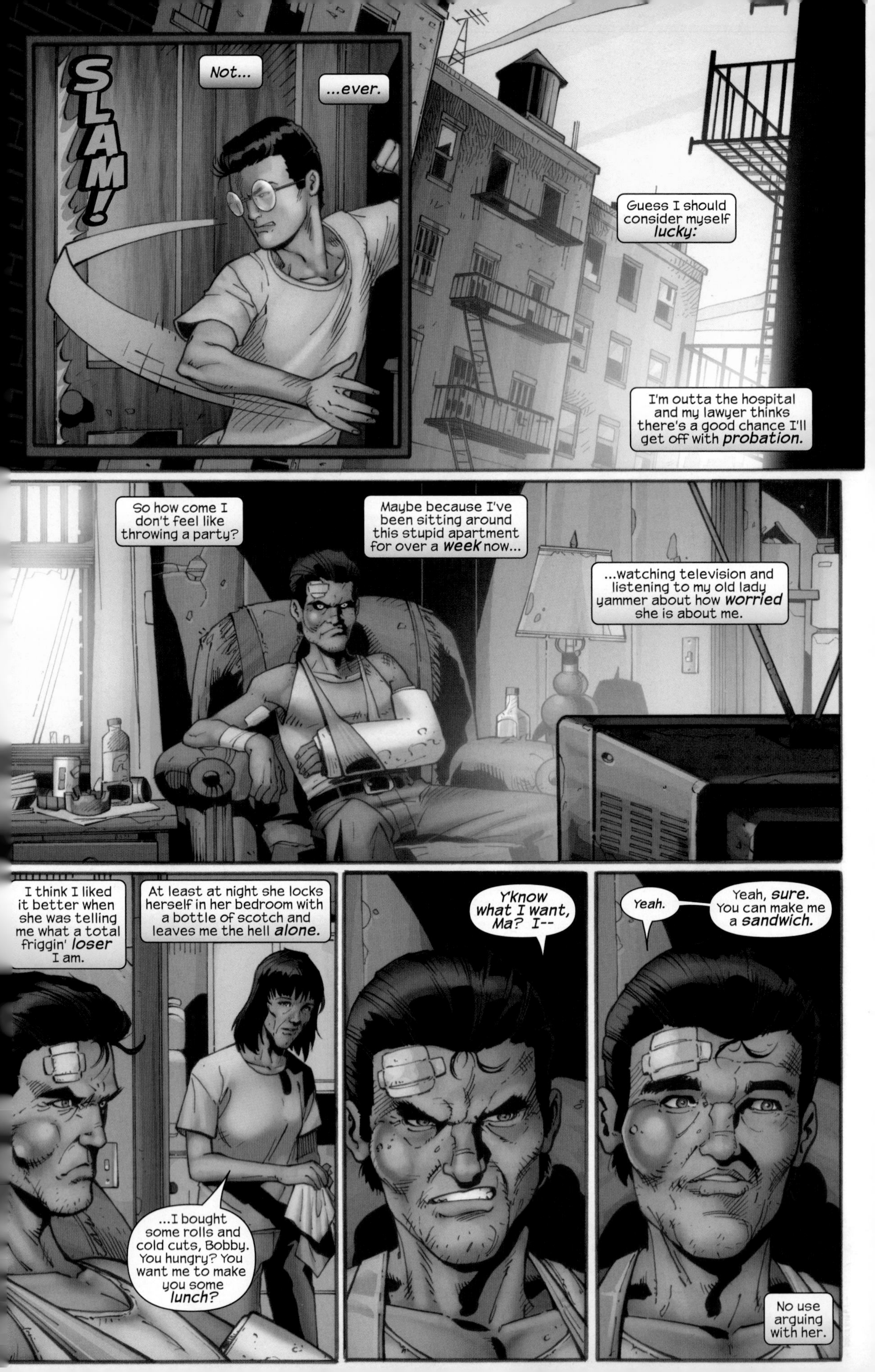
SLAM!
Not...
...ever.
Guess I should consider myself lucky:
I'm outta the hospital and my lawyer thinks there's a good chance I'll get off with probation.
So how come I don't feel like throwing a party?
Maybe because I've been sitting around this stupid apartment for over a week now...
...watching television and listening to my old lady yammer about how worried she is about me.
I think I liked it better when she was telling me what a total friggin' loser I am.
At least at night she locks herself in her bedroom with a bottle of scotch and leaves me the hell alone.
...I bought some rolls and cold cuts, Bobby. You hungry? You want me to make you some lunch?
Y'know what I want, Ma? I--
Yeah.
Yeah, sure. You can make me a sandwich.
No use arguing with her.

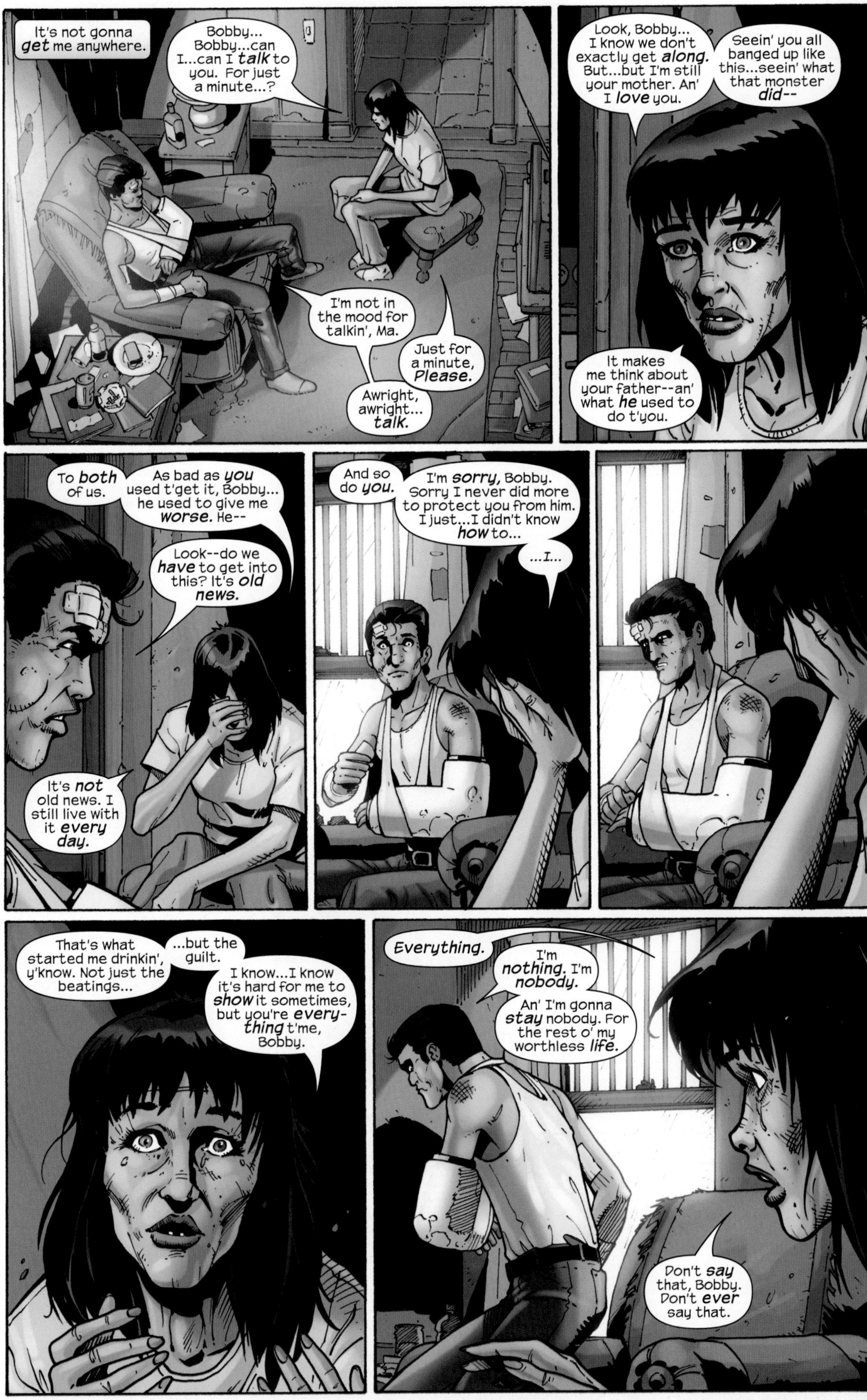
It's not gonna get me anywhere.
Bobby... Bobby...can I...can I talk to you. For just a minute...?
I'm not in the mood for talkin', Ma.
Just for a minute, Please.
Awright, awright... talk.
Look, Bobby... I know we don't exactly get along. But...but I'm still your mother. An' I love you.
Seein' you all banged up like this...seein' what that monster did--
It makes me think about your father--an' what he used to do t'you.
To both of us.
As bad as you used t'get it, Bobby... he used to give me worse. He--
Look--do we have to get into this? It's old news.
It's not old news. I still live with it every day.
And so do you.
I'm sorry, Bobby. Sorry I never did more to protect you from him. I just...I didn't know how to...
...I...
That's what started me drinkin', y'know. Not just the beatings...
...but the guilt.
I know...I know it's hard for me to show it sometimes, but you're every-thing t'me, Bobby.
Everything.
I'm nothing. I'm nobody.
An' I'm gonna stay nobody. For the rest o' my worthless life.
Don't say that, Bobby. Don't ever say that.

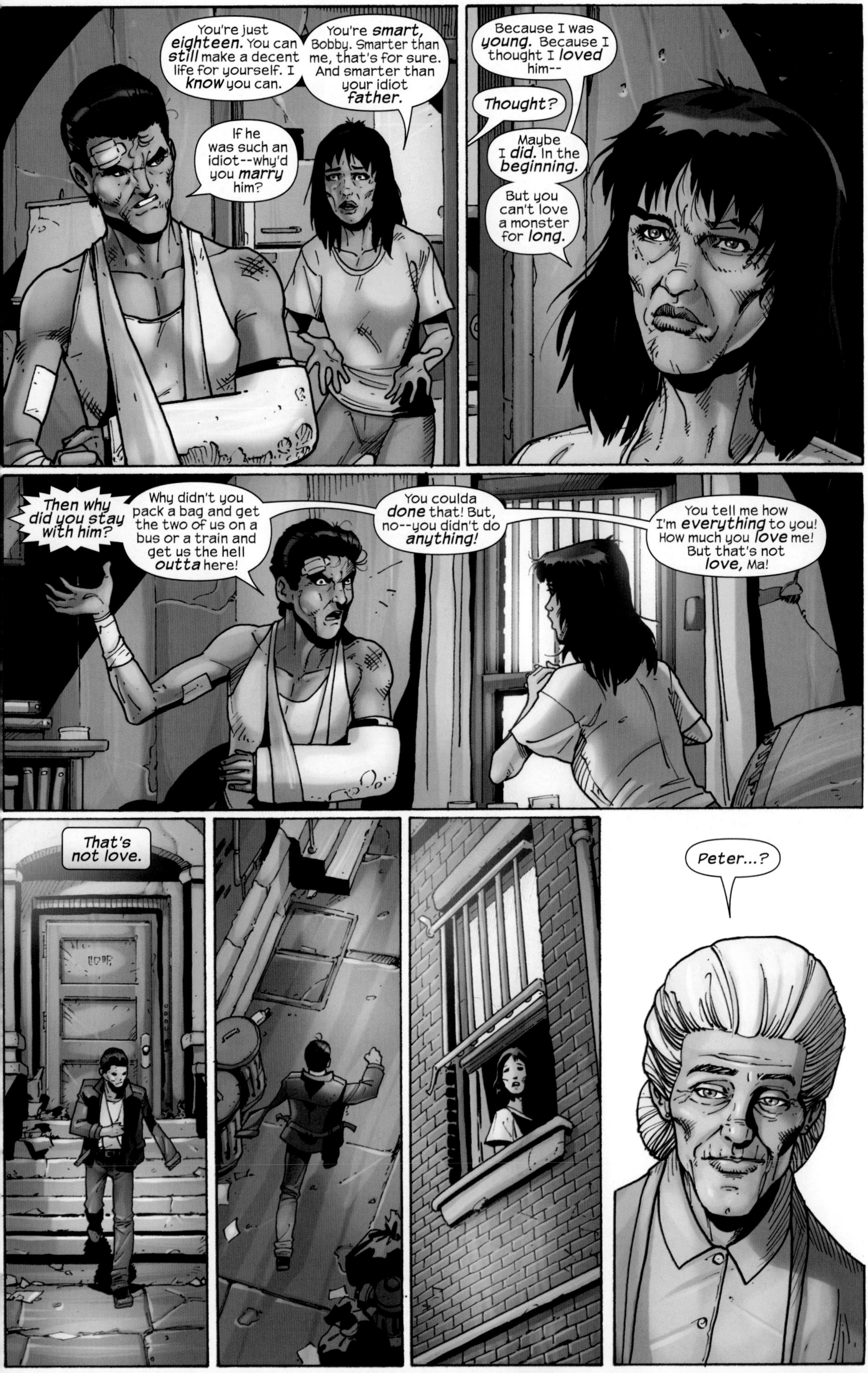

You're just eighteen. You can still make a decent life for yourself. I know you can.
You're smart, Bobby. Smarter than me, that's for sure. And smarter than your idiot father.
If he was such an idiot--why'd you marry him?
Because I was young. Because I thought I loved him--
Thought?
Maybe I did. In the beginning.
But you can't love a monster for long.
Then why did you stay with him?
Why didn't you pack a bag and get the two of us on a bus or a train and get us the hell outta here!
You coulda done that! But, no--you didn't do anything!
You tell me how I'm everything to you! How much you love me! But that's not love, Ma!
That's not love.
Peter...?

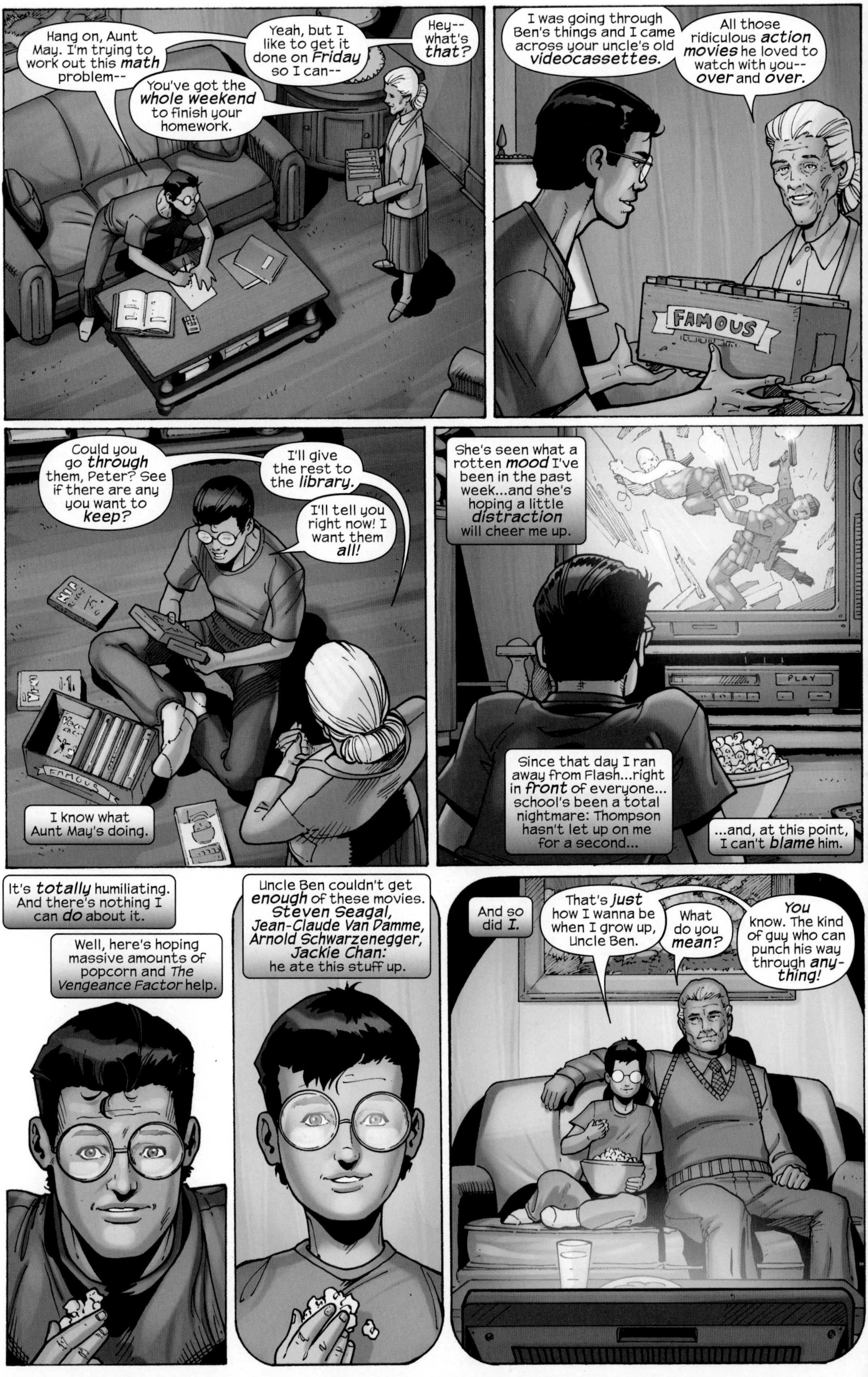

Hang on, Aunt May. I'm trying to work out this math problem--
You've got the whole weekend to finish your homework.
Yeah, but I like to get it done on Friday so I can--
Hey--what's that?
I was going through Ben's things and I came across your uncle's old videocassettes.
All those ridiculous action movies he loved to watch with you--over and over.
FAMOUS
Could you go through them, Peter? See if there are any you want to keep?
I'll give the rest to the library.
I'll tell you right now! I want them all!
I know what Aunt May's doing.
She's seen what a rotten mood I've been in the past week...and she's hoping a little distraction will cheer me up.
PLAY
Since that day I ran away from Flash...right in front of everyone... school's been a total nightmare: Thompson hasn't let up on me for a second...
...and, at this point, I can't blame him.
It's totally humiliating. And there's nothing I can do about it.
Well, here's hoping massive amounts of popcorn and The Vengeance Factor help.
Uncle Ben couldn't get enough of these movies. Steven Seagal, Jean-Claude Van Damme, Arnold Schwarzenegger, Jackie Chan: he ate this stuff up.
And so did I.
That's just how I wanna be when I grow up, Uncle Ben.
What do you mean?
You know. The kind of guy who can punch his way through any-thing!

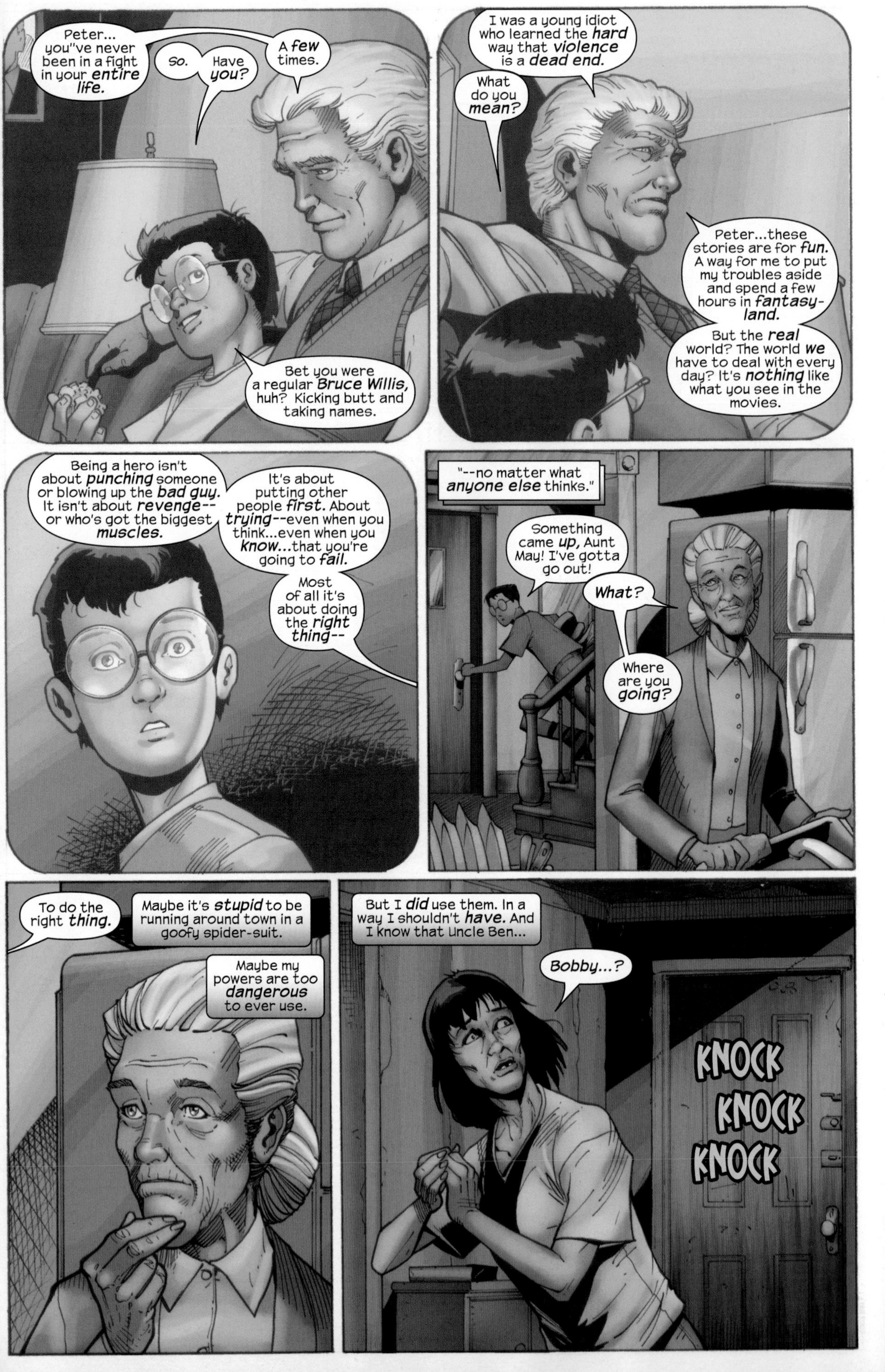

Peter... you''ve never been in a fight in your entire life.
So.
Have you?
A few times.
Bet you were a regular Bruce Willis, huh? Kicking butt and taking names.
I was a young idiot who learned the hard way that violence is a dead end.
What do you mean?
Peter...these stories are for fun. A way for me to put my troubles aside and spend a few hours in fantasy-land.
But the real world? The world we have to deal with every day? It's nothing like what you see in the movies.
Being a hero isn't about punching someone or blowing up the bad guy. It isn't about revenge-- or who's got the biggest muscles.
It's about putting other people first. About trying--even when you think...even when you know...that you're going to fail.
Most of all it's about doing the right thing--
"--no matter what anyone else thinks."
Something came up, Aunt May! I've gotta go out!
What?
Where are you going?
To do the right thing.
Maybe it's stupid to be running around town in a goofy spider-suit.
Maybe my powers are too dangerous to ever use.
But I did use them. In a way I shouldn't have. And I know that Uncle Ben...
Bobby...?
KNOCK
KNOCK
KNOCK

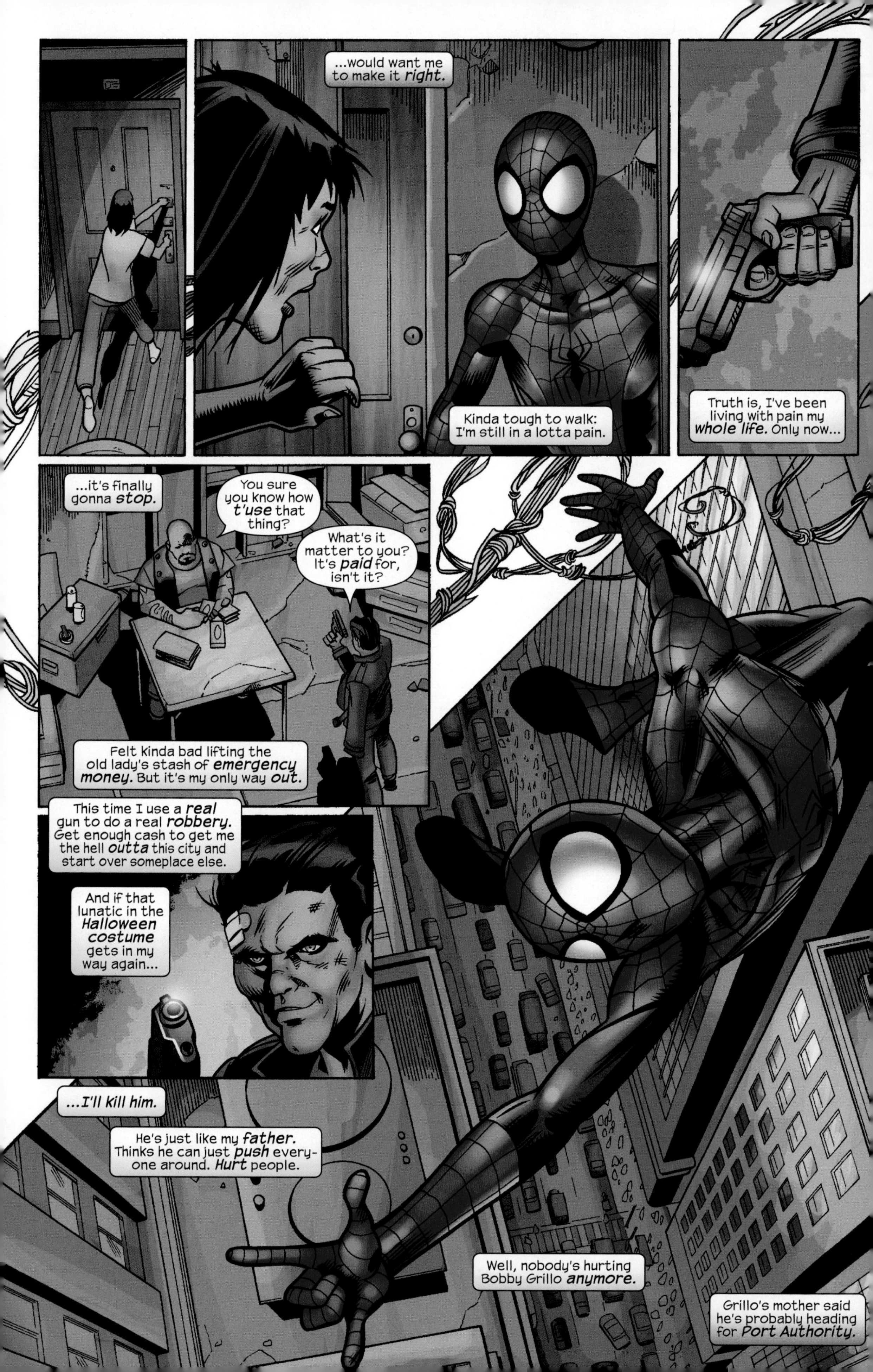

...would want me to make it *right.*
Kinda tough to walk: I'm still in a lotta pain.
Truth is, I've been living with pain my *whole life.* Only now...
...it's finally gonna *stop.*
You sure you know how *t'use* that thing?
What's it matter to you? It's *paid* for, isn't it?
Felt kinda bad lifting the old lady's stash of *emergency money.* But it's my only way *out.*
This time I use a *real* gun to do a real *robbery.* Get enough cash to get me the hell *outta* this city and start over someplace else.
And if that lunatic in the *Halloween costume* gets in my way again...
...I'll kill him.
He's just like my *father.* Thinks he can just *push* everyone around. *Hurt* people.
Well, nobody's hurting Bobby Grillo *anymore.*
Grillo's mother said he's probably heading for *Port Authority.*

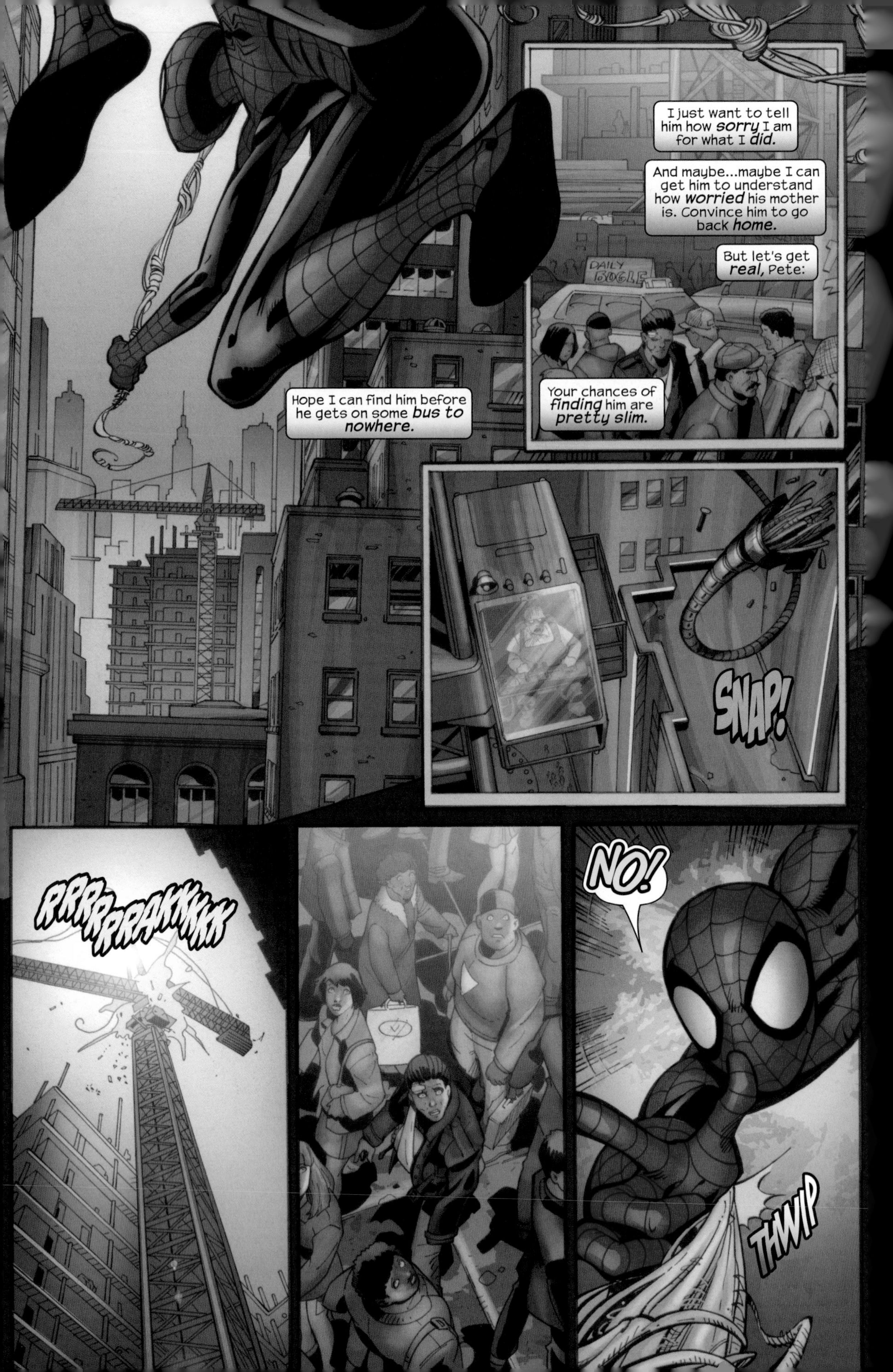

I just want to tell him how sorry I am for what I did.
And maybe...maybe I can get him to understand how worried his mother is. Convince him to go back home.
But let's get real, Pete:
DAILY BUGLE
Your chances of finding him are pretty slim.
Hope I can find him before he gets on some bus to nowhere.
SNAP!
RRRRRRAKKKKK
NO!
THWIP

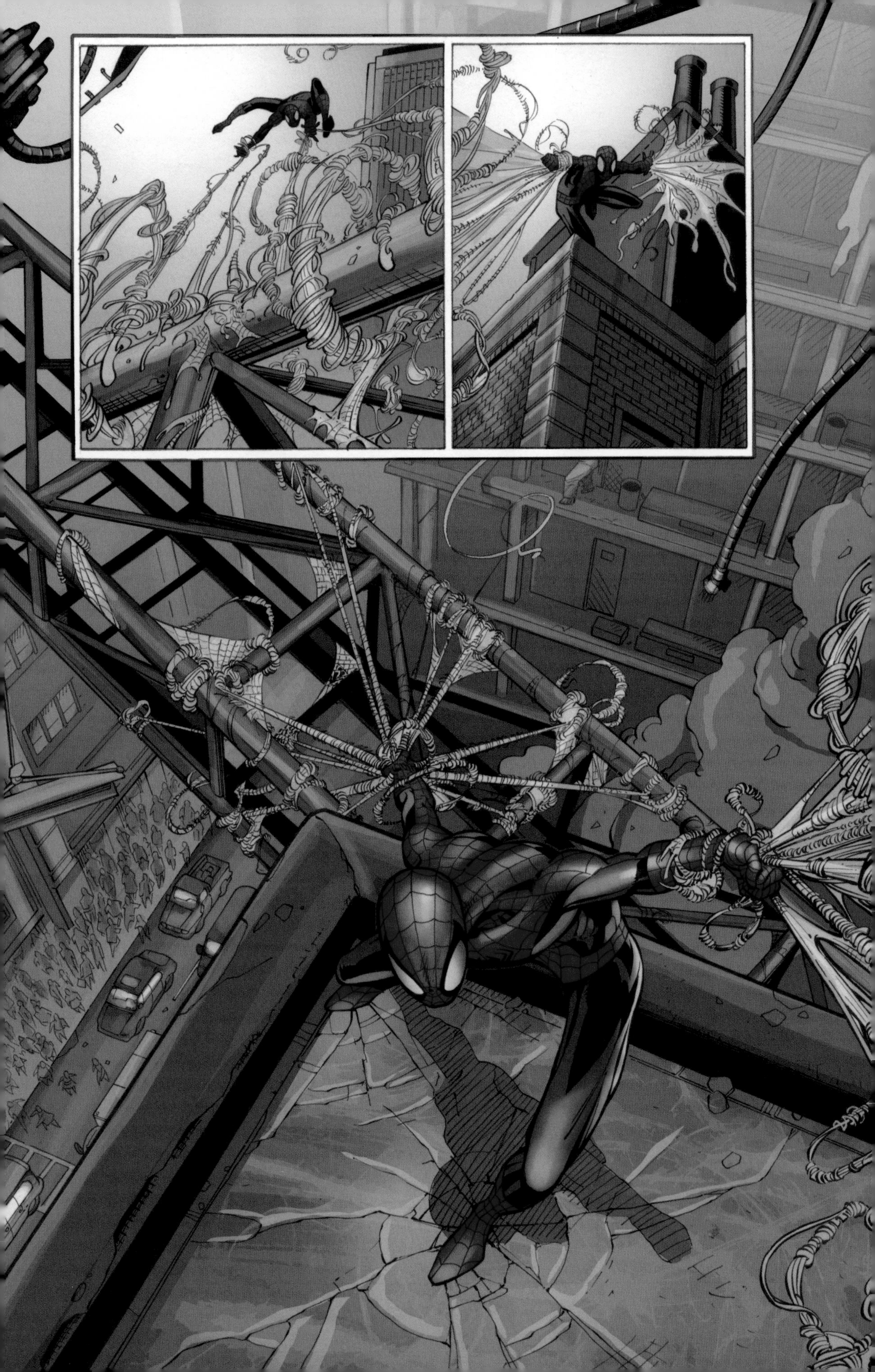

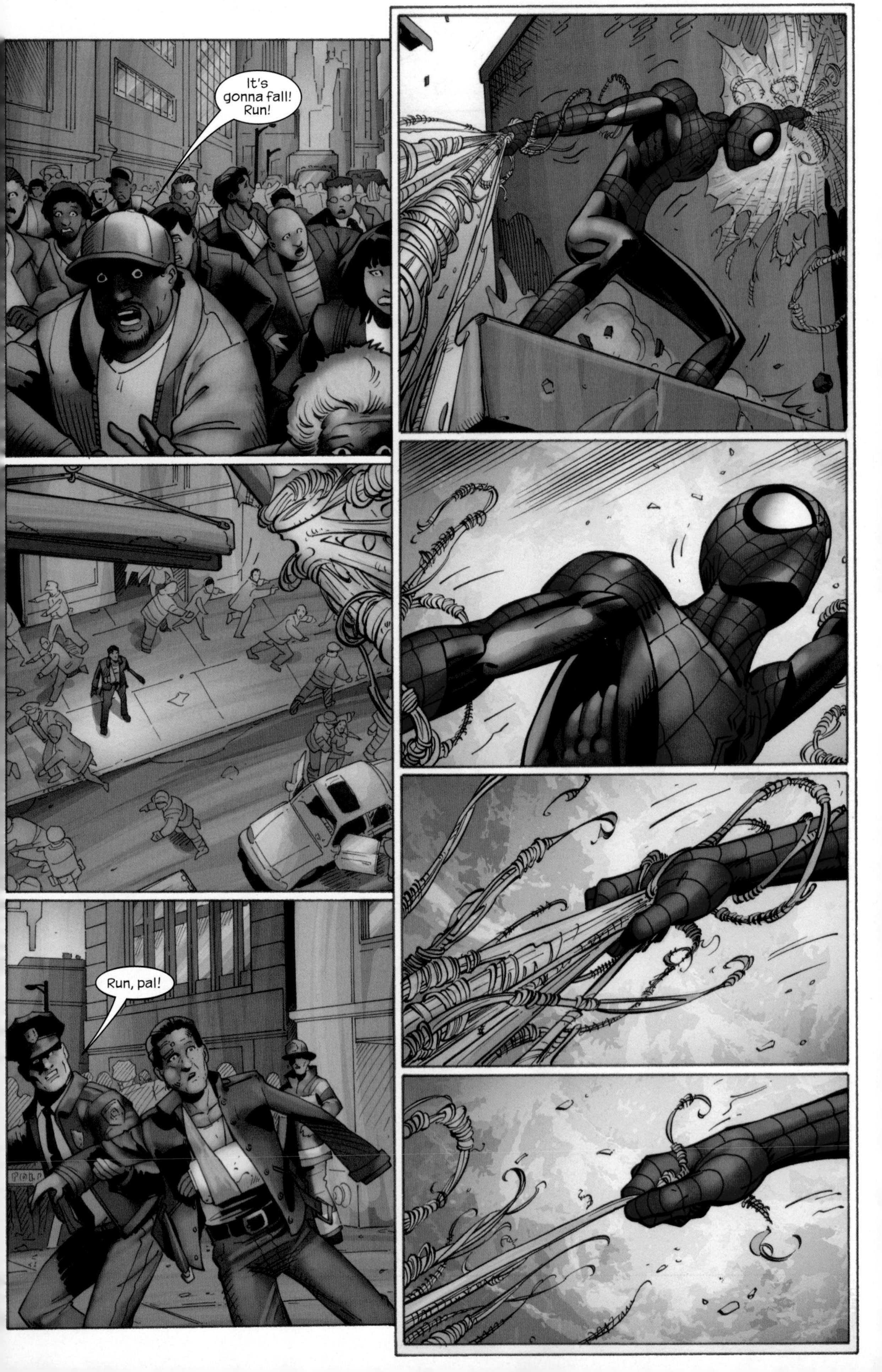
It's gonna fall! Run!
Run, pal!

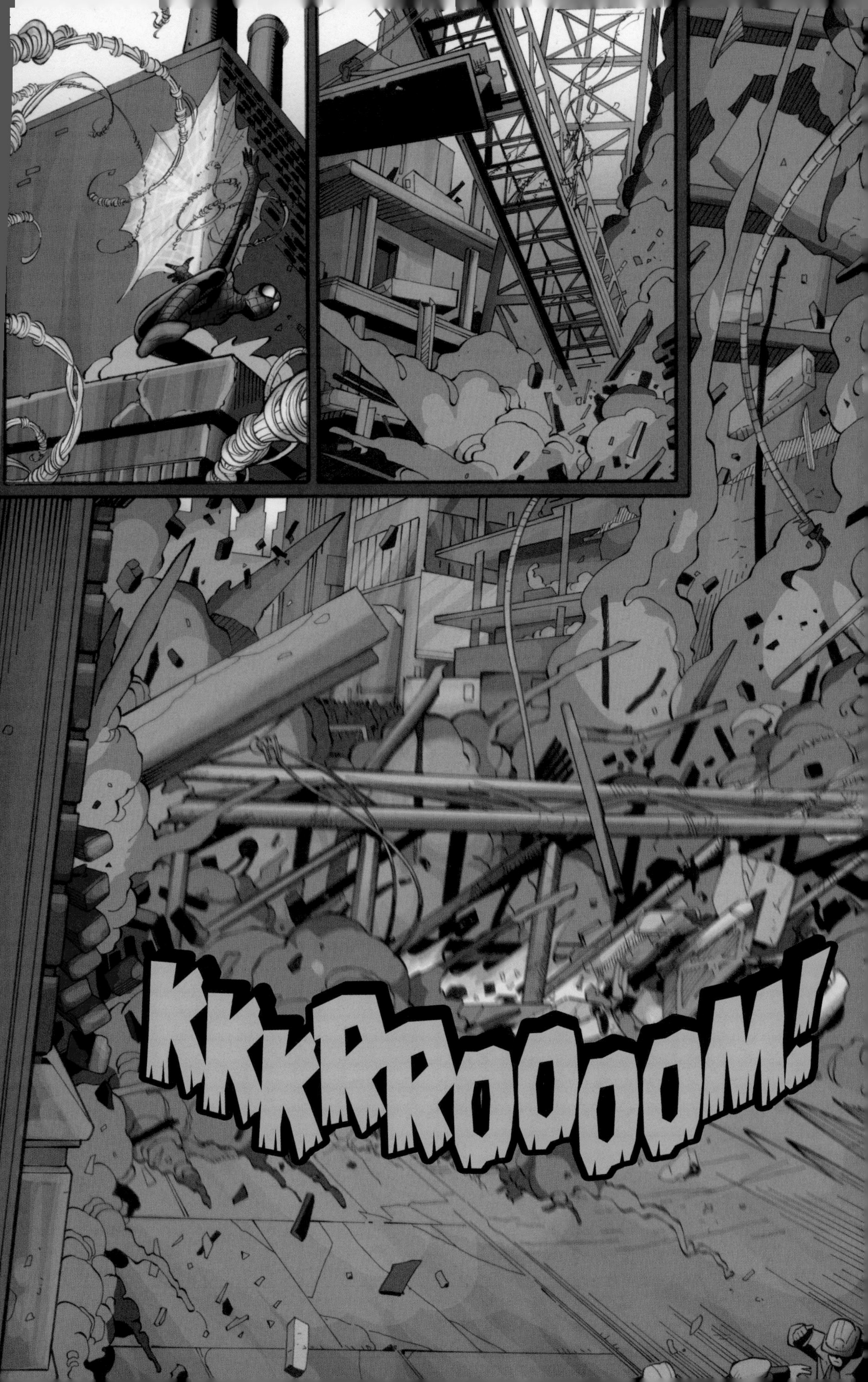
KKKRROOOOOM!

I'm *sorry.*

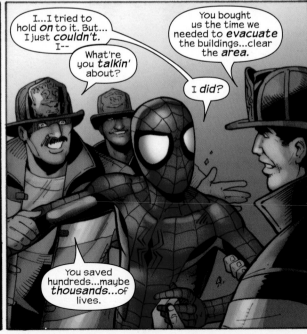

I...I tried to hold *on* to it. But... I just *couldn't.* I--

What're you *talkin'* about?

You bought us the time we needed to *evacuate* the buildings...clear the *area.*

I *did?*

You saved hundreds...maybe *thousands*...of lives.

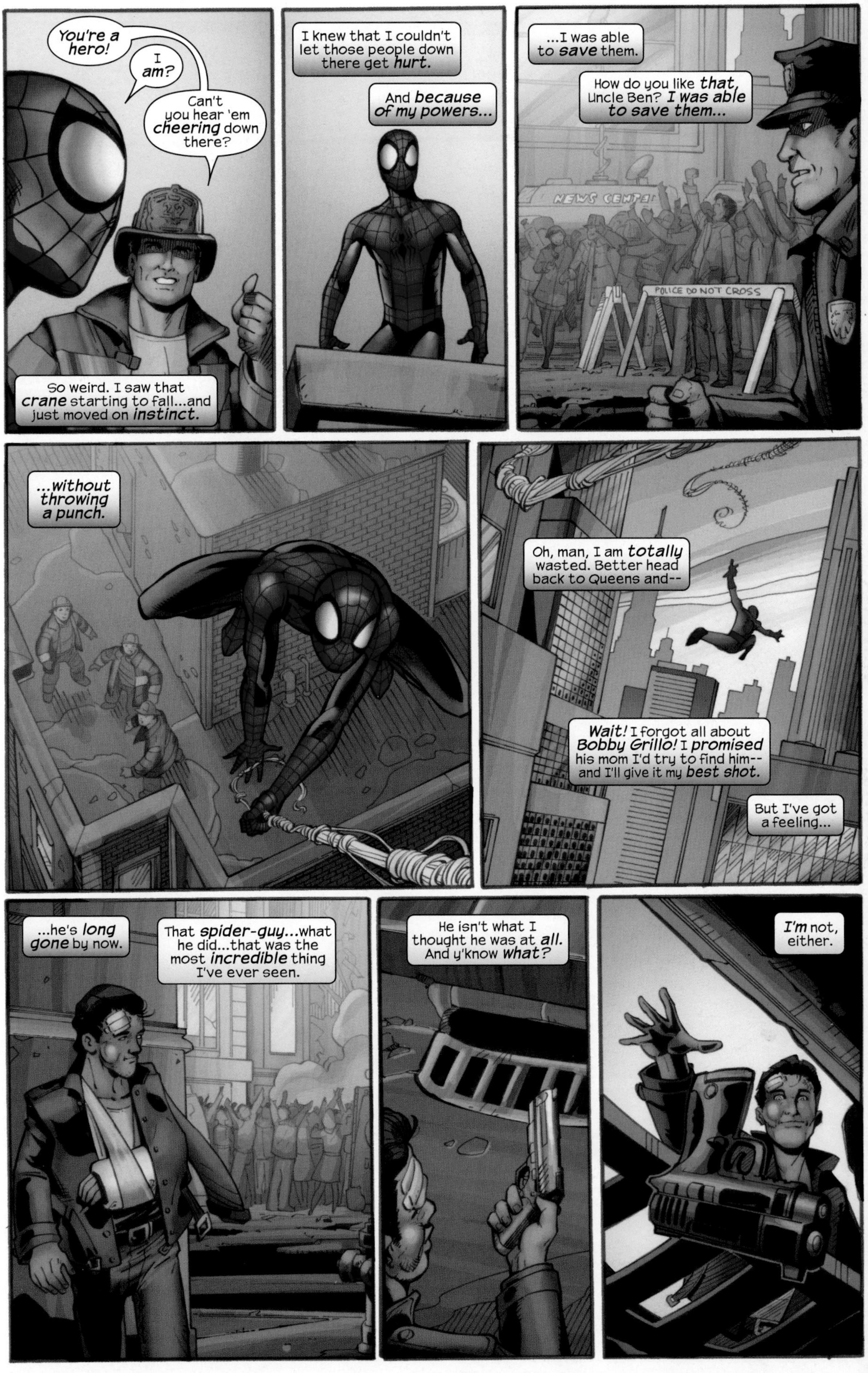
You're a hero!
I am?
Can't you hear 'em cheering down there?
So weird. I saw that crane starting to fall...and just moved on instinct.
I knew that I couldn't let those people down there get hurt.
And because of my powers...
...I was able to save them.
How do you like that, Uncle Ben? I was able to save them...
NEWS CENTE
POLICE DO NOT CROSS
...without throwing a punch.
Oh, man, I am totally wasted. Better head back to Queens and--
Wait! I forgot all about Bobby Grillo! I promised his mom I'd try to find him--and I'll give it my best shot.
But I've got a feeling...
...he's long gone by now.
That spider-guy...what he did...that was the most incredible thing I've ever seen.
He isn't what I thought he was at all. And y'know what?
I'm not, either.

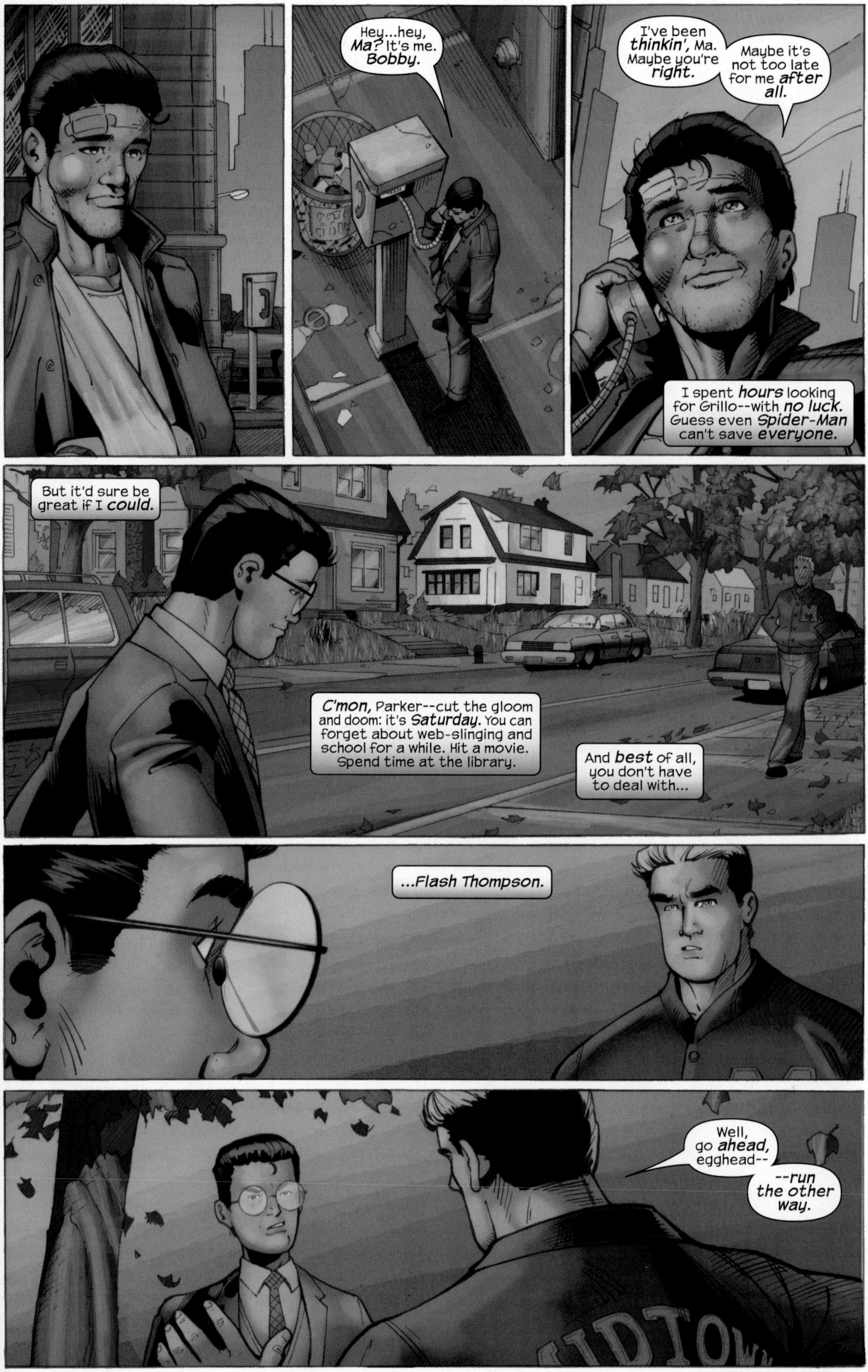

Hey...hey, Ma? It's me. Bobby.
I've been thinkin', Ma. Maybe you're right.
Maybe it's not too late for me after all.
I spent hours looking for Grillo--with no luck. Guess even Spider-Man can't save everyone.
But it'd sure be great if I could.
C'mon, Parker--cut the gloom and doom: it's Saturday. You can forget about web-slinging and school for a while. Hit a movie. Spend time at the library.
And best of all, you don't have to deal with...
...Flash Thompson.
Well, go ahead, egghead--
--run the other way.

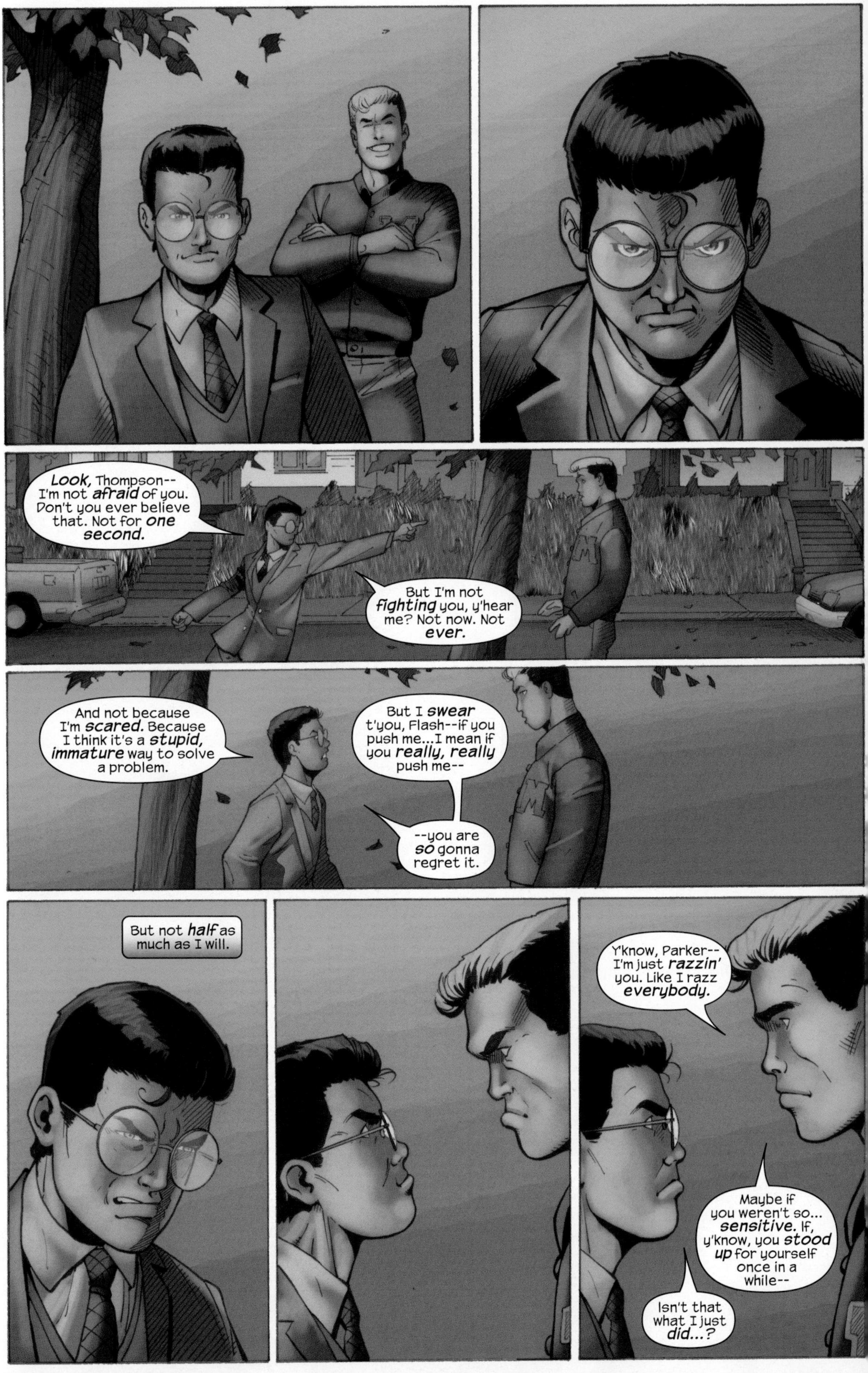
Look, Thompson--
I'm not afraid of you. Don't you ever believe that. Not for one second.
But I'm not fighting you, y'hear me? Not now. Not ever.
And not because I'm scared. Because I think it's a stupid, immature way to solve a problem.
But I swear t'you, Flash--if you push me...I mean if you really, really push me--
--you are so gonna regret it.
But not half as much as I will.
Y'know, Parker--I'm just razzin' you. Like I razz everybody.
Maybe if you weren't so... sensitive. If, y'know, you stood up for yourself once in a while--
Isn't that what I just did...?

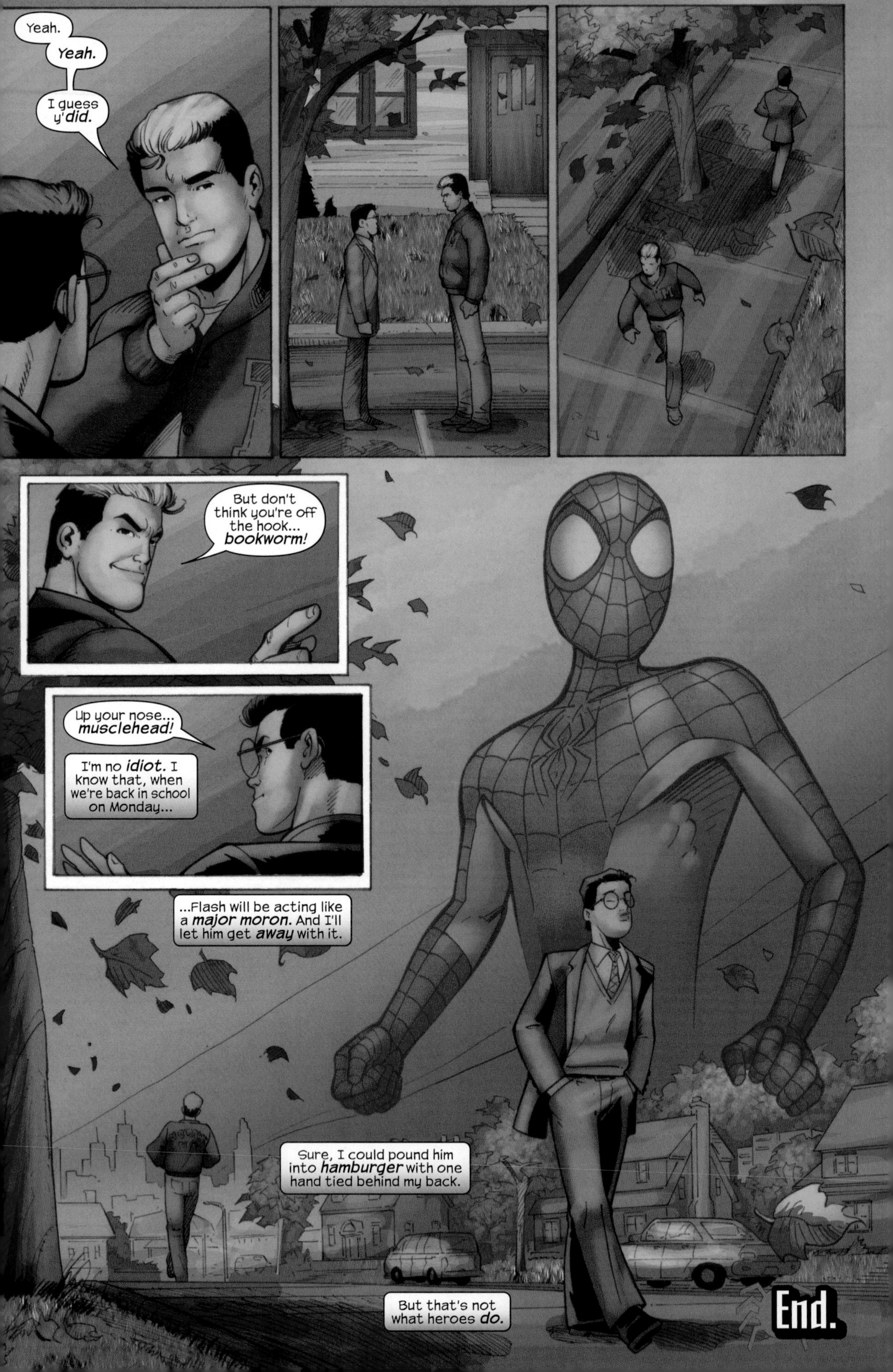
Yeah.
Yeah.
I guess y'did.
But don't think you're off the hook... bookworm!
Up your nose... musclehead!
I'm no idiot. I know that, when we're back in school on Monday...
...Flash will be acting like a major moron. And I'll let him get away with it.
Sure, I could pound him into hamburger with one hand tied behind my back.
But that's not what heroes do.
End.

You may think you know Peter Parker's sweet old **Aunt May** but you've never seen her like ***this!*** Forget everything you **think** you know and read on for what is surely the most ***shocking*** **Spider-Man** tale ever told! ***INTRODUCING*** a world where Aunt May not only knows Peter's secret identity, but a world that's about to meet...

THE AMAZING SPIDER-MA'AM

WRITER: **Abby Denson**
ARTIST: **Colleen Coover**

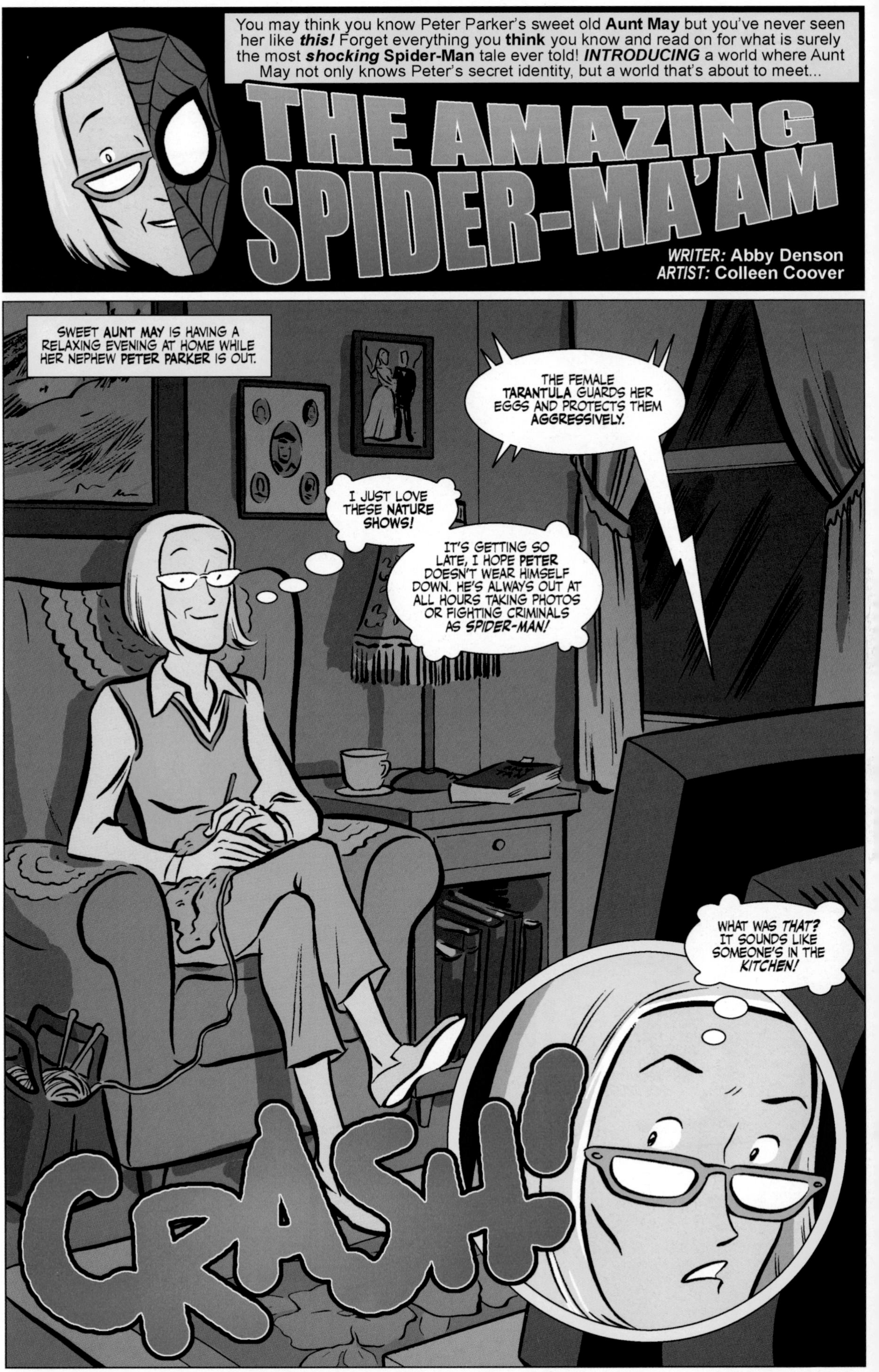

SWEET AUNT MAY IS HAVING A RELAXING EVENING AT HOME WHILE HER NEPHEW PETER PARKER IS OUT.
THE FEMALE TARANTULA GUARDS HER EGGS AND PROTECTS THEM AGGRESSIVELY.
I JUST LOVE THESE NATURE SHOWS!
IT'S GETTING SO LATE, I HOPE PETER DOESN'T WEAR HIMSELF DOWN. HE'S ALWAYS OUT AT ALL HOURS TAKING PHOTOS OR FIGHTING CRIMINALS AS SPIDER-MAN!
CRASH!
WHAT WAS THAT? IT SOUNDS LIKE SOMEONE'S IN THE KITCHEN!

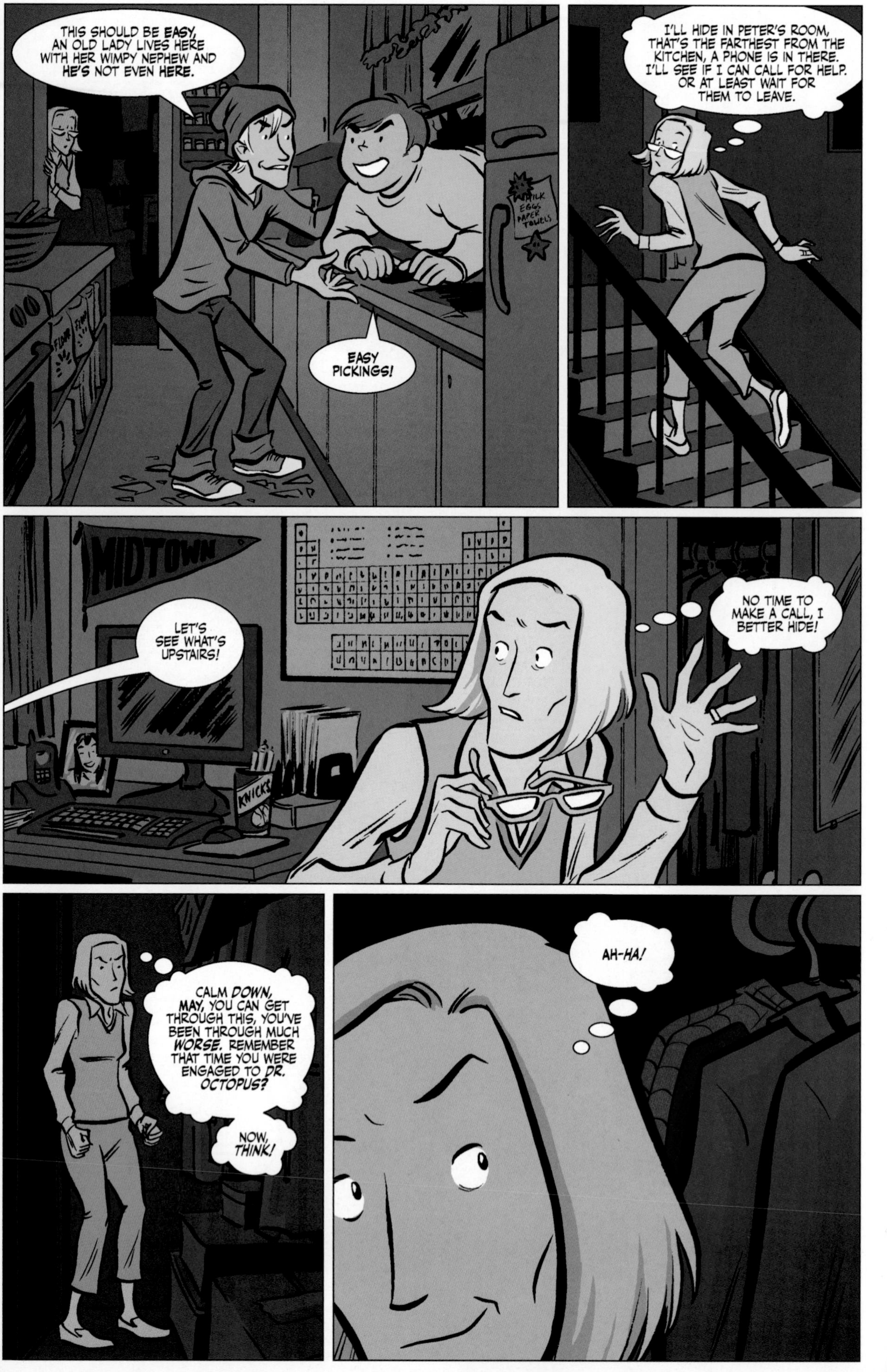
THIS SHOULD BE EASY, AN OLD LADY LIVES HERE WITH HER WIMPY NEPHEW AND HE'S NOT EVEN HERE.
EASY PICKINGS!
I'LL HIDE IN PETER'S ROOM, THAT'S THE FARTHEST FROM THE KITCHEN, A PHONE IS IN THERE. I'LL SEE IF I CAN CALL FOR HELP. OR AT LEAST WAIT FOR THEM TO LEAVE.
MIDTOWN
LET'S SEE WHAT'S UPSTAIRS!
NO TIME TO MAKE A CALL, I BETTER HIDE!
KNICKS
CALM DOWN, MAY, YOU CAN GET THROUGH THIS, YOU'VE BEEN THROUGH MUCH WORSE. REMEMBER THAT TIME YOU WERE ENGAGED TO DR. OCTOPUS?
NOW, THINK!
AH-HA!

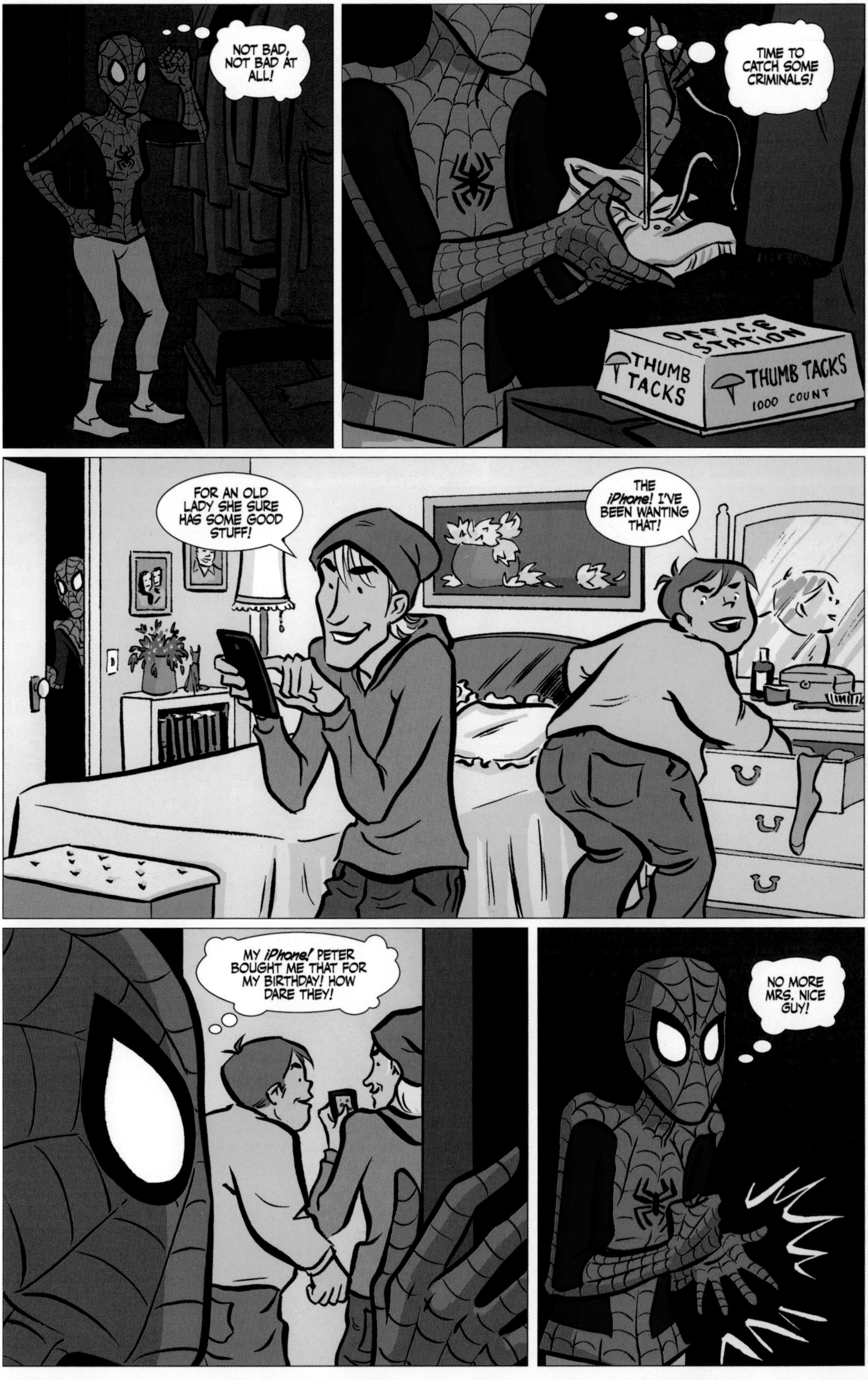
NOT BAD, NOT BAD AT ALL!
TIME TO CATCH SOME CRIMINALS!
OFFICE STATION
THUMB TACKS
THUMB TACKS
1000 COUNT
FOR AN OLD LADY SHE SURE HAS SOME GOOD STUFF!
THE *iPhone!* I'VE BEEN WANTING THAT!
MY *iPhone!* PETER BOUGHT ME THAT FOR MY BIRTHDAY! HOW DARE THEY!
NO MORE MRS. NICE GUY!

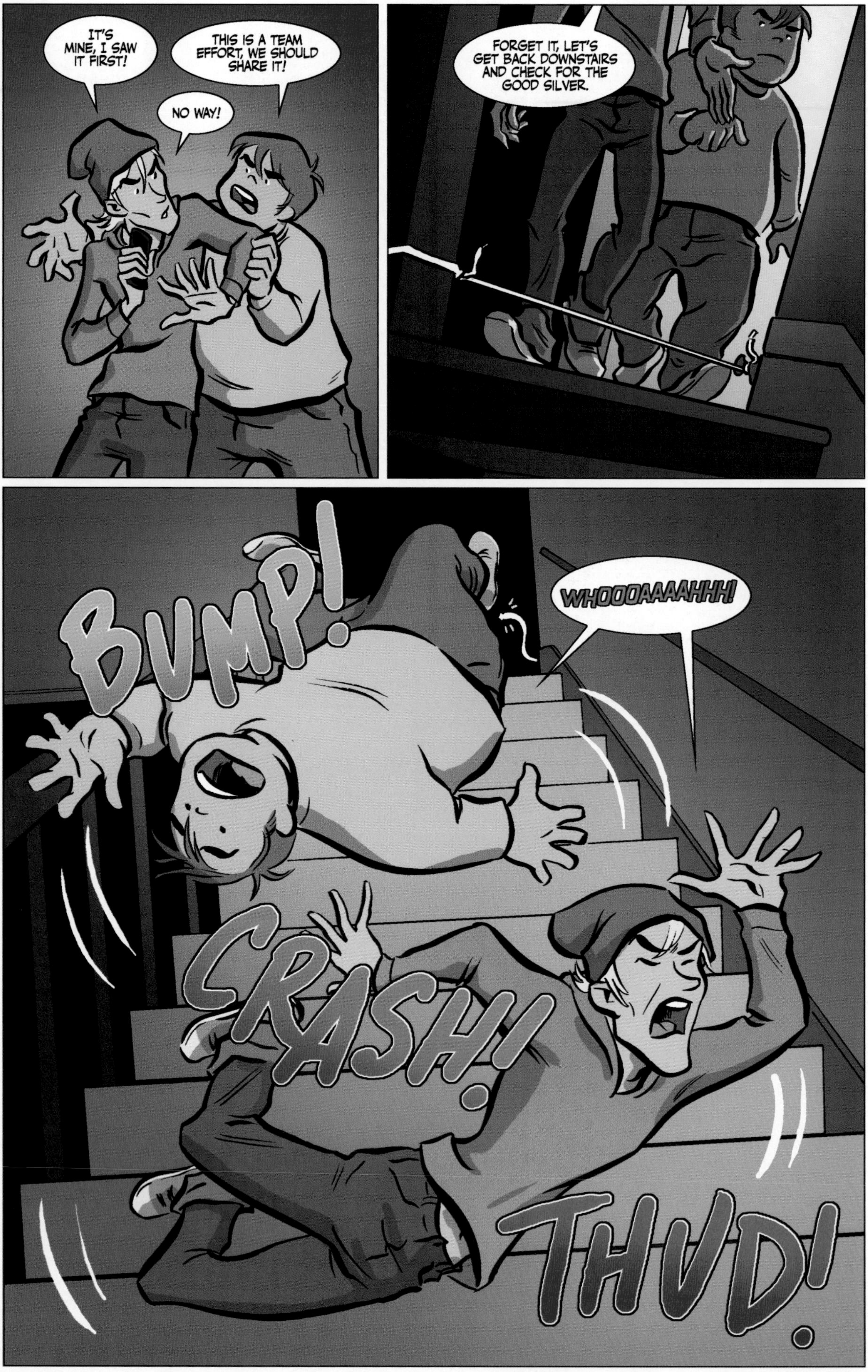
IT'S MINE, I SAW IT FIRST!
THIS IS A TEAM EFFORT, WE SHOULD SHARE IT!
NO WAY!
FORGET IT, LET'S GET BACK DOWNSTAIRS AND CHECK FOR THE GOOD SILVER.
BUMP!
WHOOOAAAAHHH!
CRASH!
THUD!

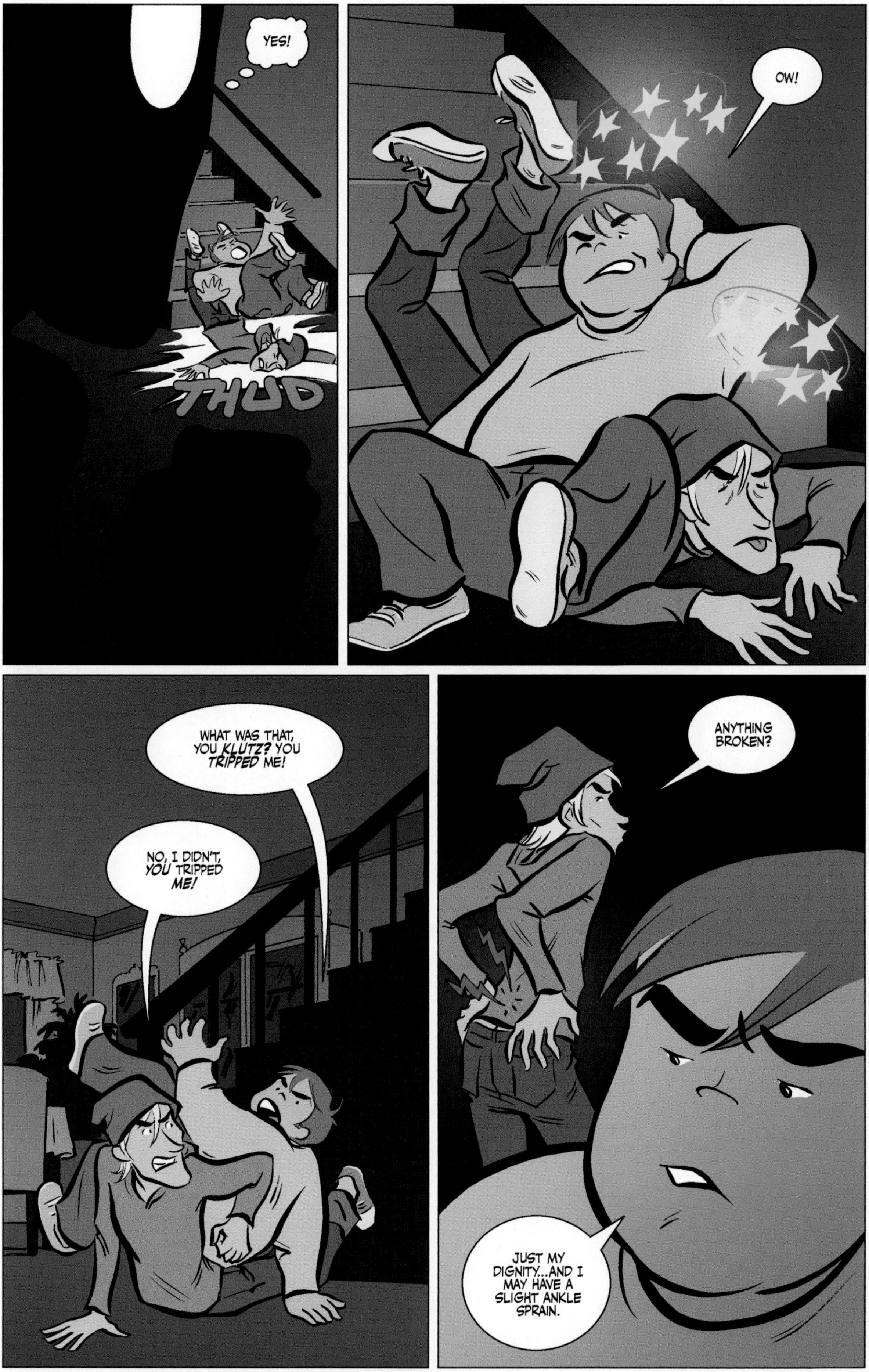
YES!
THUD
OW!
WHAT WAS THAT, YOU KLUTZ? YOU TRIPPED ME!
NO, I DIDN'T, YOU TRIPPED ME!
ANYTHING BROKEN?
JUST MY DIGNITY...AND I MAY HAVE A SLIGHT ANKLE SPRAIN.

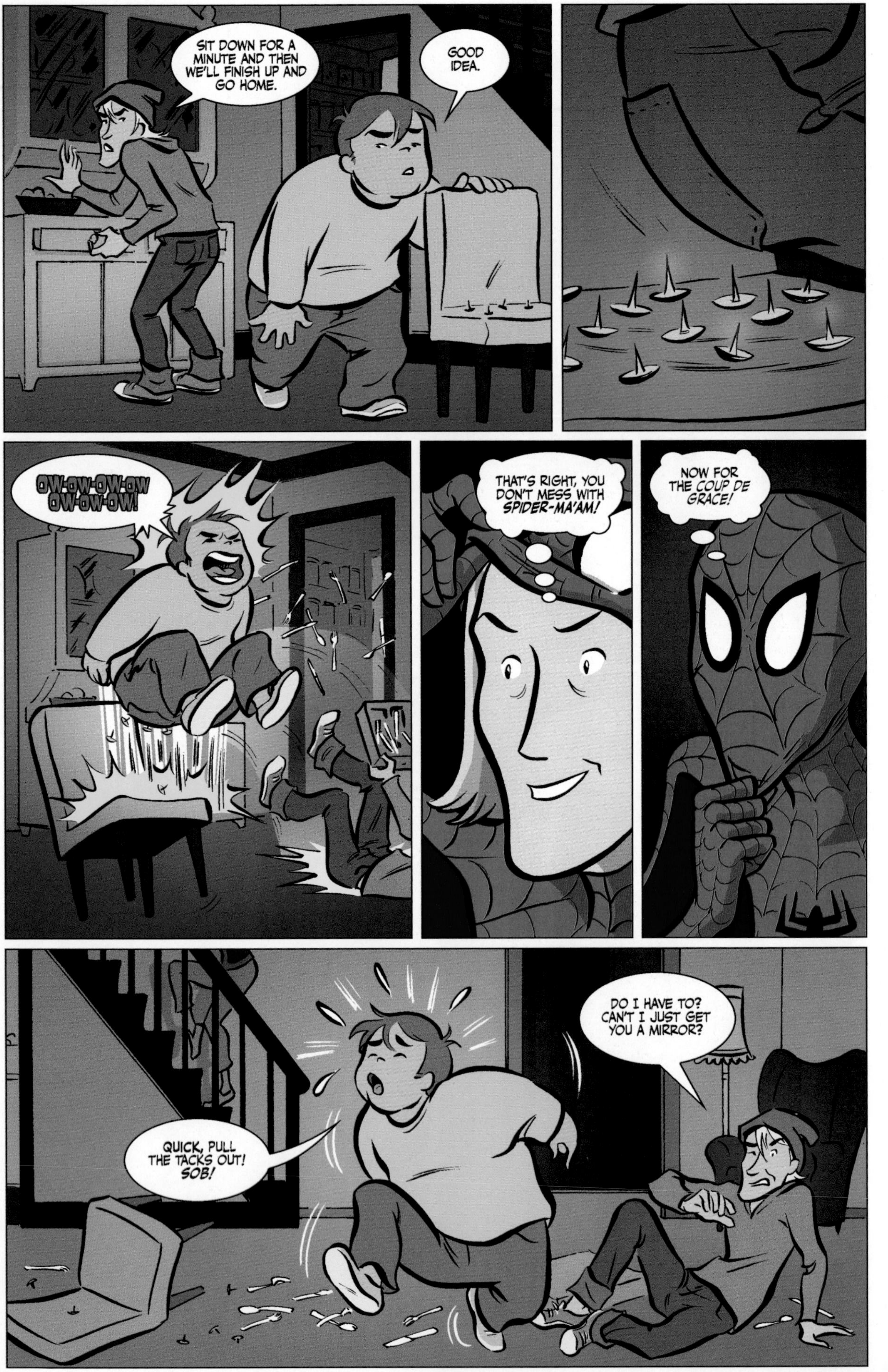
SIT DOWN FOR A MINUTE AND THEN WE'LL FINISH UP AND GO HOME.
GOOD IDEA.
OW-OW-OW-OW OW-OW-OW!
THAT'S RIGHT, YOU DON'T MESS WITH SPIDER-MA'AM!
NOW FOR THE COUP DE GRACE!
QUICK, PULL THE TACKS OUT! SOB!
DO I HAVE TO? CAN'T I JUST GET YOU A MIRROR?

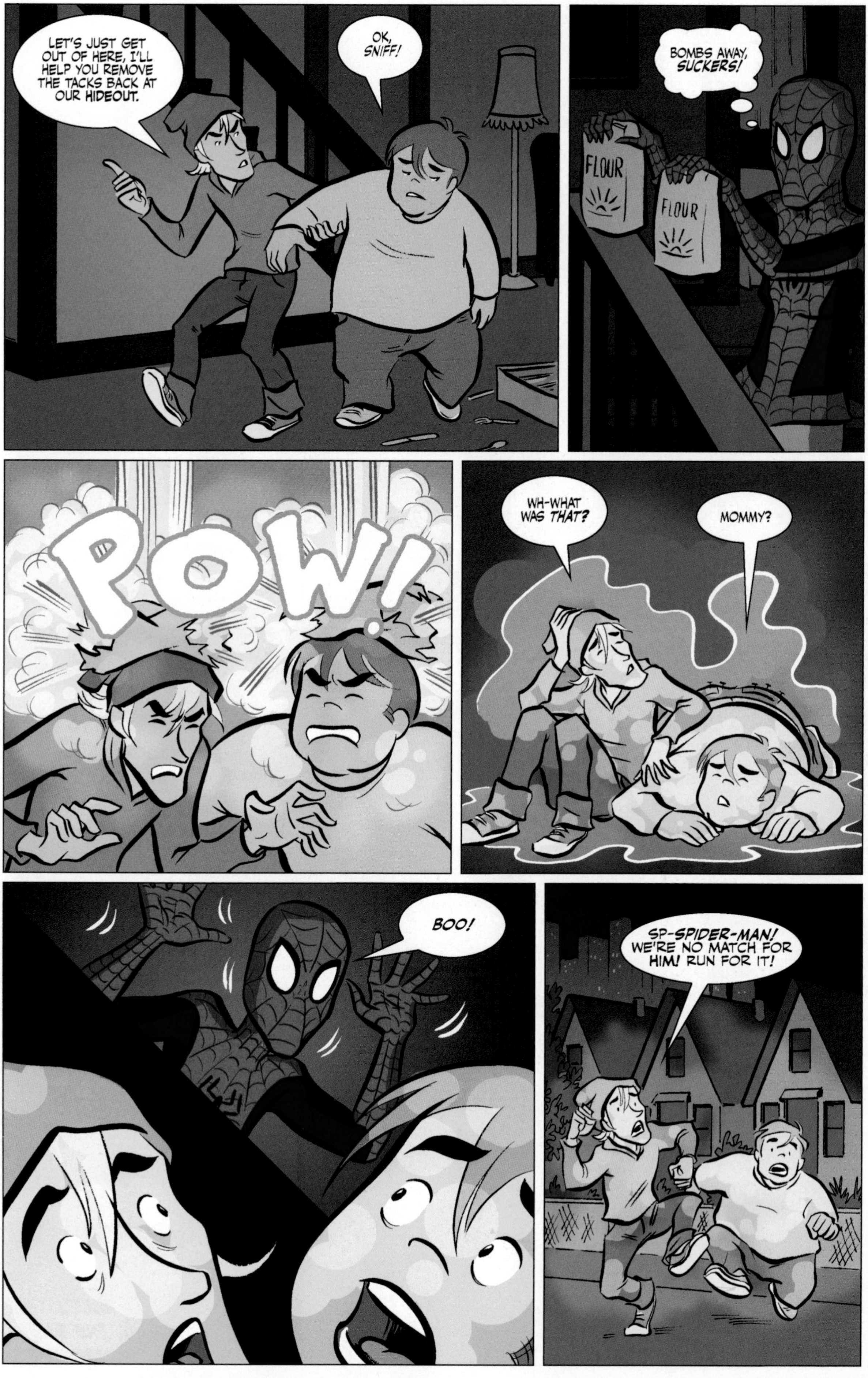
LET'S JUST GET OUT OF HERE, I'LL HELP YOU REMOVE THE TACKS BACK AT OUR HIDEOUT.
OK, SNIFF!
BOMBS AWAY, SUCKERS!
FLOUR
FLOUR
POW!
WH-WHAT WAS THAT?
MOMMY?
BOO!
SP-SPIDER-MAN! WE'RE NO MATCH FOR HIM! RUN FOR IT!

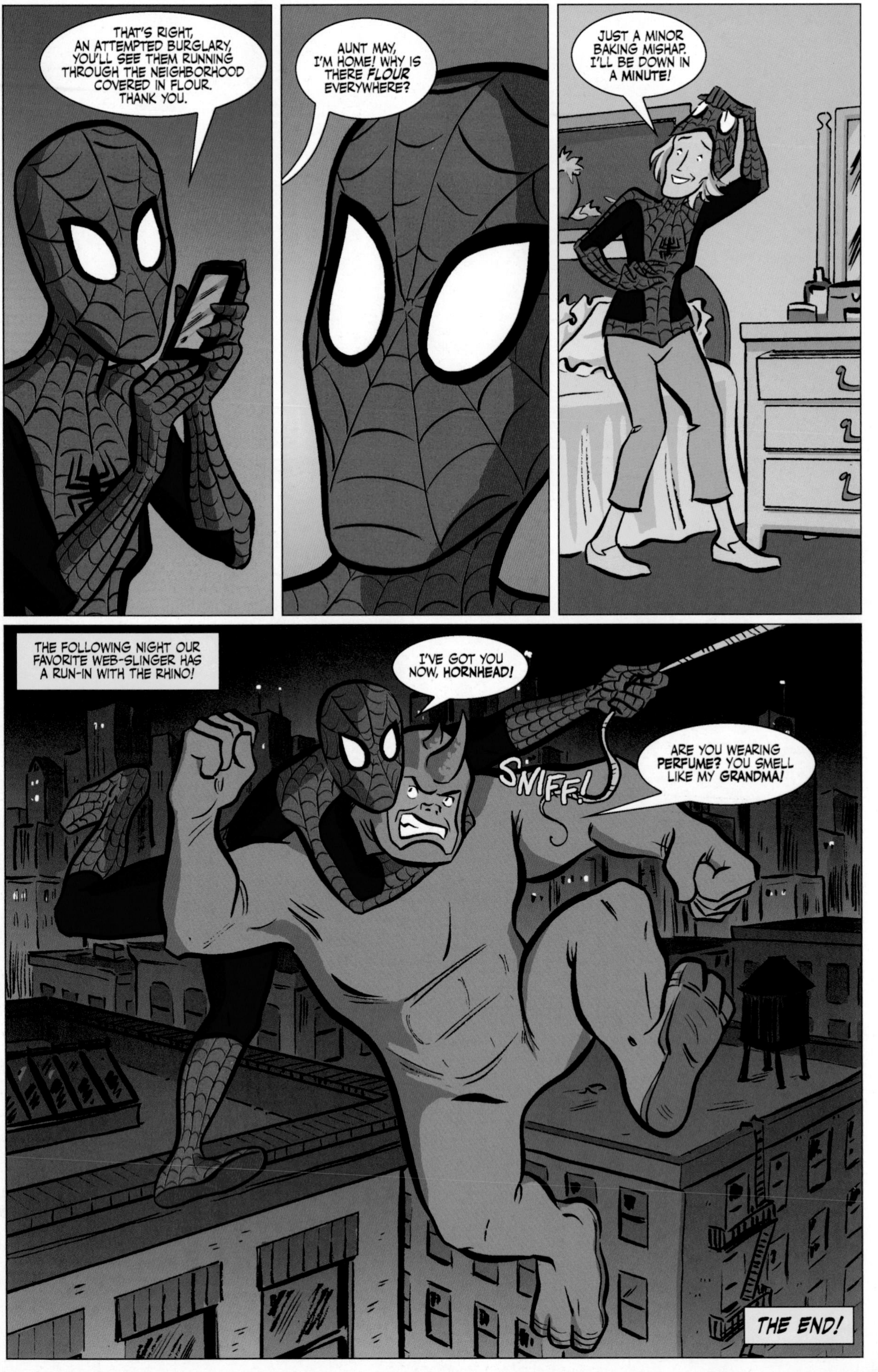
THAT'S RIGHT, AN ATTEMPTED BURGLARY, YOU'LL SEE THEM RUNNING THROUGH THE NEIGHBORHOOD COVERED IN FLOUR. THANK YOU.
AUNT MAY, I'M HOME! WHY IS THERE FLOUR EVERYWHERE?
JUST A MINOR BAKING MISHAP. I'LL BE DOWN IN A MINUTE!
THE FOLLOWING NIGHT OUR FAVORITE WEB-SLINGER HAS A RUN-IN WITH THE RHINO!
I'VE GOT YOU NOW, HORNHEAD!
SNIFF!
ARE YOU WEARING PERFUME? YOU SMELL LIKE MY GRANDMA!
THE END!

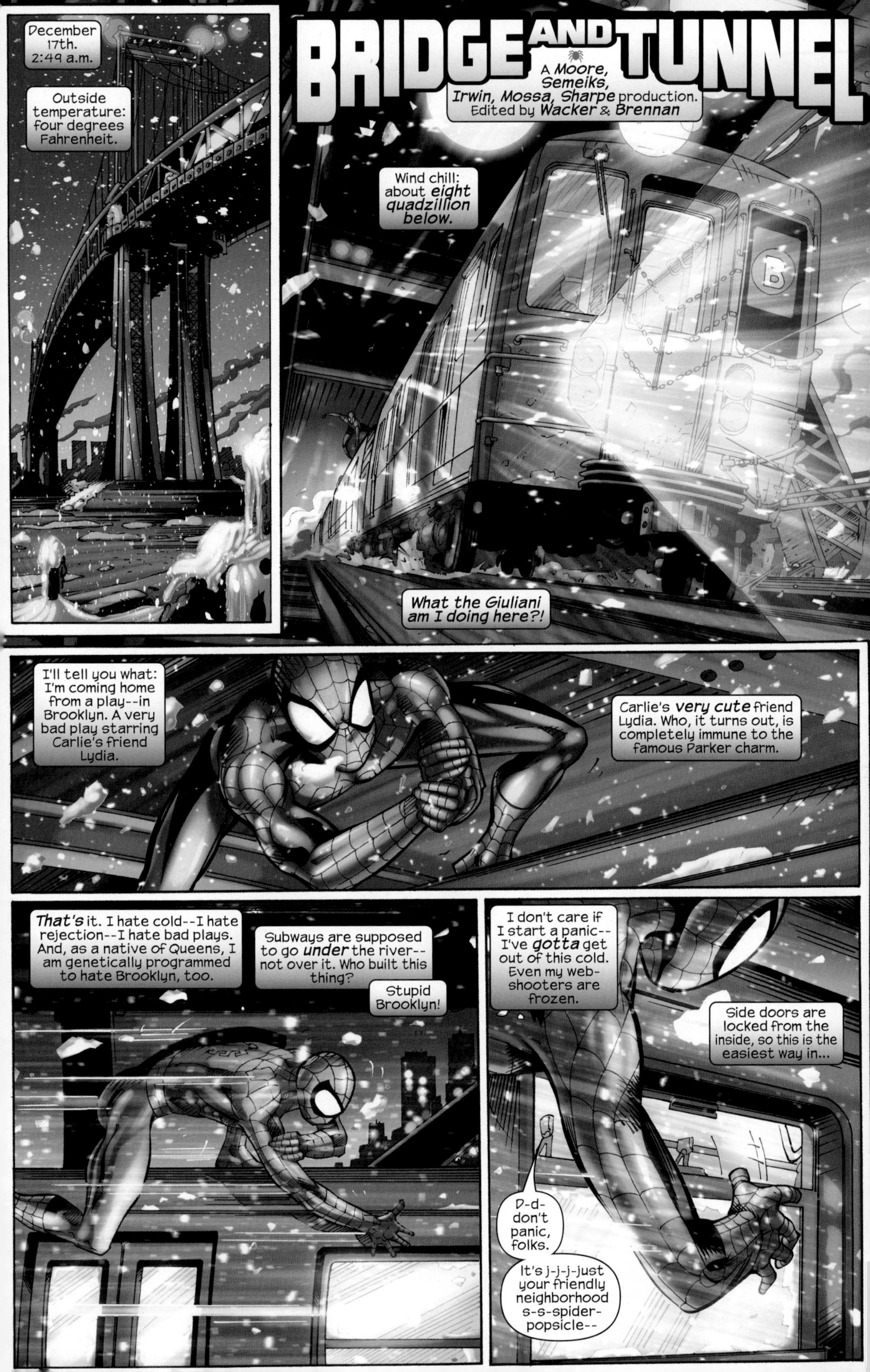
December 17th. 2:49 a.m.
Outside temperature: four degrees Fahrenheit.
BRIDGE AND TUNNEL
A Moore, Semeiks, Irwin, Mossa, Sharpe production. Edited by Wacker & Brennan
Wind chill: about eight quadzillion below.
What the Giuliani am I doing here?!
I'll tell you what: I'm coming home from a play--in Brooklyn. A very bad play starring Carlie's friend Lydia.
Carlie's very cute friend Lydia. Who, it turns out, is completely immune to the famous Parker charm.
That's it. I hate cold--I hate rejection--I hate bad plays. And, as a native of Queens, I am genetically programmed to hate Brooklyn, too.
Subways are supposed to go under the river--not over it. Who built this thing?
Stupid Brooklyn!
I don't care if I start a panic--I've gotta get out of this cold. Even my web-shooters are frozen.
Side doors are locked from the inside, so this is the easiest way in...
D-d-don't panic, folks.
It's j-j-j-just your friendly neighborhood s-s-spider-popsicle--

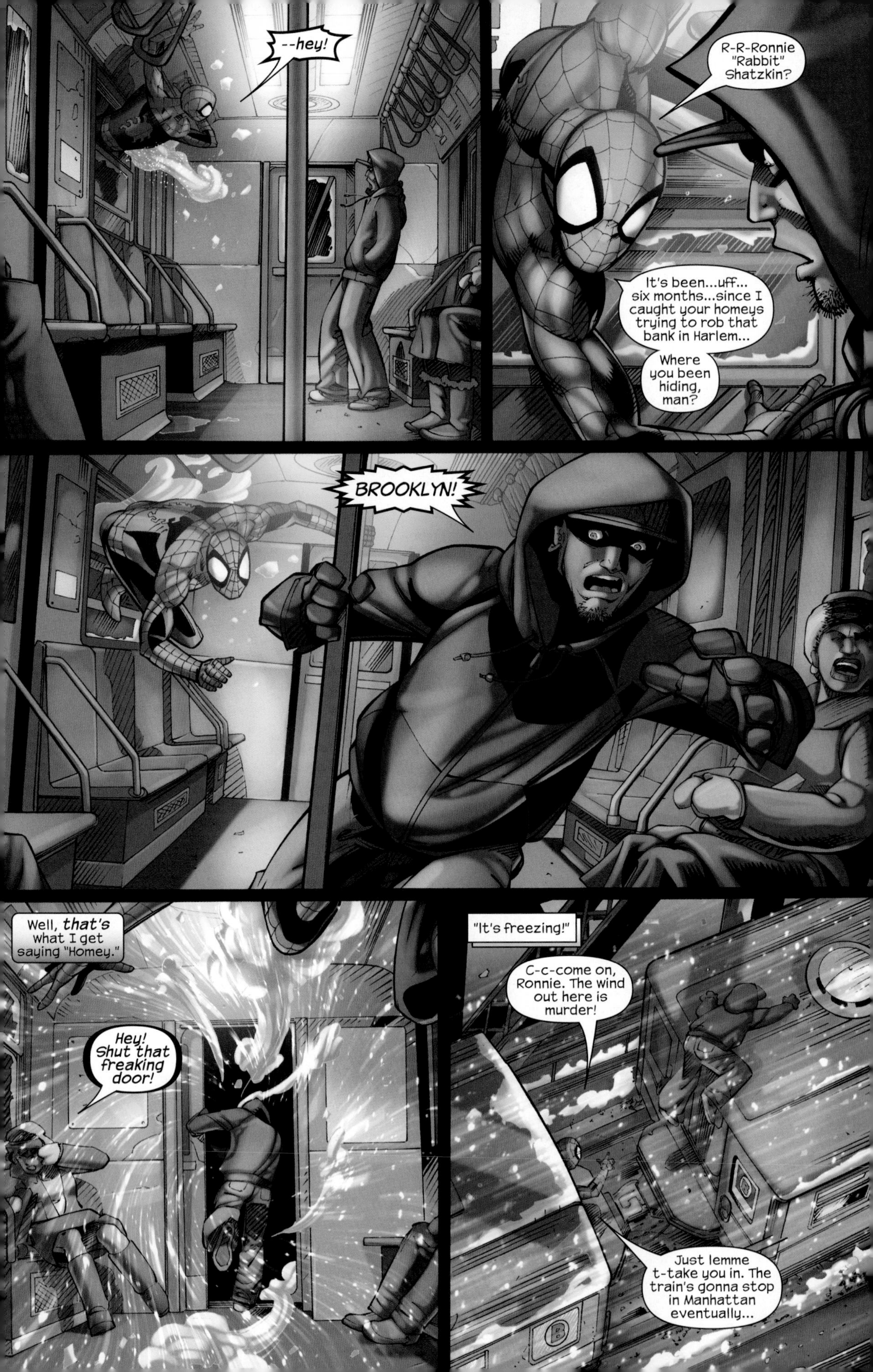
--hey!
R-R-Ronnie "Rabbit" Shatzkin?
It's been...uff... six months...since I caught your homeys trying to rob that bank in Harlem...
Where you been hiding, man?
BROOKLYN!
Well, that's what I get saying "Homey."
Hey! Shut that freaking door!
"It's freezing!"
C-c-come on, Ronnie. The wind out here is murder!
Just lemme t-take you in. The train's gonna stop in Manhattan eventually...

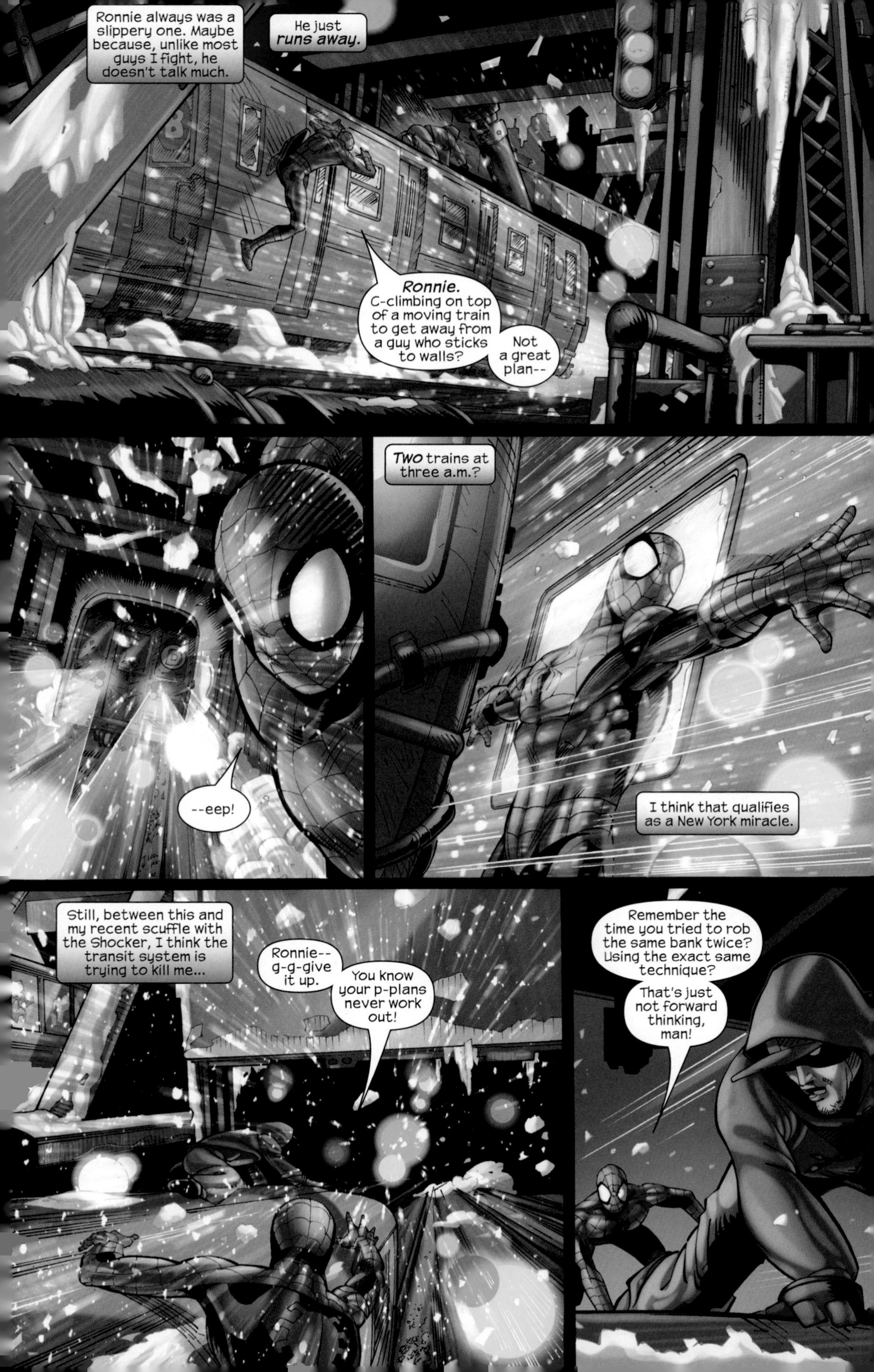

Ronnie always was a slippery one. Maybe because, unlike most guys I fight, he doesn't talk much.
He just *runs away.*
Ronnie. C-climbing on top of a moving train to get away from a guy who sticks to walls?
Not a great plan--
--eep!
TWO trains at three a.m.?
I think that qualifies as a New York miracle.
Still, between this and my recent scuffle with the Shocker, I think the transit system is trying to kill me...
Ronnie-- g-g-give it up.
You know your p-plans never work out!
Remember the time you tried to rob the same bank twice? Using the exact same technique?
That's just not forward thinking, man!

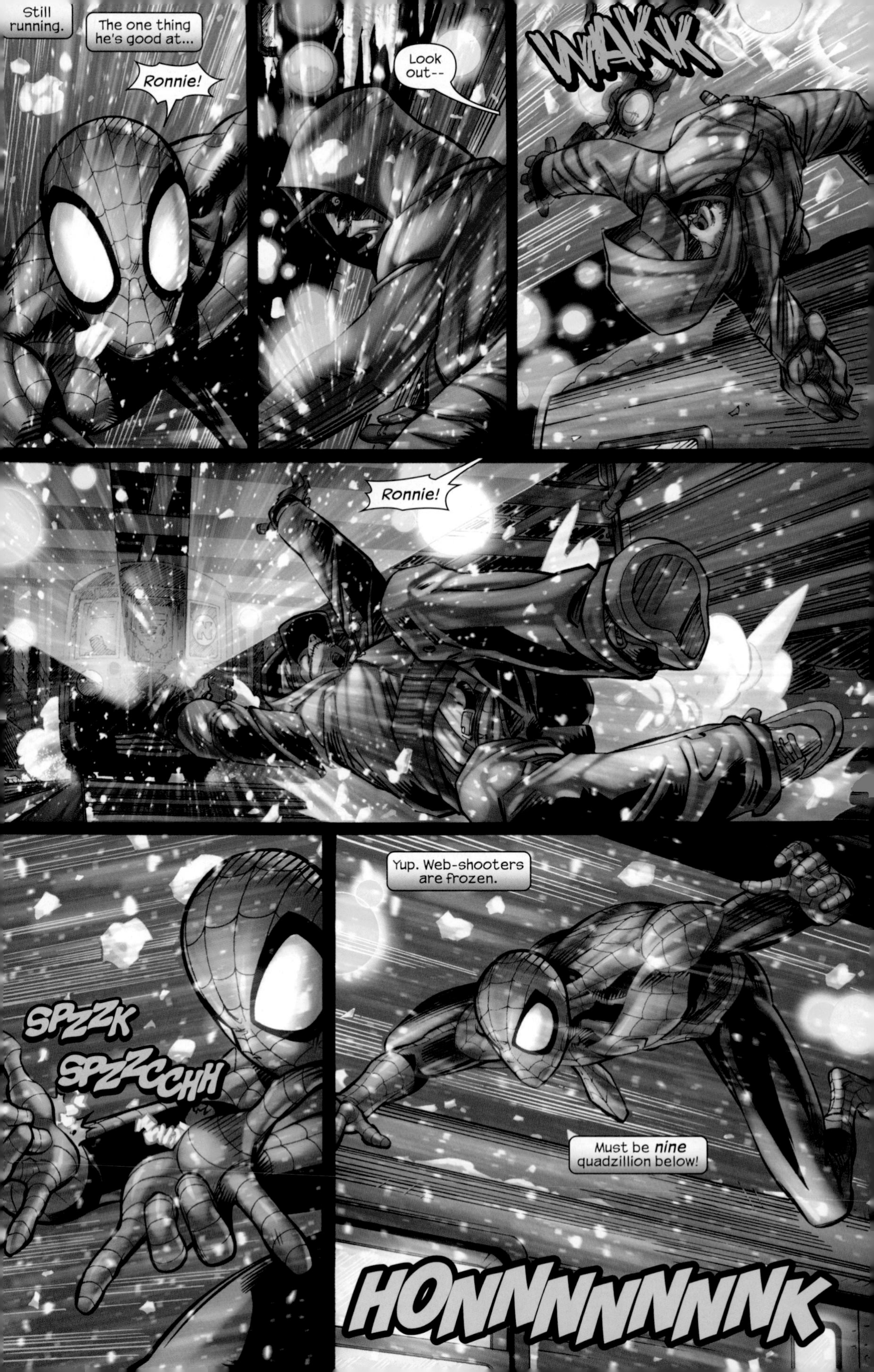

Still running.
The one thing he's good at...
Ronnie!
Look out--
WAKK
Ronnie!
Yup. Web-shooters are frozen.
SPZZK
SPZZCCHH
Must be *nine* quadzillion below!
HONNNNNNNK

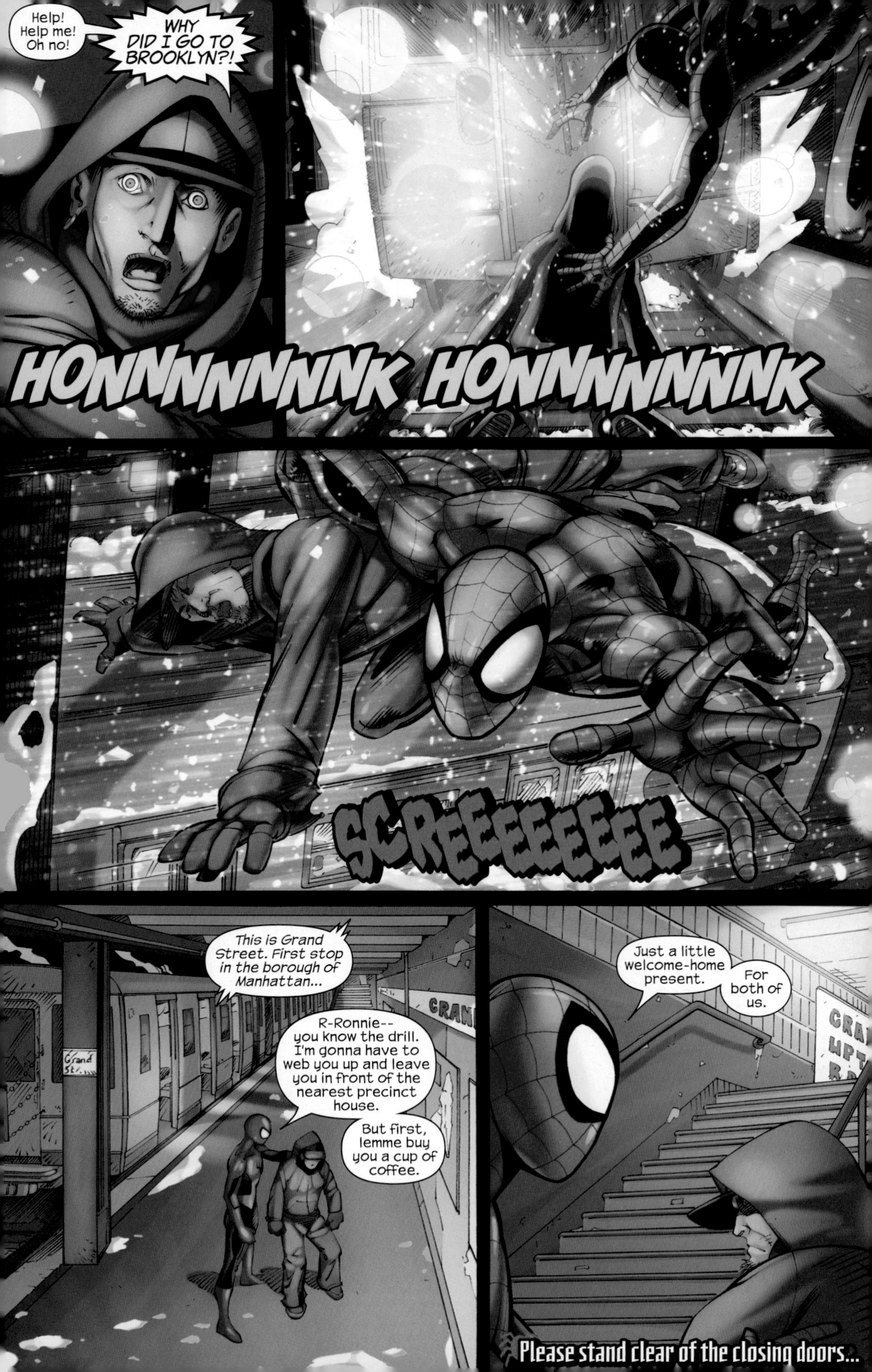

Help! Help me! Oh no!
WHY DID I GO TO BROOKLYN?!
HONNNNNNNK HONNNNNNNK
SCREEEEEEEEE
This is Grand Street. First stop in the borough of Manhattan...
Grand St.
R-Ronnie-- you know the drill. I'm gonna have to web you up and leave you in front of the nearest precinct house.
But first, lemme buy you a cup of coffee.
Just a little welcome-home present.
For both of us.
Please stand clear of the closing doors...

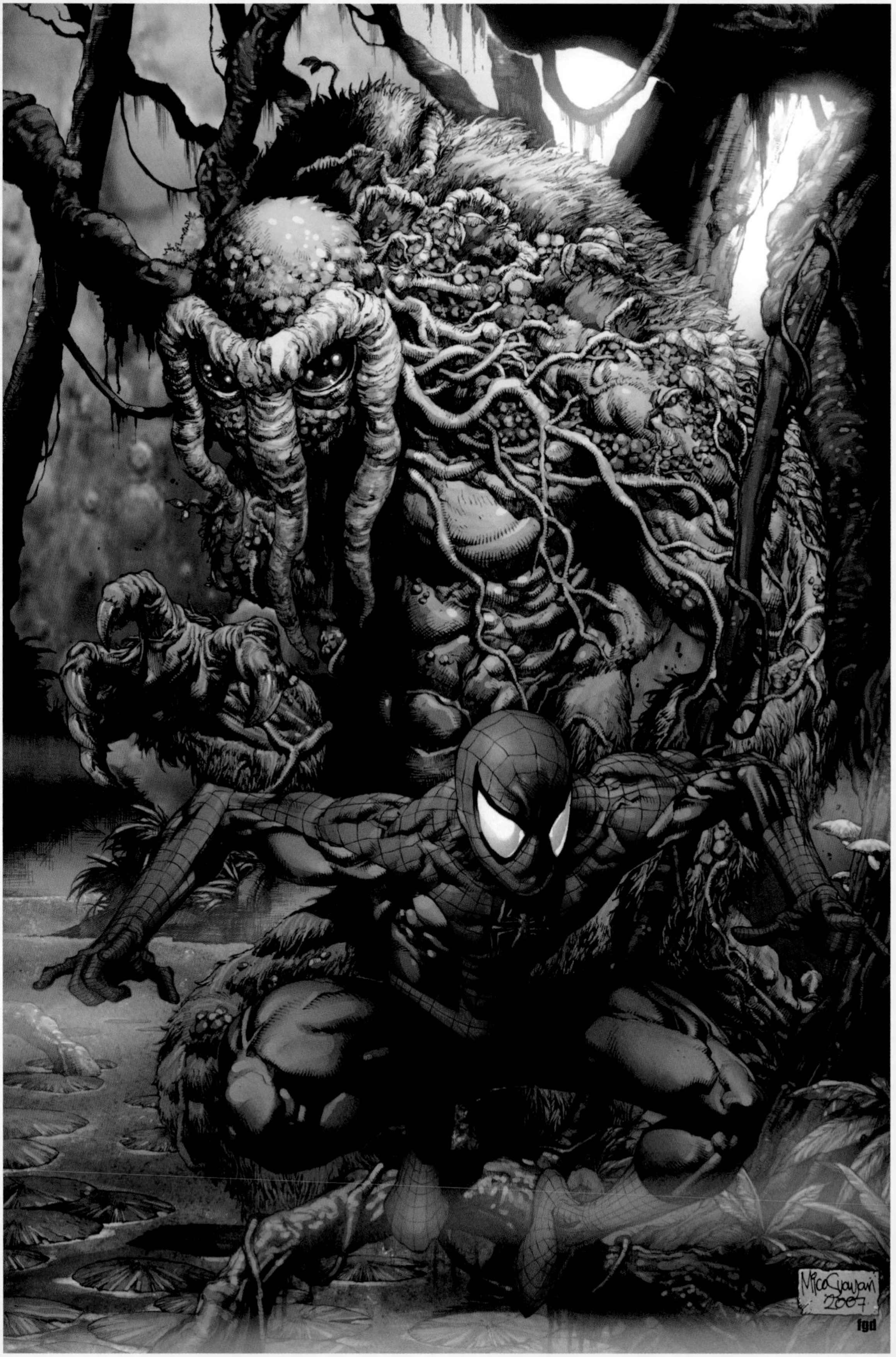
fgd

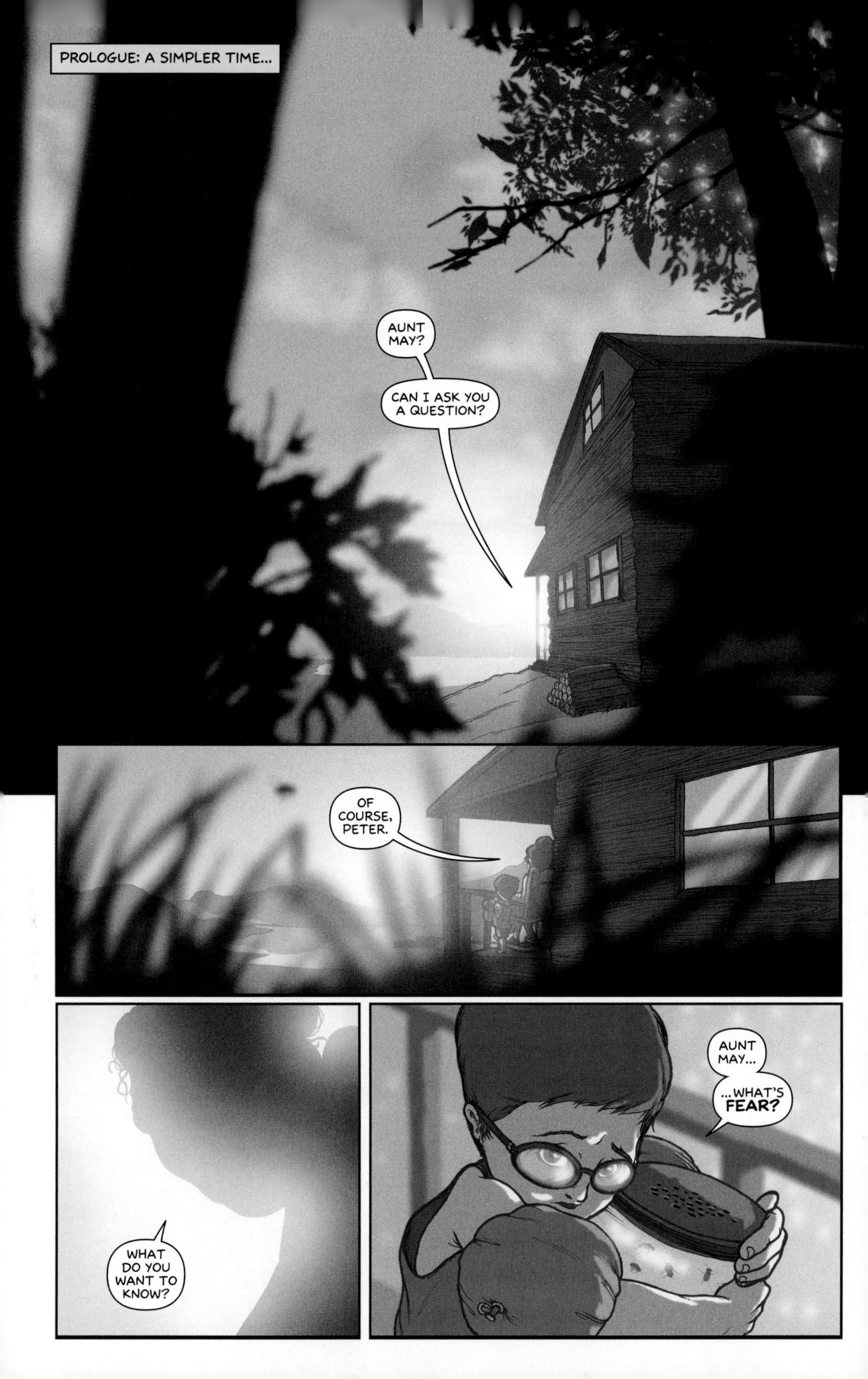
PROLOGUE: A SIMPLER TIME...
AUNT MAY?
CAN I ASK YOU A QUESTION?
OF COURSE, PETER.
WHAT DO YOU WANT TO KNOW?
AUNT MAY...
...WHAT'S **FEAR?**

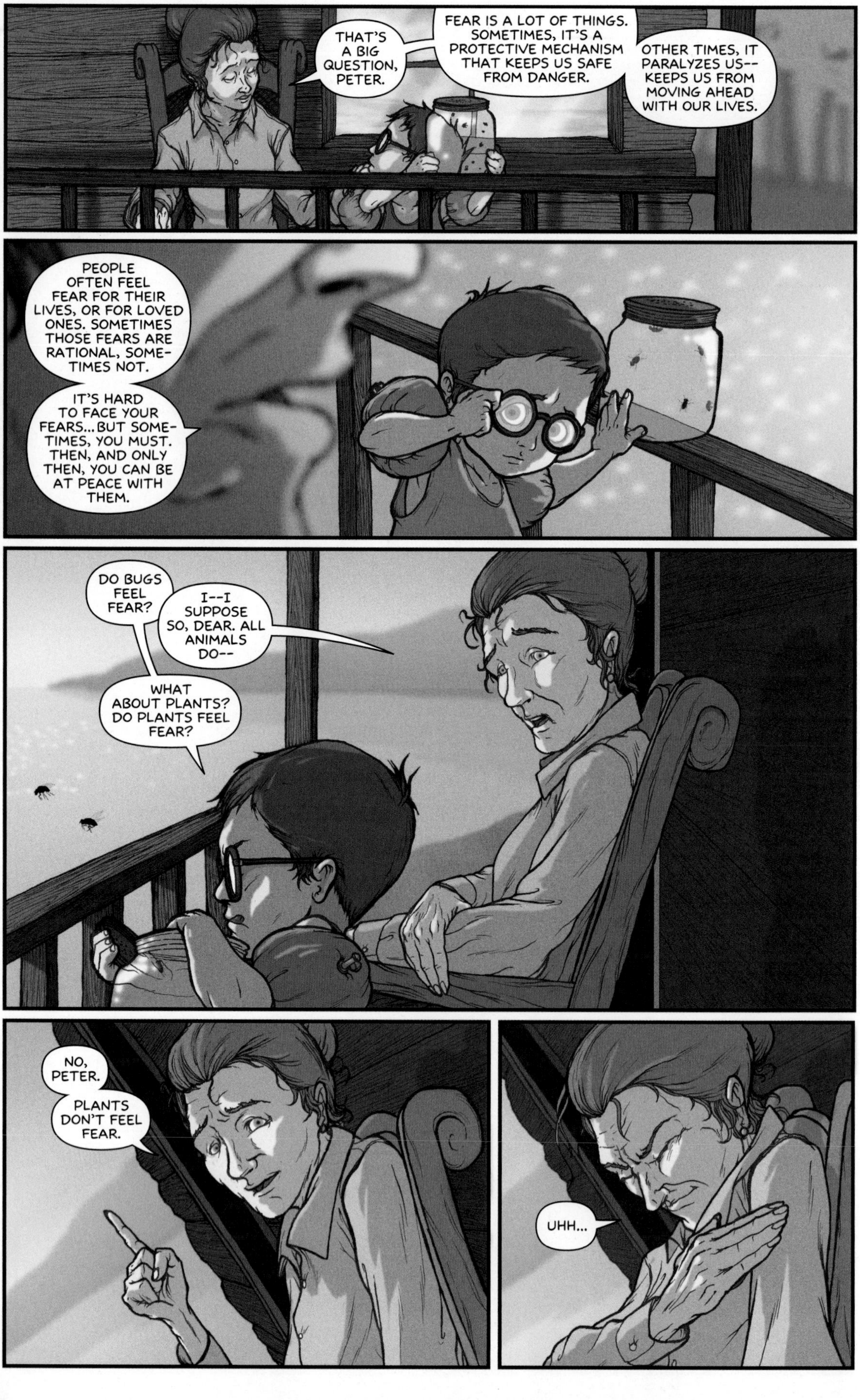
THAT'S A BIG QUESTION, PETER.
FEAR IS A LOT OF THINGS. SOMETIMES, IT'S A PROTECTIVE MECHANISM THAT KEEPS US SAFE FROM DANGER.
OTHER TIMES, IT PARALYZES US-- KEEPS US FROM MOVING AHEAD WITH OUR LIVES.
PEOPLE OFTEN FEEL FEAR FOR THEIR LIVES, OR FOR LOVED ONES. SOMETIMES THOSE FEARS ARE RATIONAL, SOME-TIMES NOT.
IT'S HARD TO FACE YOUR FEARS...BUT SOME-TIMES, YOU MUST. THEN, AND ONLY THEN, YOU CAN BE AT PEACE WITH THEM.
DO BUGS FEEL FEAR?
I--I SUPPOSE SO, DEAR. ALL ANIMALS DO--
WHAT ABOUT PLANTS? DO PLANTS FEEL FEAR?
NO, PETER.
PLANTS DON'T FEEL FEAR.
UHH...

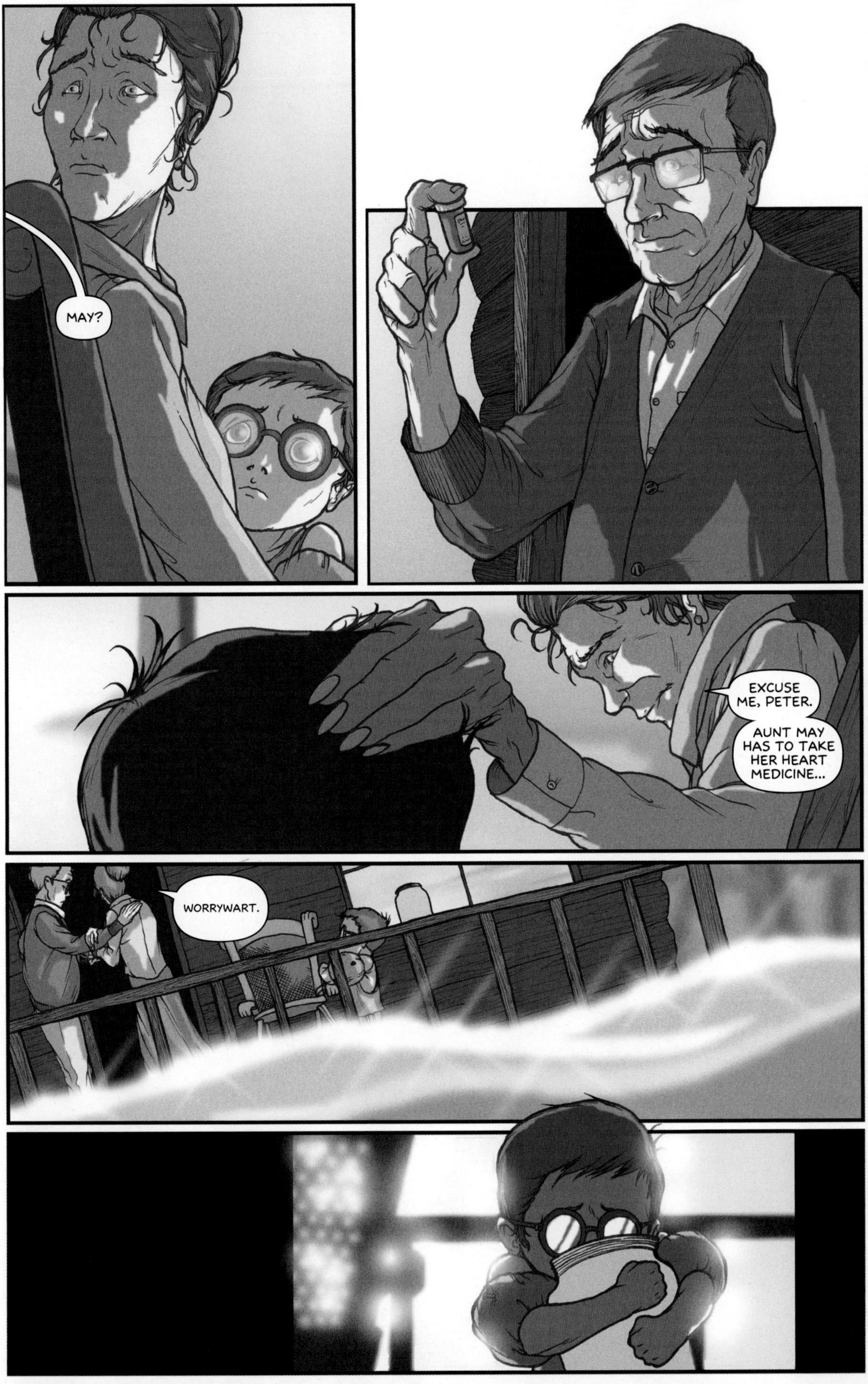
MAY?
EXCUSE ME, PETER.
AUNT MAY HAS TO TAKE HER HEART MEDICINE...
WORRYWART.

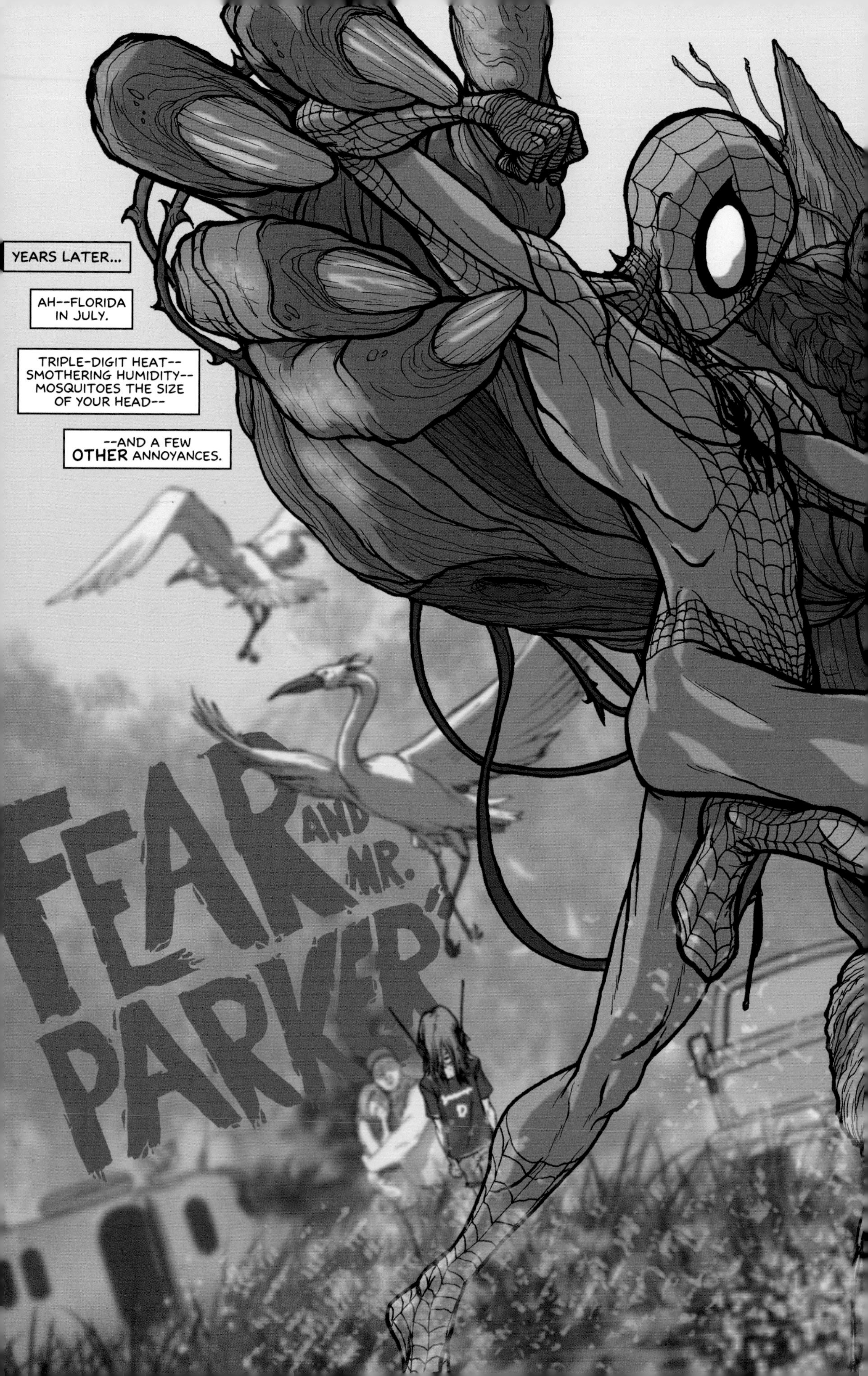

YEARS LATER...
AH--FLORIDA IN JULY.
TRIPLE-DIGIT HEAT-- SMOTHERING HUMIDITY-- MOSQUITOES THE SIZE OF YOUR HEAD--
--AND A FEW OTHER ANNOYANCES.
"FEAR AND MR. PARKER"

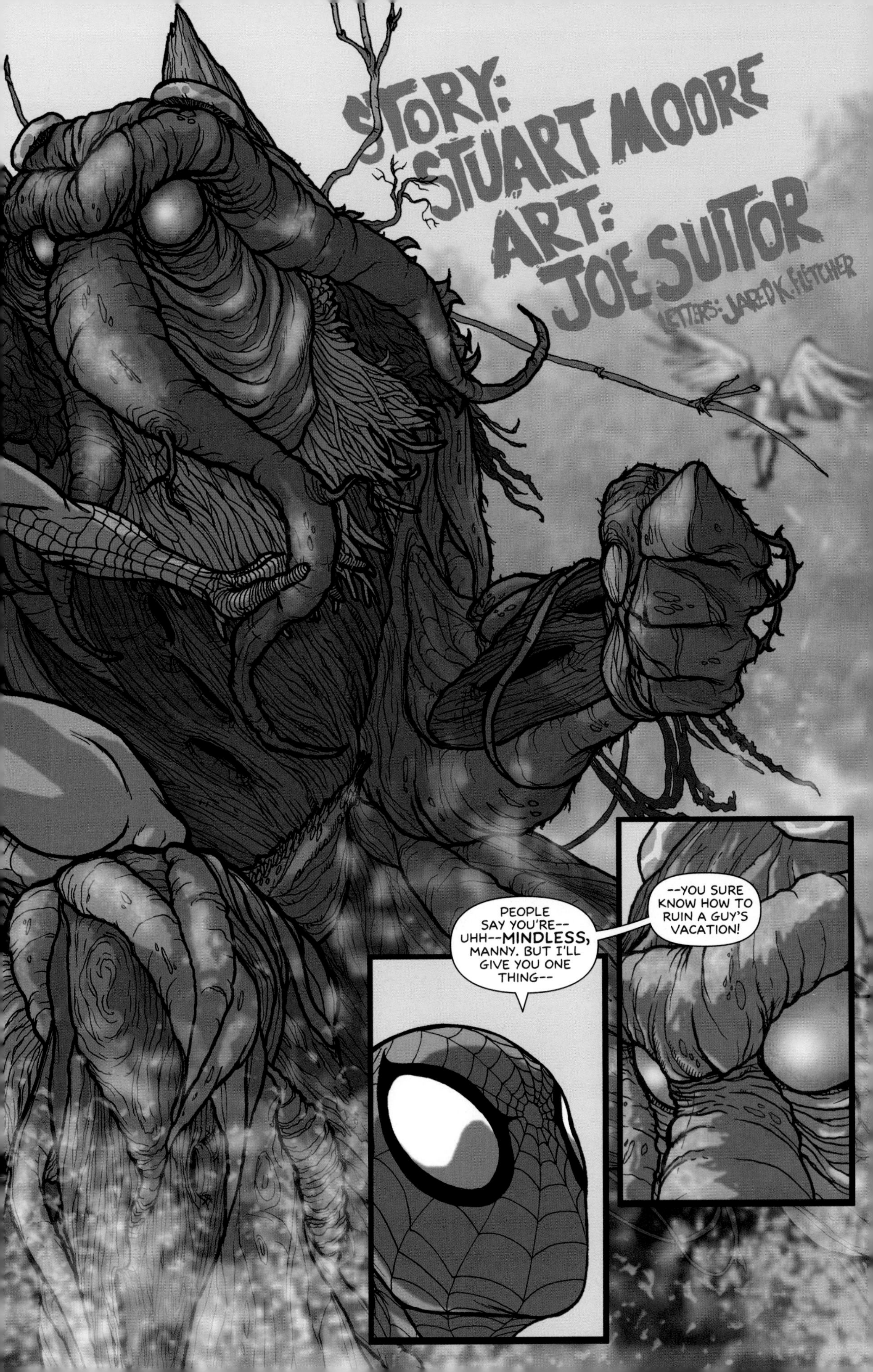
STORY:
STUART MOORE
ART:
JOE SUITOR
LETTERS: JARED K. FLETCHER
PEOPLE SAY YOU'RE-- UHH--MINDLESS, MANNY. BUT I'LL GIVE YOU ONE THING--
--YOU SURE KNOW HOW TO RUIN A GUY'S VACATION!

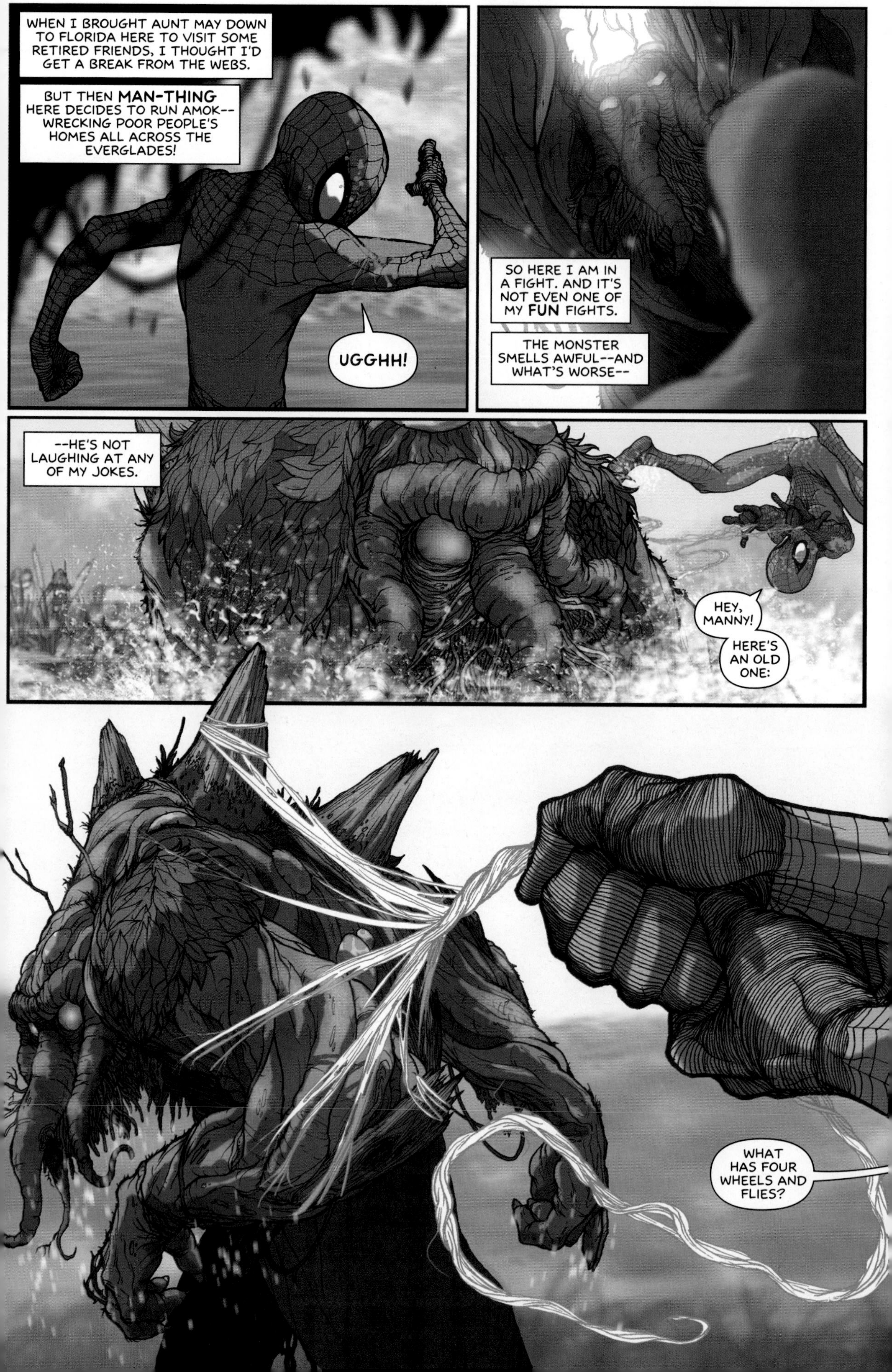
WHEN I BROUGHT AUNT MAY DOWN TO FLORIDA HERE TO VISIT SOME RETIRED FRIENDS, I THOUGHT I'D GET A BREAK FROM THE WEBS.
BUT THEN MAN-THING HERE DECIDES TO RUN AMOK-- WRECKING POOR PEOPLE'S HOMES ALL ACROSS THE EVERGLADES!
UGGHH!
SO HERE I AM IN A FIGHT. AND IT'S NOT EVEN ONE OF MY FUN FIGHTS.
THE MONSTER SMELLS AWFUL--AND WHAT'S WORSE--
--HE'S NOT LAUGHING AT ANY OF MY JOKES.
HEY, MANNY!
HERE'S AN OLD ONE:
WHAT HAS FOUR WHEELS AND FLIES?

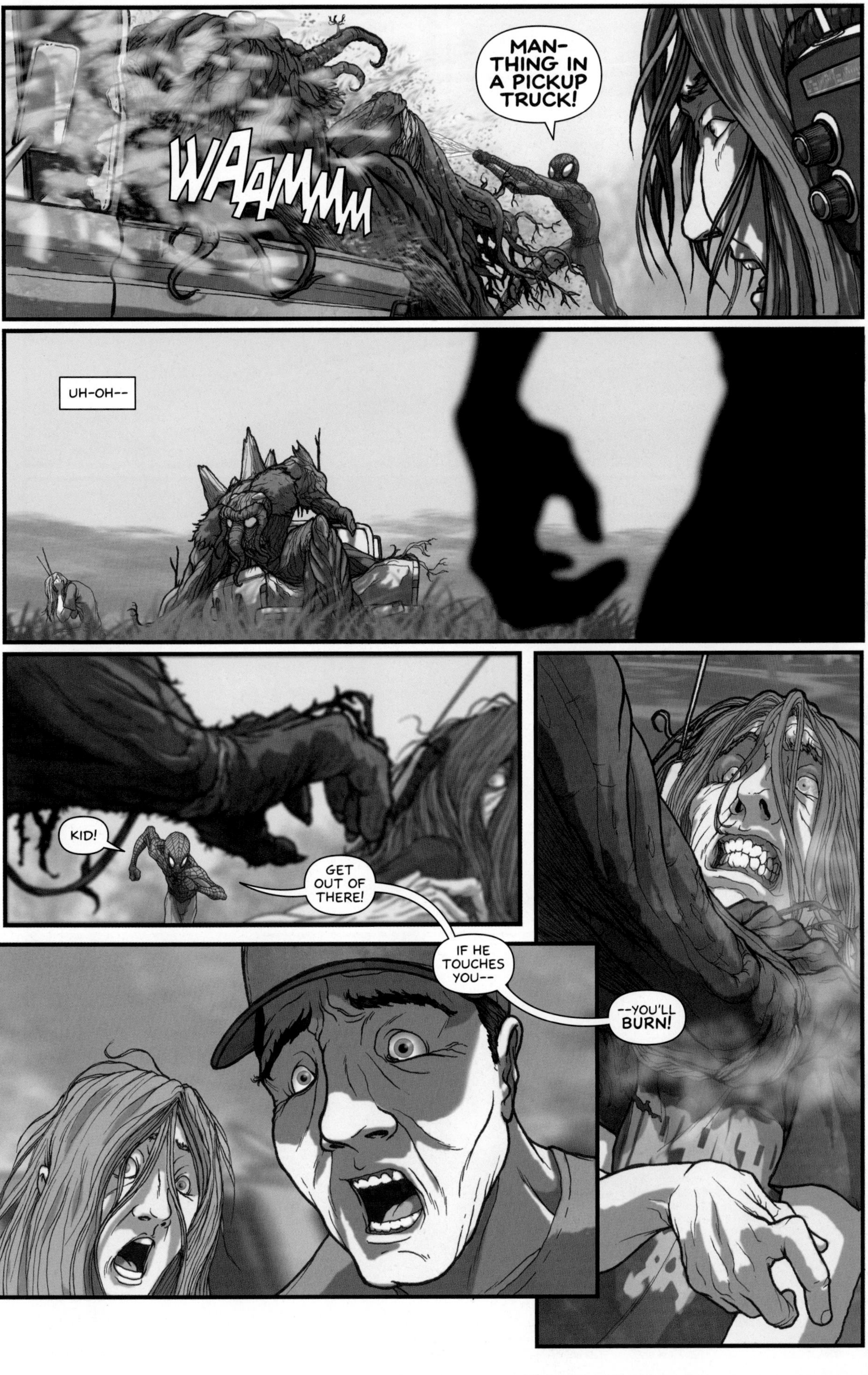
MAN-THING IN A PICKUP TRUCK!
WAAMMMM
UH-OH--
KID!
GET OUT OF THERE!
IF HE TOUCHES YOU--
--YOU'LL BURN!

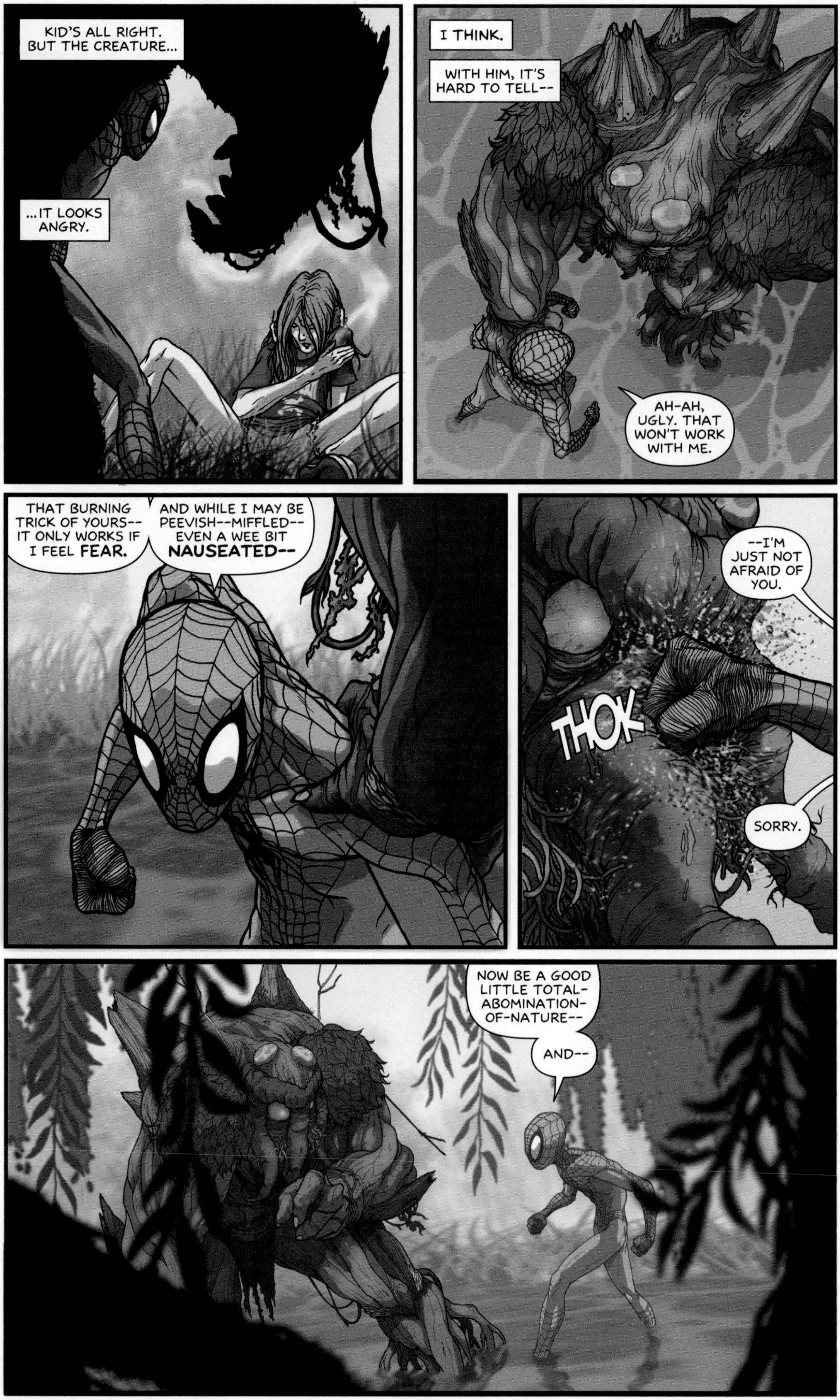

KID'S ALL RIGHT. BUT THE CREATURE...
...IT LOOKS ANGRY.
I THINK.
WITH HIM, IT'S HARD TO TELL--
AH-AH, UGLY. THAT WON'T WORK WITH ME.
THAT BURNING TRICK OF YOURS-- IT ONLY WORKS IF I FEEL **FEAR.**
AND WHILE I MAY BE PEEVISH--MIFFLED-- EVEN A WEE BIT **NAUSEATED--**
--I'M JUST NOT AFRAID OF YOU.
THOK
SORRY.
NOW BE A GOOD LITTLE TOTAL-ABOMINATION-OF-NATURE--
AND--

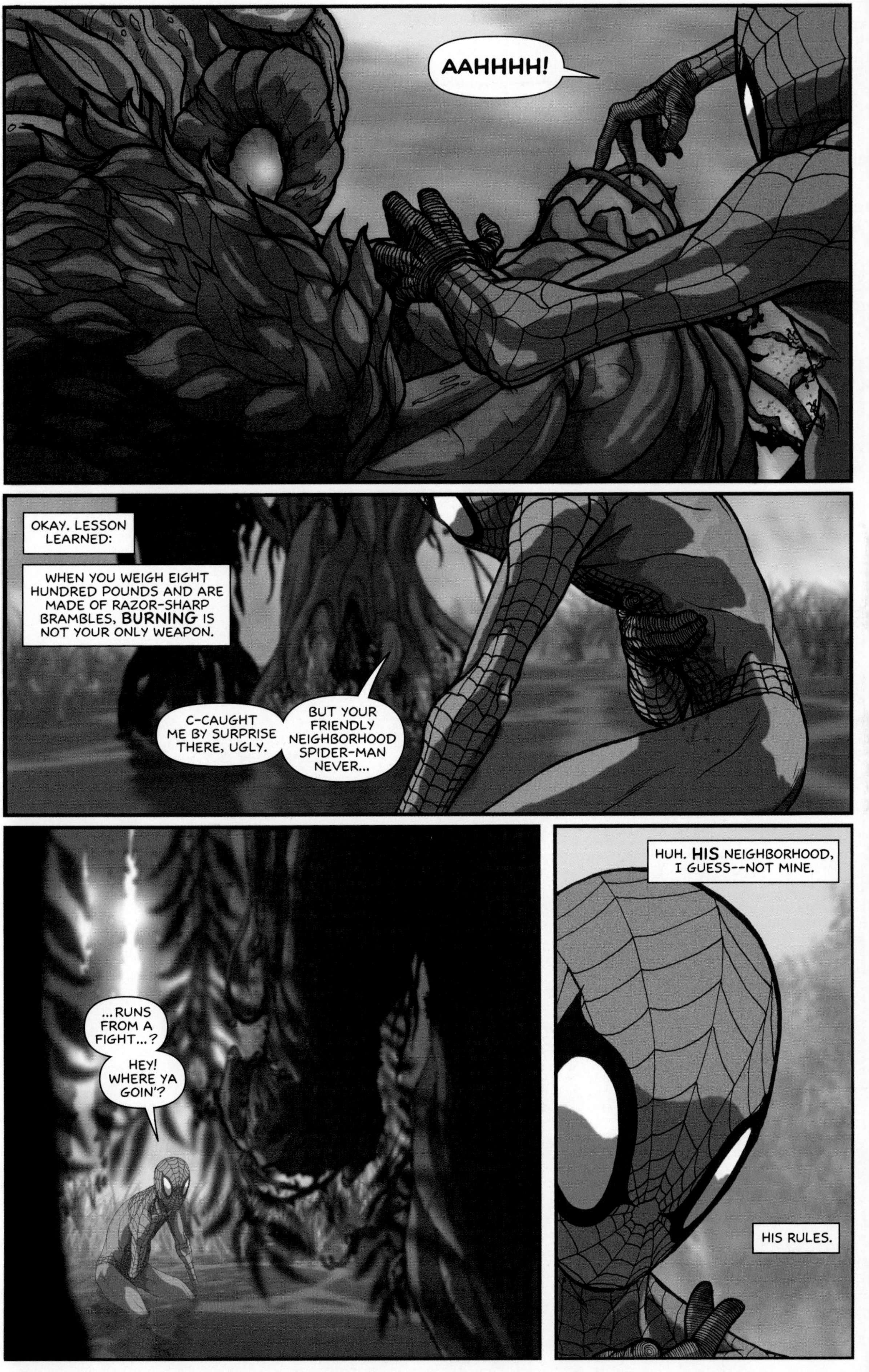
AAHHHH!
OKAY. LESSON LEARNED:
WHEN YOU WEIGH EIGHT HUNDRED POUNDS AND ARE MADE OF RAZOR-SHARP BRAMBLES, BURNING IS NOT YOUR ONLY WEAPON.
C-CAUGHT ME BY SURPRISE THERE, UGLY.
BUT YOUR FRIENDLY NEIGHBORHOOD SPIDER-MAN NEVER...
...RUNS FROM A FIGHT...?
HEY! WHERE YA GOIN'?
HUH. HIS NEIGHBORHOOD, I GUESS--NOT MINE.
HIS RULES.

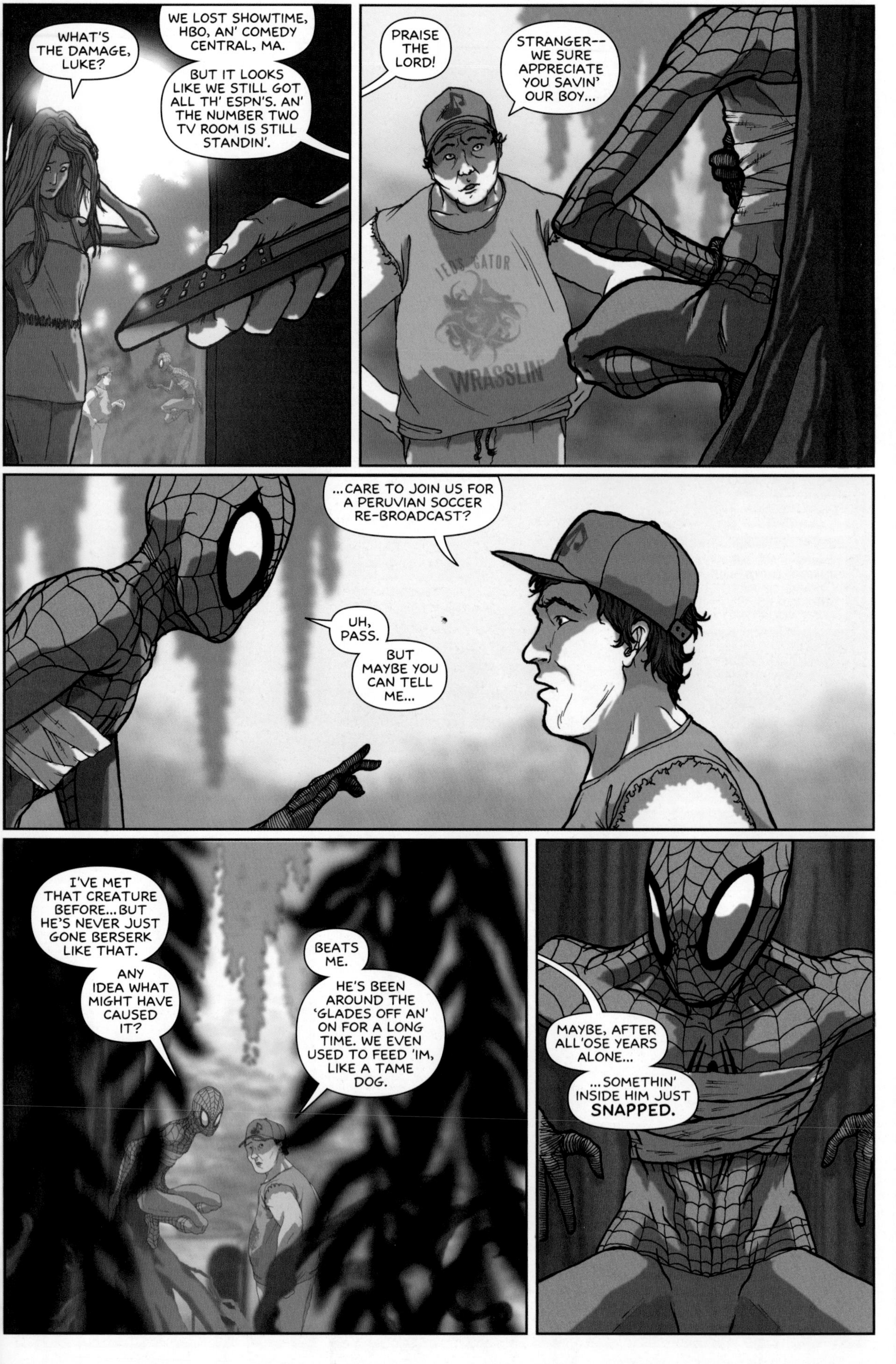
WHAT'S THE DAMAGE, LUKE?
WE LOST SHOWTIME, HBO, AN' COMEDY CENTRAL, MA.
BUT IT LOOKS LIKE WE STILL GOT ALL TH' ESPN'S. AN' THE NUMBER TWO TV ROOM IS STILL STANDIN'.
PRAISE THE LORD!
STRANGER-- WE SURE APPRECIATE YOU SAVIN' OUR BOY...
JEDS GATOR
WRASSLIN'
...CARE TO JOIN US FOR A PERUVIAN SOCCER RE-BROADCAST?
UH, PASS.
BUT MAYBE YOU CAN TELL ME...
I'VE MET THAT CREATURE BEFORE...BUT HE'S NEVER JUST GONE BERSERK LIKE THAT.
ANY IDEA WHAT MIGHT HAVE CAUSED IT?
BEATS ME.
HE'S BEEN AROUND THE 'GLADES OFF AN' ON FOR A LONG TIME. WE EVEN USED TO FEED 'IM, LIKE A TAME DOG.
MAYBE, AFTER ALL'OSE YEARS ALONE...
...SOMETHIN' INSIDE HIM JUST SNAPPED.

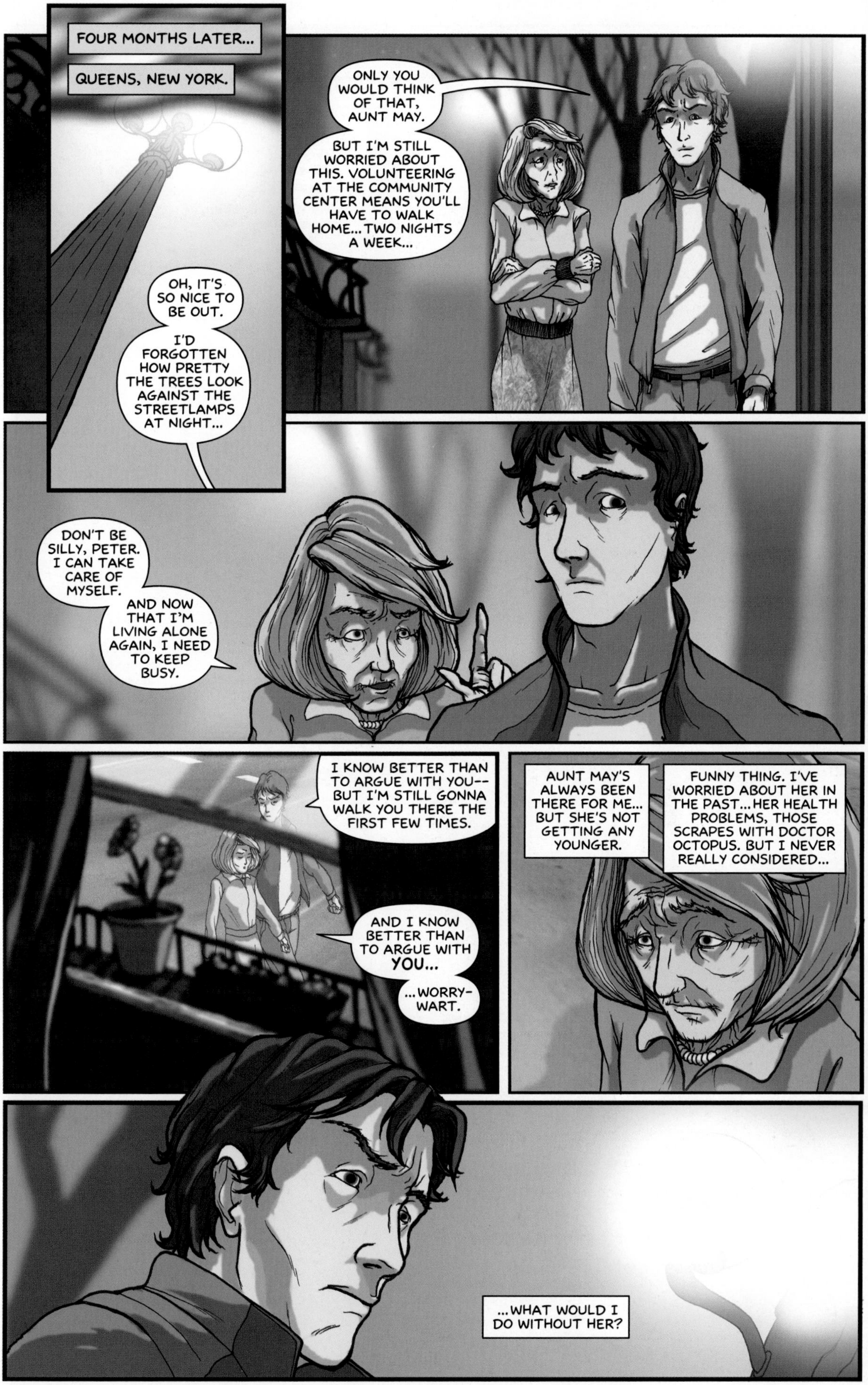
FOUR MONTHS LATER...
QUEENS, NEW YORK.
OH, IT'S SO NICE TO BE OUT.
I'D FORGOTTEN HOW PRETTY THE TREES LOOK AGAINST THE STREETLAMPS AT NIGHT...
ONLY YOU WOULD THINK OF THAT, AUNT MAY.
BUT I'M STILL WORRIED ABOUT THIS. VOLUNTEERING AT THE COMMUNITY CENTER MEANS YOU'LL HAVE TO WALK HOME...TWO NIGHTS A WEEK...
DON'T BE SILLY, PETER. I CAN TAKE CARE OF MYSELF.
AND NOW THAT I'M LIVING ALONE AGAIN, I NEED TO KEEP BUSY.
I KNOW BETTER THAN TO ARGUE WITH YOU-- BUT I'M STILL GONNA WALK YOU THERE THE FIRST FEW TIMES.
AND I KNOW BETTER THAN TO ARGUE WITH YOU...
...WORRY-WART.
AUNT MAY'S ALWAYS BEEN THERE FOR ME... BUT SHE'S NOT GETTING ANY YOUNGER.
FUNNY THING. I'VE WORRIED ABOUT HER IN THE PAST...HER HEALTH PROBLEMS, THOSE SCRAPES WITH DOCTOR OCTOPUS. BUT I NEVER REALLY CONSIDERED...
...WHAT WOULD I DO WITHOUT HER?

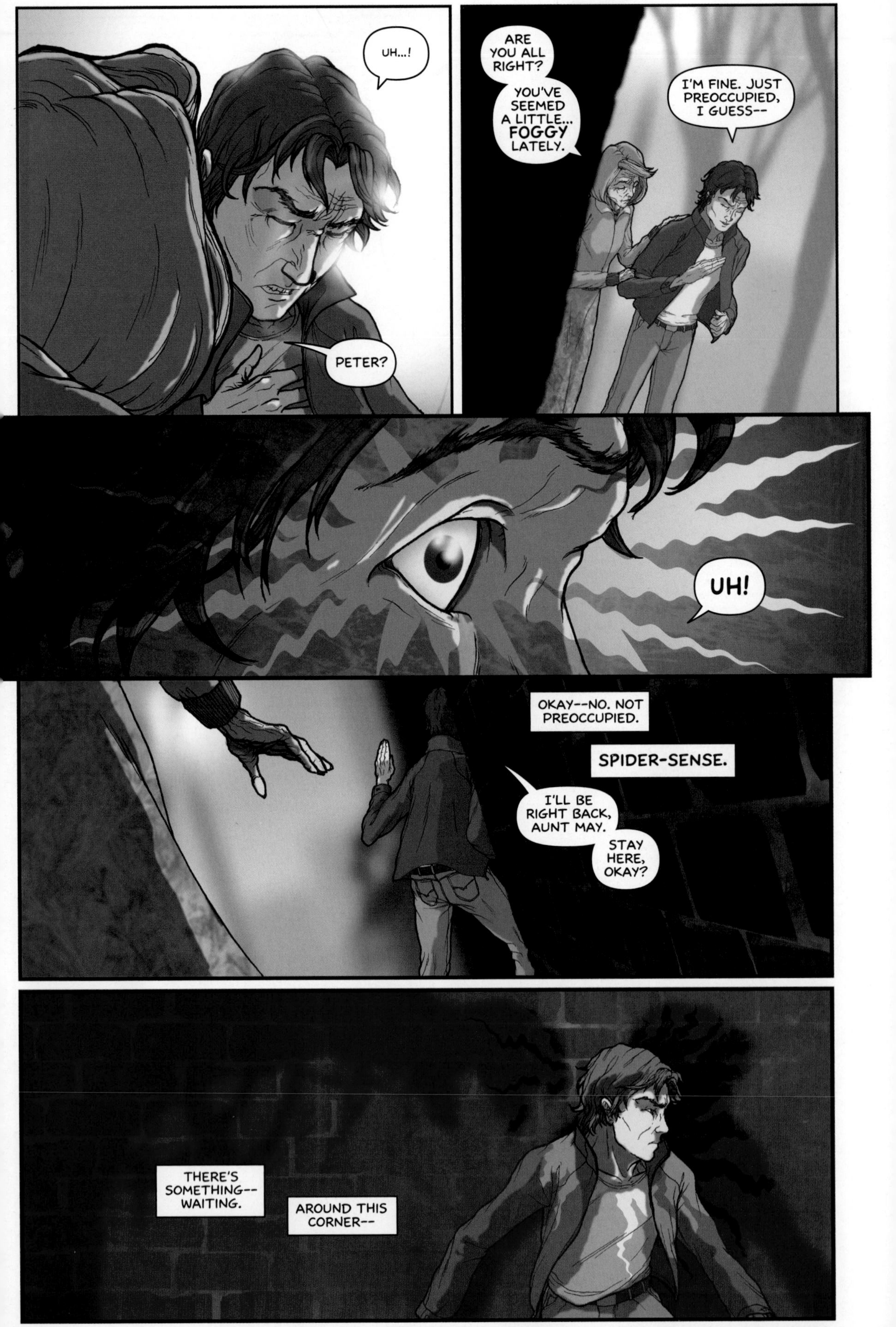
UH...!
PETER?
ARE YOU ALL RIGHT?
YOU'VE SEEMED A LITTLE... FOGGY LATELY.
I'M FINE. JUST PREOCCUPIED, I GUESS--
UH!
OKAY--NO. NOT PREOCCUPIED.
SPIDER-SENSE.
I'LL BE RIGHT BACK, AUNT MAY.
STAY HERE, OKAY?
THERE'S SOMETHING-- WAITING.
AROUND THIS CORNER--

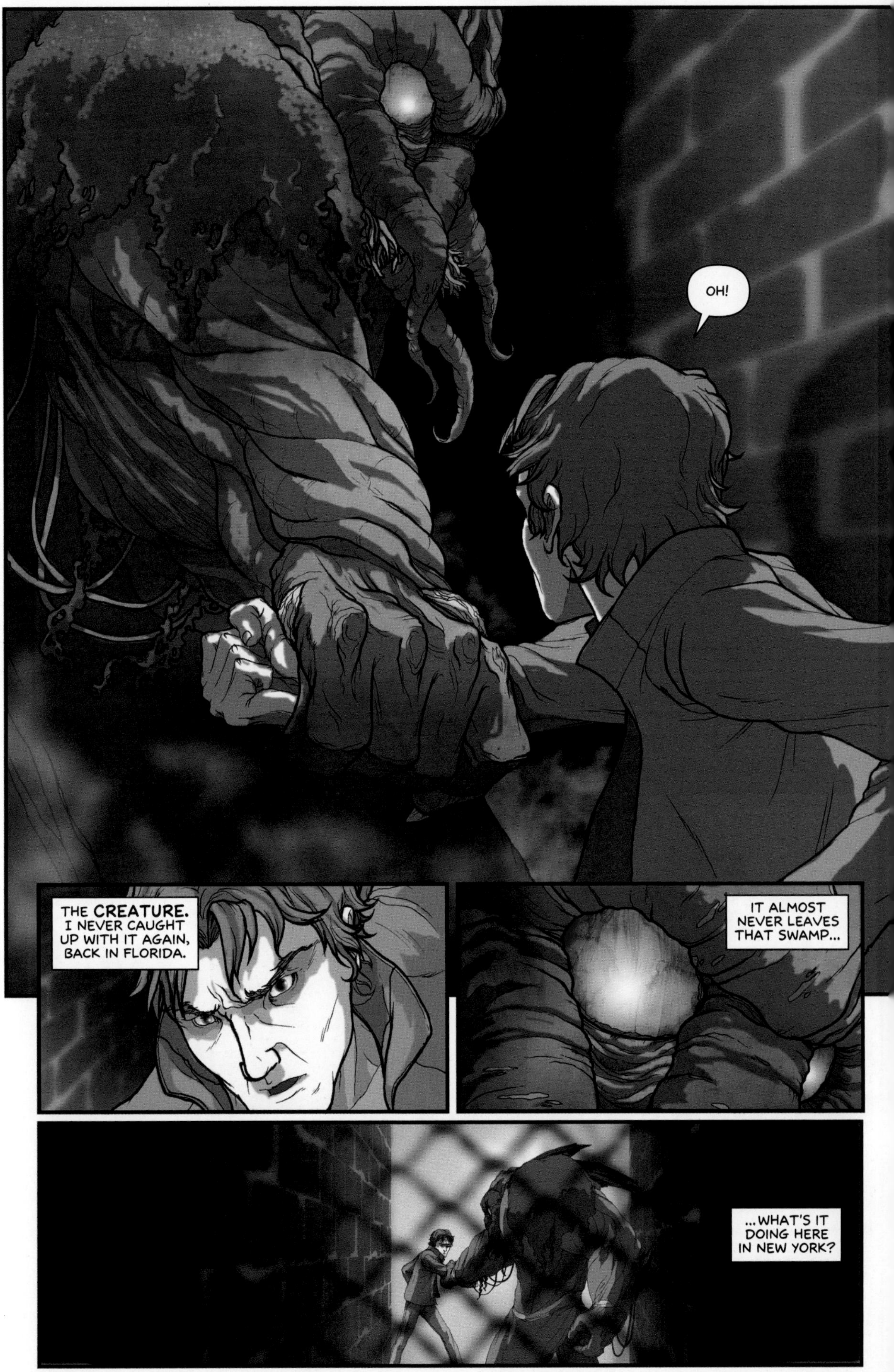
OH!
THE CREATURE. I NEVER CAUGHT UP WITH IT AGAIN, BACK IN FLORIDA.
IT ALMOST NEVER LEAVES THAT SWAMP...
...WHAT'S IT DOING HERE IN NEW YORK?

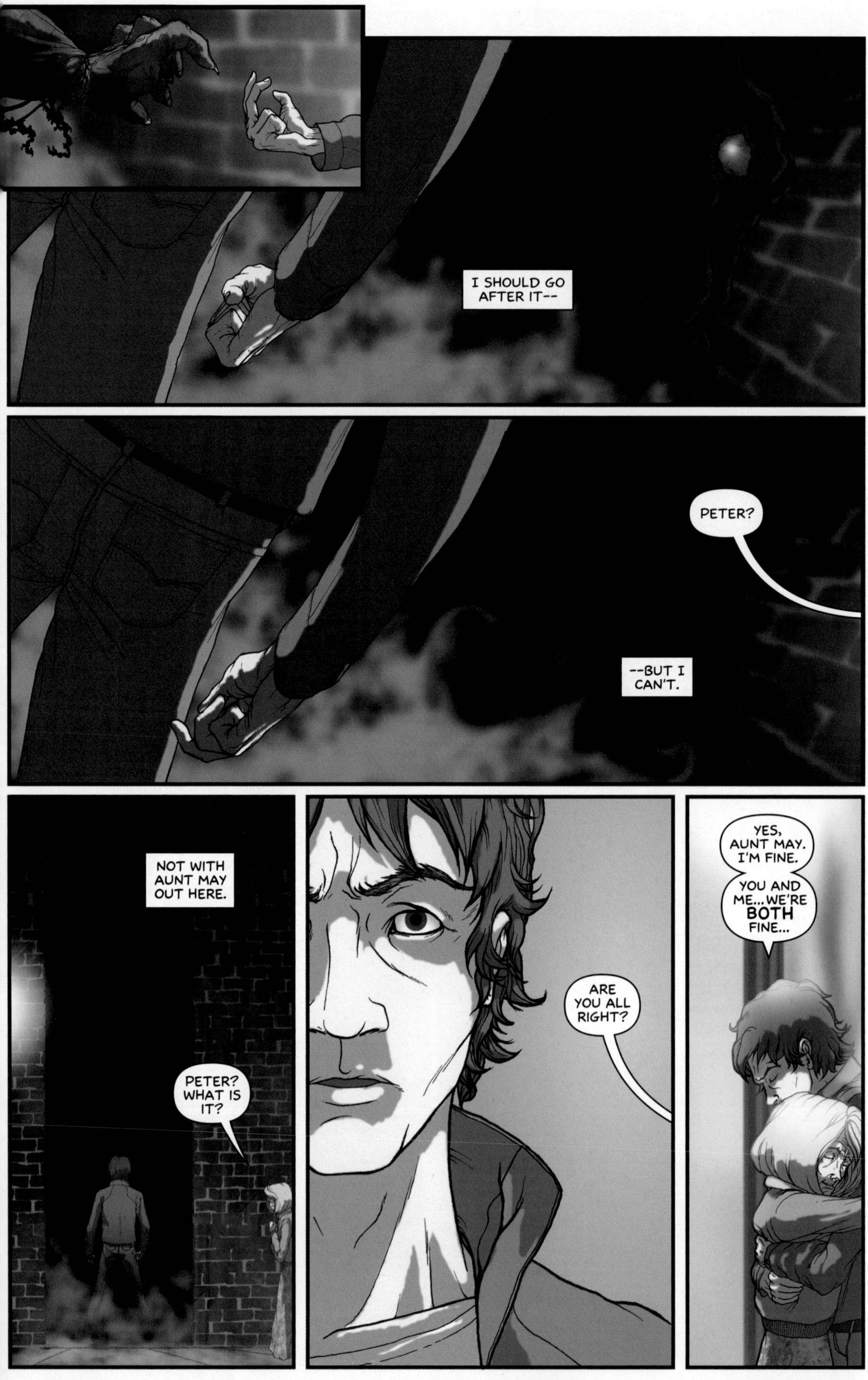
I SHOULD GO AFTER IT--
PETER?
--BUT I CAN'T.
NOT WITH AUNT MAY OUT HERE.
PETER? WHAT IS IT?
ARE YOU ALL RIGHT?
YES, AUNT MAY. I'M FINE.
YOU AND ME...WE'RE BOTH FINE...

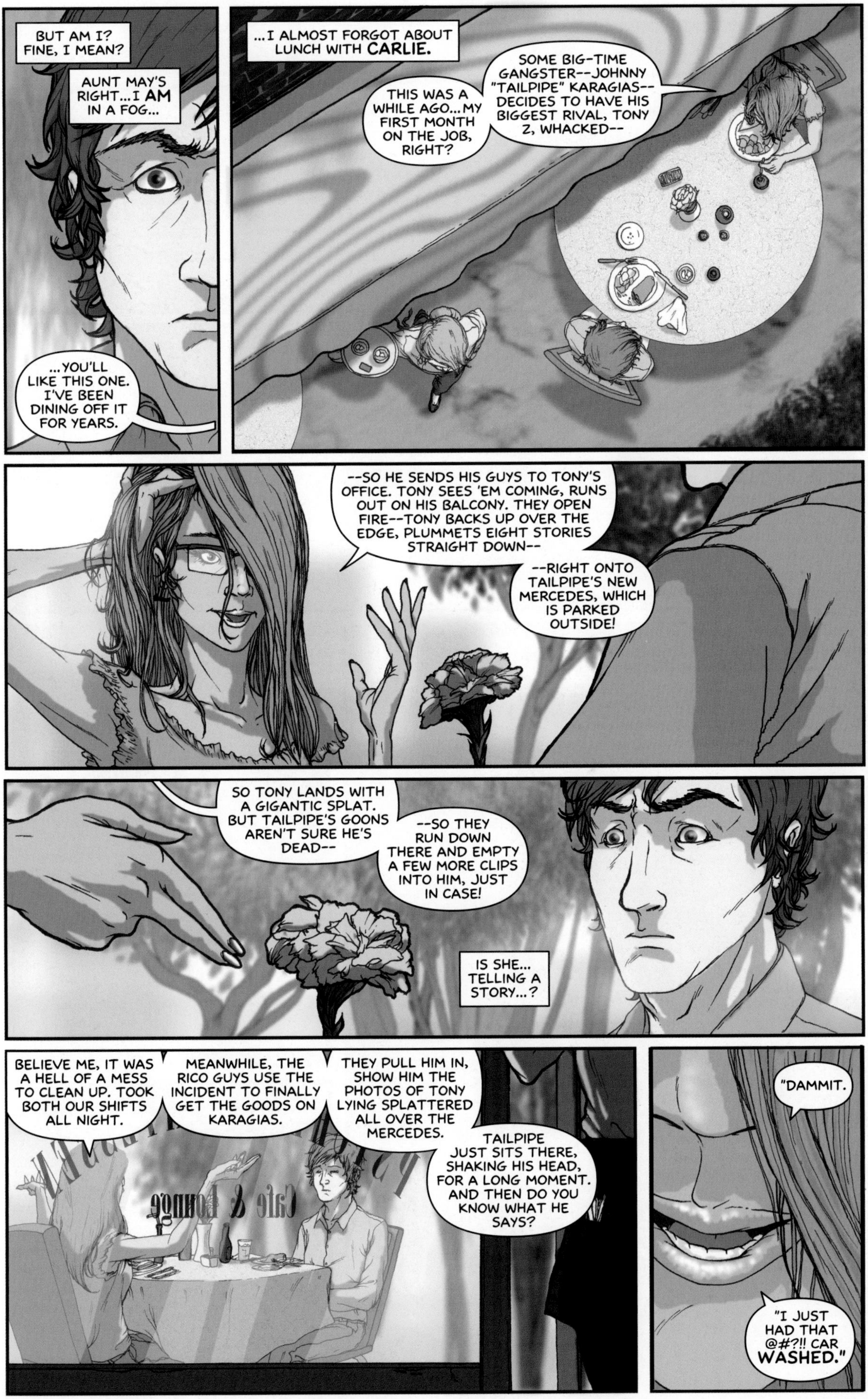
BUT AM I? FINE, I MEAN?
AUNT MAY'S RIGHT...I AM IN A FOG...
...YOU'LL LIKE THIS ONE. I'VE BEEN DINING OFF IT FOR YEARS.
...I ALMOST FORGOT ABOUT LUNCH WITH CARLIE.
THIS WAS A WHILE AGO...MY FIRST MONTH ON THE JOB, RIGHT?
SOME BIG-TIME GANGSTER--JOHNNY "TAILPIPE" KARAGIAS--DECIDES TO HAVE HIS BIGGEST RIVAL, TONY Z, WHACKED--
--SO HE SENDS HIS GUYS TO TONY'S OFFICE. TONY SEES 'EM COMING, RUNS OUT ON HIS BALCONY. THEY OPEN FIRE--TONY BACKS UP OVER THE EDGE, PLUMMETS EIGHT STORIES STRAIGHT DOWN--
--RIGHT ONTO TAILPIPE'S NEW MERCEDES, WHICH IS PARKED OUTSIDE!
SO TONY LANDS WITH A GIGANTIC SPLAT. BUT TAILPIPE'S GOONS AREN'T SURE HE'S DEAD--
--SO THEY RUN DOWN THERE AND EMPTY A FEW MORE CLIPS INTO HIM, JUST IN CASE!
IS SHE... TELLING A STORY...?
BELIEVE ME, IT WAS A HELL OF A MESS TO CLEAN UP. TOOK BOTH OUR SHIFTS ALL NIGHT.
MEANWHILE, THE RICO GUYS USE THE INCIDENT TO FINALLY GET THE GOODS ON KARAGIAS.
THEY PULL HIM IN, SHOW HIM THE PHOTOS OF TONY LYING SPLATTERED ALL OVER THE MERCEDES.
TAILPIPE JUST SITS THERE, SHAKING HIS HEAD, FOR A LONG MOMENT. AND THEN DO YOU KNOW WHAT HE SAYS?
Cafe & Lounge
"DAMMIT.
"I JUST HAD THAT @#?!! CAR WASHED."

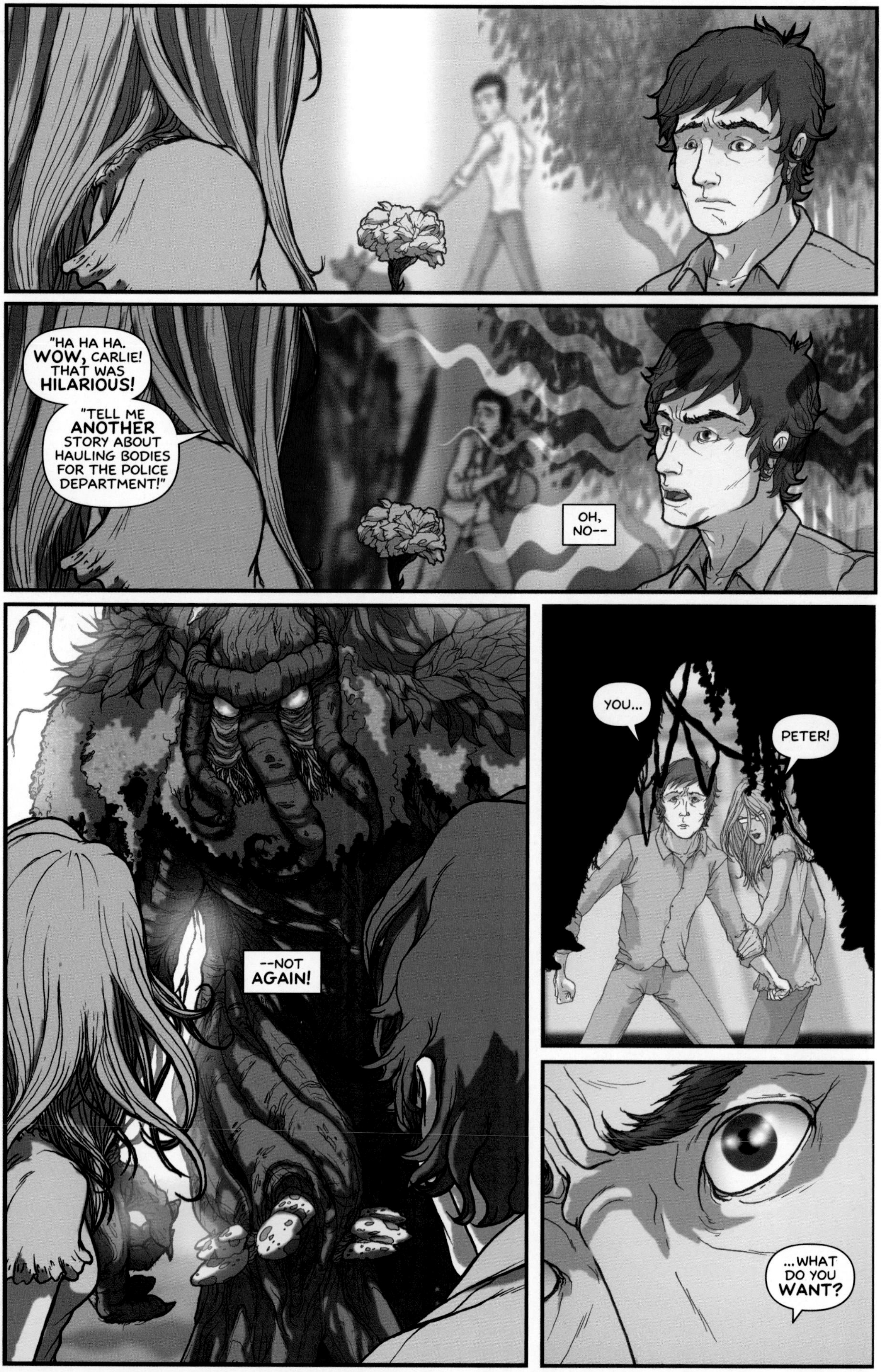
"HA HA HA. WOW, CARLIE! THAT WAS HILARIOUS!
"TELL ME ANOTHER STORY ABOUT HAULING BODIES FOR THE POLICE DEPARTMENT!"
OH, NO--
--NOT AGAIN!
YOU...
PETER!
...WHAT DO YOU WANT?

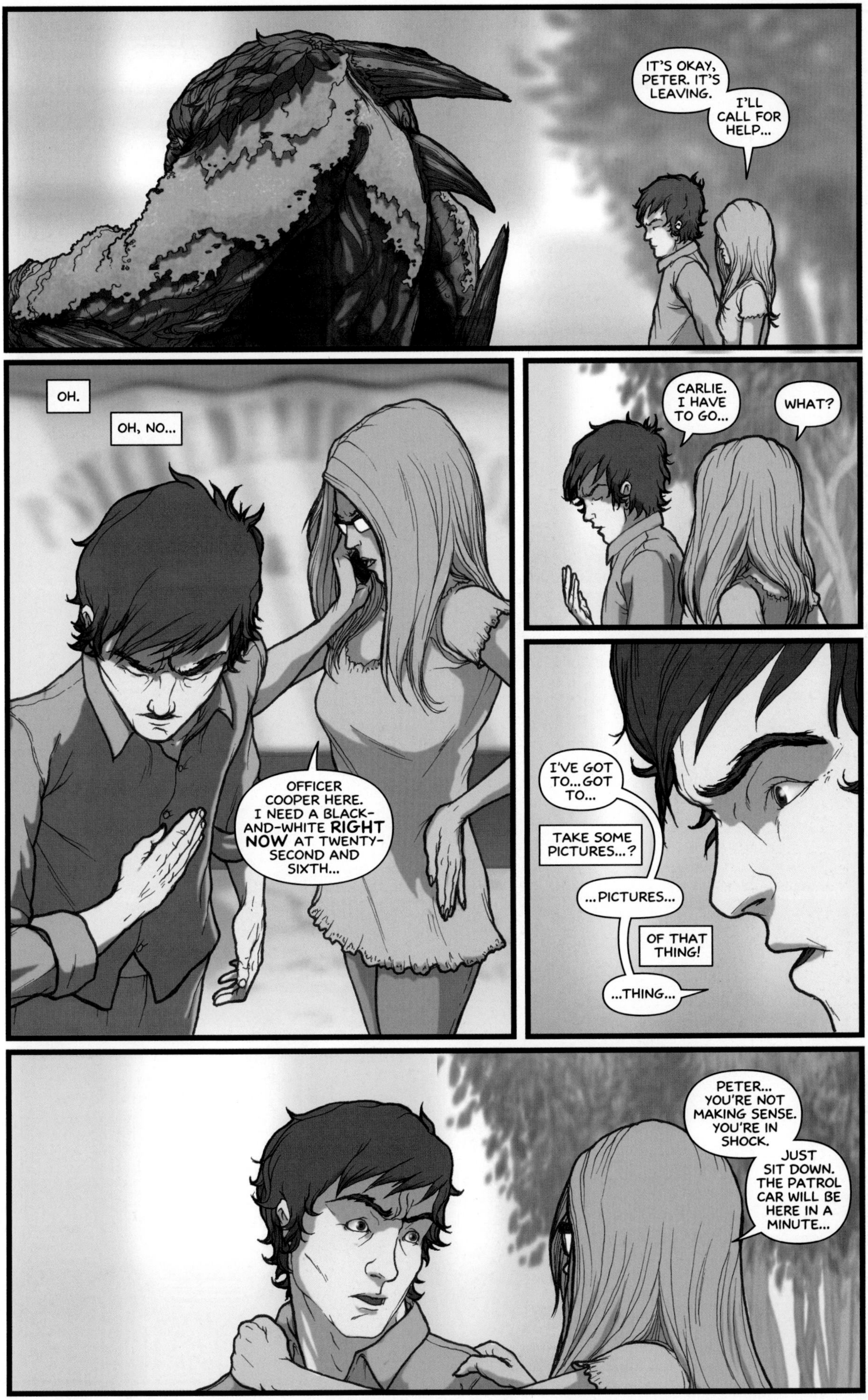
IT'S OKAY, PETER. IT'S LEAVING.
I'LL CALL FOR HELP...
OH.
OH, NO...
OFFICER COOPER HERE. I NEED A BLACK-AND-WHITE RIGHT NOW AT TWENTY-SECOND AND SIXTH...
CARLIE. I HAVE TO GO...
WHAT?
I'VE GOT TO...GOT TO...
TAKE SOME PICTURES...?
...PICTURES...
OF THAT THING!
...THING...
PETER... YOU'RE NOT MAKING SENSE. YOU'RE IN SHOCK.
JUST SIT DOWN. THE PATROL CAR WILL BE HERE IN A MINUTE...

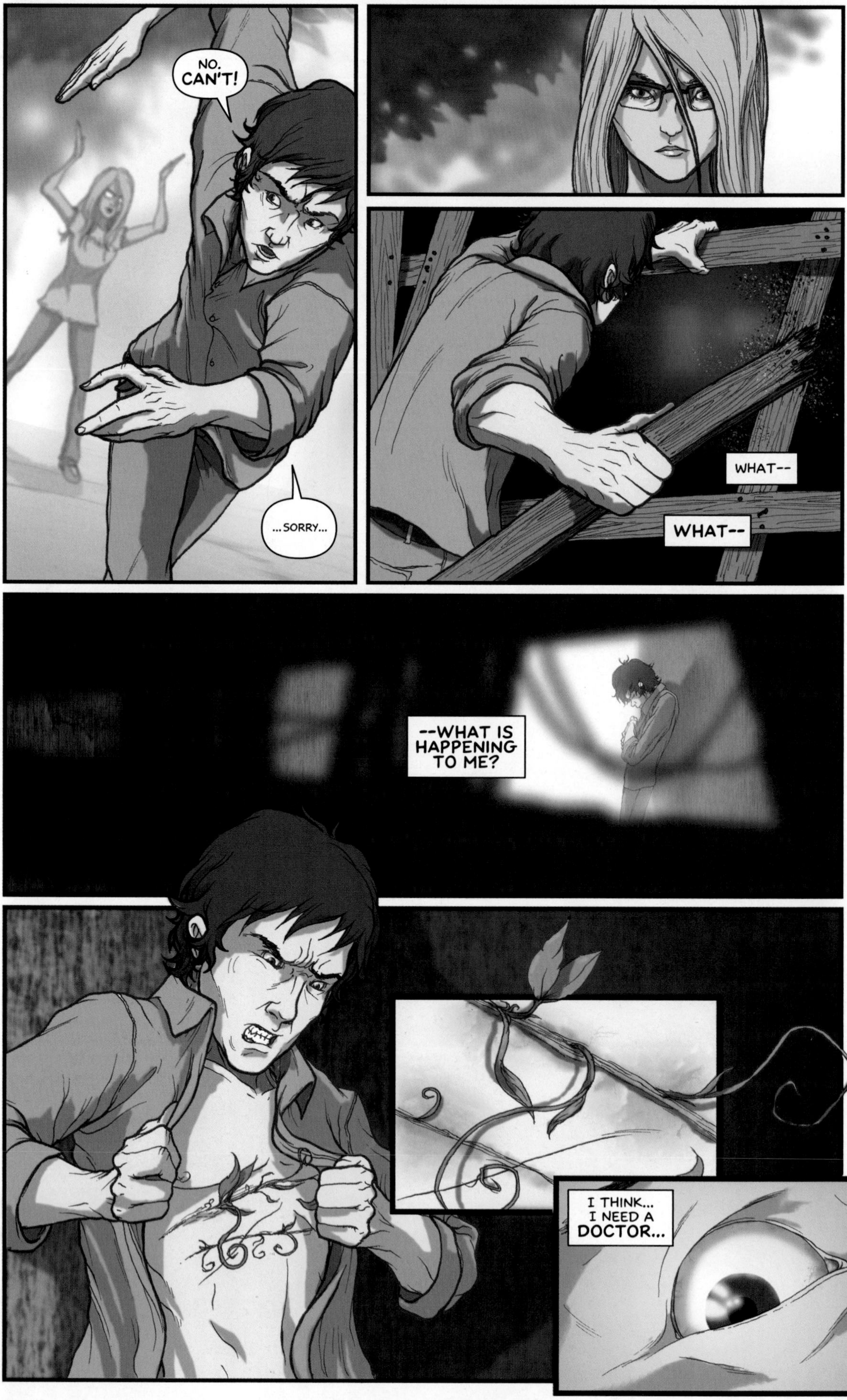

NO. CAN'T!
...SORRY...
WHAT--
WHAT--
--WHAT IS HAPPENING TO ME?
I THINK... I NEED A DOCTOR...

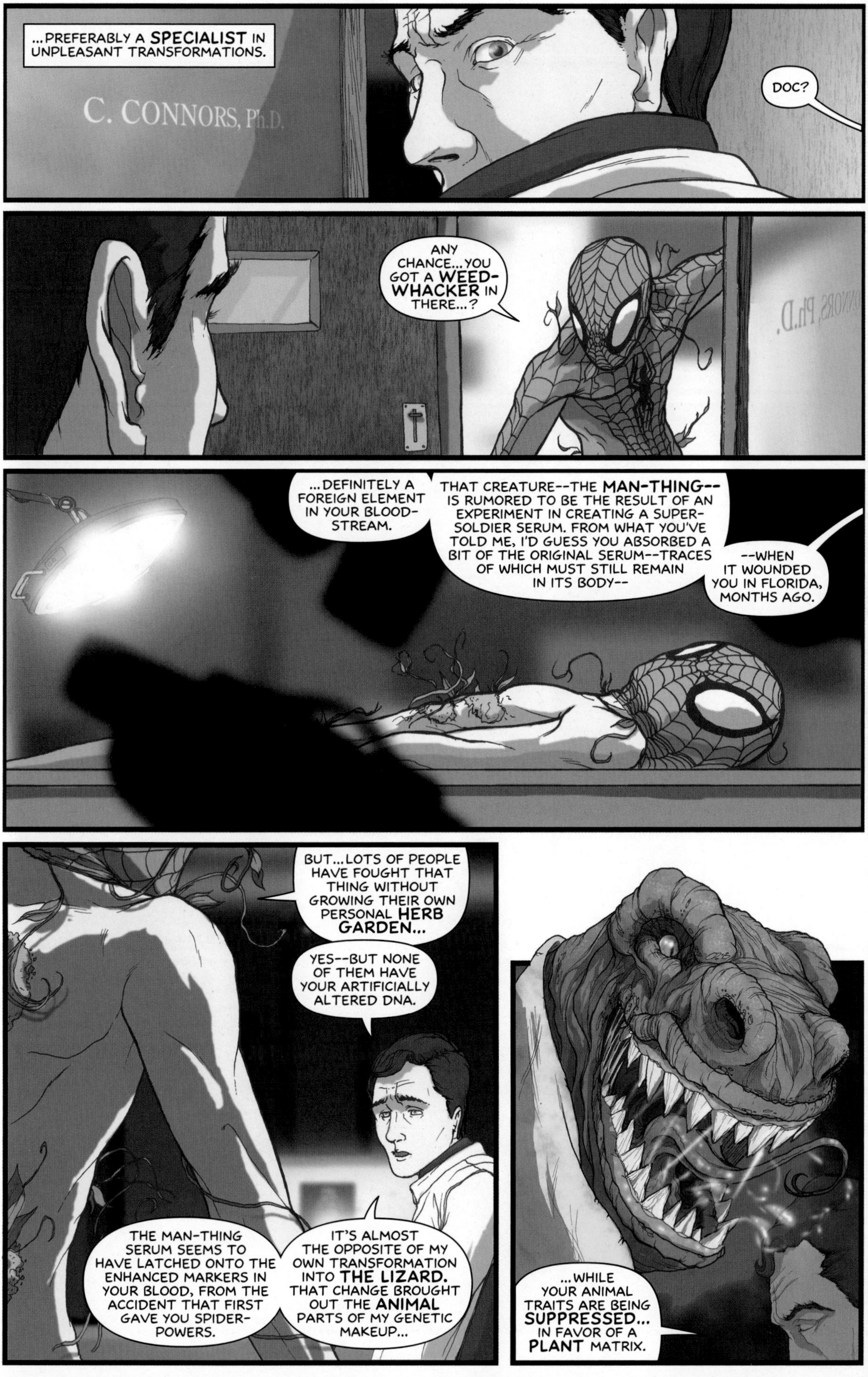
...PREFERABLY A SPECIALIST IN UNPLEASANT TRANSFORMATIONS.
C. CONNORS, Ph.D.
DOC?
ANY CHANCE...YOU GOT A WEED-WHACKER IN THERE...?
...DEFINITELY A FOREIGN ELEMENT IN YOUR BLOOD-STREAM.
THAT CREATURE--THE MAN-THING--IS RUMORED TO BE THE RESULT OF AN EXPERIMENT IN CREATING A SUPER-SOLDIER SERUM. FROM WHAT YOU'VE TOLD ME, I'D GUESS YOU ABSORBED A BIT OF THE ORIGINAL SERUM--TRACES OF WHICH MUST STILL REMAIN IN ITS BODY--
--WHEN IT WOUNDED YOU IN FLORIDA, MONTHS AGO.
BUT...LOTS OF PEOPLE HAVE FOUGHT THAT THING WITHOUT GROWING THEIR OWN PERSONAL HERB GARDEN...
YES--BUT NONE OF THEM HAVE YOUR ARTIFICIALLY ALTERED DNA.
THE MAN-THING SERUM SEEMS TO HAVE LATCHED ONTO THE ENHANCED MARKERS IN YOUR BLOOD, FROM THE ACCIDENT THAT FIRST GAVE YOU SPIDER-POWERS.
IT'S ALMOST THE OPPOSITE OF MY OWN TRANSFORMATION INTO THE LIZARD. THAT CHANGE BROUGHT OUT THE ANIMAL PARTS OF MY GENETIC MAKEUP...
...WHILE YOUR ANIMAL TRAITS ARE BEING SUPPRESSED... IN FAVOR OF A PLANT MATRIX.

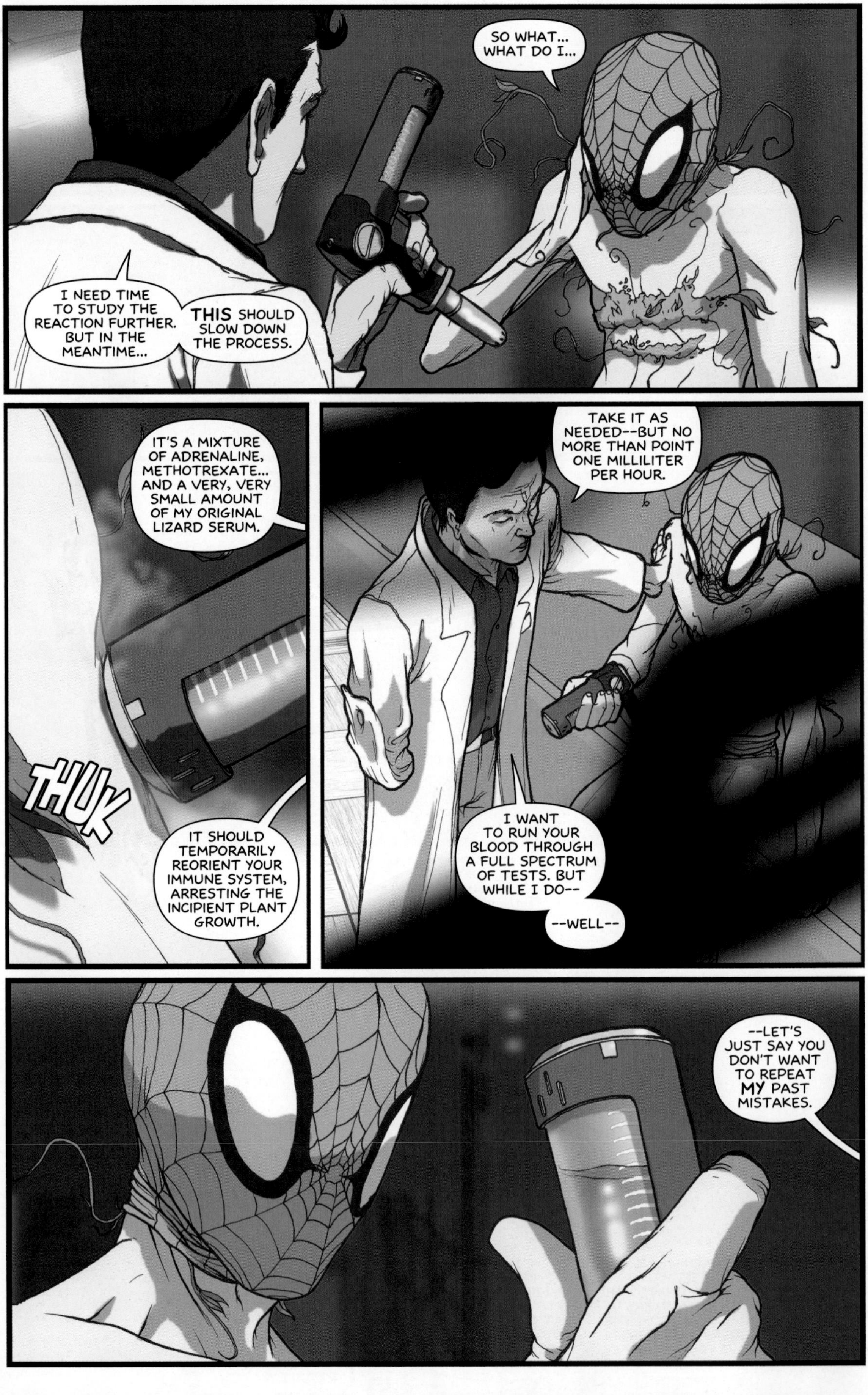

SO WHAT... WHAT DO I...
I NEED TIME TO STUDY THE REACTION FURTHER. BUT IN THE MEANTIME...
THIS SHOULD SLOW DOWN THE PROCESS.
IT'S A MIXTURE OF ADRENALINE, METHOTREXATE... AND A VERY, VERY SMALL AMOUNT OF MY ORIGINAL LIZARD SERUM.
THUK
IT SHOULD TEMPORARILY REORIENT YOUR IMMUNE SYSTEM, ARRESTING THE INCIPIENT PLANT GROWTH.
TAKE IT AS NEEDED--BUT NO MORE THAN POINT ONE MILLILITER PER HOUR.
I WANT TO RUN YOUR BLOOD THROUGH A FULL SPECTRUM OF TESTS. BUT WHILE I DO--
--WELL--
--LET'S JUST SAY YOU DON'T WANT TO REPEAT MY PAST MISTAKES.

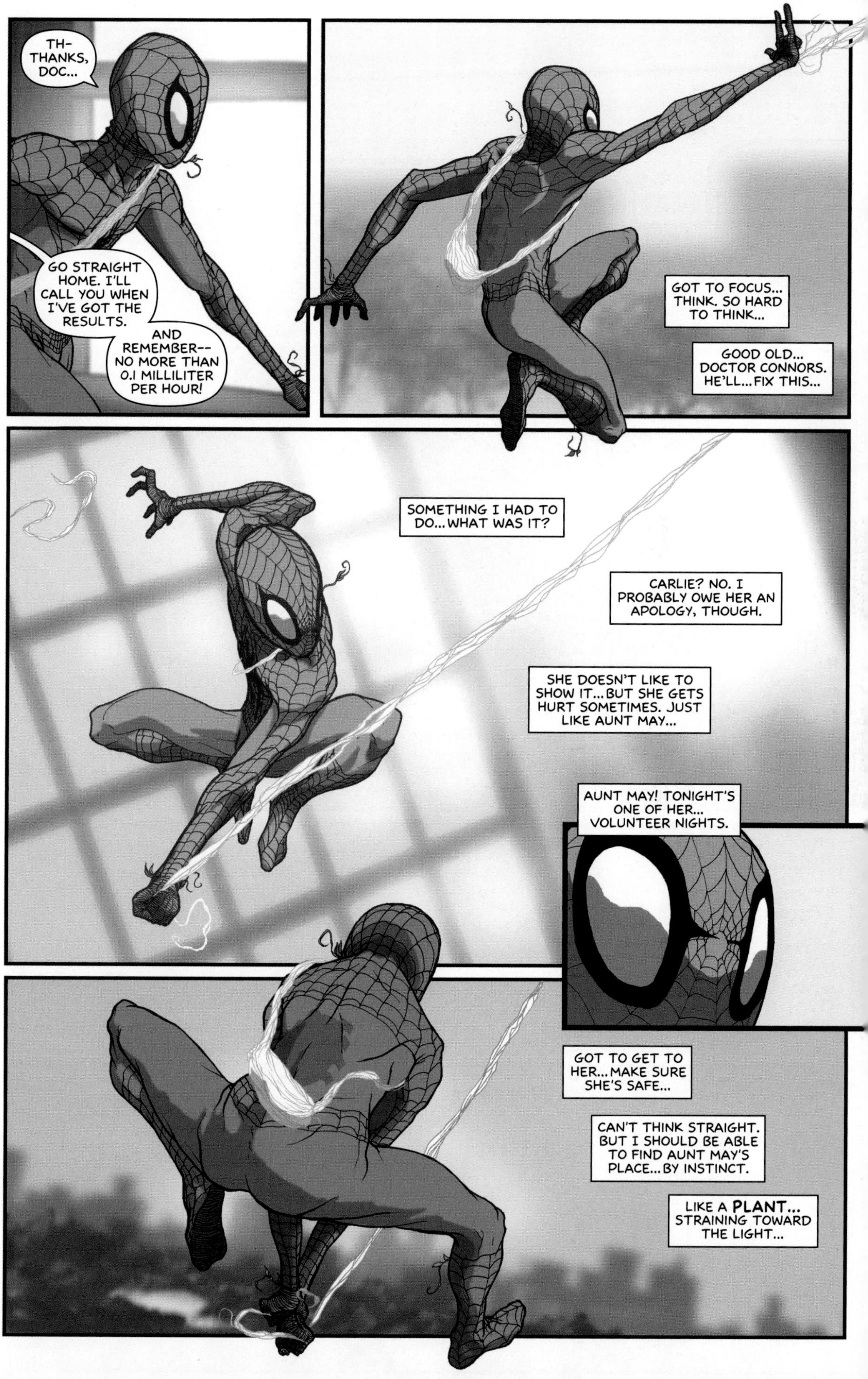
TH-THANKS, DOC...
GO STRAIGHT HOME. I'LL CALL YOU WHEN I'VE GOT THE RESULTS.
AND REMEMBER-- NO MORE THAN 0.1 MILLILITER PER HOUR!
GOT TO FOCUS... THINK. SO HARD TO THINK...
GOOD OLD... DOCTOR CONNORS. HE'LL...FIX THIS...
SOMETHING I HAD TO DO...WHAT WAS IT?
CARLIE? NO. I PROBABLY OWE HER AN APOLOGY, THOUGH.
SHE DOESN'T LIKE TO SHOW IT...BUT SHE GETS HURT SOMETIMES. JUST LIKE AUNT MAY...
AUNT MAY! TONIGHT'S ONE OF HER... VOLUNTEER NIGHTS.
GOT TO GET TO HER...MAKE SURE SHE'S SAFE...
CAN'T THINK STRAIGHT. BUT I SHOULD BE ABLE TO FIND AUNT MAY'S PLACE...BY INSTINCT.
LIKE A PLANT... STRAINING TOWARD THE LIGHT...

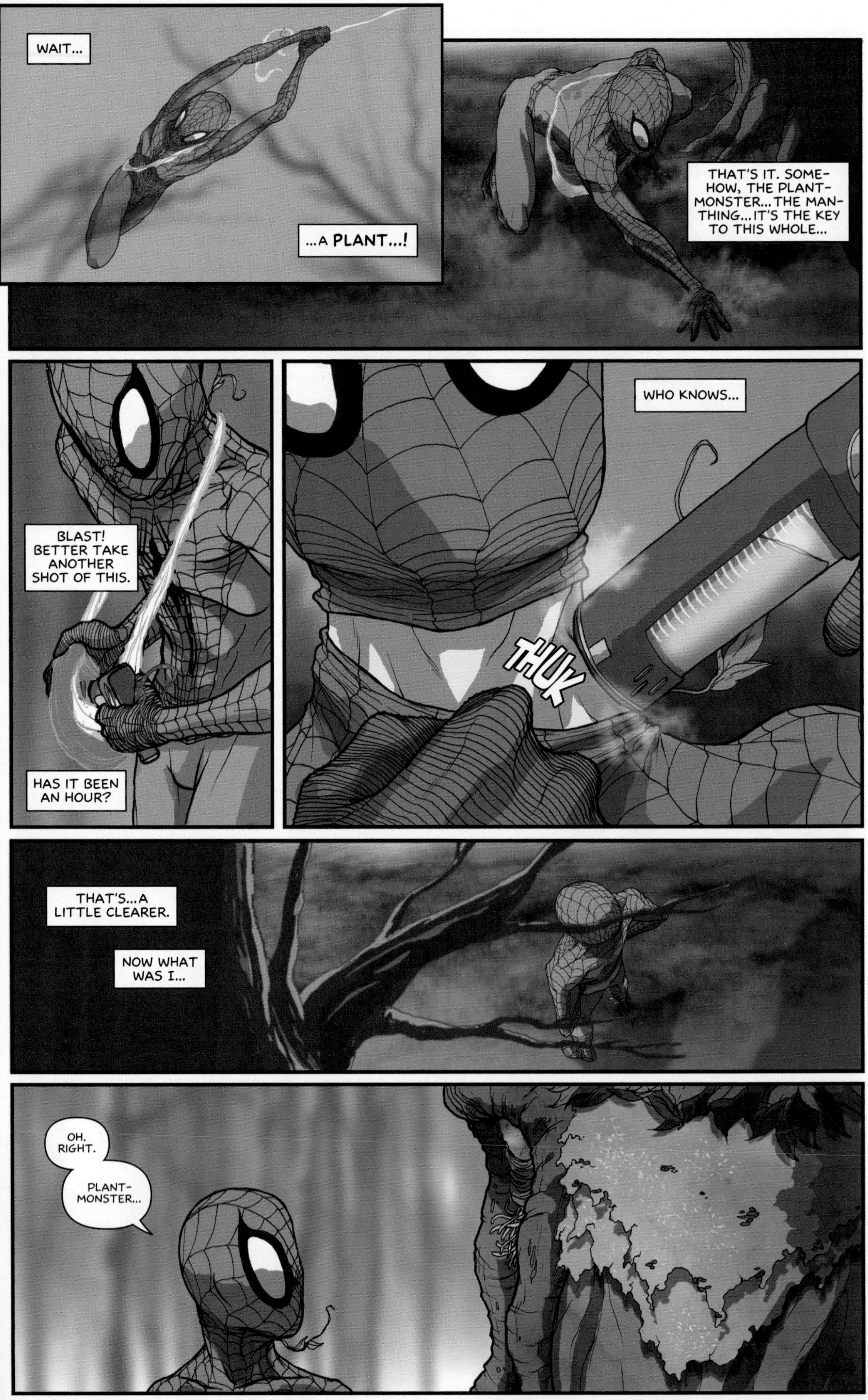
WAIT...
...A PLANT...!
THAT'S IT. SOMEHOW, THE PLANT-MONSTER...THE MAN-THING...IT'S THE KEY TO THIS WHOLE...
BLAST! BETTER TAKE ANOTHER SHOT OF THIS.
HAS IT BEEN AN HOUR?
WHO KNOWS...
THUK
THAT'S...A LITTLE CLEARER.
NOW WHAT WAS I...
OH. RIGHT.
PLANT-MONSTER...

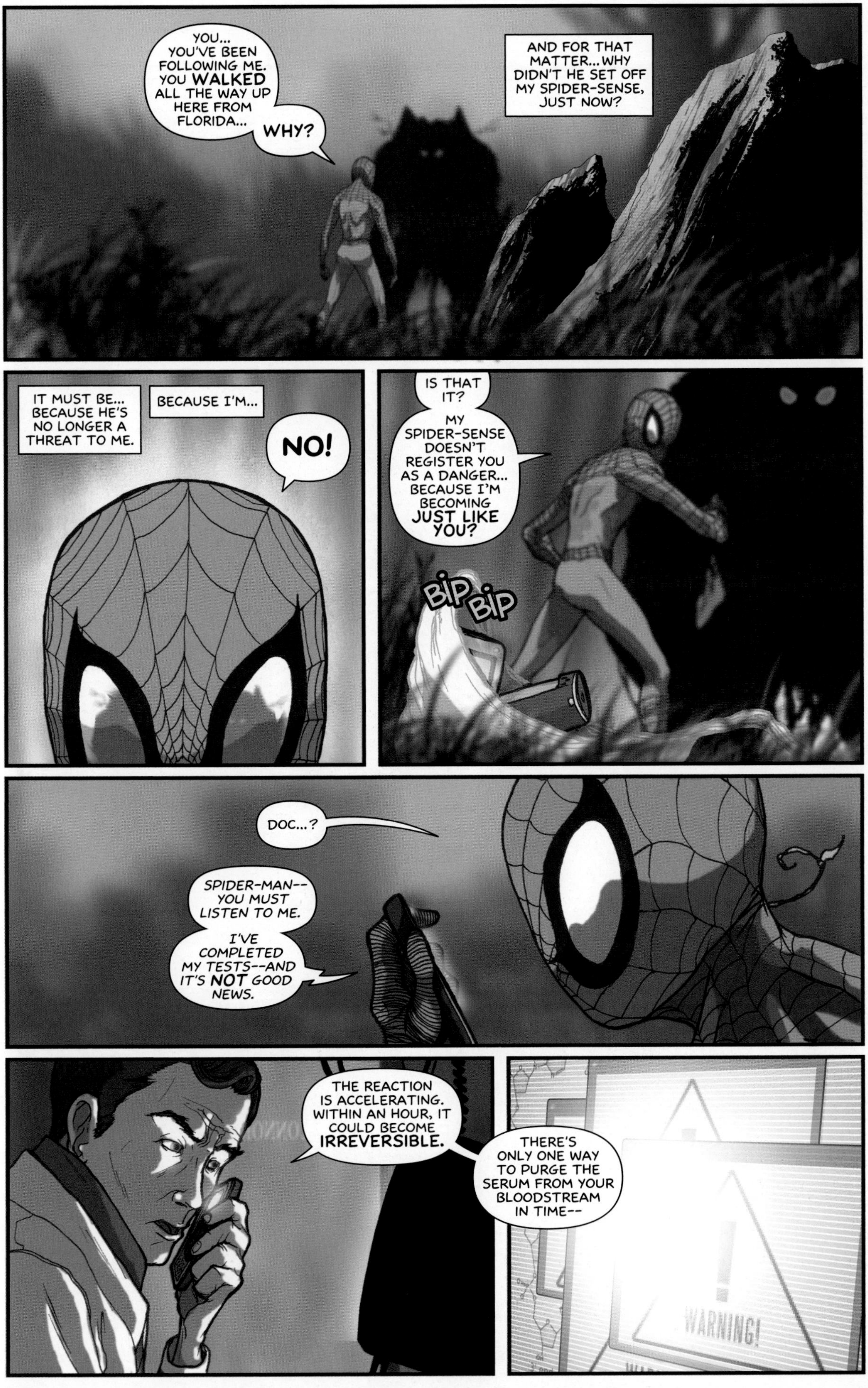
YOU... YOU'VE BEEN FOLLOWING ME. YOU WALKED ALL THE WAY UP HERE FROM FLORIDA... WHY?
AND FOR THAT MATTER...WHY DIDN'T HE SET OFF MY SPIDER-SENSE, JUST NOW?
IT MUST BE... BECAUSE HE'S NO LONGER A THREAT TO ME.
BECAUSE I'M...
NO!
IS THAT IT?
MY SPIDER-SENSE DOESN'T REGISTER YOU AS A DANGER... BECAUSE I'M BECOMING JUST LIKE YOU?
BIP BIP
DOC...?
SPIDER-MAN-- YOU MUST LISTEN TO ME.
I'VE COMPLETED MY TESTS--AND IT'S NOT GOOD NEWS.
THE REACTION IS ACCELERATING. WITHIN AN HOUR, IT COULD BECOME IRREVERSIBLE.
THERE'S ONLY ONE WAY TO PURGE THE SERUM FROM YOUR BLOODSTREAM IN TIME--
WARNING!

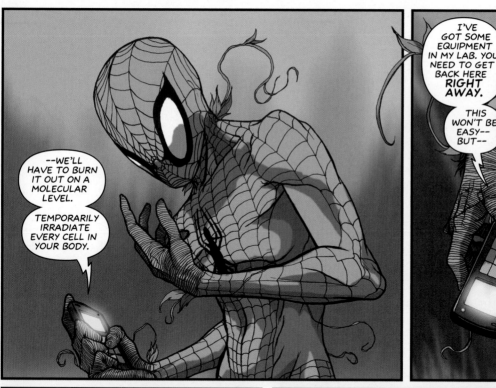

--WE'LL HAVE TO BURN IT OUT ON A MOLECULAR LEVEL.

TEMPORARILY IRRADIATE EVERY CELL IN YOUR BODY.

I'VE GOT SOME EQUIPMENT IN MY LAB. YOU NEED TO GET BACK HERE **RIGHT AWAY.**

THIS WON'T BE EASY-- BUT--

BLIP

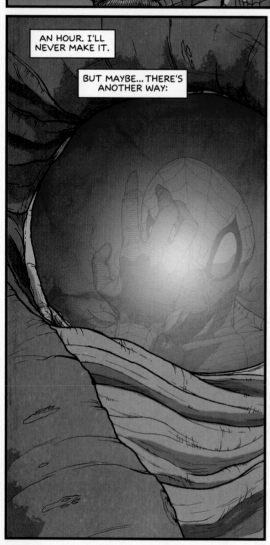

AN HOUR. I'LL NEVER MAKE IT.

BUT MAYBE... THERE'S ANOTHER WAY:

"WHATEVER KNOWS **FEAR...**

"...BURNS AT THE MAN-THING'S TOUCH."

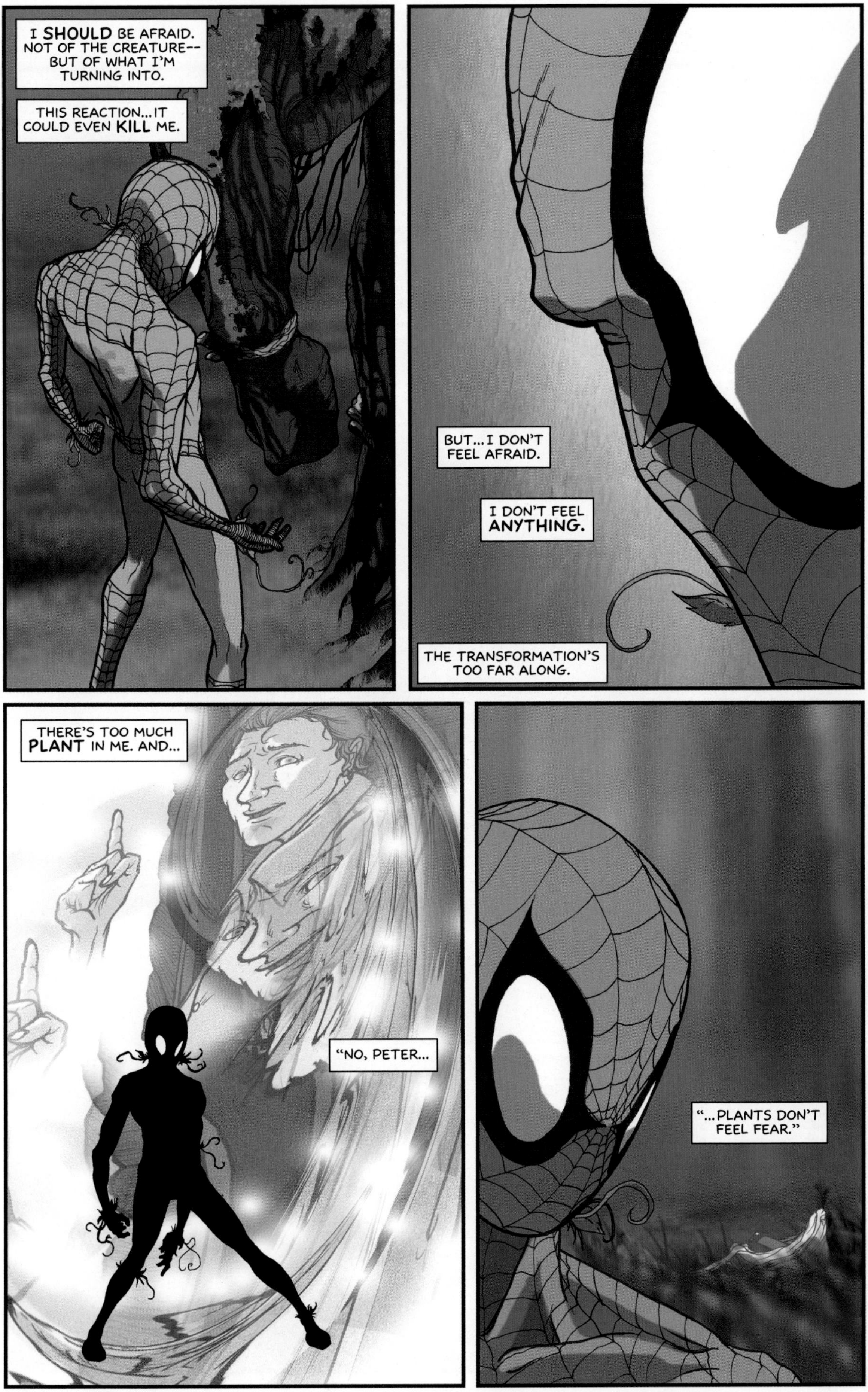
I SHOULD BE AFRAID. NOT OF THE CREATURE-- BUT OF WHAT I'M TURNING INTO.
THIS REACTION...IT COULD EVEN KILL ME.
BUT...I DON'T FEEL AFRAID.
I DON'T FEEL ANYTHING.
THE TRANSFORMATION'S TOO FAR ALONG.
THERE'S TOO MUCH PLANT IN ME. AND...
"NO, PETER...
"...PLANTS DON'T FEEL FEAR."

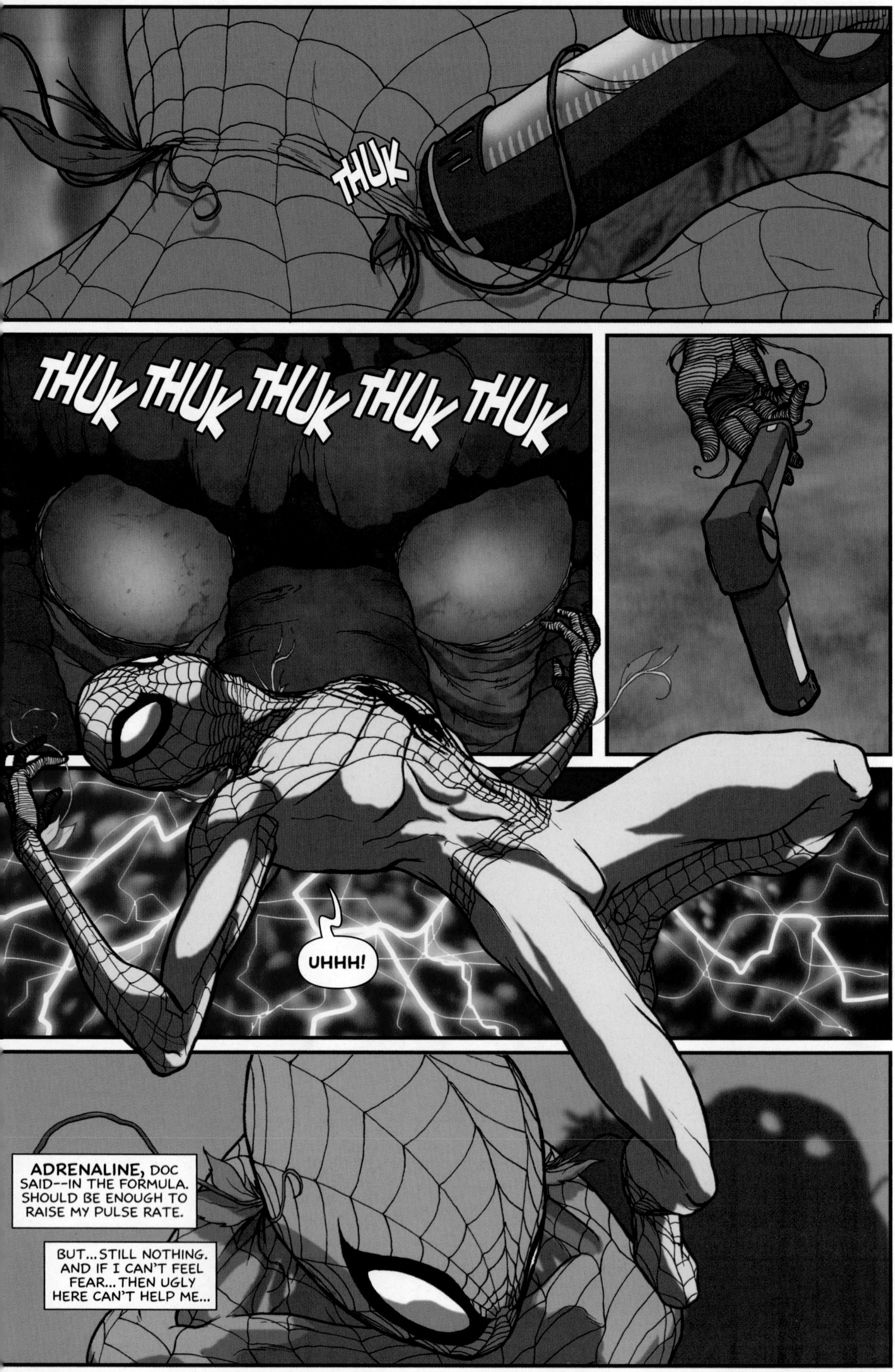
THUK
THUK THUK THUK THUK THUK
UHHH!
ADRENALINE, DOC SAID--IN THE FORMULA. SHOULD BE ENOUGH TO RAISE MY PULSE RATE.
BUT...STILL NOTHING. AND IF I CAN'T FEEL FEAR...THEN UGLY HERE CAN'T HELP ME...

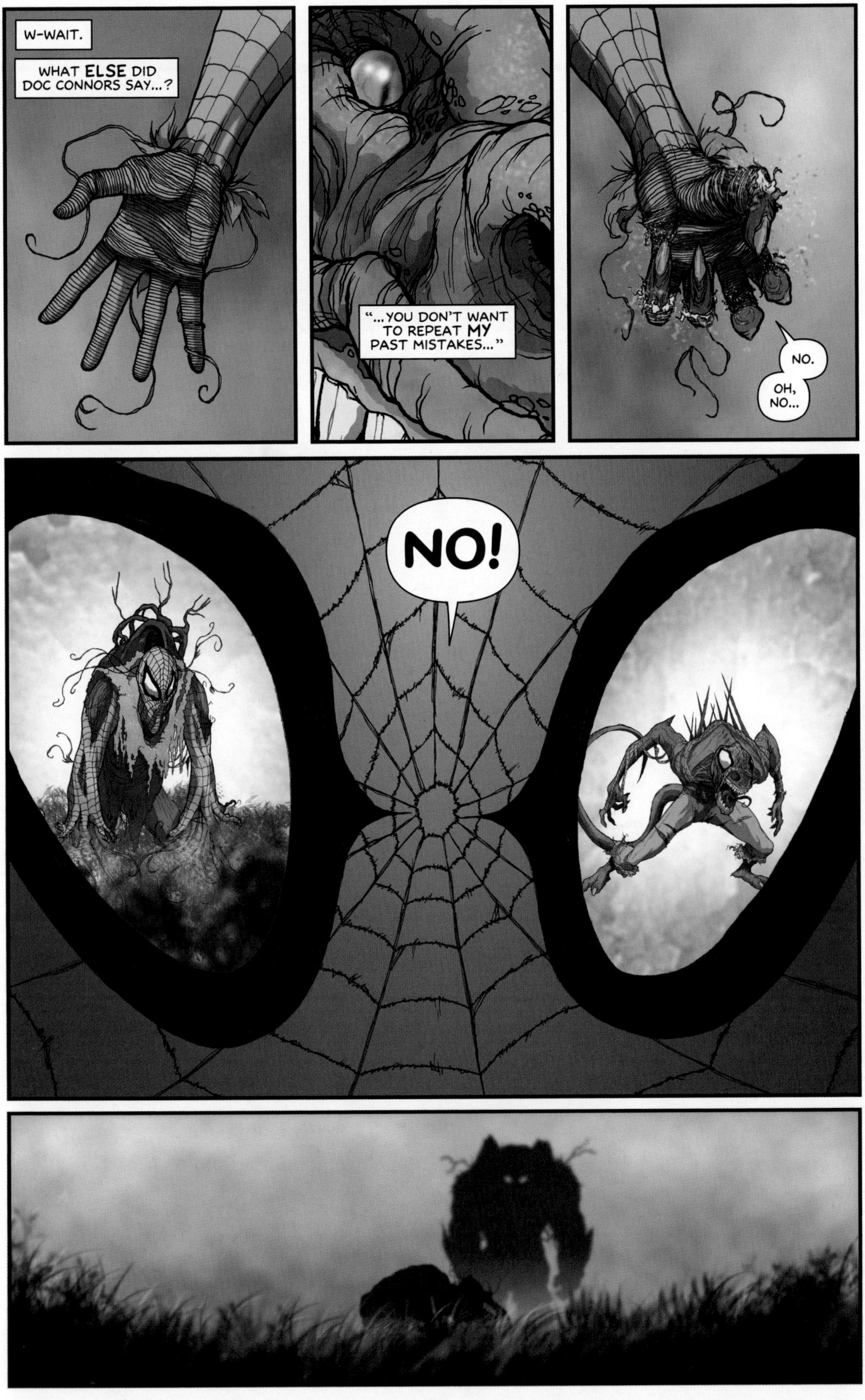
W-WAIT.
WHAT ELSE DID DOC CONNORS SAY...?
"...YOU DON'T WANT TO REPEAT MY PAST MISTAKES..."
NO.
OH, NO...
NO!

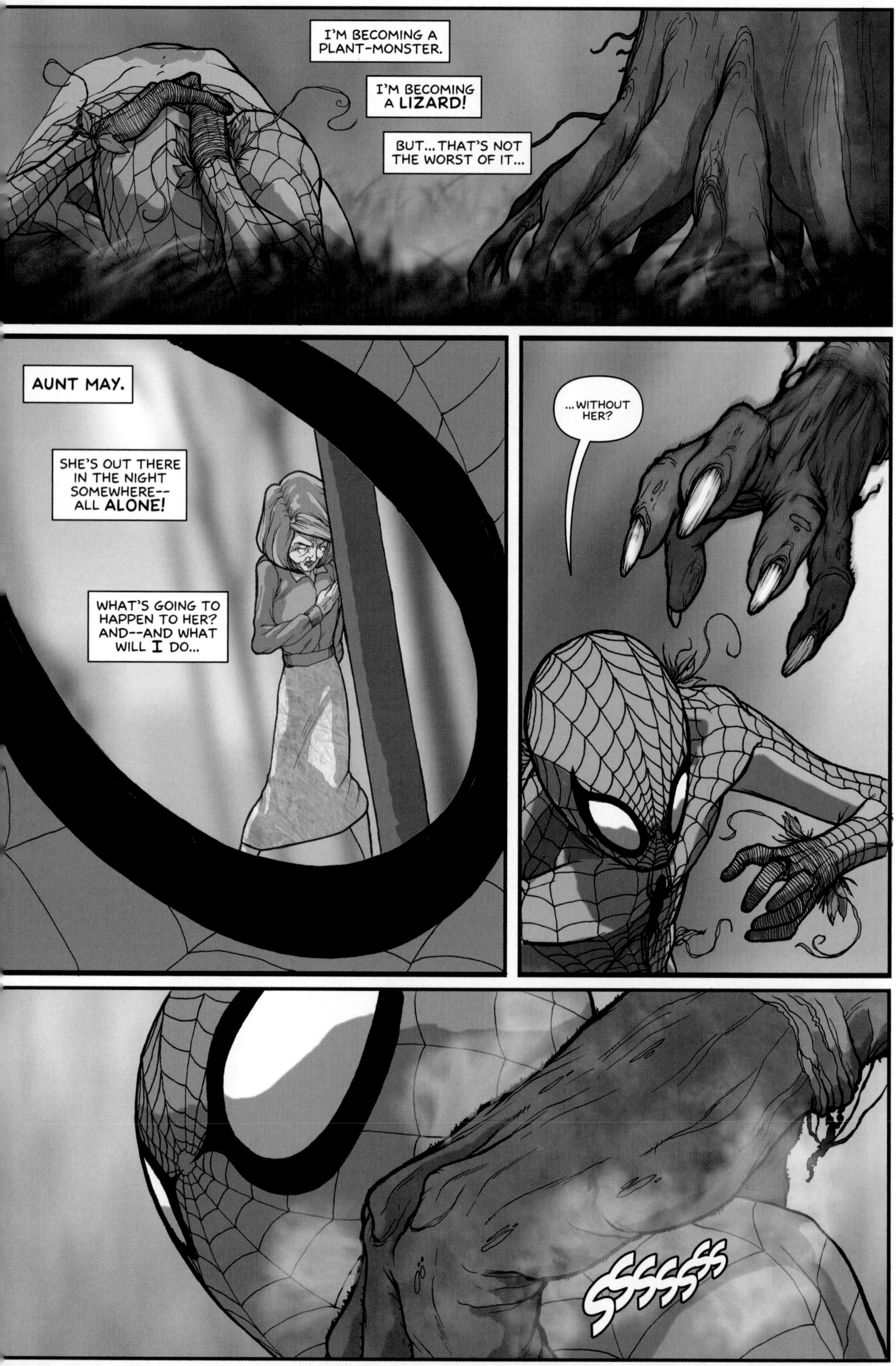
I'M BECOMING A PLANT-MONSTER.
I'M BECOMING A LIZARD!
BUT... THAT'S NOT THE WORST OF IT...
AUNT MAY.
SHE'S OUT THERE IN THE NIGHT SOMEWHERE-- ALL ALONE!
WHAT'S GOING TO HAPPEN TO HER? AND--AND WHAT WILL I DO...
...WITHOUT HER?
SSSSSS

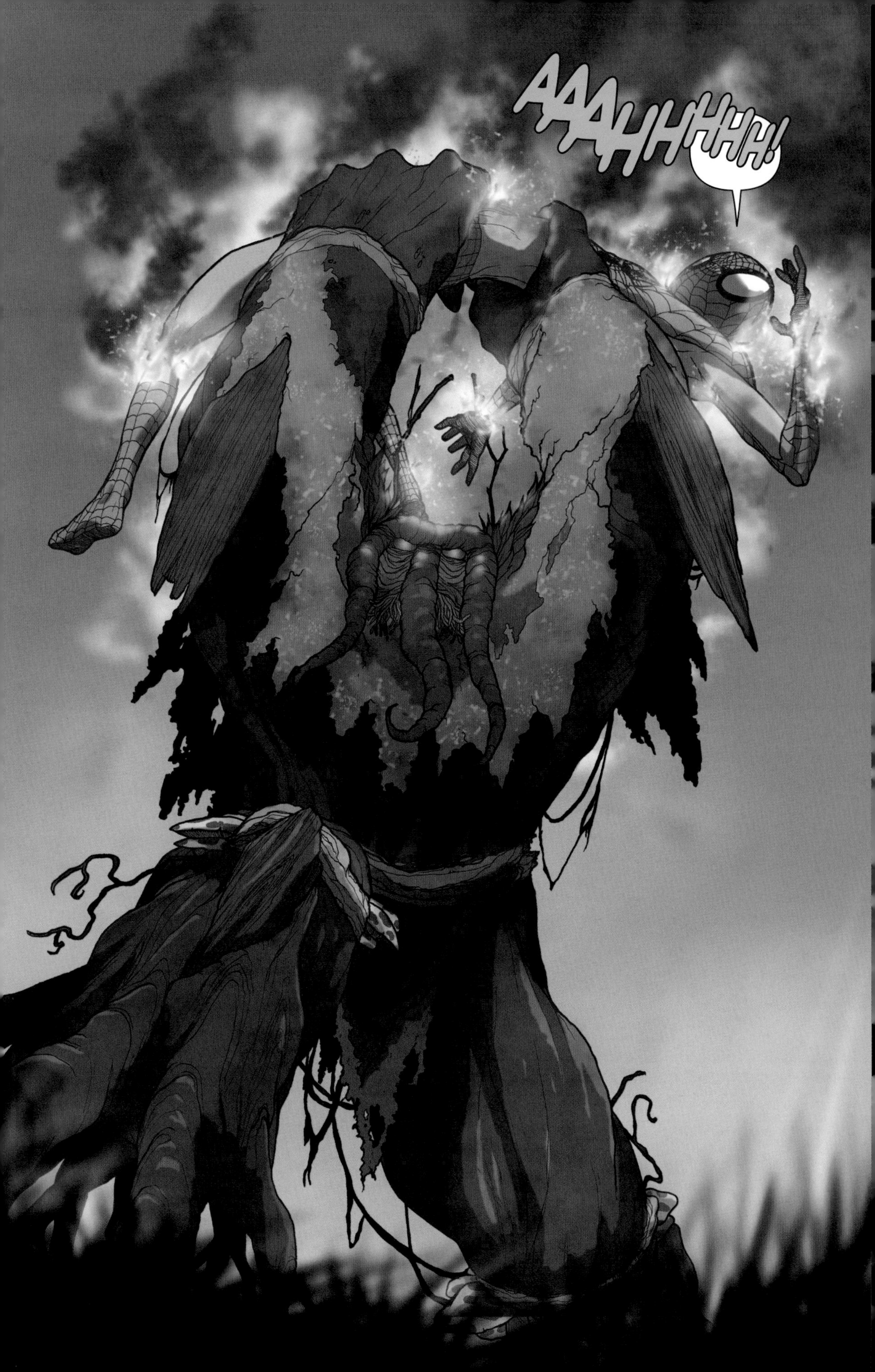
AAAHHHHH!

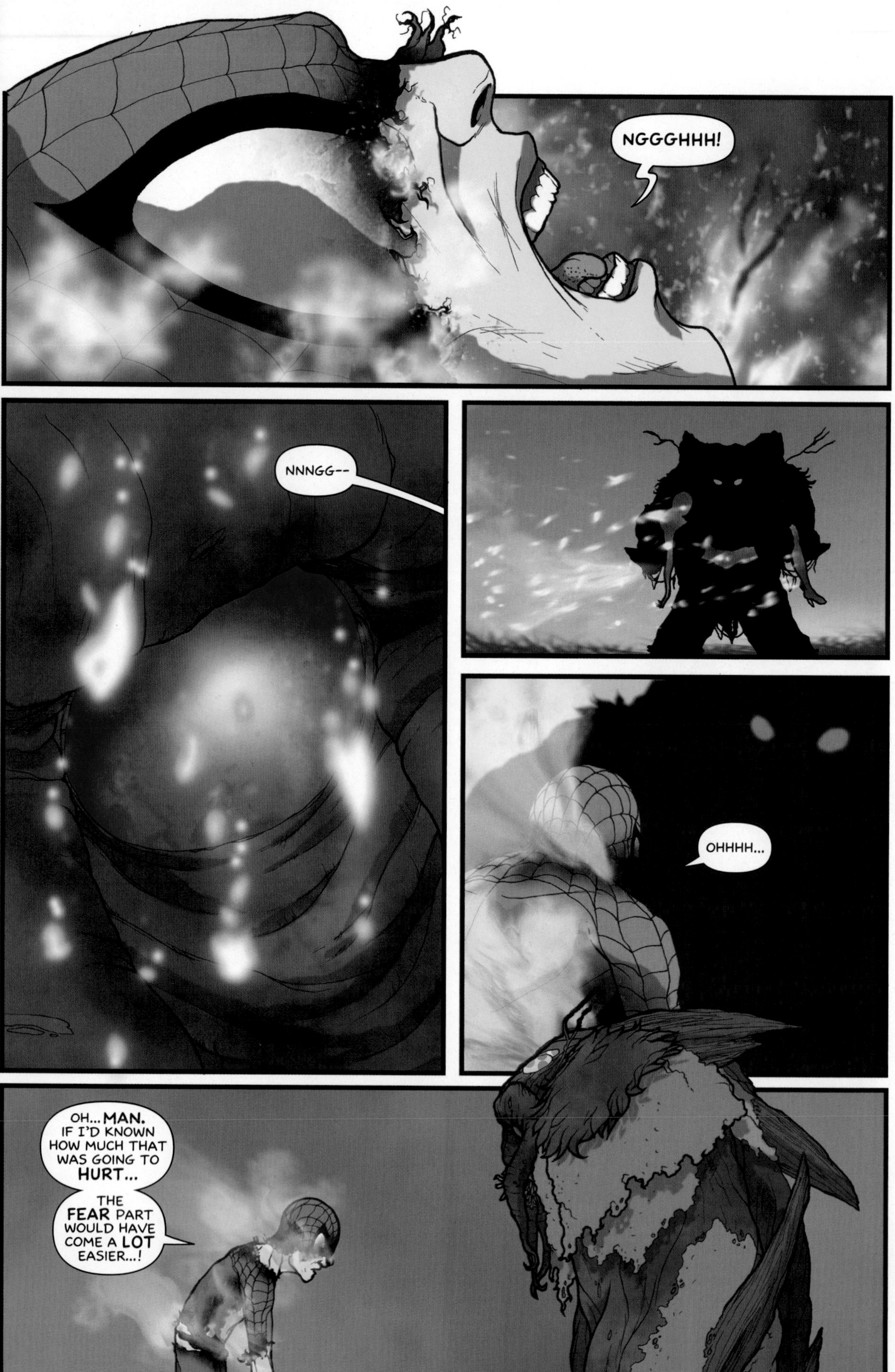
NGGGHHH!
NNNGG--
OHHHH...
OH... MAN. IF I'D KNOWN HOW MUCH THAT WAS GOING TO HURT...
THE FEAR PART WOULD HAVE COME A LOT EASIER...!

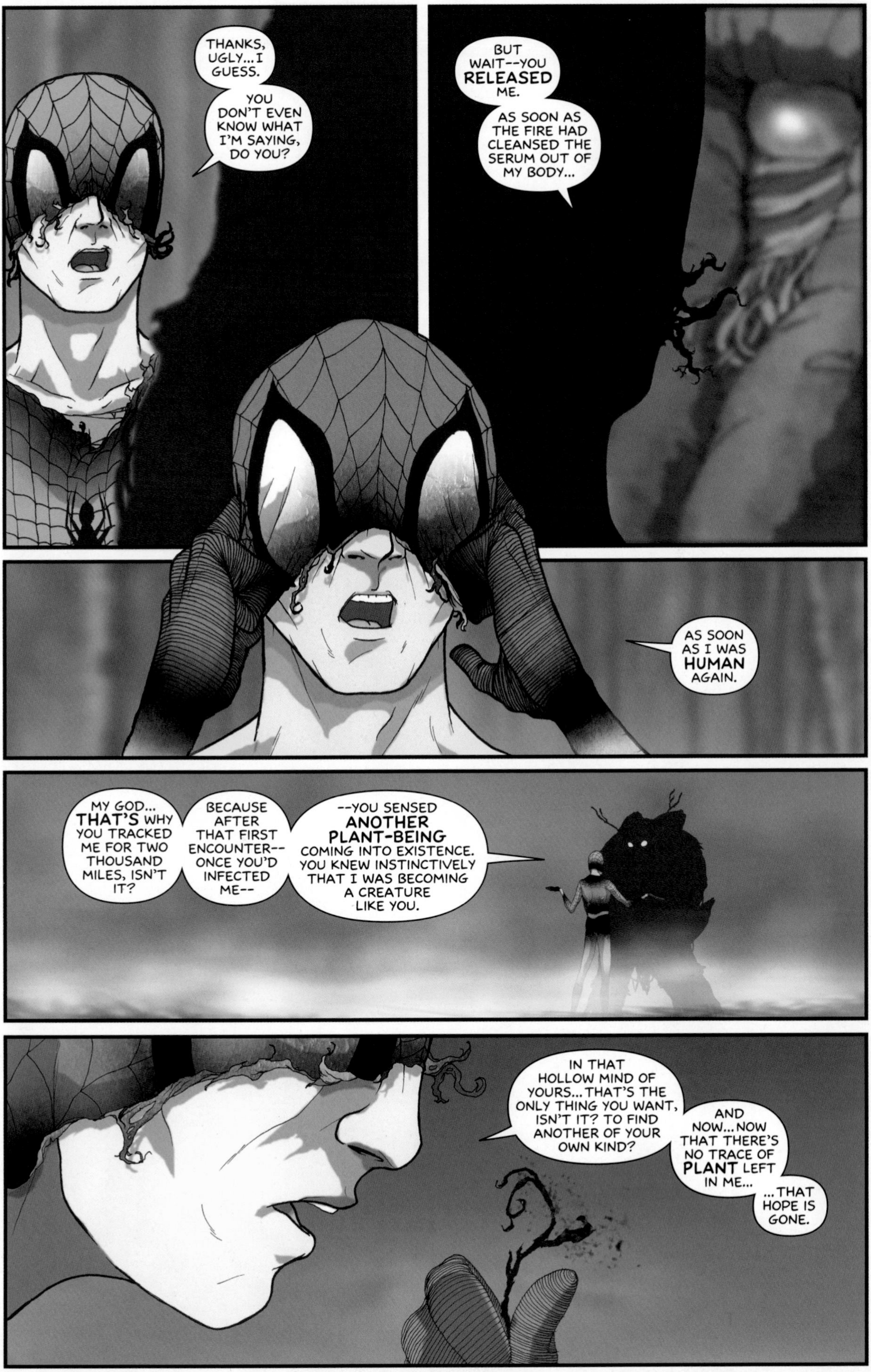
THANKS, UGLY...I GUESS.
YOU DON'T EVEN KNOW WHAT I'M SAYING, DO YOU?
BUT WAIT--YOU **RELEASED** ME.
AS SOON AS THE FIRE HAD CLEANSED THE SERUM OUT OF MY BODY...
AS SOON AS I WAS **HUMAN** AGAIN.
MY GOD... **THAT'S** WHY YOU TRACKED ME FOR TWO THOUSAND MILES, ISN'T IT?
BECAUSE AFTER THAT FIRST ENCOUNTER--ONCE YOU'D INFECTED ME--
--YOU SENSED **ANOTHER PLANT-BEING** COMING INTO EXISTENCE. YOU KNEW INSTINCTIVELY THAT I WAS BECOMING A CREATURE LIKE YOU.
IN THAT HOLLOW MIND OF YOURS...THAT'S THE ONLY THING YOU WANT, ISN'T IT? TO FIND ANOTHER OF YOUR OWN KIND?
AND NOW...NOW THAT THERE'S NO TRACE OF **PLANT** LEFT IN ME...
...THAT HOPE IS GONE.

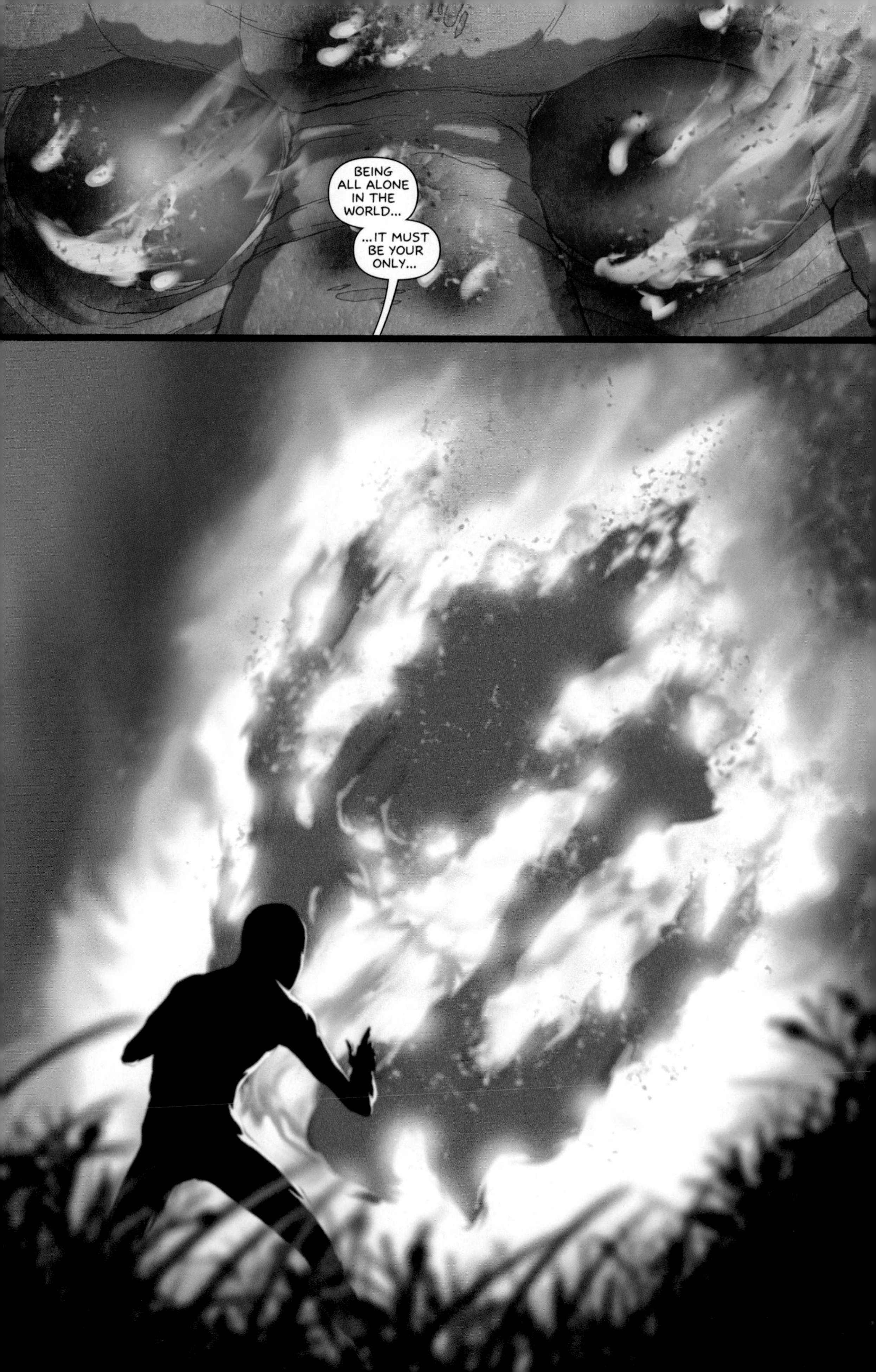
BEING ALL ALONE IN THE WORLD...
...IT MUST BE YOUR ONLY...

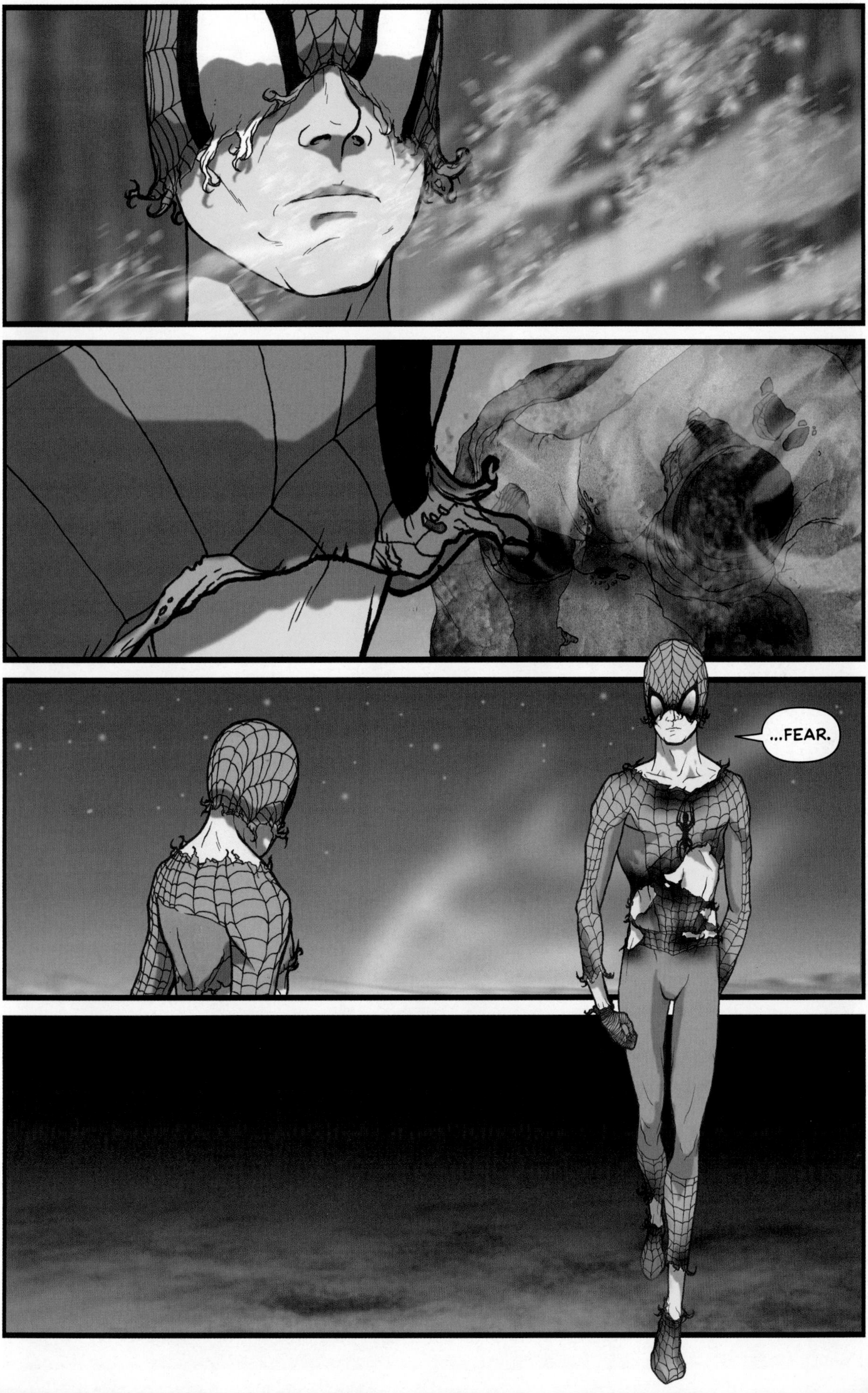
...FEAR.

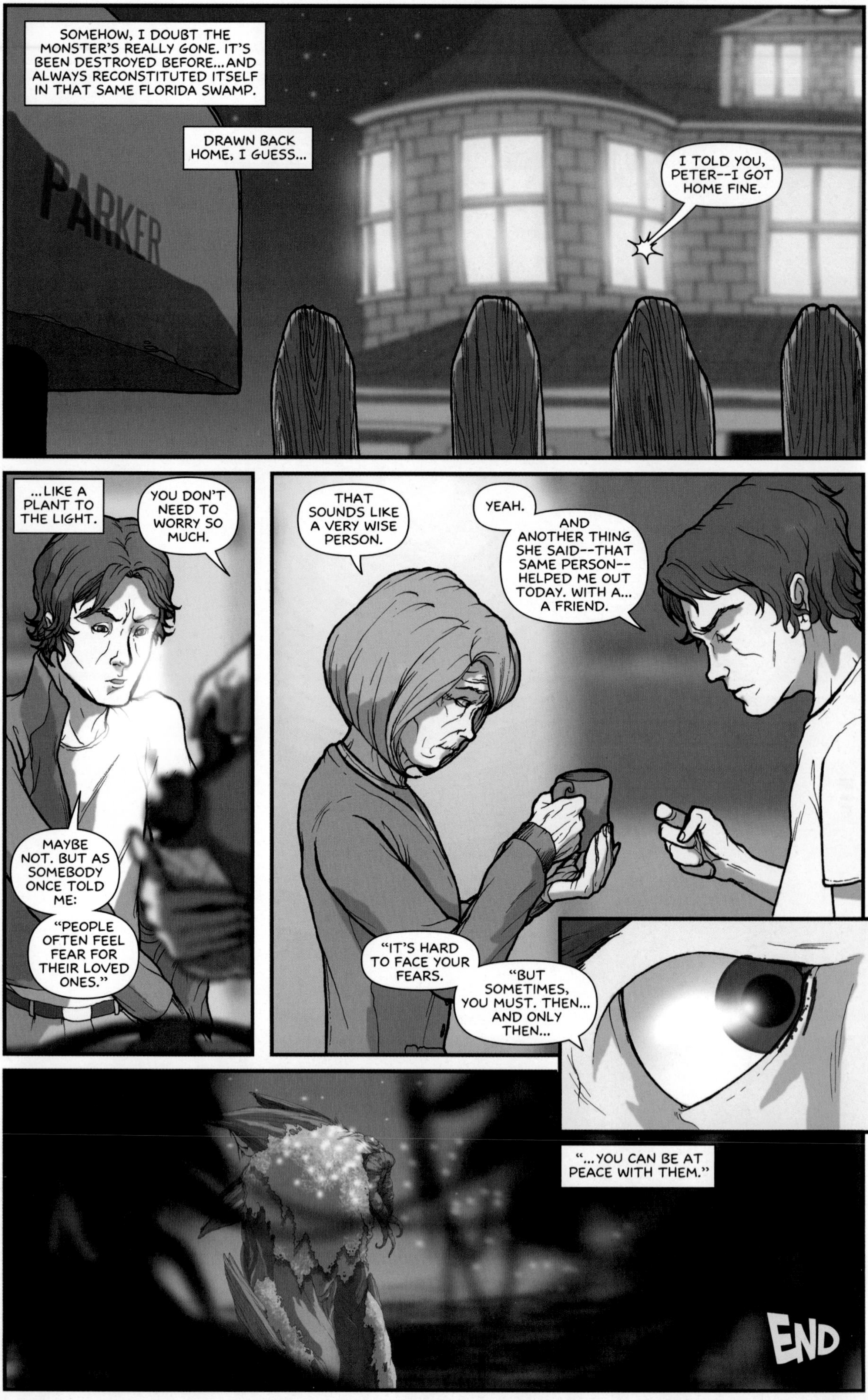
SOMEHOW, I DOUBT THE MONSTER'S REALLY GONE. IT'S BEEN DESTROYED BEFORE...AND ALWAYS RECONSTITUTED ITSELF IN THAT SAME FLORIDA SWAMP.
DRAWN BACK HOME, I GUESS...
PARKER
I TOLD YOU, PETER--I GOT HOME FINE.
...LIKE A PLANT TO THE LIGHT.
YOU DON'T NEED TO WORRY SO MUCH.
MAYBE NOT. BUT AS SOMEBODY ONCE TOLD ME:
"PEOPLE OFTEN FEEL FEAR FOR THEIR LOVED ONES."
THAT SOUNDS LIKE A VERY WISE PERSON.
YEAH.
AND ANOTHER THING SHE SAID--THAT SAME PERSON--HELPED ME OUT TODAY. WITH A... A FRIEND.
"IT'S HARD TO FACE YOUR FEARS.
"BUT SOMETIMES, YOU MUST. THEN... AND ONLY THEN...
"...YOU CAN BE AT PEACE WITH THEM."
END